# PHILOSOPHY OF PLATO AND ARISTOTLE

PHILOSOPHY
OF
PLATO AND ARISTOTLE

# The Arts of Orpheus

*by*

IVAN M. LINFORTH

ARNO PRESS
A New York Times Company
New York / 1973

Reprint Edition 1973 by Arno Press Inc.

Reprinted from a copy in
The Wesleyan University Library

PHILOSOPHY OF PLATO AND ARISTOTLE
ISBN for complete set: 0-405-04830-0
See last pages of this volume for titles.

Manufactured in the United States of America

**Library of Congress Cataloging in Publication Data**

Linforth, Ivan Mortimer, 1879-
The arts of Orpheus.

(Philosophy of Plato and Aristotle)
Reprint of the 1941 ed.
1. Orpheus. 2. Dionysus. 3. Mysteries, Religious.
I. Title: II. Series: Philosophy of Plato and
Aristotle.
BL820.07L5 1973 292'.2'11 72-9296
ISBN 0-405-04847-5

# THE ARTS OF ORPHEUS

# The Arts of Orpheus

*by*
IVAN M. LINFORTH

UNIVERSITY OF CALIFORNIA PRESS
BERKELEY AND LOS ANGELES · 1941

UNIVERSITY OF CALIFORNIA PRESS
BERKELEY, CALIFORNIA

CAMBRIDGE UNIVERSITY PRESS
LONDON, ENGLAND



PRINTED IN THE UNITED STATES OF AMERICA
BY SAMUEL T. FARQUHAR, UNIVERSITY PRINTER

ἅπαντα μὲν οὖν τὰ αἰνίγματα λύειν ἐπ' ἀκριβὲς οὐ ῥᾴδιον, τοῦ δὲ πλήθους τῶν μυθευομένων ἐκτεθέντος εἰς τὸ μέσον, τῶν μὲν ὁμολογούντων ἀλλήλοις, τῶν δὲ ἐναντιουμένων, εὐπορώτερον ἄν τις δύναιτο εἰκάζειν ἐξ αὐτῶν τἀληθές.

STRABO x, 3, 23

# CONTENTS

# Introduction

IT IS ALMOST universally assumed that there existed in the ancient world an Orphic religion which was so far distinct, unified, and coherent as to deserve recognition and a proper designation. The word Orphism has been coined in recent years as a comprehensive term for the ideas and practices which are supposed to have belonged to it. If there was such a religion, it is a fact of the greatest importance. It means that there was a body of men, unified and organized, at least to some degree, with common purposes and ideals, and devoted to common doctrines and practices. Such a body would set up a magnetic field which would profoundly affect the whole movement of thought. It would have to be reckoned with in tracing the growth and development of ideas in the whole range of religion and philosophy. We should be bound to bring into relationship with it all the ideas and practices which we find associated with the name of Orpheus in the ancient documents, and we should be justified in attaching to it conjecturally other ideas and practices not actually associated with his name, but still demonstrably akin. We should be faced with the problem of reconstructing it in all its departments as fully as the available evidence would permit.

This problem of reconstruction is precisely the problem which scholars have been endeavoring to solve for the last hundred years; but anyone who is acquainted with what they have written must be aware that with all their learning and ingenuity they have not obtained a solution which can be counted as solid and satisfactory.

With all their prolonged efforts to discover what Orphism was, and with all their determination to hold fast to the belief that back of the name there must be some reality, the Orphic religion still remains nebulous and ill defined. Perhaps no two persons would agree upon what belongs essentially to it. No account of it has been given that is free enough from conjecture to be acceptable as a true picture of the facts.

Furthermore, the way in which evidence has been used to obtain the current accounts of Orphism, unsatisfactory as they are, is open to grave suspicion. The evidence has been found in documents of two kinds, those which contain the name of Orpheus himself or some derivative of his name, and those which, though not sealed by his name, are supposed for one cause or another to supply information concerning his religion. Archaeology as well as literature provides documents of both kinds. In the documents of the first kind there is such a diversity of matter that it has been impossible to find a place for it all in a unified structure. In order to obtain something substantial and coherent it has been necessary to suppress some parts of it and to emphasize other parts without warrant above the rest. As for documents of the second kind, there is the greatest variety of opinion concerning the propriety of admitting one or another of them as evidence for Orphism. It is enough to mention the fact that the Gold Tablets from southern Italy and Crete are regarded by some as the very cornerstone for the reconstruction of Orphism, while others reject them as not Orphic at all. In fact, ideas and practices are arbitrarily attributed to an

Orphism which is largely composed of just the ideas and practices thus attributed to it, and an Orphic religion is built up of ideas and practices which are only assumed to be Orphic. Scholars cannot always resist the temptation to fatten the spare body of Orphism by dubbing conjecturally as Orphic whatever they find in religion or art that bears any resemblance to what they conceive Orphism to be; and the conjecture of the specialist becomes the certainty of the layman.

Now it may be that the general sense of frustration on the part of the students of Orphism, and the bewilderment on the part of those who read what the specialists have to say about it, is the result of misdirected effort. The whole undertaking rests on the assumption that an Orphic religion actually existed. Perhaps this assumption is erroneous. If it is, we should not be surprised at the failure to arrive at a satisfactory notion of what that religion is. Indeed, the failure does much to weaken the original assumption, which is after all not axiomatic, but of the nature of a working hypothesis. That it is no more than a hypothesis is proved by the fact that an Orphic religion is not once clearly named in all ancient literature; and if it is a hypothesis, it should be treated like one. It will stand only if it accords with all the known facts, if it "saves the appearances," and we cannot refuse to accept this test. If all the things that the ancients said about Orpheus, and the way in which they said them, and the circumstances under which they said them, can be reasonably combined in the framework of an Orphic religion and find reasonable explanation therein, the hypothesis has a high degree of probability. If not, it must be discarded, and something else must be put in its place. This does not mean that the well-attested facts which have been given a place in Orphism would be in any way altered. It means that they would fall into another pattern. It means that we could no longer think of a corporate Orphism as an undiscovered but suspected planet to whose gravitational pull we could attribute the actual perturbations in the universe of thought.

Being disposed to challenge the hypothesis, I have undertaken a fresh examination of the evidence, in the hope that, if allowed to speak for itself and not pressed to answer questions for which it has no answer, it might lead to an understanding of the facts which it reveals that would be unambiguous and convincing. By trying to learn what the men of the ancient world themselves thought they knew about Orpheus and his works, and what things in the ancient world were actually associated with his name, I have ventured to hope that I might discover, in the first place, whether there actually was an Orphic religion of whose existence men were aware, and, in the second place, if the answer is negative, what part Orpheus himself was actually conceived to have played in the religion of Greece. The question whether Orpheus himself existed or not need not be raised. There was, in general, no doubt of it in the ancient world. Indeed, it makes very little difference in the history of human thought whether the great and influential personalities ever actually lived in human bodies. Personalities like Zeus, Odysseus, and Zoroaster, and even Hamlet and Don Quixote, have been more important in the world than millions of men who have lived and died. Their reality is the reality of an idea, and the best that we can know about them is what men have thought about them. The reality of Orpheus is to be sought in what men thought and said about him.

In studying the evidence I have been guided by two principles. In the first place, I maintain that if there was an Orphic religion, we should be able to recognize and define it on the basis of the evidence which is plainly sealed with Orpheus' name. If a consistent Orphism emerges from a study of these documents, it is reasonable to bring into relationship with it ideas and practices which are similar to those attested for it, but which are not sealed with his name. If we cannot discern the nucleus of a consistent Orphism, we have no right to add such ideas and practices to a purely imaginary thing. It is only from the documents sealed with the name that one can learn what Orphic means, and only when they have supplied a sound core of knowledge can one proceed with caution to expand this knowledge with supplementary evidence of the other kind.[1] Furthermore, none of the evidence which is sealed with the name should be excluded in a fair survey. By presenting only the evidence which seems to support a preconceived theory, one may establish the theory logically; but if the premises which are supplied by partial evidence are shown to be unsound in

[1] I am aware that this procedure will meet with some disapproval. "It cannot be denied," says Nilsson ("Early Orphism and Kindred Religious Movements," *Harvard Theological Review, XXVIII* [1935], 184), "that Wilamowitz [*Glaube der Hellenen*] somewhat oversimplified the problem of criticism by not admitting testimonies other than such as expressly mention the name of Orpheus." This seems to me not so much an oversimplification as a rectification of method.

the light of the whole sum of evidence, the logical argument is at once proved useless. The evidence concerning Orpheus is particularly susceptible to misconstruction of this kind.

In the second place, the evidence must be studied chronologically. An Orphism which is determined by evidence from all the centuries that intervened between the sixth before Christ and the sixth after Christ is a timeless thing without reality, unless a genuine evolution can be recognized. The documents must be interpreted in the light of the cultural conditions from which they spring—social, religious, philosophical, literary.

Observing these two principles, I have undertaken to study as critically as possible the meaning and significance of each document, to consider the value of each author as a witness, to inquire whence he obtained the information that he supplies, to give due weight not only to what he says but also to what he leaves unsaid, to compare the statements of one with the statements of another, and thus to attempt to decide precisely what reality was in men's minds when they spoke of Orpheus or called things Orphic. The enormously complex problems which Orpheus has left to the world cannot be suddenly solved by the inauguration of a new method, but it is my hope that the observance of the principles which have been enunciated may enable one to take at least a few steps on reasonably solid ground.

Precisely what has been done in the present book is this. The evidence of the classical period is studied first, and the year 300 B.C. is arbitrarily taken as the close of the period. The propriety of recognizing a certain unity in this earlier period is manifest. When Alexander undid the gates that held the Occident and the Orient apart, the new cosmopolitan Greek world was flooded with ideas and practices which were closely enough akin to those already associated with Orpheus to produce a notable contamination, and which were of a kind that had previously trickled into Greece only in slender streams. First, then, all the documents containing the name of Orpheus, literary and archaeological, earlier than 300 B.C. are presented and discussed. They fall naturally into three groups, as they relate to the legend, the religious rites, and the poems of Orpheus. Doubtless many documents of later date also supply information which is valid for the earlier period; but their validity is conjectural, and what the contemporary documents reveal is sure and incontrovertible. Second, all the documents later than 300 B.C. concerning religious institutions and practices associated with the name of Orpheus are similarly presented. Third, a special study is made of the myth of the dismemberment of Dionysus by the Titans, which is generally regarded as peculiarly Orphic. Thus it will be seen that of the whole sum of evidence concerning Orpheus the portion which is not presented is that of a date subsequent to 300 B.C. concerning the legend and the poetry but not touching religious rites or the myth of dismemberment. The reader will not forget the existence of this neglected body of evidence and its importance, but it is hoped that the delimitations which have been contrived for the present study will not be thought such as to invalidate the results.

It is inevitable in the execution of the plan that the reader should be asked to review long marching columns of disconnected texts, and there is cause to fear that the business will be tedious. When texts are quoted in support of a particular theory, they are welcome because their significance is immediately apparent. Here, however, the texts are presented for their own sake and not to prove a theory. The purpose, it may be repeated, is to put before the reader all the evidence in chronological order, and to invite him to contemplate the picture which it presents as a whole and in the mutual relation of its parts. He will thus be in a position both to draw his own conclusions, without suspicion that something of importance has been withheld, and to judge such conclusions as may be offered.

It would naturally be expected that in dealing with a subject about which so much has been written one would begin with a statement of the present condition of the problem and a critical review of the work already done. In the present case this is impossible because, strictly speaking, there is nothing to review. The question whether there was such a thing as Orphism has not been raised. It is true that in the prolonged efforts to determine what Orphism is, sharp criticism has done something to weaken the full assurance of earlier scholars.[2] Some writers have

[2] Mention may be made, for example, of the more liberal views of André Boulanger, especially in two recent articles, "L'orphisme à Rome" (*Rev. des études latines*, XV [1937], 121–135) and a review of Guthrie's *Orpheus and Greek Religion* (*Rev. des études anciennes*, XXXIX [1937], 45–48). Liberal opinion is expressed also by P. Boyancé in his recent book, *Le culte des Muses chez les philosophes grecs* (Paris, 1937): "L'orphisme," he says (p. 28), "n'est pas une religion ésotérique, ou pour mieux dire n'est pas une religion"; but he operates throughout his book on the assumption that there was something that might be called Orphism. A stout affirmation of the opposite position may be found

been driven to acknowledge that the Orphism which they believe in is a far more shadowy and attenuated thing than it is generally supposed to be. But even with them the old hypothesis of its existence still stands. A few rude voices, like that of Wilamowitz in his last book, have shocked their feelings, but generally the only response has been a defiant reassertion of their faith in the existence of Orphism and renewed efforts to say what it is so clearly that all will believe. The vigor of their assertion, one feels, may sometimes be the result of an unconscious doubt of its truth. For these reasons, since I am ready to question the faith, I may be allowed, perhaps, to step aside in the present study from the main course of Orphic research, and, omitting a formal examination of the views which are based on the old hypothesis, proceed directly to the fundamental criticism which is implied in an inquiry concerning the validity of the hypothesis itself.

The materials for the study have been obtained almost entirely from the collections in Otto Kern's *Orphicorum Fragmenta*. The publication of this book, in 1922, gave a great impetus to Orphic studies, and has enabled students to undertake investigations which without it would have

in Macchioro's review (*Riv. Indo-Greco-Italica*, IX [1925], 3–4, 142) of Boulanger's earlier book, *Orphée. Rapports de l'orphisme et du christianisme* (Paris, 1925). Macchioro and his fellow countrymen Pettazzoni, Ribezzo, and Turchi hold what may be called the "hospitable" attitude, not only being fully confident of the existence of an Orphic religion, but admitting to it with the utmost freedom anything for which they can make out even a plausible case. Jane E. Harrison's learned but fanciful and sentimental chapters on Orpheus in her *Prolegomena to the Study of Greek Religion* (Cambridge, 1903), from which many English readers obtain their knowledge of the subject, are an extreme example of uncritical hospitality. The reader is soon aware that his feet are off the ground, and he finds himself floating, giddy and dizzy, amidst shifting and dissolving shapes.

been impossible. I am glad to have an opportunity to express my obligations to this distinguished scholar, not only for the work just named, but also for his many other writings on Orpheus and Greek religion, and for the work of his pupils whom he has inspired to carry on similar studies.

I.M.L.

# THE ARTS OF ORPHEUS

*Chapter* I

# Evidence Earlier Than 300 B.C. Concerning Orpheus

## Legend

In the museum at Delphi may be seen a sculptured metope which has been partially reconstructed from four fragments which were found by the French excavators in the foundations of the Treasury of the Sicyonians.[1] In spite of the mutilations one may clearly discern two horsemen, one at either side of the field, facing toward the front. Extending between and behind them in the lower half of the field is a ship with its side to the spectator. Standing in the right half of the field and close to the horseman on the right are two figures in front view, apparently standing in the ship, although they are disproportionately large. Each of these two persons holds a cithara in his left arm and is apparently playing upon it with his right hand. At the left of the head of the musician on the right is a vertical inscription, reading downward: ΟΡΦΑΣ. At the left of the head of the other musician, similarly, appears an inscription, which is not so clear. The style of the sculpture proves that its date was somewhat before the middle of the sixth century B.C.

It is generally recognized that the scene represented

[1] *Fouilles de Delphes*, IV, pl. 4 = *Test.* 1. (This abbreviation and the abbreviation *Fragm.* refer to the Testimonia and Fragmenta in Kern's *Orphicorum Fragmenta.*) Cf. F. Poulsen, *Delphi*, pp. 73 ff.; M. P. Nilsson, "Early Orphism and Kindred Religious Movements," *Harv. Theol. Rev.*, XXVIII (1935), 186.

belongs to the legend of the Argonauts: the two horsemen are the Dioscuri, and the ship is the Argo. Robert has tentatively restored the name of the musician on the left as Philammon. The other musician, as the inscription plainly shows, is Orpheus, who here appears for the first time in history,[2] unmistakable in name and bodily presence. He is engaged in the practice of the art which has been most closely associated with him from that time to this.

At Olympia, as well as at Delphi, there was in classical times a figure of Orpheus in stone (*Test.* 143), though it was set up nearly a hundred years later than the metope just described. It was one of a large number of statues which were dedicated by Micythus of Rhegium as a thank offering for the recovery of his son from a dangerous illness. Some time after the death of Anaxilas, the tyrant of Rhegium, of whose household he had been a member, and for whose sons he had acted as regent during their minority, he had changed his residence to Tegea in Arcadia, and it was while he was living there, perhaps as late as 460, that he had the statues made for his costly offering. These circumstances are known from Herodotus (vii, 170), Diodorus (xi, 48, 2; 66, 3), and Pausanias (v, 26); and they have been corroborated by the discovery at

[2] Kern (*Die Religion der Griechen*, II [1935], 188, n. 1), referring to an Apulian vase of the middle of the fourth century B.C., which, according to Robert, is the only Greek monument representing animals listening to the playing of Orpheus, writes thus: "Jetzt kommt aber noch eine viel ältere, kleine, boiotische Schale aus dem VII. Jahrhundert (in meinem Besitz) hinzu, auf der der bärtige, auf einer viersaitigen Lyra spielende Orpheus von sieben auf Zweigen sitzenden Vögeln und einem Reh umgeben ist. Die Schale wird in den Athenischen Mitteilungen demnächst von mir besprochen werden." If Kern is right, this is the earliest known evidence of Orpheus.

Olympia of pieces of one or more of the bases on which the statues were set, bearing fragmentary inscriptions.[3] Pausanias reports that some of the statues had been carried off by Nero, and that the remaining ones, which he saw himself, were disposed in three groups. In the first group were Amphitrite, Poseidon, Hestia, and Iphitus being crowned by Ekecheiria; in the second, Kore, daughter of Demeter, Aphrodite, Ganymedes, Artemis, Homer, Hesiod, Asclepius, and Hygieia; in the third, Agon, Dionysus, Orpheus the Thracian, and Zeus. For what reason Orpheus was included in this curious list we do not know.[4]

The earliest certain[5] occurrence of his name in literature comes a few decades later than the Delphic metope. The words ὀνομακλυτὸν Ὀρφήν occurred in a lost poem by Ibycus of Rhegium (fr. 17 Diehl = *Test.* 2), and the date of Ibycus is fixed by his presence at the court of Polycrates of Samos, whose tyranny lasted approximately from 533 to 522 B.C. The two words are quoted by the grammarian Priscian as an example of the Doric form of the name, and nothing is known of the poem in which they were found.

As early, then, as the middle of the sixth century B.C., Orpheus could be called an "illustrious" personage by a poet and be represented as a figure in an artistic composition by a sculptor. He was known as a musician and probably as an Argonaut. Further, it would have been

[3] Dittenberger-Purgold, *Die Inschriften von Olympia* (1896), Nos. 267–269.

[4] The conjectures offered by Kern (*Orpheus*, 1920, p. 4) are unconvincing.

[5] Diehl's conjectural restoration of ὀρ[φεύς in Alcaeus, fr. 80, has met with approval. Cf. Kern, *Gnomon*, XI (1935), 475 (a review of Guthrie, *Orpheus and Greek Religion*).

understood, if anyone happened to think of the matter, that as an Argonaut he belonged to the generation before that of the heroes of the Trojan War and, of course, lived long before Homer. Since he appears first as an Argonaut, let us first trace the remaining evidence for his connection with that expedition.

The earliest extant literary document in which Orpheus appears as an Argonaut is the fourth *Pythian* of Pindar, which was composed about 462 B.C. In response to the summons of Jason, as Pindar tells the tale, ten heroes came to join his company, of whom one was Orpheus. Of him it is said (*Pyth.* iv, 176 ff. Bowra = *Test.* 58): ἐξ Ἀπόλλωνος δὲ φορμιγκτὰς ἀοιδᾶν πατὴρ ἔμολεν, εὐαίνητος Ὀρφεύς. He is a lyre player, the father of song, and, as in Ibycus, an illustrious personage. But what is his relation to Apollo? Two views are expressed in the scholia on this passage.[6] According to one he is the son of Apollo, though it is pointed out that elsewhere, both in Pindar and in other authors, he is the son of Oeagrus. Other authorities, however, are cited, who also made him the son of Apollo.[7] According to the other view, which is attributed to Ammonius, Orpheus is said to be a lyre player "by grace of Apollo," as kings are said to be ἐκ Διός, not because they are his sons but because they hold their kingship from him. In the list of heroes who came at Jason's call the first three were sons of Zeus—Heracles, Castor, and Polydeuces; the next two were sons of Poseidon—Euphemus and Periclymenus; next came Orpheus; after him two

[6] These scholia are quoted on p. 8 below.

[7] For other references to Orpheus as son of Apollo see p. 22 below.

sons of Hermes—Echion and Erytus; last the two sons of Boreas—Zetes and Calais. All but Orpheus are definitely named as sons of gods, and it would seem likely that the audience listening to the ode would understand that Orpheus too was the son of a god.[8] But the language is ambiguous, and Pindar may be guilty of a mild equivocation: he may have introduced the name of Apollo in connection with Orpheus to preserve the symmetry of his list, not intending to say bluntly that they were father and son, but willing to let his listeners believe what they pleased. In the end, it is impossible to say whether he meant 'the harpist son of Apollo' or 'he who was harpist by grace of Apollo.' Nor is the ambiguity cleared up by the genealogical figure in the phrase ἀοιδᾶν πατήρ, which is equally appropriate whether Apollo is the source of his being or the source of his musical skill.

Orpheus appears again as a member of the Argonautic expedition in the *Hypsipyle* of Euripides, which was produced toward the close of the poet's life at the end of the fifth century B.C. When the Argonauts arrived at Lemnos, they found the island occupied by a community of women, who had slain all the men. Hypsipyle, the queen, however, had saved her aged father Thoas, and he had been conveyed in some way to the coast of Thrace. After the departure of the Argonauts Hypsipyle gave birth to twin sons, of whom Jason was the father. Some time later the women of the island, discovering that Hypsipyle had spared her father, sold her into slavery, and she was carried to Nemea, where she became a servant in the house

[8] In such a list as this ἐξ 'Απόλλωνος cannot mean, as Christ suggests, "from Apollonia," the city of Thrace.

of Lycurgus. On Jason's return from Colchis he found the twin sons who had been born to him and took them with him home to Iolcus. After Jason's death Orpheus, out of friendship to him, undertook the education of the boys and carried them off to Thrace. Many years later the two sons of Hypsipyle, now grown to manhood, together with Thoas, with whom they had somehow been reunited, went in search of their mother and finally found her in Nemea, where the action of the play takes place.[9] The name of Orpheus appears twice in the papyrus fragments. In a lyric passage, which was probably sung by Hypsipyle, we find the following (fr. 1, col. iii, 8–15 Italie = *Test.* 78): μέσῳ δὲ πὰρ' ἱστῷ 'Ασιὰς ἔλεγον (ἔλεγεν pap.) ἰήιον Θρῇσσ' ἐβόα κίθαρις 'Ορφέως μακροπόλων πιτύλων ἐρέτῃσι κελεύσματα μελπομένα, τότε μὲν ταχύπλουν τότε δ' εἰλατίνας ἀνάπαυμα πλάτα[s]. Orpheus, singing to the accompaniment of a "Thracian Asiatic cithara," acts as κελευστής to the rowers. The editors point out that since κίθαρις 'Ασιάς is a familiar phrase, the second epithet Θρῇσσα may legitimately be added.

The second passage is a dialogue between Hypsipyle and her son Euneus (fr. 64, col. ii, 93–107 Italie = *Test.* 79):

> (Εὔν.) 'Αργώ με καὶ τόνδ' ἤγαγ' ἐς 'Ιωλκὸν πόλιν.
> ('Υψ.) ἐπιμαστίδιόν (ἀπο- pap.) γ' ἐμῶν στέρνων.
> — ἐπεὶ δ' 'Ιάσων ἔθαν' ἐμός, μῆτερ, πατήρ —
> — οἴμοι κακὰ λέγεις, δάκρυά τ' ὄμμασιν,
> τέκνον, ἐμοῖς δίδως.
> — 'Ορφεύς με καὶ τόνδχ' ἤγαγ' εἰς Θρᾴκης τόπον.

[9] For the reconstruction of the story see the edition of the play by G. Italie (Berlin, 1923).

— τίνα πατέρι ποτὲ χάριν ἀθλίῳ
τιθέμενος; ἔνεπέ μοι, τέκνον.
— μοῦσάν με κιθάρας Ἀσιάδος διδάσκεται,
τοῦτ[ο]ν δ' ἐς Ἄρεως ὅπλ' ἐκόσμησεν μάχης.
— δι' Αἰγαίου δὲ τίνα πόρον
ἐμ[όλ]ετ' ἀκτὰν Λημνίαν;
— Θόας [κ]ομίζει σὸς πατὴρ τέκνω δύο.
— ἦ γά[ρ] σέσ[ω]στ[α]ι;
— Βα[κ]χ[ίου] γε μηχαναῖς.

One of the boys is trained by Orpheus to the art of war; the other, Euneus, is taught to play the Asiatic cithara like Orpheus himself. Of Euneus and his music we have further information. It appears that there was at Athens a family called the Εὐνεῖδαι, which took its name from Euneus, the son of Jason, and in which the arts of dancing and lyre playing were hereditary.[10] The priest of Dionysus Melpomenus, for whom one of the seats in the theater of Dionysus was reserved, was chosen from the family of the Εὐνεῖδαι.[11] It should be observed also that Thoas is said to have been saved by Dionysus. There is, however, no hint of any connection between Orpheus and Dionysus.

The remaining evidence concerning Orpheus as an Argonaut is supplied by the following scholia:

1) Schol. Apollon. i, 23 Wendel (= *Test.* 5): Ἡρόδωρος δύο εἶναι Ὀρφεῖς φησιν, ὧν τὸν ἕτερον συμπλεῦσαι τοῖς Ἀργοναύταις. Φερεκύδης δὲ ἐν τῇ ς' Φιλάμμωνά φησι καὶ οὐκ Ὀρφέα

---

[10] Hesych. Εὐνεῖδαι· γένος ἀπὸ Εὔνεω κεκλημένον, τοῦ Ἰάσονος υἱοῦ, οἷον γένος ὀρχηστῶν καὶ κιθαριστῶν κτλ.

[11] *C.I.A.*, III, 274: Ἱερέως Μελπομένου Διονύσου ἐξ Εὐνειδῶν.

συμπεπλευκέναι. ἔστι δέ, ὡς Ἀσκληπιάδης, Ἀπόλλωνος καὶ Καλλιόπης· ἔνιοι δὲ ἀπὸ Οἰάγρου καὶ Πολυμνίας. ζητεῖται δέ, διὰ τί Ὀρφεὺς ἀσθενὴς ὢν συνέπλει τοῖς ἥρωσιν· ὅτι μάντις ὢν ὁ Χείρων ἔχρησε δύνασθαι καὶ τὰς Σειρῆνας παρελθεῖν αὐτοὺς Ὀρφέως συμπλέοντος.[12]

2) Schol. Apollon. i, 31–34a Wendel (= *Test.* 5): Πιερία ὄρος Θρᾴκης, ἐν ᾗ διέτριβεν Ὀρφεύς. φησὶ δὲ Ἡρόδωρος, ὅτι παρῄνησεν ὁ Χείρων τῷ Ἰάσονι, ὅπως τὸν Ὀρφέα σὺν τοῖς Ἀργοναύταις παραλάβῃ.

3) Schol. Pind. *Pyth.* iv, 176 Drachmann (II, 139, 15 = *Test.* 58): Ἀπόλλωνος τὸν Ὀρφέα φησὶν εἶναι, ὃν καὶ αὐτὸς ὁ Πίνδαρος καὶ ἄλλοι Οἰάγρου λέγουσιν. Ἀμμώνιος δὲ σύμφωνον τὴν ἱστορίαν θέλων εἶναι . . . ὥσπερ . . . ἐκ Διὸς λέγουσιν εἶναι τοὺς βασιλεῖς, οὐχ ὅτι γόνος εἰσὶ τοῦ Διός, ἀλλ' ὅτι τὸ βασιλεύειν ἐκ Διὸς ἔχουσιν, οὕτως ἐξ Ἀπόλλωνος φορμικτὴν αὐτὸν εἶπεν· ἡγεμὼν γὰρ ὁ θεὸς τῆς κιθαρῳδίας. ὁ μέντοι Χαῖρις οὐκ ἀπιθάνως τούτους φησὶν ὠνομάσθαι τοὺς ἐκ θεῶν γεγονότας, οἷον Διοσκούρους καὶ Ἡρακλέα· οὕτω δὴ καὶ Ὀρφέα, διὰ τὸ Ἀπόλλωνος εἶναι υἱὸν γόνῳ. παρατίθεται δὲ καὶ χρησμόν τινα, ὅν φησι Μέναιχμον ἀναγράφειν ἐν τῷ Πυθικῷ . . . 'Πιέρες αἰνοπαθεῖς, στυγνὴν ἀποτίσετε λώβην Ὀρφέ' ἀποκτείναντες Ἀπόλλωνος φίλον υἱόν.' καὶ Ἀσκληπιάδης ἐν ἕκτῳ Τραγῳδουμένων ἱστορεῖ Ἀπόλλωνος καὶ Καλλιόπης Ὑμέναιον, Ἰάλεμον, Ὀρφέα.

Among the authors here referred to we find three who lived in the classical period, Pherecydes, Herodorus, and Asclepiades, and of these Pherecydes and Herodorus have something to say of Orpheus as an Argonaut. Pherecydes, who wrote about the middle of the fifth century B.C.,

[12] To this Wendel appends the note: "P add. in fine verba ταῦτα δέ φησιν Ἡρόδωρος e sch. 31/34*a* repetita" (see the following citation).

makes the surprising statement that he did not sail with the Argonauts at all, the import of which will be examined later in connection with other aspects of the legend.[13] From Herodorus, whose work entitled Ἀργοναυτικά was composed toward the end of the century, we learn that Orpheus was invited by Jason to accompany him on the recommendation of Chiron, because his aid would be required at the dangerous moment of passing the Sirens. But Herodorus also says that besides the Orpheus who sailed with the Argonauts there was another man of the same name. This, too, will receive further consideration later.

Orpheus' participation in the Argonautic expedition, as we have seen above, is the earliest incident in his legend for which we have evidence. The next earliest is the manner of his death, and the earliest description of it in literature of which we have any record was in one of the lost plays of Aeschylus. The record appears in Ps.-Eratosthenes, *Catasterismi* 24 (= *Test.* 113). Here we are told that the lyre occupies the ninth place among the stars and belongs to the Muses. Constructed originally by Hermes, it passed into the hands of Apollo, who in turn gave it to Orpheus, the son of the Muse Calliope. He increased its usefulness as a musical instrument, and it came to be believed that he could charm even stones and animals by his song. The account then continues as follows (p. 140, 1 Robert): τὸν μὲν Διόνυσον οὐκ ἐτίμα, τὸν δὲ Ἥλιον μέγιστον τῶν θεῶν ἐνόμιζεν εἶναι, ὃν καὶ Ἀπόλλωνα προσηγόρευσεν· ἐπεγειρόμενός τε τῆς νυκτὸς κατὰ τὴν ἑωθινὴν ἐπὶ τὸ ὄρος τὸ καλούμενον Πάγγαιον ἀνιὼν προσέμενε τὰς ἀνατολάς,

[13] See p. 157 below.

*ἵνα ἴδῃ τὸν Ἥλιον πρῶτον. ὅθεν ὁ Διόνυσος ὀργισθεὶς αὐτῷ ἔπεμψε τὰς Βασσαρίδας, ὥς φησιν Αἰσχύλος ὁ ποιητής, αἵτινες αὐτὸν διέσπασαν καὶ τὰ μέλη διέρριψαν χωρὶς ἕκαστον· αἱ δὲ Μοῦσαι συναγαγοῦσαι ἔθαψαν ἐπὶ τοῖς λεγομένοις Λειβήθροις.* The lyre of Orpheus was then set by Zeus among the stars as a constellation to be a memorial of him and the Muses.

The play of Aeschylus here referred to was probably one of the plays of the tetralogy known as the *Lycurgia*, which consisted of the Ἠδωνοί, the Βασσαρίδες, the Νεανίσκοι, and the Λυκοῦργος, and which was probably produced between 466 and 459. Now in view of the fact that the words *ὥς φησιν Αἰσχύλος* come in the midst of the account, immediately after the word Βασσαρίδας, and that much of what the writer has to say about the lyre obviously does not come from Aeschylus, we cannot be sure that he was attributing to Aeschylus anything more than that it was the Bassarides who tore Orpheus to pieces, whereas in other versions of the legend it was the Bacchae or simply Thracian or Macedonian women. All that we can be sure of in the story as told by Aeschylus is that Orpheus was torn to pieces by the Bassarides and that they scattered his limbs far and wide. It is probable that his tragic death resulted from the hostility of Dionysus, and since the events of the *Lycurgia* took place in Thrace it is fairly certain that the death of Orpheus occurred in that region. Beyond this we cannot go. We cannot say that the other features in the story of the *Catasterismi* were obtained from a source earlier than 300 B.C.[14]

[14] This text is fully discussed by I. M. Linforth in "Two Notes on the Legend of Orpheus," *Trans. Am. Philol. Assoc.*, LXII (1931), 11–17. To the literature there referred to should be added Leo Weber, "Orpheus," *Rhein. Mus.*, LXXXI (1932), 1–19.

Plato refers to the death of Orpheus twice. In the *Symposium* (179 D = *Test.* 60) Phaedrus, in his praise of love, says that love alone will cause one to give his life for another, and adduces the case of Alcestis as sufficient proof of this. He then recalls the cowardice of Orpheus, who did not die for his wife, but went down to Hades alive to bring her back, and was punished by the gods for his lack of courage. Ὀρφέα δὲ τὸν Οἰάγρου ἀτελῆ ἀπέπεμψαν ἐξ Ἅιδου, φάσμα δείξαντες τῆς γυναικὸς ἐφ' ἣν ἧκεν, αὐτὴν δὲ οὐ δόντες, ὅτι μαλθακίζεσθαι ἐδόκει, ἅτε ὢν κιθαρῳδός, καὶ οὐ τολμᾶν ἕνεκα τοῦ ἔρωτος ἀποθνῄσκειν ὥσπερ Ἄλκηστις, ἀλλὰ διαμηχανᾶσθαι ζῶν εἰσιέναι εἰς Ἅιδου. τοιγάρτοι διὰ ταῦτα δίκην αὐτῷ ἐπέθεσαν, καὶ ἐποίησαν τὸν θάνατον αὐτοῦ ὑπὸ γυναικῶν γενέσθαι, οὐκ ὥσπερ Ἀχιλλέα τὸν τῆς Θέτιδος ὑὸν ἐτίμησαν καὶ εἰς μακάρων νήσους ἀπέπεμψαν . . . Notice that the prominence of διὰ ταῦτα suggests that it contains the real predication of the sentence ("this was the cause of the punishment which he suffered in being slain by women"), whereas the murder of Orpheus by women is assumed to be known. Orpheus is slain by women, but we are not told who the women were or what their immediate motive was in the story which Plato has in mind.

In the myth of Er at the end of the *Republic* (x, 620 A = *Test.* 139), among the souls which gather to make their choice of lives for a new incarnation, appears the soul of Orpheus, and he like most of the others is influenced in his choice by the circumstances of his previous life: ἰδεῖν μὲν γὰρ ψυχὴν ἔφη τήν ποτε Ὀρφέως γενομένην κύκνου βίον αἱρουμένην, μίσει τοῦ γυναικείου γένους διὰ τὸν ὑπ' ἐκείνων θάνατον οὐκ ἐθέλουσαν ἐν γυναικὶ γεννηθεῖσαν γενέσθαι. Here again we have the bare statement that he was slain by women.

Isocrates, in the *Busiris* (xi, 38 = *Fragm.* 17), recalls how the poets have told blasphemous stories about the gods, attributing to them theft, adultery, and many other kinds of outrageous conduct. They have been punished for this, he says, some in one way, some in another. Orpheus, who was the worst offender, met his end by being torn to pieces: Ὀρφεὺς δ' ὁ μάλιστα τούτων τῶν λόγων ἀψάμενος, διασπασθεὶς τὸν βίον ἐτελεύτησεν. Though nothing is said about women, Orpheus is represented as being torn to pieces, as he was in the play of Aeschylus. Here, as in Plato, though no immediate motive is mentioned, an ulterior cause is recognized. In Plato Orpheus suffers because he was a lyre player too cowardly to die for his wife, in Isocrates because in his poetry he had told discreditable stories about the gods.

The death of Orpheus was a favorite subject with vase painters, and the evidence which they supply is more abundant and indeed earlier than what is found in literature. Unfortunately, evidence of this type cannot be placed before the reader. He can only be sent to the vases themselves, or the reproductions of them in drawings and photographs which have appeared in a multitude of publications.[15] No more is attempted here than to give a brief description of the prevailing types.

[15] The most convenient approach to the study of the vase paintings representing the death of Orpheus is supplied by C. Watzinger, "Kelchkrater aus Tarent im Haag. Tod des Orpheus," in Furchtwängler-Reichhold, *Griech. Vasenmalerei*, Text III (1932), 355–361, with its references to earlier literature. Guthrie, *Orpheus and Greek Religion* (1935), p. 64, gives a useful list and brief description of ten of the most important vases. See also M. P. Nilsson, "Early

Chronologically the series of vases with which we are concerned begins as early as the decade between 490 and 480. In some of the pictures Orpheus, with his lyre in his hand, is represented as fleeing from a group of Thracian women who are bent on destroying him. In others the scene portrays a slightly later moment, when Orpheus, already seized and wounded, has sunk to the ground and the women are rushing upon him to complete the slaughter. In still others we see Orpheus seated on a rock, singing to the accompaniment of his lyre and surrounded by Thracian men who are listening in rapt attention to his song; but the women are already hastening from a distance to attack him. In all the pictures the women are armed with household utensils, such as spits, mallets, and pestles, with curved Thracian knives, or with stones and clubs; in many of them they are tattooed on their arms and legs according to the Thracian custom. In the earliest vases Orpheus' costume is Greek, but in the later ones of the fifth century B.C. he appears as a Thracian, with high boots and a foxskin cap; in the vases of the fourth century B.C. he is always a Thracian. It is pointed out, however, that this need not be taken as proof of a change in the legend, because it is common to find Trojan heroes depicted as Greeks. But it is a curious circumstance that Orpheus' fellow minstrel Thamyris is always shown in Thracian costume, and the significance of Greek costume in the depiction of the Trojan heroes is somewhat weakened by the fact that Homer, in general, makes no important distinction between Trojans and Greeks. A

Orphism and Kindred Religious Movements," *Harv. Theol. Rev.*, XXVIII (1935), 188 ff.

comparison of these paintings with Aeschylus' account of the death of Orpheus reveals striking differences. The women bear none of the insignia of Dionysus, and neither their costume nor their weapons show them to be Bassarae. Furthermore, no painting represents Orpheus as being torn to pieces. It would seem, therefore, that Aeschylus has adopted, or invented, a version of the legend which is different from that which had already found expression in the vase paintings.

What was the motive for the murder? In Aeschylus' account, since the Bassarae were the murderers, it is fairly clear that they were acting under the influence of Dionysus, whatever may have been the cause of his anger. In the vase paintings, where there is no hint of the working of Dionysus, the motive is completely obscure. Plato, to be sure, says that the gods caused Orpheus to be slain by women as a punishment for cowardice; and Isocrates attributes his rending asunder to the blasphemous treatment of the gods in his poems. That they could give two totally different causes for the occurrence shows pretty clearly that the legend itself, as it was generally known in the fourth century B.C., recognized no cause, or at least no cause which was essential to the legend. But though there may have been no proper cause or justification for the murder, the women who committed it must have had some immediate motive, rational or irrational, in the minds of those who formulated the incident illustrated in the vase paintings. The evidence of classical times concerning the death itself will not carry us any farther than this.

There remains one text concerning the death of Orpheus which tells a different story. Whereas all the others agree in making him suffer a violent death at the hands of women, in this one he is slain by the thunderbolt of Zeus. There is some doubt, however, about the date of it, because it is found in a rhetorical declamation which, though it is attributed to Alcidamas, a rival of Isocrates, is probably spurious and therefore of uncertain date. The author undertakes to make out a damaging case against Palamedes, and, to do so, robs him of the glory of some of the many inventions for which he is famous. Among these is the art of writing, the credit for which he assigns to Orpheus (Ps.-Alcidamas, *Ulixes* 24, ed. Blass, *Antipho* = *Test.* 123): γράμματα μὲν δὴ πρῶτος Ὀρφεὺς ἐξήνεγκε, παρὰ Μουσῶν μαθών, ὡς καὶ ἐπὶ τῷ μνήματι αὐτοῦ δηλοῖ τὰ ἐπιγράμματα·

> Μουσάων πρόπολον τῇδ' Ὀρφέα Θρῇκες ἔθηκαν,
> ὃν κτάνεν ὑψιμέδων Ζεὺς ψολόεντι βέλει,
> Οἰάγρου φίλον υἱόν, ὃς Ἡρακλῆ ἐξεδίδαξεν,
> εὑρὼν ἀνθρώποις γράμματα καὶ σοφίην.

Now though the piece attributed to Alcidamas may be postclassical, it is not impossible that the epigram which is quoted may be early; and it has been argued that it may have been composed about 431 B.C. as a bit of propaganda to mollify the Thracians, with whom the Athenians were trying to establish friendly relations. Whatever may be the date of the epigram, it is an extraordinary document. Nowhere else, in any period, are we informed that Orpheus was the teacher of Heracles or that he was the inventor of writing, and nowhere except in Diogenes

Laertius (*Proem.* 5), who quotes the second line of the epigram, and in Pausanias (ix, 30, 5) do we find the idea that Orpheus was slain by the thunderbolt of Zeus.[16] Whenever the epigram was composed, it is even more striking proof of the instability of the legend than the divergence between Plato and Isocrates, who find two totally different causes for the murder by the women, and the divergence between Aeschylus and Isocrates on the one hand, who have Orpheus torn to pieces, and the vase paintings on the other, which represent him as killed by the crude weapons with which the women are armed.[17]

After Orpheus' participation in the expedition of the Argonauts and the circumstances of his death, the third incident in his career which we encounter in a chronological review of the evidence is his descent to Hades to recover his wife. We have already seen an allusion to this story in the *Symposium* of Plato. But this is not the earliest occurrence of it. In the *Alcestis*, which was produced in 438 B.C., Euripides puts into the mouth of Admetus, even before Alcestis has expired, but in anticipation of his bereavement after her death, the following words (357–362 = *Test.* 59):

> εἰ δ' Ὀρφέως μοι γλῶσσα καὶ μέλος παρῆν,
> ὥστ' ἢ κόρην Δήμητρος ἢ κείνης πόσιν
> ὕμνοισι κηλήσαντά σ' ἐξ Ἅιδου λαβεῖν,
> κατῆλθον ἄν, καί μ' οὔθ' ὁ Πλούτωνος κύων

[16] For a full discussion of the epigram see I. M. Linforth, "Two Notes on the Legend of Orpheus," *Trans. Am. Philol. Assoc.*, LXII (1931), 5–11.

[17] According to Schol. Eur. *Rhesus* 895, which is quoted on p. 22, Asclepiades of Tragilos denied that Orpheus had some experience which was generally attributed to him (οὐ μὴν τοιοῦτό γε πάθος ⟨οἷον λέγεται⟩ γενέσθαι). He may have meant that he was not slain by women, but it is impossible to be sure.

οὔθ' οὑπὶ κώπῃ ψυχοπομπὸς ἂν Χάρων
ἔσχον, πρὶν ἐς φῶς σὸν καταστῆσαι βίον.

Though Euripides does not say explicitly that Orpheus had gone to the lower world, but only that his gift of song was such that he could have done so and could have prevailed on the gods to restore his wife to life, there is little doubt that he is referring to a story which was already well known. Otherwise we should have to suppose that a fanciful conceit of Euripides was the germ of the whole famous story, and this is shown to be altogether unlikely by the evidence which is next to be considered. It is significant, furthermore, that in the story to which Euripides alludes Orpheus must have been successful in his undertaking. If he had failed, any reference to the matter would be inappropriate. The story, therefore, is strikingly different from the version which Vergil uses in the fourth *Georgic* and which is most familiar to the general reader.

Almost contemporary with the *Alcestis*, or possibly a little later, is the famous sculptured relief in the museum at Naples, of which several copies exist in other parts of Europe.[18] The three figures in the relief are identified by inscriptions above their heads as Hermes, Eurydice, and Orpheus. It has been suspected, but not proved, that these inscriptions were a later addition to the work. The figures of Hermes and Orpheus, however, are clearly recognizable without the inscriptions (Orpheus holds his lyre in his left hand, and, as in contemporary vase paintings, he

[18] Brunn-Bruckmann, pl. 341a = *Test.* 59. For a discussion of this relief see Gruppe in Roscher's *Lexikon*, s.v. Orpheus, p. 1194, and esp. J. Heurgon, "Orphée et Eurydice avant Virgile," *Mélanges d'archéologie et d'histoire*, XLIX (1932), 34 ff.

wears the Thracian foxskin cap and high boots), and there can be no doubt that the relief portrays some moment in the coming or going of Orpheus' wife to or from Hades.[19] Beyond this almost everything about it is obscure, and it has given rise to much controversy. No one knows who the sculptor was, the purpose for which the relief was made, or the precise meaning of the scene. It has been suggested that the moment represented is that of the death of Eurydice, when Hermes is about to lead her away and Orpheus is taking his last farewell; that the scene is in the lower world and shows us Orpheus victorious, receiving Eurydice from the hands of Hermes and about to lead her back to the light; or that Orpheus, conducting his wife to the upper world, has just looked back and is on the point of resigning her to Hermes for the second time. The last interpretation, which is the one currently accepted, has received strong support from the searching analysis of Heurgon. With the second or the third interpretation, but not with the first, we have a scene in the story of Orpheus' descent to Hades to recover his wife. The second represents him as successful, as he is also in Euripides; the third shows him on the point of failure. The best interpretation, therefore, recognizes a version of the story which is inconsistent with that alluded to in the *Alcestis*.

[19] The name of Orpheus' wife first appears in literature as Ἀγριόπη (or Ἀργιόπη) in Hermesianax (ap. Athenaeus, xiii, 597 B) at the beginning of the third century B.C.; as Εὐρυδίκεια in Moschus (iii, 124) in the first century B.C. But Εὐρυδίκη is found on one of the South Italian vases of the third century B.C. (or possibly earlier) which represent Orpheus in Hades (Santangelo, 709; *Wiener Vorlegeblätter*, Ser. E, Pl. III; A. Winkler, "Die Darstellung der Unterwelt auf unteritalischen Vasen," *Breslauer Philol., Abh.*, III, No. 5, 1888).

Plato's version in the *Symposium*[20] is still different. Orpheus descends to the lower world for his wife, but he produces a very bad impression on the gods; in their opinion he is a poor-spirited creature, as one might expect a lyre player to be; instead of dying courageously for his love, he has moved heaven and earth to get into Hades alive. Consequently they do not give him his wife, but only show him a phantom of her. He returns to the world without having accomplished his purpose, and the whole discreditable incident was the cause of the gods' punishing him with an ignominious death. As Heurgon points out,[21] Orpheus' failure to recover his wife cannot have been invented by Plato; with the legend of his success so clear in Euripides, Plato could not have said bluntly "Orpheus failed" (Ὀρφέα . . . ἀτελῆ) without explanation or apology, unless this version of the story too were already abroad. And, indeed, the Naples relief probably shows that it was. It is difficult, however, to reconcile the incident of showing Orpheus a phantom of his wife with the scene represented on the marble. Heurgon suggests that Plato really has in mind the version of the marble according to which the gods allowed Orpheus to carry his wife back to the upper world on condition that he should not look back at her until they emerged into the light, but, interpreting this to mean that they had from the beginning no real intention of giving up Eurydice, he chose to make their mocking deception more immediate and more humiliating by saying that they had never acceded to his request in any form, but had only shown him a

[20] Quoted on p. 11 above. [21] *Op. cit.*, p. 31 (see p. 17 above).

phantom. However this may be, it is clear that there were two versions of the story of Orpheus' descent to Hades: in one he succeeded by the power of his music in persuading the gods to allow him to bring his wife back to life, in the other he failed. Again, in this second version, the story was told in two ways: he failed because he did not comply with the condition that was imposed, or because the gods scornfully rejected his plea and mocked him with a phantom.

One feature in Plato's story requires special comment. The cause which moved the gods to reject Orpheus' plea was that, being a lyre player, he was lacking in manly courage. This quality of Orpheus has already been revealed in other connections. The manner of his death, helpless though he may have been in the hands of a troop of angry women, presents him in an ignominious light. Besides this, his association with the heroes of the Argo caused some surprise. In a scholium which has already been quoted[22] it is said that people wondered how it was that, "being weak" (ἀσθενὴς ὢν), he had taken part in the expedition, and the explanation is offered, probably from Herodorus, that he was needed to enable the heroes to pass the Sirens in safety, doubtless by the power of his music. Plainly, Orpheus was no hero, but only a lyre player, with a lyre player's powers and weaknesses.

Further evidence for the version of the story in which Orpheus is successful is supplied by Isocrates, who must have been writing within a few years of the time when Plato composed the *Symposium*. In the *Busiris* he criti-

[22] Schol. Apollon. i, 23 (see p. 7 above).

cizes the sophist Polycrates for his method in writing an encomium on Busiris. Busiris, says Isocrates, killed living men before their time, Orpheus brought back the dead from Hades. Besides, Busiris could not have emulated Aeolus and Orpheus, because they lived long after his time. The passage is as follows (xi, 7 f. = *Test.* 60): *οὕτω δ' ἠμέλησας, εἰ μηδὲν ὁμολογούμενον ἐρεῖς, ὥστε φῂς μὲν αὐτὸν τὴν Αἰόλου καὶ τὴν Ὀρφέως ζηλῶσαι δόξαν, ἀποφαίνεις δ' οὐδὲν τῶν αὐτῶν ἐκείνοις ἐπιτηδεύσαντα. πότερα γὰρ τοῖς περὶ Αἰόλου λεγομένοις αὐτὸν παρατάξωμεν; ἀλλ' ἐκεῖνος μὲν τῶν ξένων τοὺς ἐπὶ τὴν χώραν ἐκπίπτοντας εἰς τὰς αὑτῶν πατρίδας ἀπέστελλεν, ὁ δ' εἰ χρὴ τοῖς ὑπὸ σοῦ λεγομένοις πιστεύειν, θύσας κατήσθιεν. ἢ τοῖς Ὀρφέως ἔργοις ὁμοιώσωμεν; ἀλλ' ὁ μὲν ἐξ Ἅιδου τοὺς τεθνεῶτας ἀνῆγεν, ὁ δὲ πρὸ μοίρας τοὺς ζῶντας ἀπώλλυεν. . . . ὃ δὲ πάντων ἀτοπώτατον, ὅτι περὶ τὰς γενεαλογίας ἐσπουδακὼς ἐτόλμησας εἰπεῖν, ὡς τούτους ἐζήλωσεν, ὧν οὐδ' οἱ πατέρες πω κατ' ἐκεῖνον τὸν χρόνον γεγονότες ἦσαν.* Orpheus brought back the dead from Hades: the plural *τοὺς τεθνεῶτας* and the imperfect *ἀνῆγεν* suggest that this was a regular practice. But this form of expression may well be used, especially in the style of an encomium, to generalize the significance of a single incident; and since the only person whom Orpheus is supposed to have brought back from Hades is his wife, as far as we know from all the evidence of antiquity, we must assume that Isocrates has this instance in mind.

There are no further incidents to record in the career of Orpheus.[23] Beyond the three which have just been

[23] This statement possibly requires correction. It will be shown later (pp. 119–138) that the story of the singing head of Orpheus, which is told in postclassical texts, may have been known in classical times.

examined, his life was literally uneventful, as far as the legend is revealed by evidence before 300 B.C. What is told of him besides, relates to his parentage and descent, his profession, and the heritage which he left to the world. We have already heard something of all these matters in the documents which have been cited. It now remains to recall the information which is to be found in them, and to complete the examination by the citation of other texts.

Pindar, in the ambiguous passage of the fourth *Pythian*, which has been discussed above,[24] may or may not have declared that Orpheus was the son of Apollo. The fact was stated explicitly, however, by Asclepiades of Tragilos in the fourth century B.C. in the sixth book of his Τραγῳδούμενα, as we learn from Schol. Eur. *Rhesus* 895.[25] This interesting scholium must be quoted at length (Schwartz, II, 343 = *Test.* 22, 23): *ἰαλέμῳ: καὶ Ἀσκληπιάδης ἐν ἕκτῳ Τραγῳδουμένων ⟨εἶναι⟩ πλείους τῆς Καλλιόπης λέγει παῖδας ἐν τούτῳ· Καλλιόπῃ γὰρ τὸν Ἀπόλλωνα μιχθέντα γεννῆσαι Λίνον τὸν πρεσβύτατον καὶ τρεῖς μετ' ἐκεῖνον, Ὑμέναιον ⟨Ἰάλεμον⟩ Ὀρφέα. τῷ δὲ νεωτάτῳ τὴν μὲν ἐπιθυμίαν ⟨τῶν τῆς μητρὸς ἐπιτη⟩δευμάτων ἐμπεσεῖν καὶ περὶ τὴν μουσικὴν ⟨περιγενέσθ⟩αι πάντων· οὐ μὴν τοιοῦτό γε πάθος ⟨οἷον λέγεται⟩ γενέσθαι :—*

*ἄλλως : ἰαλέμῳ : ⟨ἱστορεῖται τὸν ἰά⟩λεμον παρωνομάσθαι ἐπὶ τιμῇ Ἰαλέμου τοῦ Ἀπόλλωνος καὶ Καλλιόπης, ὥς φησι Πίνδαρος·*[26]

[24] See p. 4.

[25] Asclepiades, fr. 6 Jacoby. The statement of Asclepiades is alluded to also in Schol. Pind. *Pyth.* iv, 176, and Schol. Apollon. i, 23, both of which are quoted above (pp. 7 f.).

[26] For the fragment of Pindar (fr. 139 Bergk) which here follows—the eleven lines at the top of p. 23—the text of Bowra (fr. 126) is printed instead of that of Schwartz.

ἔντι μὲν χρυσαλακάτου τεκέων ⟨Λατοῦς⟩ ἀοιδαὶ
ὥριαι παιανίδες· ἔντι ⟨δὲ καὶ⟩ θάλ-
λοντος ἐκ κισσοῦ στεφάνων Διονύσου
⟨διθύραμβον μ⟩αιόμεναι· τὸ δὲ κοιμίσσαν⟨το⟩ τρεῖς
. . . . . . . . . . σώματ' ἀποφθιμένων.
ἁ μὲν ἀχέταν Λίνον αἴλινον ὕμνει,
ἁ δ' Ὑμέναιον, ⟨ὃν⟩ ἐν γάμοισι χροϊζόμενον
⟨Μοῖρα⟩ σύμπρωτον λάβεν,
ἐσχάτοις ὕμνοισιν· ἁ δ' Ἰάλεμον ὠμοβόρῳ νου-
σῳ ὅτι πεδαθέντα σθένος,
υἱὸν Οἰάγρου . . .

According to Asclepiades, then, Apollo and Calliope had four sons, Linus the eldest, and after him Hymenaeus, Ialemus, and Orpheus.

The commoner tradition, however, is that the father of Orpheus was Oeagrus.[27] Pindar himself, though he may have named Apollo as the father in the fourth *Pythian*, elsewhere names Oeagrus. This we learn from the scholium on the passage; and it may be that the scholiast was thinking of the poem which contained the fragment just quoted, since the last words of the fragment are υἱὸν Οἰάγρου, and since Linus, Hymenaeus, and Ialemus, with whom Orpheus is associated by Asclepiades, appear in the verses immediately preceding. Oeagrus appears again

[27] Kern, who interprets the name of Orpheus as meaning "der einsame Sänger," finds support for his opinion in the name of Oeagrus: "zu Orpheus paßt also sein Vater vortrefflich, 'der einsam auf den Feldern Lebende,' wie der Name Oiagros wohl mit A. Fick am besten zu deuten ist" (Kern, *Orpheus*, 1920, p. 23). Fick, however, as Kern recalls (p. 16), points out that Oeagrus may also mean "der Schafe und Felder hat"; and still another possibility, which seems not to have been observed, is that οἴαγρος may have been a "wild sheep," as ὄναγρος was a "wild ass."

as the father in the *Symposium* of Plato and in the epigram quoted by Ps.-Alcidamas.[28]

That Calliope was the mother of Orpheus is attested not only by Asclepiades, but also probably by Timotheus (*Pers.* 234 ff. Wilamowitz = *Test.* 24): *πρῶτος ποικιλόμουσον 'Ορ[φε]ὺς [χέλ]υν ἐτέκνωσεν, υἱὸς Καλλιόπα[ς] Πιερίας ἔπι. Τέρπανδρος δ' ἐπὶ τῷ δέκα ζεῦξε μοῦσαν ἐν ᾠδαῖς.* This is Wilamowitz' uncertain restoration of the text. The letters which are expanded to *'Ορφεὺς χέλυν* appear in the papyrus as ΟΡΙΥΣΥΝ.

Plato, in the *Republic* (ii, 364 E), calls Musaeus and Orpheus "the offspring of the Moon and the Muses" (*Σελήνης τε καὶ Μουσῶν ἐκγόνων*). Since Musaeus is elsewhere called a descendant of the Moon and Orpheus is not, it is probable that Plato was thinking of Orpheus as the son of a Muse. In the *Rhesus* of Euripides (895) Orpheus is said to be the cousin of Rhesus, who is himself said to be the son of a Muse.[29]

It is curious that though Orpheus is more than once called the son of Oeagrus and more than once the son of Calliope, he is never until postclassical times called the son of both; the only union is that of Calliope and Apollo.

Besides the evidence which we have seen concerning Orpheus' parents, brothers, and wife, we have fortunately some information concerning the place which was assigned to him in the tables which were constructed by the genealogists of the fifth century B.C. In Proclus' *Life of Homer*

---

[28] See pp. 11 and 15 above.

[29] The passages from the *Republic* and the *Rhesus* are quoted on p. 77 and p. 61 below. For the ancestry of Musaeus see *Test.* 166 ff.

(p. 26, 14 Wilamowitz, *Vitae Homeri et Hesiodi*, in Lietzmann, *Kleine Texte*, No. 137 = Hellanicus, fr. 5 Jacoby = *Test.* 7) we find the following: Ἑλλάνικος δὲ καὶ Δαμάστης καὶ Φερεκύδης εἰς Ὀρφέα τὸ γένος ἀνάγουσιν αὐτοῦ (sc. Ὁμήρου). Μαίονα γάρ φασι τὸν Ὁμήρου πατέρα καὶ Δῖον τὸν Ἡσιόδου γενέσθαι Ἀπελλίδος τοῦ Μελανώπου τοῦ Ἐπιφράδεος τοῦ Χαριφήμου τοῦ Φιλοτέρπεος τοῦ Ἰαδμονίδα τοῦ Εὐκλέους τοῦ Δωρίωνος τοῦ Ὀρφέως. The line of descent, therefore, is as follows:

Orpheus
|
Dorion
|
Eucles
|
Iadmonides
|
Philoterpes
|
Chariphemus
|
Epiphrades
|
Melanopus
|
Apellis
|
Maion | Dius
Homer | Hesiod

Since the *Vita Romana* of Homer (p. 30, 26 Wilamowitz, *Vitae Homeri et Hesiodi* [Lietzmann, *Kleine Texte*, No. 137] = Damastes, fr. 11a Jacoby) says explicitly that according to Damastes Homer was the tenth in descent from Musaeus, who does not appear in the table just given, it is probable that Proclus' addition of Damastes' name to those of Hellanicus and Pherecydes was due to carelessness. Concerning Pherecydes we have no further evidence to prove whether the attribution of the table to him is correct or not. Hellanicus, however, whose name is the first of the three, and who is reported in other sources to have dealt with the ancestry of Homer and Hesiod (see fr. 5 Jacoby), may safely be regarded as the authority for the genealogy. The same table, with certain variants, appears also in *Certam. Hom. et Hes.* 45 ff. Allen (= *Test.* 9) and in Charax (ap. Suidas, s. v. Ὅμηρος = *F. H. G.* fr. 20 = *Test.* 9); but in these two sources the earlier ancestry of Orpheus also is given thus:

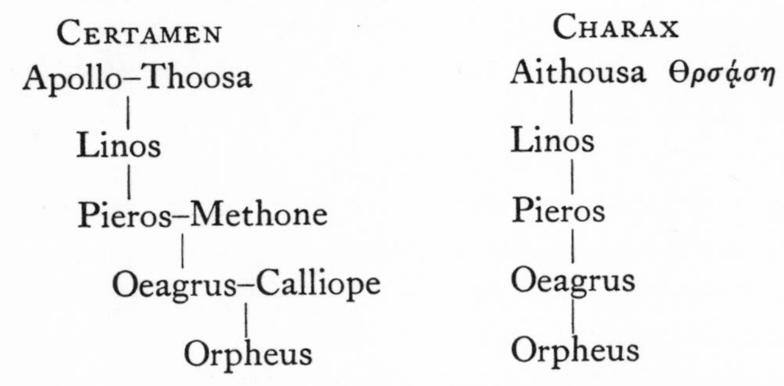


It is probable, therefore, that Hellanicus' table included the ancestors of Orpheus as well as his descendants; but in view of the variants which both precede and follow his name, it is impossible to be sure of the exact form of the table as it was composed by him.[30]

[30] For the complicated history of these genealogies see Jacoby's note on Hellanicus, fr. 5; Rohde, "Zur Chronologie der griechischen Litteraturgeschichte," *Rhein. Mus.*, XXXVI (1881), 384 ff.; and Gruppe in Roscher's *Lexikon*, s.v. Orpheus, pp. 1074 ff.

Since Hellanicus, as Rohde shows,[31] probably made Homer a contemporary of the Trojan War, Orpheus, whom he placed ten or eleven generations earlier, must have lived three centuries before the Trojan War. This is, of course, inconsistent with the story of Orpheus as an Argonaut and with the statement in the epigram given by Ps.-Alcidamas that Orpheus was the teacher of Heracles. The chronologists of later times wrestled with these inconsistencies and devised many methods of reconciling them, which need not be discussed here.[32]

There is one text which makes Orpheus a contemporary of the Idaean Dactyls and their pupil, and the introducer of *τελεταί* into Greece. This is a quotation from Ephorus in Diodorus (v, 64, 4 = *Test.* 42): *ἔνιοι δ' ἱστοροῦσιν, ὧν ἐστι καὶ Ἔφορος, τοὺς Ἰδαίους Δακτύλους γενέσθαι μὲν κατὰ τὴν Ἴδην τὴν ἐν Φρυγίᾳ, διαβῆναι δὲ μετὰ Μυγδόνος εἰς τὴν Εὐρώπην· ὑπάρξαντας δὲ γόητας ἐπιτηδεῦσαι τάς τε ἐπῳδὰς καὶ τελετὰς καὶ μυστήρια, καὶ περὶ Σαμοθρᾳκην διατρίψαντας οὐ μετρίως ἐν τούτοις ἐκπλήττειν τοὺς ἐγχωρίους· καθ' ὃν δὴ χρόνον καὶ τὸν Ὀρφέα, φύσει διαφόρῳ κεχορηγημένον πρὸς ποίησιν καὶ μελῳδίαν, μαθητὴν γενέσθαι τούτων, καὶ πρῶτον εἰς τοὺς Ἕλληνας ἐξενεγκεῖν τελετὰς καὶ μυστήρια.* This supposed incident in Orpheus' life is obviously invented to establish a connection between the teletae which he is said to have introduced in Greece and the practices of the Idaean Dactyls in Phrygia. It will be considered again in a later chapter.

Always Orpheus is a minstrel. From his first appearance on the Delphic metope the lyre is scarcely ever out of his hand. As an Argonaut he plays and sings to set

[31] *Op. cit.*, pp. 388 ff. [32] See Gruppe, *op. cit.*, pp. 1064 ff.

the time for the rowers, and he is indispensable to them in their perilous passage by the island of the Sirens. When he goes to the lower world in quest of his wife, it is by means of his song that he hopes to prevail over the gods of the dead. When the wild women who were bent upon his destruction made their attack, it was when he was in the act of playing and singing, and it was with his lyre that he sought in vain to defend himself. He was generally recognized as a Thracian, like the other legendary poets of the Pierian group—Linos, Pamphos, Thamyris, Philammon, Musaeus, Eumolpus. Before he became the pupil of the Idaean Dactyls he was exceptionally endowed with the gift of poetry and song. He was son of a Muse and servant of the Muses. By some his father was said to be Apollo, and if the god was not his father he was at least his patron. Orpheus was himself the father of song. He was numbered with other famous minstrels of legend—Philammon, Linos, Hymenaeus, Ialemus. The genealogists made him the ancestor of Homer and Hesiod.

All this has already appeared in the evidence which has been brought forward. There are many other documents, besides, which present Orpheus simply as a minstrel, without allusion to any particular exploit. These corroborate the impression which has already been produced, that the conception of Orpheus which prevailed in classical times was that of a great lyre player and singer.

Plato, in the *Ion*, numbers him among the great legendary musicians who were famous for their song and their skill with instruments (*Ion* 533 B–C = *Test.* 56): Ἀλλὰ *μήν, ὥς γ' ἐγὼ οἶμαι, οὐδ ἐν αὐλήσει γε οὐδὲ ἐν κιθαρίσει οὐδὲ ἐν κιθαρῳδίᾳ οὐδὲ ἐν ῥαψῳδίᾳ οὐδεπώποτ' εἶδες ἄνδρα ὅστις περὶ μὲν Ὀλύμπου δεινός ἐστιν ἐξηγεῖσθαι ἢ περὶ Θαμύρου ἢ περὶ Ὀρφέως ἢ περὶ Φημίου τοῦ Ἰθακησίου ῥαψῳδοῦ, περὶ δὲ Ἴωνος τοῦ Ἐφεσίου [ῥαψῳδοῦ] ἀπορεῖ καὶ οὐκ ἔχει συμβαλέσθαι ἅ τε εὖ ῥαψῳδεῖ καὶ ἃ μή.*

In the *Laws* Plato insists that no poems shall be sung at festivals except those which have been composed by good men who have performed noble deeds and who have been honored by the state. No exception shall be made to this rule, even if the music is sweeter than the hymns of Thamyras and Orpheus (*Laws* viii, 829 D–E = *Fragm.* 12): *μηδ' ἂν ἡδίων ᾖ* (sc. ἡ Μοῦσα) *τῶν Θαμύρου τε καὶ Ὀρφείων ὕμνων*. This is sometimes regarded as an allusion to Orphic poetry which was in existence in the time of Plato, and thus taken as proof that some of this poetry was in the form of hymns. This is probably erroneous for two reasons. If Plato was thinking of extant hymns of Orpheus he must also have been thinking of extant hymns of Thamyras; but we have no evidence whatever that there existed or had ever existed any hymns which were attributed to Thamyras. It is likely therefore that only the legendary poetical skill is meant. Again, from what we know of extant Orphic poetry we cannot believe that it would be referred to as a model of poetic beauty. At the same time, we may imagine that Plato would not object if his readers perceived a tacit condemnation of extant Orphic poetry as unsuitable for the public festivals. Whether Plato intends to give a hint of this by using the adjective Ὀρφείων, when the natural word after Θαμύρου is Ὀρφέως, I am unable to say.

One of the two paintings of Polygnotus in the Lesche of the Cnidians at Delphi, which were executed sometime before the middle of the fifth century B.C., represented the descent of Odysseus to Hades when he went to consult the soul of Tiresias. This picture, as we learn from Pausanias (x, 28 ff.), contained many separate scenes and a very large number of figures of famous personages who had died before Odysseus' visit. Among them is the figure of Orpheus, whose appearance is described as follows (30, 6 f. = *Test.* 69): ἀποβλέψαντι δὲ αὖθις ἐς τὰ κάτω τῆς γραφῆς ἔστιν ἐφεξῆς μετὰ τὸν Πάτροκλον οἷα ἐπὶ λόφου τινὸς Ὀρφεὺς καθεζόμενος, ἐφάπτεται δὲ [καὶ] τῇ ἀριστερᾷ κιθάρας, τῇ δὲ ἑτέρᾳ χειρὶ ἰτέας κλῶνές εἰσιν ὧν ψαύει, προσανακέκλιται δὲ τῷ δένδρῳ· τὸ δὲ ἄλσος ἔοικεν εἶναι τῆς Περσεφόνης, ἔνθα αἴγειροι καὶ ἰτέαι δόξῃ τῇ Ὁμήρου πεφύκασιν· Ἑλληνικὸν δὲ τὸ σχῆμά ἐστι τῷ Ὀρφεῖ, καὶ οὔτε ἡ ἐσθὴς οὔτε ἐπίθημά ἐστιν ἐπὶ τῇ κεφαλῇ Θρᾴκιον. τῷ δένδρῳ δὲ τῇ ἰτέᾳ κατὰ τὸ ἕτερον μέρος προσανακεκλιμένος ἐστὶν αὐτῇ Προμέδων. εἰσὶ μὲν δὴ οἳ νομίζουσι καθάπερ ἐς ποίησιν ἐπεισῆχθαι τοῦ Προμέδοντος ⟨τὸ⟩ ὄνομα ὑπὸ τοῦ Πολυγνώτου· τοῖς δὲ εἰρημένον ἐστὶν ἄνδρα Ἕλληνα ἔς τε τὴν ἄλλην ἅπασαν γενέσθαι φιλήκοον μουσικὴν καὶ ἐπὶ τῇ ᾠδῇ μάλιστα τῇ Ὀρφέως. Near by are sitting also Schedius and Pelias, the latter looking at Orpheus. Near Pelias the blind Thamyris is sitting, in a dejected attitude, with his broken lyre flung on the ground at his feet. Above Thamyris is Marsyas, seated on a rock, and by him Olympus, represented as a boy learning to play the flute. The significance of the willow tree is not clear,[33] and we can take Pausanias' guess that it represents a grove of Persephone

[33] Cf. A. B. Cook, *Zeus*, I, 527 ff.

only for what it is worth. Promedon is otherwise unknown. Nor can we recognize with certainty any connection between the scene and the incidents of the Orphic legend. It is, of course, impossible that the descent to Hades in quest of Eurydice is intended. The painter could not have made this incident contemporaneous with Odysseus' visit to the lower world. We can only suppose that Orpheus is included in the picture simply as one of the great company of illustrious dead whom the painter has chosen to portray. He is the famous minstrel, with his unfailing lyre, and he wears Grecian dress, as he does in the earlier vase paintings of the fifth century B.C. His profession is further emphasized by the proximity of the other musicians, Thamyris, Marsyas, and Olympus.

In some of the vase paintings in which Thracian women are rushing to attack Orpheus while he is playing and singing, there are also represented Thracian warriors who appear to be enraptured by his music. In one of these[34] there is also a Silenus, standing behind Orpheus, and the music seems to have the same effect upon him that it has upon the Thracian who is standing in front of him. A woman armed with a club approaches the group from behind the Silenus. Besides the paintings representing the death of Orpheus, there are others of a more peaceful type in which he appears as a musician.[35] In one picture,[36] on a black-figured vase, he is shown alone with his lyre, and there is no question of his identity, because the words

[34] *Arch. Zeitung*, XXVI (1868), Taf. 3.

[35] See Robert, *Die griechische Heldensage*, I, 399.

[36] *Arch. Zeitung*, XLII (1884), 272.

χαῖρε Ὀρφεῦ are added. In others he seems to be casting the spell of his music on listening Thracian men. Sometimes, but very seldom, animals are represented as enraptured by his music. A vase of the seventh century B.C.,[37] in which he is surrounded by seven birds and a deer, has already been mentioned as being possibly the earliest piece of evidence concerning Orpheus of any kind. In another painting,[38] of the fourth century B.C., we see Orpheus playing in the midst, with two warriors on one side of him, and two women, apparently with no hostile intent, on the other; beneath him is lying a deer, which has also yielded to the spell of his music.[39]

The magical quality of Orpheus' music, which is illustrated in these vase paintings by its effect upon Thracian warriors, a Silenus, and a deer, has already appeared in other connections. In the *Alcestis*, Admetus longed for the γλῶσσα καὶ μέλος of Orpheus that he might charm (κηλήσαντα) Persephone or her spouse and so bring back his wife to the light;[40] and according to Herodorus, Orpheus was needed by the Argonauts especially to save them from the beguiling Sirens.[41] But his power is effective not only over gods and men and animals; trees and

[37] See p. 2, n. 2, above. [38] *Mon. dell' Inst.*, VIII (1867), Tav. 43.

[39] On the back of a bronze mirror which, according to R. Eisler (*Orpheus*, 1925, p. 95), is mentioned in a catalogue of the Tyszhiéwicz Collection (*La collection Tyszhiéwicz*, Munich, 1892, p. 4), and which is reproduced by Guthrie (*Orpheus and Greek Religion*, p. 66), is portrayed a seated male figure playing a lyre, with a deer, a panther, and two birds. The mirror may date from the fifth century B.C., and the subject may be Orpheus charming animals with his music.

[40] See p. 16 above. Elsewhere in this play (962 ff.) the chorus bewail the fact that neither Asclepius nor Orpheus has supplied to men the means of overcoming Necessity. See p. 119 below.

[41] See p. 8 above.

rocks, too, and all inanimate things follow at his bidding, as may be seen in the following texts, which are contemporaneous with the vase paintings.

1) Simonides (fr. 27 Diehl = *Test.* 47): ὡς γράφει που περὶ αὐτοῦ (sc. Ὀρφέως) καὶ Σιμωνίδης οὕτως·

> τοῦ καὶ ἀπειρέσιοι
> πωτῶντ' ὄρνιθες ὑπὲρ κεφαλᾶς,
> ἀνὰ δ' ἰχθύες ὀρθοὶ κυανέου
> ἐξ ὕδατος ἅλλοντο καλᾷ σὺν ἀοιδᾷ.

2) Aeschylus, *Agamemnon* 1629 ff. (= *Test.* 48):

> Ὀρφεῖ δὲ γλῶσσαν τὴν ἐναντίαν ἔχεις.
> ὁ μὲν γὰρ ἦγε πάντ' ἀπὸ φθογγῆς χαρᾷ,
> σὺ δ' ἐξορίνας νηπίοις ὑλάγμασιν
> ἄξει· κρατηθεὶς δ' ἡμερώτερος φανεῖ.

These words are said by Aegisthus to the chorus in reply to their remonstrances. Orpheus was wont to attract all things by the delight which was inspired by his song; the chorus will be dragged off in consequence of their croaking. The passive ἄξει is contrasted with the active ἦγε.

3) Euripides, *Bacchae* 560 ff. (= *Test.* 49):

> τάχα δ' ἐν ταῖς πολυδένδρεσ-
> σιν Ὀλύμπου θαλάμαις, ἔν-
> θα ποτ' Ὀρφεὺς κιθαρίζων
> σύναγεν δένδρεα μούσαις,
> σύναγεν θῆρας ἀγρώτας.

The chorus suspect that Dionysus may be reveling in the glens of Olympus, where once Orpheus with his lyre charmed the beasts and the trees; but no connection between Orpheus and Dionysus is indicated.

4) Euripides, *Iph. Aul.* 1211 ff. (= *Test.* 50):

> εἰ μὲν τὸν Ὀρφέως εἶχον, ὦ πάτερ, λόγον,
> πείθειν ἐπᾴδουσ', ὥσθ' ὁμαρτεῖν μοι πέτρας,
> κηλεῖν τε τοῖς λόγοισιν οὓς ἐβουλόμην,
> ἐνταῦθ' ἂν ἦλθον.

The words λόγον and λόγοισιν, which are more suitable to Iphigenia than to Orpheus, mean that she wishes to be able to accomplish by speech what he accomplished by song (ἐπᾴδουσ' κηλεῖν).

5) Euripides, *Cyclops* 646 ff. (= *Test.* 83):

> ἀλλ' οἶδ' ἐπῳδὴν Ὀρφέως ἀγαθὴν πάνυ,
> ὡς αὐτόματον τὸν δαλὸν ἐς τὸ κρανίον
> στείχονθ' ὑφάπτειν τὸν μονῶπα παῖδα γῆς.

The satyr professes to know an incantation of Orpheus which will cause the beam of wood to move of itself and put out the eye of the Cyclops.

6) Euripides, *Medea* 542 ff. (= *Test.* 59);

> εἴη δ' ἔμοιγε μήτε χρυσὸς ἐν δόμοις
> μήτ' Ὀρφέως κάλλιον ὑμνῆσαι μέλος,
> εἰ μὴ 'πίσημος ἡ τύχη γένοιτό μοι,

Jason is pointing out to Medea that by leaving her obscure home in Colchis and coming to Greece she has won the fame which she deserves for her great powers. Neither wealth, he says, nor a gift of song greater than that of Orpheus has any value unless it brings distinction in the eyes of the world. The skill of Orpheus seems to occur to Jason (and to Euripides) because he is thinking of Medea's magic.

7) Plato, *Protag.* 315 A (not in Kern): *τούτων δὲ οἳ ὄπισθεν ἠκολούθουν ἐπακούοντες τῶν λεγομένων τὸ μὲν πολὺ ξένοι ἐφαίνοντο—οὓς ἄγει ἐξ ἑκάστων τῶν πόλεων ὁ Πρωταγόρας, δι' ὧν διεξέρχεται, κηλῶν τῇ φωνῇ ὥσπερ Ὀρφεύς, οἱ δὲ κατὰ τὴν φωνὴν ἕπονται κεκηλημένοι—ἦσαν δέ τινες καὶ τῶν ἐπιχωρίων ἐν τῷ χορῷ.*

Closely associated with the power of enchantment is the gift of prophecy, and this, too, Orpheus was credited with by Philochorus. Clement of Alexandria (*Strom.* i, 21, 134, 4 Stählin = *Test.* 87) says: *ἤδη δὲ καὶ Ὀρφέα Φιλόχορος* [*F. H. G.* fr. 190] *μάντιν ἱστορεῖ γενέσθαι ἐν τῷ πρώτῳ Περὶ μαντικῆς.*[42]

The review of the evidence concerning the legend of Orpheus closes[43] with a few texts in which is attributed to him the invention of certain things which were in use in the classical world. He belongs to the number of culture heroes from whom the Greeks liked to believe they had obtained the elements of their civilization. In the epigram preserved by Ps.-Alcidamas, to which reference has been made, he is credited with the invention of writing (*γράμμτα*) and poetry (if *σοφίην* may be so rendered). According to Ephorus,[44] he was the first to introduce teletae and mysteries into Greece. Mallius Theodorus (*De*

[42] Cf. also Plato, *Protag.* 316 D (= *Test.* 92), quoted and discussed below (p. 71).

[43] It is not necessary to do more than direct attention to the fact that two plays bore the name of Orpheus, one by the tragic poet Aristias of the fifth century B.C., and one by the comic poet Antiphanes in the fourth century B.C.: (1) Pollux, ix, 43 (= Aristias fr. 5 Nauck = *Test.* 253) *εἴρηται δὲ καὶ ἐν τῷ Ἀριστείου Ὀρφεῖ, 'ἦν μοι παλαίστρα καὶ δρόμος ξυστὸς πέλας'*; (2) Pollux x, 172 (= Antiphanes fr. 180 Kock = *Test.* 254): *τοῦτο* [sc. *βύσμα*] *δὲ βύστραν ἕτεροι κεκλήκασιν, ὡς . . . Ἀντιφάνης Ὀρφεῖ, 'βύστραν τιν' ἐκ φύλλων τινῶν'.*

[44] See p. 27 above.

*metris* iv, 1, p. 589, 20 Keil = *Test.* 106), writing at the end of the fourth century A.D., makes the following statement: "metrum dactylicum hexametrum inventum primitus ab Orpheo Critias adserit, Democritus a Musaeo." That the Critias referred to was the Athenian poet and politician of the end of the fifth century B.C. and that he did make this statement about the invention of the dactylic hexameter is rendered probable by some elegiacs quoted from him by Athenaeus, in which he names the origin of a number of things (i, 28 B = Critias fr. 2 Diels-Kranz). Plato includes Orpheus in a list of six culture heroes, without, however, specifying his contribution to civilization (*Laws* iii, 677 D = *Fragm.* 12): Τοῦτο ὅτι μὲν μυριάκις μύρια ἔτη διελάνθανεν ἄρα τοὺς τότε, χίλια δὲ ἀφ' οὗ γέγονεν, ἢ δὶς τοσαῦτα ἔτη, τὰ μὲν Δαιδάλῳ καταφανῆ γέγονεν, τὰ δὲ 'Ορφεῖ, τὰ δὲ Παλαμήδει, τὰ δὲ περὶ μουσικὴν Μαρσύᾳ καὶ 'Ολύμπῳ, περὶ λύραν δὲ 'Αμφίονι, τὰ δὲ ἄλλα ἄλλοις πάμπολλα, ὡς ἔπος εἰπεῖν χθὲς καὶ πρῴην γεγονότα.[45] What Plato is saying is that humanity got on for countless millennia without the blessings of civilization, and it is one or two thousand years since Daedalus, Orpheus, and the others gave their inventions to the world. The explanation of the dative Δαιδάλῳ, 'Ορφεῖ, etc., by which England is troubled, is to be found in the fact that the phrase καταφανῆ γέγονεν is chosen as the opposite of διελάνθανεν; the things which were to produce civilization had long remained hidden, but they became visible at last to the eyes of the great discoverers (εὑρέται). One

[45] This is Burnet's text. Hermann brackets ὅτι in the first line and inserts γάρ (which is found in some MSS) after μέν. Ast brackets the second γέγονεν; Hermann, followed by England, the first.

would like to know exactly what Plato had in mind for Orpheus. It is significant that music and the lyre are expressly assigned to others. If the notion that Orpheus invented writing had any vogue, this would be sufficient to give Orpheus a place in the list. If, on the other hand, Plato is thinking of the first institution of teletae, which, as we shall see, was very generally attributed to Orpheus, it is interesting to note that Plato regards them as a significant feature in human life.[46]

These last texts afford a transition from the kind of evidence which we have been examining so far to evidence of quite a different sort. We have been reviewing what men in classical times thought they knew about Orpheus himself, his life and death, his profession, and his relationships—in a word, about things of the past. Now we turn to their evidence concerning things of the present—the poetry, the institutions, the ideas, existing in classical times, which were associated with the name of Orpheus. In a proper biography of a historical personage, about whom a reasonable amount of sound documentary evidence is available, such a separation does not naturally suggest itself. The works which a man leaves to posterity, and the circumstances under which they are produced, naturally form a part of the story of his life. The case of Orpheus is strikingly different. In only a few texts have we found a collocation of the events of his legendary biography and the works which were supposed to have survived him. This can only mean that the connection

[46] Rathmann thinks that Plato meant to represent Orpheus as ἀρχηγὸς τῶν τελετῶν (*Quaestiones Pythagoreae Orphicae Empedocleae*, Diss. Halle, 1933, p. 60).

was not mythologically developed, or, if it was, that little heed was paid to it. Actually Orpheus appears as two persons,[47] the legendary figure whose career we have followed, and the author of poetry and institutions which will be examined in the following chapters.

## Rites

1) The earliest text containing an allusion to anything like Orphic religion is supplied by Herodotus, in his account of the curious customs of the Egyptians. The passage tells us little, and, unfortunately, the little it has to tell is not perfectly clear. Since the meaning of the Greek is not beyond question, it will be necessary to give careful attention to its interpretation before any conclusions can be drawn from it.

The Egyptians, says Herodotus (ii, 79), follow the customs which they have inherited from their ancestors and do not adopt foreign customs from abroad. There are certain resemblances, however, which he points out, between Egyptian customs and the customs of other nations. There is a particular song, or tune, for example, which is sung not only in Egypt, but in Phoenicia, in Cyprus, in Greece, and elsewhere. Herodotus is puzzled to know where the Egyptians got it; but they maintain that it originated in Egypt. Again, young men in Egypt show certain marked forms of respect to their elders which are also observed by the Lacedemonians (συμφέ-

[47] It would seem that Herodorus had something like this in mind when he said that there were two men called Orpheus, of whom one had sailed with the Argonauts (see p. 7 above). This, however, must be considered later in connection with other evidence (see p. 157 below).

ρονται δὲ καὶ τόδε ἄλλο Αἰγύπτιοι Ἑλλήνων μούνοισι Λακεδαιμονίοισι). The common gesture of salutation, however, which is used in Egypt is never found in Greece (τόδε μέντοι ἄλλο Ἑλλήνων οὐδαμοῖσι συμφέρονται). A third point of resemblance between Greece and Egypt is found in certain prohibitions concerning the use of wool. The Egyptians wear linen chitons and, over them, white garments of wool; but wool is not worn in the temples, nor is it buried with the dead, because this is forbidden by religion (ἐνδεδύκασι δὲ κιθῶνας λινέους . . . ἐπὶ τούτοισι δὲ εἰρίνεα εἵματα λευκὰ ἐπαναβληδὸν φορέουσι. οὐ μέντοι ἔς γε τὰ ἱρὰ ἐσφέρεται εἰρίνεα οὐδὲ συγκαταθάπτεταί σφι· οὐ γὰρ ὅσιον). Similar prohibitions against the use of wool are also found in Greece, as Herodotus explains in the following words (ii, 81 = *Test.* 216), which come immediately after the Greek which has just been quoted: ὁμολογέουσι δὲ ταῦτα τοῖσι Ὀρφικοῖσι καλεομένοισι καὶ Βακχικοῖσι, ἐοῦσι δὲ Αἰγυπτίοισι καὶ Πυθαγορείοισι. οὐδὲ γὰρ τούτων τῶν ὀργίων μετέχοντα ὅσιόν ἐστι ἐν εἰρινέοισι εἵμασι θαφθῆναι. ἔστι δὲ περὶ αὐτῶν ἱρὸς λόγος λεγόμενος.

This text, which is of interest to us because of the words τοῖσι Ὀρφικοῖσι καλεομένοισι, has been the subject of prolonged discussion, and there is no unanimity among scholars in its interpretation.[48]

[48] Besides the editions of Herodotus the following may be consulted: Gomperz, *Sitzungsber. der Wiener Akad.*, phil.-hist. Cl., CXIII (1886), 1032; Maass, *Orpheus* (1895), pp. 164 ff.; Knapp, "Orpheusdarstellungen," *Jahresber. Gymnas. in Tübingen* (1895), p. 5, n. 4; Rohde, "Orpheus," *Kleine Schriften*, II, 304, and *Psyche* (1925), II, 107; Gruppe, in Roscher's *Lexikon*, s.v. Orpheus, pp. 1105 f.; Kern, *Orpheus* (1920), p. 3, n. 5, and p. 10; Wilamowitz, *Der Glaube der Hellenen*, II (1932), 189; Zeller, *Philosophie der Griechen* (1920), I, 64, n. 1, and 390, n. 3; Pley, "De lanae in antiquissim. rit. usu," *Religionsgeschichtliche Versuche und Vorarbeiten*, XI (1911), No. 2, p. 96;

The first question relates to the gender of the datives in the phrase *τοῖσι Ὀρφικοῖσι . . . Πυθαγορείοισι*. Is Herodotus speaking of Ὀρφικά and Βακχικά or of Ὀρφικοί and Βακχικοί? Ὀρφικά in the sense of 'Orphic poetry,' as we shall see, is common enough in classical times; but it does not seem likely that Herodotus is thinking of poetry here. In the sense of 'Orphic rites' it is not found earlier than Strabo (x, 3, 16). Ὀρφικοί as a substantive does not appear before Achilles Statius in the second century A.D.[49] Either Orphics or Orphic rites, however, must be meant; and since Orphic rites could conceivably be called Egyptian and Orphics could not, we must conclude, it would seem, that the adjectives are all to be understood as neuters.

It is also argued that the phrase *τούτων τῶν ὀργίων* is further proof that they are neuters. As a matter of fact, the use of this phrase would be reasonable enough even if the preceding adjectives were masculines. *τούτων* cannot, of course, be taken as a possessive genitive modifying *τῶν ὀργίων*, as Rathmann proposes, but agrees with *ὀργίων*. *τούτων τῶν ὀργίων* is in effect the genitive of *τὰ τούτων ὀργία* and is used to avoid the impossibly awkward *τῶν τούτων ὀργίων*: 'these rites' would easily be understood to mean 'the rites of these people.'

The reason why the gender of the datives is in any way open to question is that if the subject of ὁμολογέουσι is the

Rathmann, *Quaestiones Pythagoreae Orphicae Empedocleae*, Diss. Halle, 1933, pp. 52–55; Leo Weber, "Zu Herodot ii, 81," *Philol. Woch.*, LIII (1933), 1180–1183; Rathmann, "Zu Herodot ii, 81," *Philol. Woch.*, LIV (1934), 1178–1184; Krueger, *Quaestiones Orphicae*, Diss. Halle, 1934; P. Boyancé, *Le culte des Muses chez les philosophes grecs* (Paris, 1937).

[49] *Introd. in Aratum* 4, p. 33, 17 Maass = *Fragm.* 70.

Egyptians there is some incongruity in asserting that persons are in agreement (ὁμολογέουσι) with things. Leo Weber feels this incongruity so keenly that he insists on taking ταῦτα as the subject of ὁμολογέουσι, explaining the irregularity of the plural verb by pointing out that though ταῦτα is a neuter it comprises several things—Egyptian costume, and the prohibition of wool both in cult and in burial. The point of agreement, however, between Greeks and Egyptians seems to be only the prohibition in burial. Rathmann, arguing against Weber, undertakes to show by statistics that a plural verb is impossible with ταῦτα as its subject in Herodotus. These statistics are not convincing, and it must be admitted that Herodotus could, if he wished, use a plural verb with ταῦτα. But the subject of ὁμολογέουσι is the Egyptians. It is impossible for anyone who has just read the preceding page, in which the Egyptians are the prevailing subject, and in which the phrase συμφέρονται τόδε has been used twice, to understand the subject of ὁμολογέουσι to be anything but the Egyptians and ταῦτα to be anything but an adverbial accusative. One who is reading and not construing cannot go back and revise his understanding after he has observed that the following datives must be neuter. The incongruity must stand, whether we like it or not, and we must acknowledge that the sentence is not written so well as it might be. Let us leave this question for the moment and proceed to the second point of obscurity.

Do the four adjectives refer to one or to more than one set of things? Are the Orphica and Bacchica identical, or two different kinds of orgia? Are both Egyptian and

Pythagorean, or is one Egyptian and the other Pythagorean? Various ways of sorting out the adjectives have been proposed. Most scholars, including Rohde, Gruppe, Gomperz, Kern, and Knapp, have thought they all refer to a single kind of ὄργια, which are called Orphic and Bacchic, but which are really Egyptian and Pythagorean. Zeller does not accept this view. Herodotus, he says, would not have called the Orphic-Bacchic religion Pythagorean, because he also asserts that it was introduced by Melampus, who was much older than Pythagoras, and because the doctrine of metempsychosis was borrowed by the Pythagoreans from the Orphics. As for the latter point, it is only a conjecture; we really know nothing about it. The former is of little significance, because Melampus introduced only the φαλλοφορία (ii, 49). However, to meet his own objections, Zeller proposes to place a comma before Πυθαγορείοισι, as Stallbaum had done in his edition of 1824. This means that there were *two* kinds of ὄργια: the Orphic-Bacchic, which came from Egypt, and the Pythagorean. Gomperz and Maass very properly point out that with this phrasing an article is required before Πυθαγορείοισι. Maass himself, who is concerned to prove that there was no connection between Bacchus and primitive Orphism, proposes a third interpretation, and discerns *three* kinds of ὄργια—Orphic, Bacchic (which originated in Egypt), and Pythagorean. The article, he says, can well be omitted in the coördination of three ideas. But this reading is so forced as to be almost impossible, and besides, as Gruppe remarks, it destroys the contrast, evidently intentional, between καλεομένοισι and ἐοῦσι.

Of these three interpretations only the first is really tolerable grammatically. But even so there are still difficulties. After being once told that the Egyptian custom corresponds to the Greek custom, we are surprised to read that the form of religion in which the custom prevailed was itself Egyptian. Again, Πυθαγορείοισι comes as a shock when it is equated with Βακχικοῖσι, however much the latter may be restricted to a particular species called Orphic.

Leo Weber[50] offers an interpretation so subtle that it must be presented in his own words if it is to be understood at all. "Wie Αἰγυπτίοισι und Πυθαγορείοισι inhaltlich sich vollkommen deckende Begriffe nicht sein können, vielmehr mit dem zweiten durch Hinzufügung des Teiles das zuerst genannte Ganze Αἰγυπτίοισι näher bestimmt wird, so gilt das gleiche auch für die beiden vorhergehenden nomina, die gleichfalls mit καὶ verbunden sind, dessen ursprünglich adverbiale Bedeutung 'auch' in beiden Gliedern noch sichtlich hervortritt. Herodot würde damit also sagen: wie einem bestimmten aigyptischen Brauch Pythagoreisches entspricht, so ist in den Βακχικά auch ähnliches wie in den sogenannten 'Ορφικά enthalten; beide decken sich also inhaltlich ebensowenig miteinander wie das zweite Paar." His translation of the sentence is (p. 1183): "es stimmt aber solches überein mit dem sogenannten Orphischen, auch Bakchischen, das aigyptisch, auch pythagoreisch ist." The meaning of this is so elusive that even when it has been expounded it is difficult, if not impossible, to discern it in Herodotus' words.

[50] *Op. cit.*, p. 1181.

It is not likely that he put such a tax on the ingenuity of his readers.

Enough has been said to show that no way of handling the sentence that has yet been proposed has succeeded in making it satisfactory. It is curious that Herodotus, who was obviously writing for people who did not already know what he had to tell them, should have left the matter in such obscurity.

Nothing has been said so far about the condition of the text in the manuscripts. Since almost all scholars who have sought in the passage information about Greek religion have dealt with it in the form quoted, which may be regarded as the vulgate, it has seemed best to discuss their views on the basis of the text which they used. As a matter of fact, the sentence appears in one form in the manuscripts of the Florentine family (ABC) and in another form in the manuscripts of the Roman family (RSV). The latter have the text as it appears in the vulgate except that ὁμολογέει is read instead of ὁμολογέουσι. The former have ὁμολογέουσι but they omit the words καὶ Βακχικοῖσι ἐοῦσι δὲ Αἰγυπτίοισι. Unfortunately, though scholarly opinion inclines a little to the belief that the Florentine family is slightly superior to the Roman, this superiority is not so clearly made out that we should be justified in preferring it on *a priori* grounds.

It will be seen that the incongruity between the subject of the introductory verb and the succeeding neuter adjectives, which is disturbing in the vulgate, disappears in both manuscript readings. In ABC τοῖσι Ὀρφικοῖσι καλεομένοισι καὶ Πυθαγορείοισι are easily understood as masculines and so accord with the plural ὁμολογέουσι; in RSV, where the adjectives must be neuter, the introductory verb is in the singular with ταῦτα as its subject. As far as the verb is concerned, therefore, either manuscript reading is preferable to the vulgate. It seems strange that Weber should choose to defend the plural verb with ταῦτα as its subject rather than to adopt the entire Roman reading outright exactly as it stands.

It will also be seen that all the awkwardness and uncertainty about the relation between the four adjectives in the vulgate remain in the Roman reading and disappear in the Florentine. The language of the manuscripts of the Florentine family is altogether more reasonable and intelligible than the language of the Roman family.

Mr. A. D. Nock argues that ὀργίων in the next sentence cannot well refer to Πυθαγορείοισι, but can refer to Ὀρφικοῖσι and Βακχικοῖσι.[51] If he means that is impossible because Πυθαγορείοισι is masculine, the objection has been answered above. If he means that the Pythagoreans had no orgia, several things may be said: (1) the orgia need not be orgia of both Orphics and Pythagoreans; (2) if we can attribute orgia to Orphics on the basis of this text, even though there is no other allusion to Orphic orgia in classical times, so we can also attribute them to Pythagoreans; (3) there is after all no objection to attributing orgia to Pythagoreans, since the word may mean anything done in the name of religion and need not imply that the things done are either orgiastic or secret: what other more suitable word could Herodotus have found

[51] *Conversion* (1933), p. 277, note to p. 26.

for the things done by the Orphics and the things done by the Pythagoreans in the name of religion?

If Herodotus wrote the sentence as it stands in the Roman family, the scribe who wrote the archetype of the Florentine family not only omitted καὶ Βακχικοῖσι ἐοῦσι δὲ Αἰγυπτίοισι, but also changed ὁμολογέει to ὁμολογέουσι. Now the omission might be accidental or intentional, but in either case the scribe would not have been likely to alter the verb.

If Herodotus wrote the sentence as it stands in the Florentine family, καὶ Βακχικοῖσι ἐοῦσι δὲ Αἰγυπτίοισι must have been an interpolation in the Roman archetype, and, since the addition immediately made all the adjectives neuter, ὁμολογέουσι was changed to ὁμολογέει to accord with the gender of the adjectives. Since the addition to the text, unlike the omission, could not have been made inadvertently, the scribe might well have had an eye to the verb.

If the doubtful words were an interpolation in the Roman archetype, we may guess that the source of them was a scholium written by someone who was acquainted with the mythological theory that Dionysus and Osiris were identical and that Bacchic rites had originated in Egypt. There is much said on this subject in the earlier books of Diodorus. The scholium would have been intended to inform the reader either that in addition to Orphic and Pythagorean institutions there was a third Greek institution, the Bacchic, itself Egyptian in origin, which resembled the Egyptian in its prohibition against wool, or that the Orphic and Pythagorean institutions, possibly only the Orphic, were Bacchic and in origin Egyptian. Introduced into the text, the words of the scholium produce a perplexing jumble.

Now, besides the present passage in Herodotus, the prohibition against the use of wool is attested for the Graeco-Roman world in only one other place.[52] This is in Apuleius, who says (*Apologia* 56 = *Test.* 217): "Wool, an outgrowth from the body of a particularly sluggish creature, taken, as it is, from the body of a sheep, has been regarded as a form of clothing unsuited for sacred purposes ever since it was so proscribed in the rules of Orpheus and Pythagoras" (quippe lana, segnissimi corporis excrementum, pecori detracta iam inde Orphei et Pythagorae scitis profanus uestitus est). There is just a chance, since the prohibition is mentioned by Herodotus and by Apuleius, and by no one else, that Apuleius obtained his information from Herodotus. If he did, it seems probable that, since he names only Orphic and Pythagorean doctrines, he read the text of Herodotus in the shorter version.

All things considered, a fairly strong argument can be made out for the reading of the manuscripts of the Florentine family. An editor of Herodotus would have to choose what he would print in his text. But for the present purpose the words which appear in the longer version of the Roman family fall under such heavy suspicion that they cannot be admitted as evidence from Herodotus, and no inference concerning his ideas about Orphics can be safely drawn except from the shorter version.

[52] Pley, *op. cit.* (see p. 39 above), p. 96.

Besides the troublesome sentence which we have been considering, there is one more point in the text before us which raises a question. What is the antecedent of αὐτῶν in the phrase περὶ αὐτῶν? What was it about which a tale was told, and who told it? The words which are possible as antecedents are εἵμασι and ὀργίων. It is probably not ὀργίων, because Herodotus is interested here in the single practice of avoiding wool in burial; nor is it likely to be εἰρινέοισι εἵμασι alone. It is best to refer it to the same antecedent as that of ταῦτα above (ὁμολογέουσι δὲ ταῦτα κτλ.), that is, not to a particular word, but to precisely the notion of a prohibition against wool—in Egypt. It seems to be generally taken for granted that the sacred tale is one which explains the prohibition against wool in certain groups in Greece. A reader who is primarily concerned with what the passage has to tell about Greek conditions naturally falls into this view. Herodotus, however, is writing about Egypt; and it is more likely that the sacred tale is the Egyptian explanation of the Egyptian avoidance of wool, the same kind of aetiological story that Herodotus refers to repeatedly in his account of Egypt.[53] We cannot, therefore, accept Kern's statement that Herodotus speaks of an Orphic-Pythagorean ἱρὸς λόγος.[54]

The whole passage, in the form which may be relied upon, may now be translated thus: "The Egyptians agree

[53] See I. M. Linforth, "Herodotus' Avowal of Silence in His Account of Egypt," *Univ. Calif. Publ. Class. Philol.*, VII (1924), 269–292.

[54] *Orpheus* (1920), p. 3, n. 5: "Es ist wohl bisher kaum beachtet worden, daß Herodot ii. 81 auch von einem orphisch-pythagoreischen ἱρὸς λόγος spricht." Cf. also *Orphicorum Fragmenta* (1922), p. 249: "quem Orphei librum Herodotus significaverit, obscurum est."

in this with the Orphics, as they are called, and with the Pythagoreans; for it is similarly against the rule for anyone who takes part in these rites to be buried in woolen garments. These customs are the subject of a sacred legend which is told by the Egyptians."

The conclusions that can be drawn from this are meager but important. We see that there were persons in the middle of the fifth century B.C. who were known as Orphics, or, at all events, if the longer version is right, persons who were devoted to what were known as Orphica. They practiced orgia of some kind, but there is no hint of the nature of the orgia. It was a rule that those who took part in the orgia should not be buried in woolen garments. There must have been at least a loose, local organization among them, because the requirements concerning burial must have been carried out by persons who had been fellow participants in the orgia with the deceased person. Though the passage is always accepted as proof of the identity of the Orphic and Dionysiac mysteries, it must be denied that it supplies any reliable evidence for this, since the only possible evidence is found in the longer version, which lies under grave suspicion, and even there it cannot be taken as certain that the Orphica and the Bacchica are identical. If the shorter version is right, there were also persons who were known as Pythagoreans, of whom the same things may be said as of the Orphics. The Orphics and the Pythagoreans may have formed a single set, however widely scattered, which was called by both names; or they may have been two distinct sets, resembling one another in one particular custom, whether there was any other resemblance or not. Whether the orgia of the Orphics were the same as the orgia of the Pythagoreans, we cannot say.

2) In the *Hippolytus* of Euripides, when Theseus has learned of Phaedra's death and been convinced by the accusation inscribed on the tablet she holds in her dead hand that his son has been guilty of improper approaches to her, he denounces him to his face in a long and violent speech (936–980). In the midst of it is a passage of particular significance for things Orphic, as follows (943–957 Murray = *Test.* 213):

> σκέψασθε δ' ἐς τόνδ', ὅστις ἐξ ἐμοῦ γεγὼς
> ᾔσχυνε τἀμὰ λέκτρα κἀξελέγχεται
> πρὸς τῆς θανούσης ἐμφανῶς κάκιστος ὤν. 945
> δεῖξον δ', ἐπειδή γ' ἐς μίασμ' ἐλήλυθας,
> τὸ σὸν πρόσωπον δεῦρ' ἐναντίον πατρί.
> σὺ δὴ θεοῖσιν ὡς περισσὸς ὢν ἀνὴρ
> ξύνει; σὺ σώφρων καὶ κακῶν ἀκήρατος ;
> οὐκ ἂν πιθοίμην τοῖσι σοῖς κόμποις ἐγὼ 950
> θεοῖσι προσθεὶς ἀμαθίαν φρονεῖν κακῶς.
> † ἤδη νυν αὔχει καὶ δι' 'αψύχου βορᾶς
> σίτοις † καπήλευ', 'Ορφέα τ' ἄνακτ' ἔχων
> βάκχευε πολλῶν γραμμάτων τιμῶν καπνούς·
> ἐπεί γ' ἐλήφθης. τοὺς δὲ τοιούτους ἐγὼ 955
> φεύγειν προφωνῶ πᾶσι· θηρεύουσι γὰρ
> σεμνοῖς λόγοισιν, αἰσχρὰ μηχανώμενοι.

The despair which Murray feels about lines 952 and 953 is shared by Wilamowitz. Nothing but an inspiration, he says, can mend the passage: σίτοις is impossible because of the number; καπήλευε demands an object, and since no object which is even tolerable can be found, it too falls under suspicion. Diels (Diels-Kranz, *Fragmente der Vorsokratiker*, I [1934], 4), followed by Kern, prints his own emendation, σῖτ' ἐκκαπήλευ', understanding something like τοῖς ἔξω βεβήλοις with it, and taking σῖτα as equivalent to σίτησιν. For ἐκκαπηλεύειν he compares Philostratus, *Vita Apollon. Tyan.* i, 15 τὸν γὰρ σῖτον οἱ δυνατοὶ ξυγκλείσαντες εἶχον, ἵν' ἐκκαπηλευθείη τῆς χώρας. 'Sell subsistence to outsiders,' which seems to be what Diels' words mean, is altogether cryptic. A number of other emendations which have been proposed need not be discussed, especially as a conjectural restoration of the lines would have no value as evidence. Méridier retains the manuscript reading and translates: "Avec ton régime végétarien fais étalage de ta nourriture."

καπήλευε is almost certainly sound. The verb can be used independently without an object (cf. Herodotus ii, 35: αἱ μὲν γυναῖκες ἀγοράζουσι καὶ καπηλεύουσι; i, 155, πρόειπε δ' αὐτοῖσι κιθαρίζειν τε καὶ ψάλλειν καὶ καπηλεύειν παιδεύειν τοὺς παῖδας), and, since it often has a derogatory sense, it can easily mean here 'play the part of a petty tradesman who cries his wares and makes dishonest statements about them.' The significance of it as applied to Hippolytus lies in the attribution to him of dishonesty and insincerity in his assumption of peculiar virtue. Creon accuses Teiresias of fraud in somewhat similar language in Sophocles, *Antigone* 1034 ff.:

κοὐδὲ μαντικῆς
ἄπρακτος ὑμῖν εἰμι, τῶν δ' ὑπαὶ γένους
ἐξημπόλημαι κἀμπεφόρτισμαι πάλαι.

So in *Oedipus Tyrannus* 388 f., Teiresias is called a mercenary impostor,

> δόλιον ἀγύρτην, ὅστις ἐν τοῖς κέρδεσιν
> μόνον δέδορκε, τὴν τέχνην δ' ἔφυ τυφλός.

σίτοις, however, must be wrong, in spite of Méridier, and in spite of Liddell and Scott (1930), where s.v. καπηλεύω the manuscript reading is quoted with the translation "drive a trade, chaffer with your vegetable food." In the singular it would carry exactly the same meaning as ἀψύχου βορᾶς, but the plural normally means 'provisions' or 'supplies,' as for an army; and a dative, which is very awkward with καπήλευε, only repeats the preceding phrase. Though both σῖτος and βορά can mean 'food' in general, σῖτος very often and βορά less frequently, the proper meaning of σῖτος is 'grain' and foods prepared from grain, whereas βορά is properly the food of carnivorous beasts (see Liddell and Scott, s.v., with the citations). ἀψύχου βορᾶς is, therefore, an oxymoron, which may have seemed to some ancient scholiast to require a note. If σίτοις λέγει, or some such note, was written in the margin of a manuscript, σίτοις may have replaced in some later copy the word preceding καπήλευε. It is idle to guess what the lost word may have been.

Something must be said about two other words in these lines. καπνούς is explained by the familiar usage in which it means 'something unsubstantial, insignificant, worthless.' So Aeschylus, fr. 399 Nauck πιστὸν οὐδὲν μᾶλλον ἢ καπνοῦ σκιά; Sophocles, *Phil.* 946 κοὐκ οἶδ' ἐναίρων νεκρὸν ἢ καπνοῦ σκιάν; Aristophanes, *Clouds* 320 καὶ λεπτολογεῖν *ἤδη ζητεῖ καὶ περὶ καπνοῦ στενολεσχεῖν*; Plato, *Rep.* ix, 581 D *οὐ τὴν μὲν ἀπὸ τῶν χρημάτων ἡδονὴν φορτικήν τινα ἡγεῖται* (sc. *ὁ φιλότιμος*), *καὶ αὖ τὴν ἀπὸ τοῦ μανθάνειν, ὅ τι μὴ μάθημα τιμὴν φέρει, καπνὸν καὶ φλυαρίαν.*

It is generally taken for granted that the word *βάκχευε* affords a clear indication that the practices associated with the name of Orpheus were of a Dionysiac character. There is, of course, no doubt that the word is used often enough to describe the conduct of the worshipers of Dionysus. In Herodotus' description of the public participation of the Scythian Scyles in the orgiastic Greek cult (iv, 79) the word occurs repeatedly; for example: *Σκύθαι δὲ τοῦ βακχεύειν πέρι Ἕλλησι ὀνειδίζουσι· οὐ γάρ φασι οἰκὸς εἶναι θεὸν ἐξευρίσκειν τοῦτον ὅστις μαίνεσθαι ἐνάγει ἀνθρώπους*, and *παρήιε σὺν τῷ θιάσῳ ὁ Σκύλης καὶ εἶδόν μιν βακχεύοντα οἱ Σκύθαι.* It may, therefore, mean here, 'go on with orgiastic worship of Dionysus.' Méridier[55] insists that it should be so understood. "Comme Dionysos était la grande divinité de l'orphisme, il paraît naturel de garder ici à *βακχεύω* sa valeur propre." Whether Dionysus was or was not the principal divinity of Orphism (and we shall see that the answer to this question is not so certain as is generally supposed), at all events there is no clear evidence before the third century B.C. of a connection between Orpheus and Dionysus save in the *Bassarae* of Aeschylus, where the relation is one of hostility. The only other hint of a connection is in the passage of

[55] "Euripide et l'orphisme," *Bull. de l'Assoc. G. Budé*, No. 18, janvier 1928, p. 16. In this article Méridier amplifies the discussion of the present passage which he had already presented in his edition of 1927 (p. 20, n. 1). He accepts many ill-founded assumptions concerning Orphism which need not be discussed in this connection.

Herodotus which we have just examined, and that we have seen reason to reject. It is our present business to discover what the testimonies concerning Orpheus actually disclose, without allowing ourselves to be affected by preconceptions. Now βακχεύειν is frequently used of mad behavior in general, where there is no connection whatever with the cult of Dionysus. In the *Antigone* of Sophocles it is used of the rage of Capaneus against Thebes (135 ff. ὃς τότε μαινομένᾳ ξὺν ὁρμᾷ βακχεύων ἐπέπνει ῥιπαῖς ἐχθίστων ἀνέμων). Euripides uses it in the *Ion* to describe the reeling of the poisoned dove (1203 f. εὐθὺς εὔπτερον δέμας ἔσεισε κἀβάκχευσεν), in the *Hercules Furens* (966) of the mad Heracles, and twice in the *Orestes* (411, 835) of the paroxysms induced by the visions of the conscience-stricken sufferer. In Plato's *Phaedrus* (234 D), after Socrates has heard Phaedrus read aloud the speech of Lysias he confesses that he has been carried away by the enthusiasm of the reader: ἑπόμενος συνεβάκχευσα μετὰ σοῦ τῆς θείας κεφαλῆς. These passages show that the word could be used without any reference whatever to Dionysus or orgiastic ritual. We cannot say, therefore, that the use of the word here proves that Theseus had in mind some Dionysiac cult, or even any form of orgiastic ritual whatever. It may be simply a term of reprobation, expressing, like αὔχει, καπήλευε, and καπνούς, Theseus' extravagant and ironical condemnation of the conduct of Hippolytus.

Let us consider the thoughts that surge through the mind of Theseus in his passion of grief and anger. Recalling Hippolytus' pretension to be σώφρων and to be devoted to a blameless life in the open, enjoying the favor of Artemis, he accuses him of false pride, hypocrisy, and fraud. "Hitherto," he says (946 f.), "you have held yourself superior, and you still proudly refuse to look at me. But now you have no excuse for not looking me in the face, because you have been humbled by the pollution into which you have come."[56] Since Hippolytus is really different from other people, though in a harmless way, Theseus berates him with this peculiarity (ὡς περισσὸς ὢν ἀνήρ 948). Then, by an anachronism which Euripides allows, he is reminded of a class of people who would be known to the Athenian audience of the day for their peculiar practices and their proud claims and their hypocrisy. "Go on!" he says in effect to Hippolytus, "Add to your nonsense by taking up the absurdities and impostures of these people who make so much of Orpheus! You have been caught and unmasked, and you can no longer deceive me." Euripides was struck by the analogy between what Athenians thought of the followers of Orpheus, whom he himself also had had occasion to observe, and what he conceived Theseus would be likely to think of Hippolytus in the play.

These peculiar people have certain definite characteristics: they are vegetarians (δι' ἀψύχου βορᾶς); they may be said to regard Orpheus as their lord ('Ορφέα τ' ἄνακτ' ἔχων); they make use of a great number of books, for which they have a high regard. Since we know from other sources that Orpheus was held to be the author of books, and that the regimen of a vegetarian was called an

[56] This interpretation of the lines explains the person of ἐλήλυθας, which Musgrave wished to change to ἐλήλυθα.

'Ορφικὸς βίος,[57] we may safely conclude that these three characteristics were united in a single set of persons, who may properly be regarded as followers of Orpheus. Like any group of people who observe peculiar practices of their own choice, they felt, no doubt, that they had a certain advantage and superiority over others. There is no indication of what advantage they thought they enjoyed except that of being peculiar. Theseus naturally represents them in a bad light and accuses them of base motives. They are like dishonest and knavish hucksters who will do anything for their own gain (καπήλευε); their conduct is crazy and irrational (βάκχευε); their proud demeanor is only a cloak that enables them to prey on society (θηρεύουσι γὰρ σεμνοῖς λόγοισιν, αἰσχρὰ μηχανώμενοι). Euripides could not have written these lines if his audience had not been acquainted with the practices of the followers of Orpheus, and if the popular attitude toward them had not been, to some degree at least, one of scorn and suspicion. Even their books are mocked by Theseus for containing nothing but empty vaporing, for all their number.

It will have been observed that the interpretation which has been adopted for the imperatives καπήλευε and βάκχευε and their attendant participles is not the familiar one. They are generally supposed to mean: '*Continue* with your practices as a follower of Orpheus,'—which is, of course, equally possible grammatically. "Un point incontestable," says Méridier, "c'est que Thésée représente expressément son fils comme un Orphique." So he

[57] Plato, *Laws* vi, 782 C. See p. 98 below.

does, indeed, if his words are taken in the sense which is generally attributed to them. Violent as he is in his anger, he could scarcely assert that Hippolytus is a follower of Orpheus unless he knew him to be so. But this interpretation introduces insuperable difficulties. Not only is there no real evidence elsewhere in the play that Hippolytus was an Orphic; there are clear indications of contrast between the life of Hippolytus and certain practices associated with the name of Orpheus. Méridier and others who have labored to discover some proof that Hippolytus was an Orphic recall that he had been initiated in the Eleusinian Mysteries (v. 25) and point to the supposed connection between those mysteries and Orpheus. But there was nothing peculiar among Athenians in this initiation, and Hippolytus' journey to Athens for the purpose is simply the familiar device of bringing about a meeting of prospective lovers at a festival. It is also said that since Orpheus in certain versions of the legend is represented as rejecting the love of women, Hippolytus is here following in his footsteps. In the myth of Er (Plato, *Rep.* x, 620 A = *Test.* 139) the soul of Orpheus chooses to be born as a swan because of his hatred of women. But this means that he will not have a woman for a mother since women have murdered him. In the elegiacs of Phanocles preserved by Stobaeus (iv, 20, 47 = *Test.* 77) we are told that Orpheus introduced boy-love among the Thracians and that the women murdered him because he would have nothing to do with them. But this is obviously a device to account for the old story of the murder.[58] In Vergil (*Georg.* iv, 516; cf. Ovid,

[58] See p. 14 above.

*Met.* x, 78 = *Test.* 76) it is grief for the failure to recover his wife that causes Orpheus to shun the society of women; he had had a wife and had loved her deeply. There is not much resemblance in all this to the attitude of Hippolytus. Besides, there is nothing to prove that celibacy was required of the followers of Orpheus.[59] It is idle to look for other indications of a similarity between the habits of Hippolytus and the Orphic way of life. The clear contradiction between Orphic vegetarianism (*δι' ἀψύχου βορᾶς*) and the lusty joy Hippolytus takes in the hunt and in the hunter's breakfast that follows (vv. 108 ff.) is enough to prove that he was no follower of Orpheus and that his father had no thought that he was. One who slays animals for sport is no Orphic. But still Maurice Croiset[60] maintains that he was a representative of the nobler type of Orphism, and André Boulanger,[61] who holds that the Orphic sect consisted not of small communities, but of isolated ascetics, asserts that the figure of Hippolytus is modeled upon them. There is, in fact, nothing in the play to show that Hippolytus was an Orphic and much to show that he was not. We shall have to recognize, therefore, that the words of Theseus supply all the evidence concerning Orpheus which is to be discovered in

[59] Eugen Fehrle ("Die kultische Keuschheit im Altertum," *Religionsgeschichtliche Versuche und Vorarbeiten*, VI [1910], 226) says: "Besonders waren es die orphischen Gemeinden, in denen schon vom Anfang des sechsten Jahrhunderts ab strenge Askese gelehrt wurde." He also refers to Dieterich, *Abraxas* (1891), p. 1, who says: "Ein Jahr nachher macht Euripides seinen Hippolytos zum orphischen Misogyn und Vegetarianer." These are unsupported assertions.

[60] "Le mouvement religieux en Grèce du vii^e au vi^e siècle," *Revue des cours et conférences*, XXIII (1921–22), 683.

[61] In his excellent article, "L'orphisme à Rome," *Rev. des études latines*, XV (1937), 121–135.

the play. Even if Euripides intended us to believe that Hippolytus was an Orphic and that Theseus was aware of the fact, it would be impossible for us to distinguish among the ideas and practices which belong to the subtle and intricate character of Hippolytus those which might properly be called Orphic.

The facts about Orpheus which we have succeeded in disentangling from the immediate associations of the play may now be repeated. There were people in Athens in the fifth century B.C. who avoided animal food,[62] who regarded Orpheus in some sense as their lord, and who made use of a great number of books, to which they attached a high value. They felt that they had some advantage and superiority over others; but it is not clear what advantage they thought they enjoyed other than that of being peculiar. The Athenians in general were acquainted with these peculiar people and their peculiar practices, and many looked on them with scorn and suspicion.

We have now had two glimpses, in Herodotus and Euripides, of persons with whom the name of Orpheus was associated: those who took Orpheus as their lord, and those who were known as Ὀρφικοί. The common denominator suggests that they formed a single recognizable group, and the characteristics which are attributed to them in the two texts, though they are different, are not incongruous. Herodotus may or may not have known the Orphics of Athens, and the Athenian Orphics may or may not have observed the regulations concerning burial.

[62] Cf. Johannes Haussleiter, "Der Vegetarismus in der Antike," *Religionsgeschichtliche Versuche und Vorarbeiten*, XXIV (1935), 79–96 (Die Orphiker und ihre Vorläufer).

We cannot say that there was an organization wide enough to include them all. Nor can we say for what cause the name of Orpheus was attached to them. But we may with some assurance speak of Ὀρφικοί of the Herodotus-*Hippolytus* type with the characteristics which appear in the two texts.

3) Both authorship and date of the *Rhesus*, which is included among the works of Euripides, are uncertain. Some scholars regard it as a genuine production of Euripides; others assign it to an unknown author of the fourth century B.C.; others, again, hold that it is an archaizing work of the Alexandrian age. It is not necessary here to renew the long controversy. The play is so generally regarded as at least a work of the classical period that it is properly included in a review of the evidence concerning Orpheus in this period; but though it is convenient to introduce it in connection with the other evidence from Euripides, it should not be forgotten, if the question of chronology should become important, that its precise place in the chronological series is not determined.

At the close of the play, after the death of Rhesus, the grief-stricken Muse who is his mother appears as the *deus ex machina* to resolve the mystery of his death, to reveal the strange fortune which is in store for him, and to assume charge of his obsequies. She relates first the story of his birth and his untimely fate. She and her sisters were on the way to Mount Pangaeum to meet Thamyris, the son of Philammon, in a musical contest, when perforce in the bed of the river Strymon she conceived her child. On his birth she gave him into the care of his father, who in turn entrusted him to the water nymphs. He became the first king of Thrace, and he would have lived long and prospered had he not disobeyed his parents and yielded to the solicitation of the Trojan envoys who implored him to come to their assistance. The Muse then proceeds to show with some bitterness who was immediately responsible for his death, as follows (938-949 = *Test.* 91):

> *καὶ τοῦδ', 'Αθάνα, παντὸς αἰτία μόρου,*
> *—οὐδὲν δ' 'Οδυσσεὺς οὐδ' ὁ Τυδέως τόκος*
> *ἔδρασε δράσας — μὴ δόκει λεληθέναι.* 940
> *καίτοι πόλιν σὴν σύγγονοι πρεσβεύομεν*
> *Μοῦσαι μάλιστα κἀπιχρώμεθα χθονί,*
> *μυστηρίων τε τῶν ἀπορρήτων φανὰς*
> *ἔδειξεν 'Ορφεύς, αὐτανέψιος νεκροῦ*
> *τοῦδ' ὃν κατακτείνεις σύ· Μουσαῖόν τε, σὸν* 945
> *σεμνὸν πολίτην κἀπὶ πλεῖστον ἄνδρ' ἕνα*
> *ἐλθόντα, Φοῖβος σύγγονοί τ' ἠσκήσαμεν.*
> *καὶ τῶνδε μισθὸν παῖδ' ἔχουσ' ἐν ἀγκάλαις*
> *θρηνῶ· σοφιστὴν δ' ἄλλον οὐκ ἐπάξομαι.*

After some words from Hector, in which he promises to do high honor to Rhesus in his burial, the Muse continues (962–973; not in Kern):

> *οὐκ εἶσι γαίας ἐς μελάγχιμον πέδον·*
> *τοσόνδε Νύμφην τὴν ἔνερθ' αἰτήσομαι,*
> *τῆς καρποποιοῦ παῖδα Δήμητρος θεᾶς,*
> *ψυχὴν ἀνεῖναι τοῦδ'· ὀφειλέτις δέ μοι* 965
> *τοὺς 'Ορφέως τιμῶσα φαίνεσθαι φίλους.*
> *κἀμοὶ μὲν ὡς θανών τε κοὐ λεύσσων φάος*
> *ἔσται τὸ λοιπόν· οὐ γὰρ ἐς ταὐτόν ποτε*
> *οὔτ' εἶσιν οὔτε μητρὸς ὄψεται δέμας·*

κρυπτὸς δ' ἐν ἄντροις τῆς ὑπαργύρου χθονὸς 970
ἀνθρωποδαίμων κείσεται βλέπων φάος,
Βάκχου προφήτης ὥστε Παγγαίου πέτραν
ᾤκησε, σεμνὸς τοῖσιν εἰδόσιν θεός.

The Muse lays the blame for Rhesus' death upon Athena, and she is deeply resentful because she herself and her sisters have been more intimately associated with Athena's city of Athens than with any other city and have shown it higher regard than they have shown to any other. Besides the general distinction of Athens in the arts which the Muses have taught her, she recalls the relations which exist between them through Orpheus and Musaeus. Musaeus, who was a revered citizen of Athens, had attained his eminence by the special favor of Apollo and the Muses. Conversely, Orpheus, who was himself the son of a Muse and the cousin of Rhesus, had conferred a notable benefaction on Athens: *μυστηρίων τε τῶν ἀπορρήτων φανὰς ἔδειξεν*. The author might have made the Muse say bluntly that Odysseus and Diomedes had slain Rhesus; but he chooses to carry the blame back to Athena in order that he may have an occasion to introduce Athens and her glory in connection with a quite alien legend. The device is ingenious and managed with great skill. One is reminded of the easier shift to Athens at the end of the *Iphigenia Taurica*.

The aetiology of the second passage is obscure, but what the Muse says (except in the last two lines) is plain enough. She will prevail upon Persephone to release the soul of Rhesus, so that he shall not have to go to the lower world. Instead, he will continue to exist in the upper world (βλέπων φάος) as an ἀνθρωποδαίμων, lying hidden in a cave in a land with veins of silver. The Muse is confident that Persephone will accede to her request because she is under some obligation to show honor to any friend of Orpheus.

Three questions demand consideration: (1) What mysteries are referred to? (2) What is the nature of the obligation of Persephone to Orpheus? (3) Who is the βάκχου προφήτης?

The words μυστηρίων τῶν ἀπορρήτων φανὰς ἔδειξεν mean: "he devised and introduced the secret mysteries with their torches." ἔδειξεν is used for the compound κατέδειξεν, which is commoner in this sense.[63] The 'torches of the mysteries' is used, by synechdoche, for the mysteries themselves. The most significant thing about the statement is that, since the institution of these mysteries is cited by the Muse as a benefaction to the Athenians, they must have been mysteries on which the Athenians set a high value and which belonged essentially to them. Otherwise there would be no point in the allusion. Though Lobeck[64] holds that the reference need not be more explicit than to mysteries in general, no more valuable to the Athenians than to the rest of the world, Gruppe[65] expresses his belief that the Eleusinian Mysteries must be intended. Maass[66] maintains that the allusion is to the Lesser Mysteries which were celebrated at Agrae, about which

[63] Cf. Aristoph. *Frogs* 1030, and Ps.-Demosth. xxv, 11, quoted below on pp. 67 and 99; and Plato, *Laws* iii, 677 D, quoted above (p. 36), where though neither δεῖξαι nor καταδεῖξαι appears, the idea that an *invention* is something *revealed*, first to the inventor and then by him to the world, is well illustrated.

[64] *Aglaophamus*, I, 239.

[65] Roscher's *Lexikon*, s.v. Orpheus, p. 1096.

[66] *Orpheus* (1895), pp. 72 ff.

very little is known. Without admitting either of these conjectures as certain, we must insist that the mysteries which Orpheus is said to have established were an *honored Athenian cult*, neither a cult which was undistinguished in Athens nor one which meant no more to Athens than to other cities.

When, a little later, the Muse expresses her reliance on some obligation by which Persephone is bound to her nephew Orpheus, it would be overcritical to question the connection of this with the earlier passage. What Orpheus had done for Persephone was to ordain mysteries in her honor at Athens. Maass holds that the special mention of Persephone is an argument in favor of the mysteries at Agrae, where she was preëminent, whereas Demeter was more important at Eleusis. But it was Persephone and not Demeter who, as queen of the lower world, had power to release the soul of Rhesus, and if the audience had already understood in the earlier passage an allusion to the Eleusinian Mysteries, they would not have been disturbed here by the mention of Persephone, who shared with her mother the worship at Eleusis.

Concerning the *βάκχου προφήτης* various opinions have been expressed, and the matter is complicated by an uncertainty in the text. Instead of *ὥστε* the second hand in the Palatinus has *ὅστε*. With *ὅς τε*, the *βάκχου προφήτης* can be no one but Rhesus himself.[67] With *ὥστε*, the words mean: "even as the prophet of Bacchus hath taken up

[67]Perdrizet ("Cultes et mythes du Pangée," *Annales de l'Est*, XXIV [1910], 1) adopts this reading, and draws the daring conclusions that we learn from the present play what was thought of Rhesus by the Orphic sect in Athens in the middle of the fourth century B.C., and that the soul of Rhesus

his abode among the rocks of Pangaeum, a god revered by those who know." Maass[68] asserts without hesitation that the prophet is Orpheus. He is evidently led to this assumption by the Thracian and Bacchic character of the prophet, but he finds the decisive proof in the words *τοῖσιν εἰδόσιν*, which he understands to mean "the initiates." The avoidance of the name, he says, is due to a religious scruple. It may freely be admitted that Orpheus was known as a Thracian in the fifth century B.C., and that in postclassical texts he was associated with Bacchus and Mount Pangaeum. Indeed, this association was probably recognized in the *Bassarae* of Aeschylus.[69] But *τοῖσιν εἰδόσιν* need not mean "initiates"; and even if it does, it need not mean initiates in any mysteries specially connected with Orpheus. There is no hint at all of any connection between Orpheus, who has already been mentioned, and the *βάκχου προφήτης*, and there is no reason

---

was supposed to have presented itself before Persephone with an Orphic formula such as those found on the Gold Tablets (*Fragm.* 32). The arguments in support of these statements cannot be refuted, because there are none.

[68] *Orpheus* (1895), pp. 66–71, 134–139. The view of Maass is accepted by J. Rempe (*De Rheso Thracum heroe*, Diss. Münster, 1927, pp. 26 ff.), who discusses the passage at length and gives references to earlier literature on the subject, and by Leo Weber ("Orpheus," *Rhein. Mus.*, LXXXI [1932], 8), who offers a highly imaginative account of the origins of Orphic religion, deriving it from a cult of a god Orpheus on Mount Pangaeum.

[69] Maass does not hesitate to say (pp. 138 f.): "das Begräbnis des Orpheus auf dem Pangaion, sein dionysisches Prophetenamt daselbst und seine Göttlichkeit stand im aischyleischen Drama, wie es im 'Rhesos' steht." He even reconstructs the close of the play by imagining that Apollo or the Muse appeared and declared that the lyre of the dead Orpheus would be given to Musaeus. This is the source of the statement in the *Rhesus* (945) that Musaeus had enjoyed the special favor of Apollo and the Muses! And the reliance of the Muse on her relationship to Orpheus in her plea to Persephone is only a silly distortion of the plea of the mother of Orpheus for her own son, which must have been the original version in Aeschylus! Guesses so wild as this do not help the cause of scholarship.

to suppose that Orpheus is intended any more than any other Thracian worthy. The final disproof of Maass' theory, however, is the quite unparalleled statement that Orpheus was a god. Nock,[70] pointing out that Orpheus was "not *σεμνὸς τοῖσιν εἰδόσιν θεός*, certainly not consciously regarded as such," suggests that the *προφήτης* was an unidentified figure like Zalmoxis. This is by all odds the most reasonable interpretation, and, though in the end we cannot say who the prophet of Bacchus was, we can at least be reasonably sure that he was not Orpheus. The possibility that he was Orpheus is so slender that the lines are deprived of any immediate interest in the present review of the evidence.

What we learn from the whole passage which has been under consideration is this. Orpheus ordained mysteries in Athens. These mysteries were secret; they were characterized by the use of torches; they were celebrated in honor of Persephone. They were highly esteemed and belonged essentially to Athens; they were, therefore, almost certainly a state cult.

A comparison of this evidence with what has already been discovered in Herodotus and the *Hippolytus* yields some interesting and important results. The mysteries of the Rhesus are probably not identical with the *'Ορφικά* of Herodotus, because if Herodotus had been referring to an essentially Athenian institution he would almost certainly have named the locality. They are surely not the same as the *'Ορφικά* of the Hippolytus, because Euripides could not have undertaken to show that Hippolytus

[70] *Class. Rev.*, XL (1926), 184 ff.

was peculiar and contemptible by representing him as a devotee of an honored Athenian cult. It is to be concluded, therefore, that the name of Orpheus could be, and was, associated with more than one particular religious institution. This conclusion leads inevitably to a capital principle which must be observed in judging the evidence concerning Orpheus: it is not to be assumed that every form of religion which is associated with his name belongs to a single particular religious institution. If we wish to speak of Orphism or the Orphic religion, we must understand thereby something different from this. We must not regard all Orphic items, even though they are sealed by his name, as fractions of a single whole which can be added together to produce that whole simply because they have a common denominator. Whatever meaning we may attach to the word Orphic, we cannot use it to characterize an idea or a practice as belonging to a single Orphic institution, as if there were only one.

4) In the *Frogs* of Aristophanes, Aeschylus, defending his own sturdy qualities as a poet and berating Euripides with the demoralizing influence of his tragedies, invites him to consider the edifying works of the good old standard poets (1030–1036 = *Test.* 90):

> σκέψαι γὰρ ἀπ' ἀρχῆς
> ὡς ὠφέλιμοι τῶν ποιητῶν οἱ γενναῖοι γεγένηνται.
> Ὀρφεὺς μὲν γὰρ τελετάς θ' ὑμῖν κατέδειξε φόνων τ' ἀπέχεσθαι,
> Μουσαῖος δ' ἐξακέσεις τε νοσῶν καὶ χρησμούς, Ἡσίοδος δὲ
> γῆς ἐργασίας, καρπῶν ὥρας, ἀρότους· ὁ δὲ θεῖος Ὅμηρος
> ἀπὸ τοῦ τιμὴν καὶ κλέος ἔσχεν πλὴν τοῦδ' ὅτι χρήστ' ἐδίδαξεν,
> τάξεις ἀρετὰς ὁπλίσεις ἀνδρῶν;

Orpheus, like Hesiod and Homer, has been of service to the world; and two benefactions are expressly mentioned: he has instituted τελεταί, and he has taught men to abstain from bloodshed. The word τελεταί,[71] though it may be used of any kind of religious ceremony, is applied mostly to rites in which the prime purpose is not to worship the gods (θεραπεύειν τοὺς θεούς), but to procure peace for the soul of the participant. The teletae which Orpheus has instituted are clearly teletae of this sacramental type. Such means of grace are a blessing to men. But precisely what teletae is Aeschylus thinking of? We have seen that it is no answer to say simply Orphic teletae. In fact, we have seen two forms of ceremonial evidently quite distinct but both associated with the name of Orpheus: the orgia of the people who avoid woolen garments in burial, and the Athenian mysteries in which Persephone was worshiped. The teletae that Aeschylus speaks of may be either of these, or both, or other Orphic teletae that we have not heard of, or all Orphic teletae taken together. But we have no right to limit the reference even to these. The true explanation may be, not that some teletae out of all were Orphic, but that all alike were Orphic, in the sense that Orpheus first gave teletae to the world and was the originator of this great remedy for human disquietude. Unfortunately, Aristophanes' bare words do not enable us to decide between these various possibilities, but with further evidence we may be in a position to determine where the probability lies.

The other thing that Orpheus had done was to teach men to refrain from bloodshed. Here again we cannot be

[71] See p. 101, n. 87, below.

quite sure what Aristophanes has in mind. Since φόνος can be used both of the slaughter of men and of the slaughter of animals, both possibilities must be considered; and both men and animals may be slain for use as food. There are, therefore, three separate possibilities: (1) Orpheus taught men to refrain from murder; (2) he put an end to cannibalism; (3) he replaced flesh with cereals as the staple of human diet; or these three may all be thought of as one process in the growth of civilization. That men in classical times were aware of such a process is shown by a long fragment of the tragic poet Moschion (fr. 6 Nauck), where we have a description of the transition from the time when men lived like beasts among the caves of the mountains and slew one another for food, to an ordered state of society in which they enjoy the blessings of Demeter and Bacchus. It may be that the brief words φόνων ἀπέχεσθαι were sufficient to remind the audience of a form of the legend in which Orpheus, not Prometheus, was the culture hero who brought these great things to pass. Horace, in the *Ars Poetica* (391 ff.), shows that he is aware of such a legend when he says:

> silvestris homines sacer interpresque deorum
> caedibus et victu foedo deterruit Orpheus,
> dictus ob hoc lenire tigris rabidosque leones.

But the association of the two features, *sacer interpresque* and *caedibus deterruit*, bears so close a resemblance to Aristophanes' line, and the plural *caedibus* is so clear an echo of φόνων, that we might well suppose that Horace had recently been reading the *Frogs*—which would not be surprising when he was writing on the art of poetry.

However this may be, φόνων ἀπέχεσθαι is an admirable summary statement of the great change in human life, and the production of such a change may well be mentioned as a great benefaction to men. But it must be admitted that there is no support in classical evidence for Orpheus as the culture hero who changed men from savages to agriculturists.[72]

If we look for help in contemporary evidence, we are immediately reminded of the vegetarian diet attested for the followers of Orpheus by Euripides in the *Hippolytus*. Rohde (*Psyche*, II, 125, n. 3) holds that Aristophanes means nothing more than this, and that Horace misunderstood him. But to have imposed a rule against animal food on a set of peculiar people whom Euripides could hold up to scorn does not seem enough to justify Aristophanes in naming it as one of the benefactions which put Orpheus in the same class with Homer and Hesiod. Besides, φόνων ἀπέχεθαι, "to abstain from bloodshed," is a strange phrase to use if it is to mean no more than "avoid animal food." It is more likely that Horace is right, and that though certain fanatics carried Orpheus' principles to the extreme, everyone knew of the reformation he had introduced in the world by persuading men to give up their old savage habit of slaughtering both animals and one another for food.

[72] This very legend does appear, however, in Themistius, *Or.* xxx, 349 B (= *Test.* 112). Kern (*Orpheus*, 1920, p. 32) thinks that the legend was engendered in late times by late Orphic poems on agriculture; but it may be old. On the whole subject see Preller, "Die Vorstellungen der Alten, besonders der Griechen, von dem Ursprunge und den ältesten Schicksalen des menschlichen Geschlechts," *Philologus*, VII (1852), 1-60, and Uxkull-Gyllenband, "Griechische Kultur-Entstehungslehren," *Bibliothek für Philosophie*, XXVI (Berlin, 1924).

After all, Aristophanes' line demands more than it gives. It tells us nothing certain about Orpheus that we did not know before, and what it does say stands in need of elucidation. We must make the most of the little that it tells: Orpheus was one of the standard poets, who had all been of service to humanity, and his service lay in the institution of teletae and the discouragement of bloodshed.

5) When, in the *Protagoras* of Plato, Socrates and his young friend Hippocrates, who wishes to put himself under the tuition of the great sophist, arrive at the house of Callias, Socrates suggests to Protagoras that he may wish to take up the subject of Hippocrates' education in private. Protagoras is grateful for Socrates' considerateness, because he admits that a sophist in a strange city is in a somewhat delicate position. But he has decided that the wisest course is to practice his profession openly and without concealment. Sophistic, he says, is an ancient art, which men have practiced in the past under the guise of other arts to avoid obloquy; but they have not succeeded, because people have always known what they have really been about. To avoid the appearance of dishonesty he proclaims himself boldly a sophist.

In the following passage he gives examples of men who were sophists without confessing it (316 D = *Test* 92): ἐγὼ δὲ τὴν σοφιστικὴν τέχνην φημὶ μὲν εἶναι παλαιάν, τοὺς δὲ μεταχειριζομένους αὐτὴν τῶν παλαιῶν ἀνδρῶν, φοβουμένους τό ἐπαχθὲς αὐτῆς, πρόσχημα ποιεῖσθαι καὶ προκαλύπτεσθαι, τοὺς μὲν ποίησιν, οἷον Ὅμηρόν τε καὶ Ἡσίοδον καὶ Σιμωνίδην, τοὺς δὲ αὖ τελετάς τε καὶ χρησμῳδίας, τοὺς ἀμφί τε Ὀρφέα καὶ

*Μουσαῖον· ἐνίους δέ τινας ᾔσθημαι καὶ γυμναστικήν, οἷον Ἴκκος τε ὁ Ταραντῖνος καὶ ὁ νῦν ἔτι ὢν οὐδενὸς ἥττων σοφιστὴς Ἡρόδικος ὁ Σηλυμβριανός, τὸ δὲ ἀρχαῖον Μεγαρεύς· μουσικὴν δὲ Ἀγαθοκλῆς τε ὁ ὑμέτερος πρόσχημα ἐποιήσατο, μέγας ὢν σοφιστής, καὶ Πυθακλείδης ὁ Κεῖος καὶ ἄλλοι πολλοί.*

What Protagoras means by sophistic appears clearly a little later (317 B) when he acknowledges that he is a sophist and that his business is education (*ὁμολογῶ τε σοφιστὴς εἶναι καὶ παιδεύειν ἀνθρώπους*). He does not teach any particular subject, he teaches men. In the educational faculty he is a professor without portfolio. It is his function to prepare men directly for the world and a successful life in it, without complicating the matter by requiring a knowledge of special subjects. He recognizes that the old-fashioned teachers had good intentions at heart and clung to the old ways only because they did not dare to come out boldly and proclaim themselves professors of life.

That Homer, Hesiod, Musaeus, and Orpheus were great teachers as well as great poets was recognized also by Aristophanes, as we have seen. But whereas Aristophanes represents them as teachers of particular subjects, Protagoras holds that they were educators in the wider sense like himself, using their special arts as a screen to conceal their ulterior purposes. In Aristophanes they are all referred to as poets; Protagoras names Homer and Hesiod as typical of the art of poetry, but Orpheus and Musaeus are typical of the art which is occupied with teletae and chresmodiae. This does not mean that they were not also poets. Aristophanes was interested for the moment only in poets; Protagoras is interested in the various activities which are educational in their effect, and mentions representative practitioners in each activity.

That Protagoras found sound educational value, even as he understood education, in poetry, gymnastic, and music, is not surprising, because they were traditional modes of instruction and could not be said to have failed utterly in their purpose. What educational value did he find in the work of those who occupied themselves with teletae and chresmodiae? Nestle[73] simply mentions the fact that in the seventh and sixth centuries B.C. ecstatic seers were called *σοφοί*, quoting Plut. *Solon* 12 (of Epimenides) *σοφὸς περὶ τὰ θεῖα τὴν ἐνθουσιαστικὴν σοφίαν*. But Protagoras implies that the sophistic of Orpheus and Musaeus, as well as that of Homer and Hesiod, the gymnastic teachers, and the music teachers, was a sophistic comparable to his own, not a particular *σοφία* in each case. As a solution to the problem the conjecture is offered that when Plato found a place for teletae and chresmodiae in his list of educational activities, he was intending to designate by these words the activity which we in this connection should denominate by the modern word 'religion.' The public religion of cults and festivals was not thought of as an instrument of instruction; but the teletae and chresmodiae, being concerned with the individual, his relation to the gods, and his own destiny, took the place of that aspect of religion in the modern world. The fact that they involved the use of books gave them something more in the way of doctrinal substance than was to

[73] In the Cron-Deuschle edition, 6th ed., 1910, p. 1.

be found in the state cults. Whether they had any direct moral influence or not, they would be effective in molding the lives of those who participated in them and believed in their importance.

In this religion of teletae and chresmodiae Orpheus and Musaeus are named as leaders. There are two points to notice in the phrase τοὺς ἀμφί τε Ὀρφέα καὶ Μουσαῖον. In form it is only a variant of the preceding phrase, οἷον Ὅμηρόν τε καὶ Ἡσίοδον καὶ Σιμωνίδην. As there were more poets besides these three, so there were more men who had been occupied with teletae and chresmodiae. Orpheus and Musaeus were only typical of the profession. One suspects that the activity itself was more important than the particular men who were engaged in it. Under such conditions there might easily be confusion in the tradition of what the several men had individually accomplished. Second, Plato's language indicates that teletae and chresmodiae were intimately associated as the work of a single class of men, and that neither one nor the other is to be attributed to Orpheus or to Musaeus alone. It is true that in Aristophanes teletae belong to Orpheus, chresmoi and remedies for disease to Musaeus, but classical and later evidence sometimes reverses the roles.[74]

What is significant for Orpheus in the passage is rather the manner than the matter of the allusion. He appears, with Musaeus, as the representative of a class of men who

---

[74] Philochorus, quoted on p. 35 above, said that Orpheus was a mantis; and when Diodorus (iv, 25, 1) says that Musaeus was in charge of the Eleusinian Mysteries at the time of Heracles' initiation, he may be quoting from Herodorus (see I. M. Linforth, "Diodorus, Herodorus, Orpheus," in *Classical Studies Presented to Edward Capps*, Princeton, 1936, pp. 217–222).

were occupied, as founders or poets, with teletae and chresmodiae, and whose work played a part, together with poetry, gymnastic, and music, in the traditional process of education.

6) In the course of the great passage in the second book of the *Republic*, which is calculated to make the defense of justice in the later books as difficult as possible, Plato has occasion to say something of teletae and their function, and he mentions the name of Orpheus in connection with them. It will be necessary first to summarize the contents of the passage (363 A–366 B) in which the allusion occurs.

After Glaucon has recounted the arguments of those who hold that the life of the unjust man is better than that of the just man, Adeimantus, to make the case in favor of justice still weaker, proceeds to show the weakness of the position of those who maintain that justice is *better* than injustice. The defenders of justice, he says, recommend it, not for itself, but for the good things which are won by the reputation for justice among men, and for the rewards which are bestowed on the just by the gods. They point to the blessings which the gods reserve for the just in this world (363 A–B), in the next world (363 C), and in the fortunes of their descendants, and to the disasters that overtake the unjust in the next world (363 D) and in this (363 E). These arguments, though they show that the just are rewarded and the unjust punished, cannot be accepted as proof that justice is really better than injustice, because they show only that justice is valuable as a means to an end.

Adeimantus next brings forward the widely prevalent view that, though justice may be better than injustice, injustice really makes life more agreeable and more successful (364 A). Even the gods, they say, grant better fortune to the unjust than to the just, and, besides, they are not inexorable in the punishment of injustice. This is illustrated by the practices of the *ἀγύρται* and *μάντεις*, who profess to have special power from the gods to cure men of the consequences of their misdeeds or the misdeeds of their ancestors,[75] and to be able to injure the enemy of a client, whether the enemy is a good man or not, by forcing the gods to do their will (364 B–C). These views, that vice is easy and virtue hard, and that the gods can be beguiled, are further supported by quotations from Hesiod and Homer and by reference to the books of Musaeus and Orpheus and the doctrines of the men who use them in their ritual (364 D–E). Even the fear of punishment after death is meaningless, because we have the authority of cities and of prophets for the assurance that we can escape it by means of the teletae and the *λύσιοι θεοί*.

In order to determine precisely what is revealed by this passage concerning Orpheus and Orphic institutions, we must undertake to disentangle what Plato knew about them from the tissue of thought which he is weaving for his own purposes. Especially, the marked tone of disapproval with which he speaks of all means of nullifying the consequences of sin must not color our judgment of the value

[75] Evidently, people were often terrified at what might happen to them on account of the misdemeanors of their ancestors. To such people the dramas of the hereditary curse must have had a particularly poignant interest.

set upon them by others. The teletae which he disparages, others, as we have already seen, regarded as blessings to mankind.

Within the several pages whose contents have been summarized there are four short texts which are of immediate importance for our purposes. Let us examine first the single sentence in which the name of Orpheus appears (364 E3 – 365 A3 = *Fragm.* 3), almost every word of which requires comment: *βίβλων δὲ ὅμαδον παρέχονται Μουσαίου καὶ Ὀρφέως, Σελήνης τε καὶ Μουσῶν ἐκγόνων, ὥς φασι, καθ' ἃς θυηπολοῦσιν, πείθοντες οὐ μόνον ἰδιώτας ἀλλὰ καὶ πόλεις, ὡς ἄρα λύσεις τε καὶ καθαρμοὶ ἀδικημάτων διὰ θυσιῶν καὶ παιδιᾶς ἡδονῶν εἰσὶ μὲν ἔτι ζῶσιν, εἰσὶ δὲ καὶ τελευτήσασιν, ἃς δὴ τελετὰς καλοῦσιν, αἳ τῶν ἐκεῖ κακῶν ἀπολύουσιν ἡμᾶς, μὴ θύσαντας δὲ δεινὰ περιμένει.*

Observe, first, the prominence of the word *βίβλων*. Three illustrations have been given of the popular opinion that injustice is easy and safe: the practices of the *ἀγύρται* and *μάντεις*, a quotation from Hesiod, and a quotation from Homer. One might expect the new sentence to begin *Μουσαίου δὲ καὶ Ὀρφέως*, contrasting these poets with the preceding ones. There seems to be a false emphasis on "books," because one feels the idea to be already latent in the reference to Homer and Hesiod. What is the cause of this emphasis, which, of course, in the language of Plato cannot be false? Two causes can be discerned. In the first place, whereas the poems of Homer and Hesiod, the great classics, are known to the people by heart or through the recitation of rhapsodes, the works of Musaeus and Orpheus are accessible only to the reader, or to the participant in the teletae, who perhaps heard them read. In the second place, the fact that the persons who conducted the teletae used books in some way means that they depended on the sanctity of the written word. Like the chresmologoi they depended for their authority upon the written scrolls which they could exhibit. Whether the books which were attributed to Musaeus and Orpheus contained a formal expression of the doctrine of remission of sins, or whether they were simply symbolical of the teletae in which they were used and in which the doctrine was implicit, we cannot say.

The old Homeric word ὅμαδος means a 'din of many voices.' It is commonly understood to mean here, without any authority, a 'multitude.' The πολλῶν γραμμάτων καπνούς of the *Hippolytus* is probably the source of this notion. Lobeck proposed to emend to ὁρμαθόν, a 'string' or 'cluster,' and finds some support for the word in Theophrastus, *Char.* vi, 8 ὁρμαθοὺς γραμματειδίων ἐν ταῖς χερσίν. This is ingenious, but it cannot be accepted. We must take the word we have, and take it in its true sense. When Plato says a 'din of books' he means books whose gabbling recitation produces a din or hubbub, and the same kind of jargon perhaps that Euripides describes under another figure as καπνούς. So a visitor to a mosque, hearing the books of the Koran recited aloud by a crowd of students, might call them a βίβλων ὅμαδον. So Aeschines, who reads the books in his mother's ritual, as Demosthenes tells us (xviii, 259), is a good howler.

παρέχονται is used in its regular sense, 'adduce as evidence.' But who are to be thought of as the subject? The only possible antecedent is the general class of people who hold remarkable views about the attitude of the gods toward human misconduct. They were last named explicitly in the sweeping phrase πάντες ἐξ ἑνὸς στόματος ὑμνοῦσιν (364 A). But when we get to θυηπολοῦσιν, though no new subject has been named, it is restricted to the particular persons who conduct teletae. This means that Plato expects the reader to make a similar restriction in παρέχονται. He might have written οἱ δὲ καὶ βίβλων ὅμαδον παρέχονται, but βίβλων was eager to come out first.

The phrase καθ' ἃς θυηπολοῦσιν is baffling. We do not know what was in the books or how they were used. They may have contained liturgies; they may have contained myths, which were dramatized in the teletae or interpreted symbolically by the practitioners; or they may have contained a miscellany, like the Bible, neither entirely liturgical nor entirely mythological, but yet serving as authority.

That the teletae were recommended not only to individuals, but also to cities, and presumably employed by them, as we shall see in the fourth text to be discussed, is a very significant fact. It shows not only that their value was publicly recognized, but also that they were not the possession of a limited religious sect. Though the practitioners must have been specialists, like μάντεις and χρησμολόγοι, their services were available for all who felt themselves in need of them.

In the phrase λύσεις τε καὶ καθαρμοὶ ἀδικημάτων, ἀδικήματα plainly means the abiding effects of wrongdoing. ἀδικήματα are offenses of any kind which are reprobated by the moral sense; but since the offenders are conscious of sin in consequence of them, they believe that the offenses remain with them as permanent disabilities. The misdeed committed in the past is still potent, and is a very real blight on a man's life. It may be felt as a tightness which calls for release (λύσις), or as a stain which demands cleansing (καθαρμός). Under another figure it may be a sickness which must be cured (ἀκεῖσθαι 364 C). In whatever form it is felt, the thing itself can be removed by teletae.

All that we are told here of the method of the teletae, besides the use of books, is in the words διὰ θυσιῶν καὶ παιδιᾶς ἡδονῶν. This may mean that the ceremonies which produced such tremendous results were really rather fun, like a game, and so, to any serious-minded person like Plato, contemptible; or that they actually involved children's games. One is reminded of the ῥομβός and the ἀστράγαλοι in the myth of Dionysus; but whether teletae based upon that myth were in use in the fourth century B.C. or not (and they may well have been), it is not admissible to find an allusion to them here. The spirit of mockery is similar to that in the phrase μεθ' ἡδονῶν τε καὶ ἑορτῶν, which is used a little earlier (364 C), and there is nothing there about a game. If the παιδιαί were ceremonial games Plato would have said it more clearly, and the games in the myth of Dionysus imply very little in the way of ἡδονή. Besides, teletae involving that myth would seem to be quite inappropriate for ministering to the needs of ailing cities.

The next question relates to the words ζῶσιν and

*τελευτήσασιν*. Do these two words denote two sets of people, the living and the dead, or do they denote one set of people, while they are still alive and after they have died? If the first, the meaning is that teletae may be performed for the benefit of people who are still alive and for the benefit of people who are already dead. If the second, the benefit of the teletae is said to be enjoyed by the participants immediately while they are still alive, and to continue in effect even after they die. Grammatically either interpretation is possible, but it is difficult to see why, if the first was intended, Plato did not write *τοῖς ἔτι ζῶσιν* and *τοῖς τελευτήσασιν*. Those who adopt the first interpretation[76] with its significant religious implication are principally influenced by an Orphic fragment of unknown date which is quoted by Olympiodorus in the sixth century A.D. (*In Plat. Phaedon.* p. 87, 15 Norvin = *Fragm.* 232):

> *ἄνθρωποι δὲ τεληέσσας ἑκατόμβας*
> *πέμψουσιν πάσῃσιν ἐν ὥραις ἀμφιέτῃσιν*
> *ὄργια τ' ἐκτελέσουσι λύσιν προγόνων ἀθεμίστων*
> *μαιόμενοι· σὺ δὲ τοῖσιν ἔχων κράτος, οὕς κ' ἐθέλῃσθα,*
> *λύσεις ἔκ τε πόνων χαλεπῶν καὶ ἀπείρονος οἴστρου.*

It is not certain, however, that even here the orgia are performed in behalf of the poor souls of the departed. The poet may be saying, in a clumsy way, "seeking remission of (the *ἀδικήματα* which have been inherited from) wicked ancestors." Kern,[77] in fact, understands the words so; but

[76] Cf. Rohde, *Psyche*, II, 128, n. 5. Shorey translates thus: "... that there really are remissions of sins and purifications for deeds of injustice, by means of sacrifice and pleasant sport for the living, and that there are also special rites for the defunct, which they call functions ..."

[77] *Orpheus* (1920), p. 46.

he also recognizes an allusion to the wicked Titans—the common ancestors of the human race, according to some late Orphic fragments. This may be right. But if Plato and the late fragments are talking about the same thing, it is probably not right, because Plato speaks of the sins of ancestors who cannot be the Titans. The phrase *εἴτε τι ἀδίκημά του γέγονεν αὐτοῦ ἢ προγόνων* (364 B), being conditional, implies that a man may or may not be afflicted with the sins of his ancestors; but there can be nothing conditional about the Titans, since all men alike, according to the doctrine, suffer for the Titans' sin. Again, in 366 A the phrase *ἢ αὐτοὶ ἢ παῖδες παίδων* shows that Plato has in mind the transmission of guilt from generation to generation, not some original sin which afflicts all humanity. The only support, therefore, for the first interpretation is weak and remote. The second interpretation accords with the natural construction of the words (the participles agree with *αὐτοῖς* or *ἡμῖν* understood) and is made certain by the last words of the sentence, *μὴ θύσαντας δὲ δεινὰ περιμένει*. The teletae are performed by the living to insure their own happiness after death.[78]

In the words *ἃς δὴ τελετὰς καλοῦσιν* an etymological connection is doubtless suggested between *τελετὰς* and *τελευτήσασιν*. Those who adopt the first of the interpretations which have just been discussed conclude that only the rites for the dead are called *τελεταί*. Shorey's transla-

[78] Guthrie (*Orpheus and Greek Religion*, London, 1935, p. 214) disposes effectively of the notion of prayers for the dead. Nilsson, however ("Orphism and Kindred Religious Movements," *Harv. Theol. Rev.*, XXVIII [1935], 229), continues to say that the Orphics "professed that their initiations were able to save those too who were already suffering their punishments in the Underworld."

tion, indeed, implies that the 'sacrifices and ceremonies which resemble child's play' are used only for purification and release in this life and that they are not the same as the teletae which are effectual for the dead. This is manifestly erroneous. The word teletae, than which there is no more general term, applies to both kinds of ceremonies (if there were two kinds), or to the single ritual which served both purposes. The teletae are performed with a view to procuring a happy state for one and the same person before and after death; but since the terrors of the next world greatly outweigh the known discomforts of this life, and the chief value of the teletae is prophylactic, the etymology is not unreasonable (though, of course, not sound), whether made by Plato or someone else; and it is naturally mentioned in immediate connection with *τελευτήσασιν*.

The sentence closes with the statement that "if we do not perform these sacrifices, appalling things await us." If all who are unpurified by teletae suffer terrible things in Hades, and if the purifications are intended to remove the stain of wrongdoing, then all men must be guilty of wrongdoing. This means that all men have either done wrong themselves or inherited guilt from their ancestors. This brings us again to the possibility that Plato has in mind the original sin of the Titans, under which all humanity labored. Where this doctrine appears, however, the penalty which men suffer for the sin of the Titans is generally conceived to be the imprisonment of the soul in flesh through a series of recurrent births. This, at any rate, is not thought of here. If, on the other hand, Plato was aware of a doctrine that all men are doomed to suffer after death for the reason that all men alike bear a load of guilt, we should certainly have had something more than this slight allusion to the matter in his whole discourse on the value of justice and injustice. It would have been an admirable point for Adeimantus if he could have shown that according to this view justice is utterly futile because no degree of justice could save a man from punishment after death. Let us consider the case of the old man Cephalus with whom Socrates converses in the introduction to the *Republic* (i, 330 D). When one begins to realize, he says, that death is drawing near, he is seized with apprehension that there may be some truth in the stories that he has laughed at hitherto, which tell about conditions in Hades and give warning that men who have sinned in this life are punished there. If these stories had told that all alike, whether they had sinned or not, were doomed to misery, unless they were saved through the teletae, anyone in the credulous state described by Cephalus would have been little concerned about his own personal sins; he would avail himself promptly of the one remedy that was offered, on the chance that it might be efficacious. When Cephalus recalls the grounds for an old man's fears, he gives no hint of this most alarming doctrine at all, the condemnation of the entire human race for inherited sin. It is fair to conclude that this doctrine did not form a part of the well-known stories about rewards and punishments in Hades, and that if it did exist in obscure corners and Adeimantus had wished to allude to it, he would have used language more open and explicit.

A more probable explanation of the passage is this. Men naturally look forward to death with fear and horror and consequently form an unpleasant conception of the state after death; and since all men must die, all anticipate this unpleasantness. If the unpleasantness can be avoided and a pleasant state assured, through the instrumentality of the teletae, it is only natural that those who are specially interested in teletae and recommend their use should emphasize the horrors that await the uninitiated. For this it is not necessary to urge a doctrine of original sin; the natural fear of death and its elaboration by the mythopoeic imagination are sufficient. To this is added, to be sure, the notion that wrongdoers are punished in the next world for their misdeeds in life, so that the teletae are understood to insure men not only against the natural terrors of the hereafter, but also against the special punishment which they have incurred by their own misconduct. This notion is fortified by the general belief that even in this life men suffer under serious liabilities for misdeeds of every sort, μιάσματα which can be cured by καθαρμοί.

The second of the texts requiring discussion comes about a page earlier than the first and runs as follows (363 C3–E3 = *Fragm.* 4): Μουσαῖος δὲ τούτων νεανικώτερα τἀγαθὰ καὶ ὁ ὑὸς αὐτοῦ παρὰ θεῶν διδόασιν τοῖς δικαίοις· εἰς Ἅιδου γὰρ ἀγαγόντες τῷ λόγῳ καὶ κατακλίναντες καὶ συμπόσιον τῶν ὁσίων κατασκευάσαντες ἐστεφανωμένους ποιοῦσιν τὸν ἅπαντα χρόνον ἤδη διάγειν μεθύοντας, ἡγησάμενοι κάλλιστον ἀρετῆς μισθὸν μέθην αἰώνιον. οἱ δ' ἔτι τούτων μακροτέρους ἀποτείνουσιν μισθοὺς παρὰ θεῶν· παῖδας γὰρ παίδων φασὶ καὶ γένος κατόπισθεν *λείπεσθαι τοῦ ὁσίου καὶ εὐόρκου. ταῦτα δὴ καὶ ἄλλα τοιαῦτα ἐγκωμιάζουσιν δικαιοσύνην· τοὺς δὲ ἀνοσίους αὖ καὶ ἀδίκους εἰς πηλόν τινα κατορύττουσιν ἐν Ἅιδου καὶ κοσκίνῳ ὕδωρ ἀναγκάζουσι φέρειν, ἔτι τε ζῶντας εἰς κακὰς δόξας ἄγοντες, ἅπερ Γλαύκων περὶ τῶν δικαίων δοξαζομένων δὲ ἀδίκων διῆλθε τιμωρήματα, ταῦτα περὶ τῶν ἀδίκων λέγουσιν, ἄλλα δὲ οὐκ ἔχουσιν.*

What is said about teletae in the first text considered is appropriately included by Adeimantus in that portion of his argument in which the popular view is set forth that, though injustice is admittedly a bad thing, it is still possible to enjoy the fruits of it with impunity. In the text now before us, in which he describes the other popular view, namely, that justice is good because it brings good results, and injustice bad because it leads to evil, he introduces ideas which obviously bear some relation to the teletae. The general subject of the teletae and the ideas associated with them is thus torn apart and made to yield illustrations of two discreditable aspects of popular morality. The connection between the two passages is signalized by the words *δεινὰ περιμένει* in the later text, which recall summarily a part of what is found in the earlier one, and by the name of Musaeus, which appears in both, Musaeus and his son in the first, Musaeus and Orpheus in the second. Who the son was, no one knows for certain. Eumolpus is named in some genealogies. Though Musaeus sometimes appears as the son of Orpheus, Orpheus never appears as the son of Musaeus. The father of Orpheus is always Apollo or Oeagrus. Plato may, however, have followed a genealogy otherwise unattested and understood Musaeus to be his father.

When διδόασιν, ἀγαγόντες, and the succeeding verbs and participles are grammatically made predicates of Musaeus and his son, the meaning, of course, is that they give the world to understand that such are the things that occur in Hades. This form of speech is common enough in Plato. But it does not tell us how these doctrines were actually made known. From the mention of books in 364 E one might conclude that they were published in that form, but it is worth noticing that this is not explicitly stated.

In the second sentence there is a curious turn of emphasis which seems to be generally overlooked. The first things that happen to good men after their death are expressed by three aorist participles: they are conducted to Hades, they are given places on couches, they are made members of a symposium with others like themselves—and then they stay there forever after with wreaths on their heads. ἐστεφανωμένους stands first in its colon and bears the emphasis, which is intended to leave the reader with a picture in his mind of a company of people wearing garlands to all eternity. The colon ends with the word διάγειν and the sense is complete. What follows (a dash should be introduced) is obviously not a part of the doctrine of Musaeus, but a slurring comment added by Adeimantus. μεθύοντας is so much stronger and more significant than ἐστεφανωμένους that if drunkenness had been part of Musaeus' doctrine μεθύοντας would have come first. Being placed where it is, it is intolerably weak unless it is given the force which has been suggested. Plutarch, to be sure (*Comp. Cim. et Lucull.* 521 B), says: Πλάτων ἐπισκώπτει τοὺς περὶ τὸν Ὀρφέα, τοῖς εὖ βεβιωκόσι φάσκοντας ἀποκεῖσθαι γέρας ἐν Ἅιδου μέθην αἰώνιον. But Plutarch and all postclassical writers lack the fine sense of order which adds infinitely to the delicacy of expression in classical Greek prose, and consequently give a blunted and mistaken report of what Plato said.

The words τῶν ὁσίων in this sentence are sometimes pressed to mean more than they do. ὅσιος is a common adjective in general use and describes a person who is 'void of offense,' 'one whose moral record is clear.' It is vaguer and wider in range than the more precise δίκαιος, but in effect the words are synonymous. Plato, writing on justice, naturally uses δίκαιος most frequently, but ὅσιος appears from time to time in the same sense. So τοῖς ὁσίοις in 363 A is followed two lines later by τοῖς δικαίοις with exactly the same meaning. In the phrase τοῦ ὁσίου καὶ εὐόρκου in 363 D, ὁσίου plainly has no technical application. Immediately after, in τοὺς ἀνοσίους καὶ ἀδίκους, the two adjectives do not differ in meaning. Plato's view of the matter is this. Men are δίκαιοι or ἄδικοι according to their conduct; οἱ δίκαιοι are ὅσιοι, and οἱ ἄδικοι are ἀνόσιοι. But οἱ ἄδικοι, according to the pretensions of the teletae, can be cleansed of their ἀδικήματα. Then, since it would be too much to call them δίκαιοι, they are called by the vaguer term ὅσιοι. Strictly, then, the συμπόσιον τῶν ὁσίων is composed of the δίκαιοι, and of the ἄδικοι who have been cleansed of their ἀδικήματα. But τῶν ὁσίων, which is quite unemphatic, is scarcely more than a pronominal echo of τοῖς δικαίοις, which just precedes it, as if αὐτῶν had been written—"they are made members of a symposium with others like themselves." There is no justification in taking the word in the restricted and technical sense of 'saints,' meaning thereby the members of a self-righteous sect.[79]

The words *οἱ δέ* at the beginning of the next sentence introduce a statement of the views of persons other than Musaeus and his son.[80] But who then are to be taken as the subject of *κατορύττουσι* and *ἀναγκάζουσι*? Probably Musaeus and his son come into force again, so that we are given the companion piece to their picture of the banquet of the just. But perhaps we have no right to attribute these things to Musaeus in particular. They may simply be current ideas—*οἱ λεγόμενοι μῦθοι περὶ τῶν ἐν Ἅιδου*, as Cephalus says.

Having studied the first two texts and observed their relationship, we may now consider the third, which stands between the two (364 B5 – C5 = *Fragm.* 3): *ἀγύρται δὲ καὶ μάντεις ἐπὶ πλουσίων θύρας ἰόντες πείθουσιν ὡς ἔστι παρὰ σφίσι δύναμις ἐκ θεῶν ποριζομένη θυσίαις τε καὶ ἐπῳδαῖς, εἴτε τι ἀδίκημά*

[79] As Guthrie remarks (*Orpheus and Greek Religion*, p. 160), punishments are not primarily for the uninitiated, but for the unrighteous (*ἄδικοι καὶ ἀνόσιοι*); 'uninitiated' would not have suited the argument.

[80] Rohde (*Psyche*, II, 129, n. 3) says: "Plato . . . stellt diesen [Musaeus and his son] mit *οἱ δέ* andere entgegen, die anderes verhiessen, vielleicht andere orphische Gedichte." He refers to Servius ad Verg. *Aen.* iii, 98, "sane hic versus Homeri est, quem et ipse de Orpheo sustulit, item Orpheus de oraculo Apollinis Hyperborei." Vergil's line is: "et nati natorum et qui nascentur ab illis"; Homer's line is *καὶ παίδων παῖδες, τοί κεν μετόπισθε γένωνται*. Servius may or may not have found the same line, or a similar line, in an Orphic poem; if he did, it was probably borrowed from Homer, whose words seem to be echoed in Plato. Rohde continues: "Aber Musaeus, wie er bei Plato stets eng mit Orpheus verbunden vorkommt, vertritt zweifellos auch hier orphische Dichtung (unter seinem Namen hatte man eine Literatur wesentlich orphischen Characters)." But what is Orphic poetry except poetry attributed by the ancients to Orpheus? Why should Plato say Musaeus and his son if he means Orpheus?

του γέγονεν αὐτοῦ ἢ προγόνων, ἀκεῖσθαι μεθ' ἡδονῶν τε καὶ ἑορτῶν, ἐάν τέ τινα ἐχθρὸν πημῆναι ἐθέλῃ, μετὰ σμικρῶν δαπανῶν ὁμοίως δίκαιον ἀδίκῳ βλάψει ἐπαγωγαῖς τισιν καὶ καταδέσμοις, τοὺς θεούς, ὥς φασιν, πείθοντές σφισιν ὑπηρετεῖν. This text, it will be recalled, falls in Adeimantus' exposition of the popular belief that though justice is better than injustice in the abstract, the blessing of the gods rests on the unjust rather than on the just, and they can be moved to cancel whatever ill effects injustice may cause. The practices of the ἀγύρται and μάντεις provide an instance of the operation of these principles. They profess to have special power from the gods to cure any ἀδικήματα, personal or hereditary, from which their clients are suffering, and to be able, by their influence with the gods, to injure the enemy of a client, however just a man he may be. This special power which they have from the gods must be constantly recruited (ποριζομένη) by sacrifices and incantations; but as far as their clients are concerned, the cure is performed under the circumstances of a holiday merrymaking. The harm that they profess to do the enemy of a client is accomplished by the usual ritual of magic. Their motives are entirely mercenary, and their whole business is to fleece the rich.

What relation do these gentry bear to those who conduct teletae in accordance with books of Musaeus and Orpheus? An unprejudiced reader must acknowledge that the two sets are not identical. The ἀγύρται and μάντεις are dealt with in a single sentence. With ἐπάγονται in the next sentence the subject reverts to those who hold the general views which Adeimantus is expounding. They find authority for their position in Hesiod, Homer, and the books of Musaeus and Orpheus.[81] Obviously a new thing is introduced with the mention of these books, not a continuation of what has been said about the *ἀγύρται* and *μάντεις*. There is, of course, a manifest resemblance between the two sets, because they both illustrate the moral laxity of the gods and both undertake to remove the evil effects of misdemeanor by painless and agreeable methods. But in these things they both resemble Homer, too. The most important difference between them is that the first set make irresponsible claims of personal power, the second rest on the authority of books and conduct their ceremonies in accordance with these books. The first set is in business to make money; nothing of this sort is imputed to the second. The second set is distinctly more respectable than the first. They are quite wrong in their religious attitude, Plato believes; but so are Homer and Hesiod and all who believe in the forgiveness of sins through prayer and sacrament. But except for the words *παιδιᾶς ἡδονῶν* he says nothing particularly contemptuous of them. The second set are in some sort followers of Musaeus and Orpheus; the first, as far as Plato's evidence goes, are not.

The last text to be considered is as follows (366 A4–B2 = *Fragm.* 3): "*Ἀλλὰ γὰρ ἐν Ἅιδου δίκην δώσομεν ὧν ἂν ἐνθάδε ἀδικήσωμεν, ἢ αὐτοὶ ἢ παῖδες παίδων.*" *Ἀλλ', ὦ φίλε, φήσει λογιζόμενος, αἱ τελεταὶ αὖ μέγα δύνανται καὶ οἱ λύσιοι θεοί, ὡς αἱ μέγισται πόλεις λέγουσι καὶ οἱ θεῶν παῖδες ποιηταὶ καὶ προφῆται τῶν θεῶν γενόμενοι, οἳ ταῦτα οὕτως ἔχειν μηνύουσιν.*

[81] Jebb (on Theophr. *Char.* xxviii [xvi], 29) makes *ἀγύρται καὶ μάντεις* subject of *παρέχονται.*

This text supplies no information which we have not already obtained from the previous ones, though it is shown to be bound up with the first by the words *οἱ θεῶν παῖδες ποιηταὶ καὶ προφῆται γενόμενοι*, which plainly refer to such persons as Orpheus, Musaeus, and the son of Musaeus—though there is no reason to suppose that there were not others who might have been named. It is worth observing, however, that the blight of an *ἀδίκημα* is again recognized as hereditary by the words *ἢ αὐτοὶ ἢ παῖδες παίδων*, in which the possibility of the original sin of the Titans is excluded. By the words *λύσιοι θεοί* we need not suppose that any particular gods are intended, though a number of gods could be named who bore the epithet *λύσιος* or other epithets with a similar meaning. Plato is probably thinking again of the lines of Homer which he quoted a little earlier (364 D), and he substitutes the familiar word *λύσιοι* for the uncommon *λιστοί*. Thus he repeats the two generally accredited means of procuring remission of sins, the teletae and the simple prayers and sacrifices of Homer. Again, *αἱ μέγισται πόλεις* is an echo of *πόλεις* in 364 E. The teletae are not used by cities to insure happiness after death; but the fact that they use them for other purposes of cleansing and remission gives them an authority which recommends them to individuals as a means of future salvation. Finally, the word *λέγουσι* does not require us to believe that the poets actually make these explicit statements in their poems, any more than that the cities speak. It is enough that the poets are used as authorities by the men who conduct the teletae, whatever may have been their contents.

Having now examined the general bearing of the arguments of Adeimantus, and having studied with some care the language of Plato in order to determine, where there is any reason for doubt, precisely what he does, and what he does not, say and imply, we are prepared to appraise the passage as a whole for the evidence which it affords concerning the subject in which we are interested. Let us undertake to formulate the conclusions that may safely be drawn.

There was a belief in Athens, and probably elsewhere, in the fourth century B.C. that misdeeds imposed dangerous liabilities on the offenders. One who was conscious of wrongdoing felt a sense of tightness and constriction, a sense of impurity, a sense of disease. His life was disordered, and he was apprehensive of harm. He feared the consequence of his guilt both in this world and after death. Nor was it his own misdeeds alone that caused him alarm. The sins of his ancestors might still be potent to endanger him, as if they had been his own. How widespread these feelings were, we cannot say. It is not likely that in the healthy life of every day many men were so affected, or that any were so affected all the time. The superstitious were naturally more prone to these fears; all would be open to them at the approach of death; and they might be roused in the minds of the rich by quacks who hoped to profit by alleviating them. But we may well believe that there were many more than these. Even whole cities might fall a prey to such fears and look for means of relieving themselves of the misdeeds which they felt to afflict them.

Under these conditions the ordinary methods of prayer and sacrifice were available to appease the anger of the gods which was stirred by the wrongs done, and so to remove the evil consequences. But it is not surprising that sick souls felt the need of some means of relief which would be more powerful and effectual than the simpler processes of religion. Such means were provided, and, as is natural, those who provided the means encouraged the use of them. There were unscrupulous men who professed to be able to procure special powers from the gods that enabled them to cure past misdeeds by the processes of magic. These men relied only on the presumptuous assertion of their own power. But there were others in better standing who offered cures which were no more disagreeable, but who based their whole procedure on the authority of the written words of poets who were the offspring of gods and therefore commanded respect. The ceremonies conducted by them were called by the technical name of teletae.

Those who submitted themselves to the ministration of the teletae were taught to believe that they received remission and cleansing from the evil consequences of their sins while they were still alive, and that they would be saved from punishment for these sins after death. Of the ceremonies we learn only that they involved sacrifice, a rather childish and not disagreeable ritual, and perhaps recitation from the authoritative books. We are not told what the books contained. Probably some books by the same or similar authors described the rewards of good men after death and the punishment of bad men. The good, according to them, might look forward to the enjoyment of a perpetual banquet after death; the bad must expect to be sunk in mud or to be compelled to carry water in a sieve. Such books as these, or these with others, may have been the books used in the ritual.

Nothing is said about secrecy in the teletae. This may be simply because Adeimantus had no occasion to mention it. He is interested to recall only those things which are significant to illustrate the popular attitude toward the forgiveness of sins. But he speaks of the ceremonies as if he had seen them (and not as a participant), and as if he could tell us more if he wished. The contents of the books would also be known, if they were recited in the ritual, and certainly many, if not all, of the poems of Musaeus and Orpheus were accessible to readers. If there was some element of secrecy (as there may well have been), we do not learn of it here, at all events.

Beyond the few essential features, we have no right to assume that teletae were all alike, or that all made use of the same books. The men who conducted them may well have been quite independent and have recognized no common allegiance. There is nothing to indicate that they were organized in any sort of institution, and they have no common designation. There is even less probability that their clients were associated with them in anything like a congregation of the faithful. They were eager in their profession, recommending their offices to cities and individuals alike, and their motives must have been, at least in part, honest. They probably had a genuine belief in the saving power of their rites.

What is Orpheus' part in it all? He and Musaeus were authors of books which practitioners of teletae offered as evidence in support of their pretensions. This is all. Orpheus is not even named as an authority for the rewards and punishments after death.[82] It is true that Plutarch, reporting what Plato says in the present passage (see pp. 87 f.), attributes the doctrine of eternal drunkenness to *τοὺς περὶ τὸν Ὀρφέα*. We have seen reason above to question his interpretation of Plato's words in one respect, and there is reason likewise to question them here. Plato does not attribute the doctrine in question to Orpheus, but to Musaeus and his son. Possibly Plutarch may have chosen to use the name of Orpheus in his phrase *τοὺς περὶ τὸν Ὀρφέα* as typical of those who held such doctrines; possibly he had himself found the doctrine or something like it in an Orphic poem. The significant thing is that Plato does not name Orpheus as his authority, and that in his whole account of teletae and the doctrines associated with them there is no such emphasis on Orpheus as is implied in Plutarch's phrase. The implications of his language must not be overlooked. In the one place where he mentions Orpheus' name he refers to books of Musaeus and Orpheus which somehow supplied authority for teletae. If he had used Orpheus' name

[82] This is emphasized by Paul Tannery (*Rev. de philologie*, XXV [1901], 315 f.). Concerning the passage in Plutarch (*Comp. Cim. et Lucull.* 521 B) he writes thus: "Enfin si . . . Plutarque dit *τοὺς περὶ τὸν Ὀρφέα*, en parlant de ceux que Platon a raillés comme promettant aux justes une ivresse éternelle dans l'Hadès, alors que c'est Musée et Eumolpe que Platon a nommés expressément, je ne puis voir là, soit qu'une inadvertance de Plutarque, soit qu'une preuve que l'expression *οἱ περί* ne désigne point précisément, ainsi qu'on l'enseigne d'ordinaire, la personne dont le nom à l'accusatif suit la préposition *περί*."

alone, we should have evidence of a more or less well-defined religious institution which could be called Orphic. If no name at all appeared, we should be free to call the institution Orphic, if other arguments proved this to be true. But when the name of Orpheus is coupled with the name of Musaeus and is not even given first place, it is reasonably certain that Plato did not recognize the ideas and practices which he is describing as constituting a definite religion bearing the name of Orpheus. This is entirely consistent with his words in the passage from the *Protagoras*, discussed above, where he speaks of Orpheus, Musaeus, and others who were concerned with teletae and chresmodiae (*οἱ ἀμφί τε Ὀρφέα καὶ Μουσαῖον*). Others, like Aristophanes, may have chosen to regard Orpheus as the originator of all teletae, and in this sense all teletae can be called Orphic. But there is no evidence in the present passage that the world was aware of the existence of a distinct set of ideas and practices which was called Orphic.[83]

7) In a passage of the sixth book of the *Laws*, where Plato is considering the indefinite length of time during which civilization has been developing, he remarks that even today the practice of human sacrifice survives in many places, whereas, on the other hand, we hear of peoples whose custom it was not even to sacrifice animals, but to use only bloodless offerings (*Laws* vi, 782 C = *Test.* 212): *τὸ δὲ μὴν θύειν ἀνθρώπους ἀλλήλους ἔτι καὶ νῦν*

[83] G. W. Dyson ("Orphism and the Platonic Philosophy," *Speculum Religionis, Essays Presented to Claude G. Montefiore*, Oxford, 1929) has a discussion of this passage, which, though it is open to criticism in some points, is still excellent.

*παραμένον ὁρῶμεν πολλοῖς· καὶ τοὐναντίον ἀκούομεν ἐν ἄλλοις, ὅτε οὐδὲ βοὸς ἐτόλμων μὲν γεύεσθαι, θύματά τε οὐκ ἦν τοῖς θεοῖσι ζῷα, πέλανοι δὲ καὶ μέλιτι καρποὶ δεδευμένοι καὶ τοιαῦτα ἄλλα ἁγνὰ θύματα, σαρκῶν δ' ἀπείχοντο ὡς οὐχ ὅσιον ὂν ἐσθίειν οὐδὲ τοὺς τῶν θεῶν βωμοὺς αἵματι μιαίνειν, ἀλλὰ Ὀρφικοί τινες λεγόμενοι βίοι ἐγίγνοντο ἡμῶν τοῖς τότε, ἀψύχων μὲν ἐχόμενοι πάντων, ἐμψύχων δὲ τοὐναντίον πάντων ἀπεχόμενοι.* These people who neither sacrificed animals nor ate their flesh lived lives which Plato calls *Ὀρφικοί τινες λεγόμενοι βίοι*. The plural is used, not because more than one kind of Orphic life is thought of, but because each individual in the community lived such a life. Does this mean that this manner of life in the past was called an Orphic life, or that it so closely resembled a modern manner of living which was called Orphic that the same name might be applied to it with propriety? Grammatically either is possible, but the latter is favored by the presence of *τινες*, which makes the phrase mean "a kind of Orphic life, as it is called." The Orphic life may have implied something more than the avoidance of animal food; but this was an important feature of it, and justified the use of the term for the people of the past who avoided animal food. We have already seen that the Orphic life was well known in Athens, because Theseus scornfully recommended to Hippolytus that he should take it up; and the tone of Plato's allusion to it indicates that it would be familiar to his readers.

8) The next text to be examined is found in the speech which is known as the First Speech against Aristogeiton. This speech is included among the works of Demosthenes,

but it is generally regarded as spurious. The question of authenticity affects the evidence which it supplies concerning Orpheus in only one point: if Demosthenes is the author the date is certain; otherwise it cannot be fixed with precision, though presumably it was contemporary with Demosthenes.[84] The situation which is presented in the speech is this. Aristogeiton, who had been condemned to pay certain fines to the state, had failed to do so. In spite of this, though it was against the law for a man who had not paid a fine to speak in the assembly, he continued to do just this, bringing in indictments and making trouble. Finally, however, an action was brought against him, in the course of which the speech which is attributed to Demosthenes was delivered, and it is directed to a general condemnation of the life of Aristogeiton. It is time, says the speaker, to put a stop to his lawless and outrageous conduct, which the people have tolerated hitherto. The author then continues as follows: *ὑμᾶς τήμερον ὀρθῶς δεῖ δικάσαι, τὴν τὰ δίκαι' ἀγαπῶσαν Εὐνομίαν περὶ πλείστου ποιησαμένους, ἣ πάσας καὶ πόλεις καὶ χώρας σῴζει· καὶ τὴν ἀπαραίτητον καὶ σεμνὴν Δίκην, ἣν ὁ τὰς ἁγιωτάτας ἡμῖν τελετὰς καταδείξας Ὀρφεὺς παρὰ τὸν τοῦ Διὸς θρόνον φησὶ καθημένην πάντα τὰ τῶν ἀνθρώπων ἐφορᾶν, εἰς αὐτὸν ἕκαστον νομίσαντα βλέπειν οὕτω ψηφίζεσθαι, φυλαττόμενον καὶ προορώμενον μὴ καταισχῦναι ταύτην, ἧς ἐπώνυμός ἐστιν ὑμῶν ἕκαστος ὁ ἀεὶ δικάζειν λαχών* . . . ([Dem.] xxv, 11 = *Fragm.* 23).[85] The purpose of

---

[84] See Rich. Schläfke, *De Demosthenis quae dicuntur adversus Aristogiton. orationibus*, Diss. Greifswald, 1913.

[85] Weil, who defends the authenticity of the speech as a whole, brackets the passage here quoted, beginning with *τὴν ἀπαραίτητον*. "J'attribue à un très ancien interpolateur toute cette amplification jusqu'à la fin du § 11. . . . On

the author is to increase the solemnity of his appeal by an allusion to a passage in an Orphic poem in which it is said that Dike sits by the throne of Zeus and keeps watch on the conduct of men. He makes the allusion still more impressive by recalling that Orpheus was the originator of the most holy teletae. We have already seen the word καταδεῖξαι in the same sense in Aristophanes, and the simple δεῖξαι in the *Rhesus*. The superlative ἁγιωτάτας, expressing the high regard in which the teletae were held, gives a suitable emphasis for the author's purpose. There is no reason to suppose that any particular teletae are meant. It is quite unnecessary to assume, as Gruppe does,[86] that the author has in mind the Eleusinian Mysteries. We have, in fact, an utterance exactly parallel to that in the *Frogs*. It is striking that the teletae are mentioned just when the speaker wishes the audience to believe that Dike is inexorable. If Plato gives a fair picture of the teletae, their very function was to circumvent justice. But the present speaker gains more by turning the thoughts of his listeners to the dangers of the immoral state which calls for the purgation of the teletae, than he loses by the slight chance that anyone will perceive the incongruity. As far as the teletae themselves are concerned, inconsistency of this kind is quite characteristic of religion.

9) A statement of Ephorus concerning the relation be-

---

chercherait vainement dans ce discours un autre exemple d'une période aussi embarrassée et aussi surchargée. Diké est de trop après Eunomie, et la solennité du ton, l'onction avec laquelle il est parlé du vieil Orphée, tranche avec l'allure générale de ce morceau."

[86] In Roscher's *Lexikon*, s.v. Orpheus, p. 1096.

tween Orpheus and the Idaean Dactyls is reported by Diodorus, in a passage which has already been quoted (v, 64, 4; see p. 27 above). There it is said that the Dactyls, who originated in Phrygia and from there crossed into Europe, practiced incantations, teletae, and mysteries, and that Orpheus, who was naturally gifted in poetry and music, became their pupil and was the first to introduce teletae and mysteries among the Greeks. The opinion here expressed concerning Orpheus is not essentially different from what we have seen before in the *Rhesus*, Aristophanes, and Ps.-Demosthenes. They all represent him as the originator of teletae. Ephorus' only modification of this is to say that he was the originator of teletae in Greece and that he had learned the art from the Phrygian Dactyls. The change was probably due to the growing habit of finding a foreign origin for everything in the Greek world. The resemblance between the performances attributed to the Dactyls and the teletae which were known in Greece was enough to suggest that the one was the source of the other, and since the Greek teletae were said to have been instituted by Orpheus, the obvious step was to make him the pupil of the Dactyls.

10) Among the types described by Theophrastus in his *Characters* is included that of the Superstitious Man, and it is not surprising to find that this personage is excessively addicted to the use of teletae: *καὶ ὅταν ἐνύπνιον ἴδῃ, πορεύεσθαι πρὸς τοὺς ὀνειροκρίτας, πρὸς τοὺς μάντεις, πρὸς τούς ὀρνιθοσκόπους, ἐρωτήσων τίνι θεῶν ἢ θεᾷ εὔχεσθαι δεῖ. καὶ τελεσθησόμενος πρὸς τοὺς 'Ορφεοτελεστὰς κατὰ μῆνα πο-*

*ρεύεσθαι μετὰ τῆς γυναικός* (*ἐὰν δὲ μὴ σχολάζῃ ἡ γυνή, μετὰ τῆς τίτθης*) *καὶ τῶν παίδων* (*Char.* xvi, 11 f. Diels = *Test.* 207).[87] There can be little doubt that the teletae to which the Superstitious Man had recourse were of the type described by Plato in the *Republic*. Only, whereas the ordinary man would avail himself of them in a serious emergency, the Superstitious Man thought it best to take the treatment once a month. Evidently this was regarded as a very short interval. It is curious that he always took his wife or the children's nurse with him. It would seem as if the presence of a woman seemed to him somehow desirable.[88] Those who conducted the teletae seem to have been established in a regular way of business, since the man knew where they were to be found; they were different from Plato's peddlers who knocked at rich men's doors.

The word Ὀρφεοτελεστής is new. Are we to suppose that it indicates a special type of teletae which were called Orphic to distinguish them from others? The difficulty with this is that it supplies as the designation for a special type of teletae a name which according to Plato's

[87] A thorough discussion of this passage may be found in Hendrik Bolkestein, "Theophrastos' Character der Deisidaimonia als religionsgeschichtliche Urkunde," *Religionsgeschichtliche Versuche und Vorarbeiten*, XXI (1929), 2, pp. 52–63. The meaning of the words *τελετή* and *τελεῖν* is here studied in some detail, and the conclusion is that Theophrastus uses *τελεσθησόμενος* to mean "um sich reinigen zu lassen." This limitation of meaning is somewhat arbitrary, and I should prefer to allow the broader sense "to subject himself to the effectual treatment of the sacramental rite"—whatever the rite may be.

[88] Bolkestein (p. 62) suggests that, though Theophrastus uses only men as types of character, he recognizes that women are more superstitious than men and makes an opportunity to bring out this fact by introducing the wife and the nurse. This is not convincing. A single passing allusion in the whole essay is not sufficient for the purpose; and besides, we get the impression that the women accompany the man only to satisfy his whims.

account might well be used of all, since the books of Orpheus, with others, were authoritative in them. It is more likely that Theophrastus and Plato are referring to exactly the same thing, all unofficial teletae which rest on the authority of books, but that they place a different emphasis on the two principal authors of the books. In Plato Musaeus is the more prominent; the word used by Theophrastus puts Orpheus forward. Whoever coined Ὀρφεοτελεστής must have chosen to think of Orpheus as the titular authority for teletae. This is not surprising when we recall how often we have seen him named as their originator. The word is really tautological, like "Bible Christians." But there is a reason for the phrase "Bible Christians"; what is the reason for Ὀρφεοτελεστής? Two reasons may be suggested. The natural word for those who conducted teletae would be τελεσταί. This word is found, but it is very infrequent. μάντεις, ἀγύρται, γόητες, μάγοι—these and others are common enough. But there is no familiar word with the meaning of τελεστής; writers often resort to οἱ τελοῦντες. The reason for the avoidance of τελεστής is that it lacked precision, like τέλος and τελέω. A τελεστής is simply 'one who brings to fulfillment'; and such a word could not be trusted to mean 'a conductor of teletae' unless the context revealed the sense. But if the name of Orpheus is prefixed the sense is indubitable. The other reason that may be suggested is the desire to specify unofficial teletae in distinction from the great state mysteries. The essential thing about the unofficial teletae is the use of authoritative books, which are attributed to Orpheus and others; and since Orpheus was perhaps oftener thought of as a poet than as the culture hero who originated all teletae and mysteries, and since his poems were well known, the word Ὀρφεοτελεστής would suggest book teletae in distinction from the teletae of the great mysteries where the tradition of the cult was sovereign.

## Poems

### THE EXISTENCE OF ORPHIC POETRY AND THE REPUTATION OF THE AUTHOR

It was believed by most people in the fifth and fourth centuries B.C., though not by all (as we shall see later), that Orpheus was one of the great classical poets, not unworthy to be named with Homer and Hesiod; and poems existed in manuscript form of which he was generally held to be the author. This we know from texts which have already been cited from the *Frogs* of Aristophanes, from Ps.-Demosthenes, from the *Republic* of Plato, and from the *Hippolytus* of Euripides. Other texts which attest the same facts may now be quoted.

What may be an allusion to the earliest appearance of Orphic poetry in history is found in a doubly ambiguous sentence in Suidas (s.v. Φερεκύδης = *Test.* 228): Φερεκύδης, Ἀθηναῖος, πρεσβύτερος τοῦ Συρίου, ὃν λόγος τὰ Ὀρφέως συναγαγεῖν. Besides the confusion which prevails in Suidas concerning the several persons named Pherecydes, there is obscurity in the very language of this brief statement. The antecedent of ὃν may be Pherecydes of Athens or Pherecydes of Syros, and τὰ Ὀρφέως may be actual poems or simply ideas connected with teletae or found in poems.

Either Pherecydes of Syros, in the sixth century B.C., or Pherecydes of Athens, in the fifth century B.C., collected the poems of Orpheus or in his own works brought together Orphic materials of some sort. Any one of these statements would be interesting, if we could trust it, but it would add little to our knowledge of Orpheus. In any case, the tradition, as λόγος shows, was very faint when Suidas was writing in the tenth century A.D.

Clement of Alexandria, speaking of the readiness with which Greek authors stole other men's ideas, quotes a passage from the sophist Hippias, who says plainly that he has obtained his material from earlier writers (*Strom.* vi, 15, 2 Stählin = *Test.* 252 = Hippias fr. 6 Diels-Kranz): τούτων ἴσως εἴρηται τὰ μὲν Ὀρφεῖ, τὰ δὲ Μουσαίῳ, κατὰ βραχὺ ἄλλῳ ἀλλαχοῦ, τὰ δὲ Ἡσιόδῳ, τὰ δὲ Ὁμήρῳ, τὰ δὲ τοῖς ἄλλοις τῶν ποιητῶν, τὰ δὲ ἐν συγγραφαῖς τὰ μὲν Ἕλλησι, τὰ δὲ βαρβάροις· ἐγὼ δὲ ἐκ πάντων τούτων τὰ μάλιστα [καὶ] ὁμόφυλα συνθεὶς τοῦτον καινὸν καὶ πολυειδῆ τὸν λόγον ποιήσομαι. A number of emendations have been proposed for κατὰ βραχὺ ἄλλῳ ἀλλαχοῦ. It is difficult to see how these words can have any particular application to Musaeus or to Musaeus and Orpheus. If a change is to be made, the simplest is to move the four words to a place immediately after βαρβάροις, so that they would summarize the preceding—"in a word, by one writer in one place, by another in another." It is also possible that they are a scholium which has intruded into the text. Stählin, by putting a comma after Μουσαίῳ, makes the phrase sound like a summary, but a summary in the midst of a list is strange. In any case, Hippias includes Orpheus in the stereotyped list of classical poets which we have already seen in Aristophanes, and the four poets are named in the same order—Orpheus, Musaeus, Hesiod, Homer.

Curiously enough, the same order is observed by Socrates at the end of Plato's *Apology*, when he is thinking of the delight of meeting these great men of old (*Apol.* 41 A = *Test.* 138): ἢ αὖ Ὀρφεῖ συγγενέσθαι καὶ Μουσαίῳ καὶ Ἡσιόδῳ καὶ Ὁμήρῳ ἐπὶ πόσῳ ἄν τις δέξαιτ' ἂν ὑμῶν;

In the *Ion* of Plato, also, the poets are mentioned in the same order, though Hesiod is absent (*Ion* 536 A–B = *Test.* 244): καὶ ὁ μὲν τῶν ποιητῶν ἐξ ἄλλης Μούσης, ὁ δὲ ἐξ ἄλλης ἐξήρτηται—ὀνομάζομεν δὲ αὐτὸ κατέχεται τὸ δέ ἐστι παραπλήσιον· ἔχεται γάρ—ἐκ δὲ τούτων τῶν πρώτων δακτυλίων, τῶν ποιητῶν, ἄλλοι ἐξ ἄλλου αὖ ἠρτημένοι εἰσὶ καὶ ἐνθουσιάζουσιν, οἱ μὲν ἐξ Ὀρφέως, οἱ δὲ ἐκ Μουσαίου· οἱ δὲ πολλοὶ ἐξ Ὁμήρου κατέχονταί τε καὶ ἔχονται. ὧν σύ, ὦ Ἴων, εἷς εἶ καὶ κατέχει ἐξ Ὁμήρου . . . Socrates has been comparing the inspiration of a Muse to the power of a magnet. As the attraction of the magnet can support a series of iron rings, each one attached to the one above it, so the inspiration of the Muse passes through the poet to the rhapsode or actor and thence to the spectator or listener. One line of attraction passes from Orpheus to those who are especially moved by his poetry, another from Musaeus, another from Homer: can we say that there were also public recitations of the poetry of Orpheus and Musaeus? Unfortunately, Plato's words do not allow us to answer this with certainty. In the sentence which is quoted he may be thinking, not of the rhapsodes only, who were inspired by the several poets, but of *all* recipients of this inspiration. If this be so, he may have in mind the stimulating effect of Orpheus and Musaeus upon the private reader and upon those who participated in the teletae, rather than the effect produced upon an audience by the public recitation of rhapsode. It is regrettable that we cannot be sure about this, because if we knew that Orpheus was recited to public audiences for their amusement, we should know more than we actually do know concerning the nature of Orphic poetry.

The comic poet Alexis, in the fourth century B.C., has occasion to give what appears to be a list of standard authors such as may be found in any library: Orpheus is first, Hesiod second; Musaeus is absent (*Athenaeus* iv, 164 B–C = Alexis fr. 135 Kock = *Test.* 220):

> βιβλίον
> ἐντεῦθεν ὅ τι βούλει προσελθὼν γὰρ λαβέ,
> ἔπειτ' ἀναγνώσει πάνυ γε διασκοπῶν
> ἀπὸ τῶν ἐπιγραμμάτων ἀτρέμα τε καὶ σχολῇ.
> 'Ορφεὺς ἔνεστιν, 'Ησίοδος, τραγῳδίαι,
> Χοιρίλος, Ὅμηρος, 'Επίχαρμος, συγγράμματα
> παντοδαπά.

Emendations proposed to correct the grammar in the first line and the meter in the last need not be discussed here.

## SUBJECT MATTER OF THE POEMS

Let us now bring together certain texts which bear evidence of poetry directly associated with the name of Orpheus and which give at the same time some indication of its nature. As we have seen, little is to be learned from the allusion in the *Hippolytus*: Theseus speaks of the contents of the books honored by the followers of Orpheus as nonsensical, but he speaks as a scoffer and we do not even know that the books were by Orpheus. Nor does the passage in the *Republic* which tells of the books used in connection with the teletae say anything explicitly about their contents. We cannot even say, on the basis of this text alone, that there were poems of Orpheus which described the rewards and punishments awaiting men in the next world, though such poems were attributed to Musaeus. But there is another passage in Plato, which has been thought to give supplementary information.

1) In the *Timaeus*, after his account of the creation of the visible gods, Plato says that it is beyond his powers to determine the origin of the gods of religion and mythology; in this matter he can only follow the earlier authorities, who professed that they were themselves the offspring of gods. We cannot, he says somewhat playfully, reject their testimony: they must know who their forefathers were, and as sons of gods they must be believed; besides, the law requires that we accept the evidence of relatives in family matters (*Tim.* 40 D–E = *Fragm.* 16): Περὶ δὲ τῶν ἄλλων δαιμόνων εἰπεῖν καὶ γνῶναι τὴν γένεσιν μεῖζον ἢ καθ' ἡμᾶς, πειστέον δὲ τοῖς εἰρηκόσιν ἔμπροσθεν, ἐκγόνοις μὲν θεῶν οὖσιν, ὡς ἔφασαν, σαφῶς δέ που τούς γε αὑτῶν προγόνους εἰδόσιν· ἀδύνατον οὖν θεῶν παισὶν ἀπιστεῖν, καίπερ ἄνευ τε εἰκότων καὶ ἀναγκαίων ἀποδείξεων λέγουσιν, ἀλλ' ὡς οἰκεῖα φασκόντων ἀπαγγέλλειν ἑπομένους τῷ νόμῳ πιστευτέον. οὕτως οὖν κατ' ἐκείνους ἡμῖν ἡ γένεσις περὶ τούτων τῶν θεῶν ἐχέτω καὶ λεγέσθω. Γῆς τε καὶ Οὐρανοῦ παῖδες 'Ωκεανός τε καὶ Τηθὺς ἐγενέσθην, τούτων δὲ Φόρκυς Κρόνος τε καὶ 'Ρέα καὶ ὅσοι μετὰ τούτων, ἐκ

δὲ Κρόνου καὶ Ῥέας Ζεὺς Ἥρα τε καὶ πάντες ὅσους ἴσμεν ἀδελφοὺς λεγομένους αὐτῶν, ἔτι τε τούτων ἄλλους ἐκγόνους. The words τοῖς εἰρηκόσιν ἔμπροσθεν, ἐκγόνοις μὲν θεῶν οὖσιν, ὡς ἔφασαν bear a marked resemblance to the words in the *Republic* (ii, 364 E): Μουσαίου καὶ Ὀρφέως, Σελήνης τε καὶ Μουσῶν ἐκγόνων, ὥς φασι. But this is not enough to prove that Plato means precisely Musaeus and Orpheus in the *Timaeus*. Many poets may have called themselves the "offspring of the Muses." It is possible that this may have been the regular practice of the poets whose books were accepted as authoritative in the teletae; and Plato may have been thinking of this *class* of poets, among whom Musaeus and Orpheus would be included. In any case, he attributes the genealogy to more than one poet; he may have found it in one and attributed it to all, or he may have found an identical genealogy in more than one, or he may have put together an eclectic genealogy out of some or all of the poems. Among the shifting early genealogies none is found exactly like this one. We certainly cannot say that it was either in a poem by Orpheus or in a poem by Musaeus, or even in any poem which was used in connection with the teletae. All we can say is that there were poets who professed to be the offspring of gods; that Musaeus and Orpheus were of this number; and that some or all of them had written of the genealogy of the gods.[89]

2) Clement of Alexandria, in chapter 21, Book I, of the *Stromata*, undertakes to show, at great length and with great learning, that the wisdom of Moses was much more

[89] Some scholars say that this text is certainly Orphic (e.g., Schuster, Gruppe), others that it is not (e.g., Tannery, Kern). It should probably not be introduced here at all. The name of Orpheus does not appear in it.

ancient than the wisdom of the Greeks. In the course of his discussion he points out that the works of Orpheus, which were supposed to descend from great antiquity, were believed by the critics to be actually not earlier than the sixth century B.C. What he says here makes this one of the most important texts concerning the names of the Orphic poems and their supposed authors. Now, since Clement lived five hundred years after the close of the classical period, and many things had occurred in the interval, we are not concerned at present with his text as a whole. But there is included in the text an indirect quotation from the versatile poet and prose writer of the fifth century B.C., Ion of Chios, which supplies evidence of the first importance for classical times. The passage runs as follows (*Strom.* i, 21, 131 Stählin = *Test.* 183, 222): Ναὶ μὴν 'Ονομάκριτος ὁ 'Αθηναῖος, οὗ τὰ εἰς 'Ορφέα φερόμενα ποιήματα λέγεται εἶναι, κατὰ τὴν τῶν Πεισιστρατιδῶν ἀρχὴν περὶ τὴν πεντηκοστὴν ὀλυμπιάδα εὑρίσκεται, 'Ορφεὺς δέ, ὁ συμπλεύσας 'Ηρακλεῖ, Μουσαίου διδάσκαλος· 'Αμφίων γὰρ δυσὶ προάγει γενεαῖς τῶν 'Ιλιακῶν, Δημόδοκος δὲ καὶ Φήμιος μετὰ τὴν 'Ιλίου ἅλωσιν (ὃ μὲν γὰρ παρὰ τοῖς Φαίαξιν, ὃ δὲ παρὰ τοῖς μνηστῆρσι) κατὰ τὸ κιθαρίζειν εὐδοκίμουν. καὶ τοὺς μὲν ἀναφερομένους εἰς Μουσαῖον χρησμοὺς 'Ονομακρίτου εἶναι λέγουσι, τὸν Κρατῆρα δὲ τὸν 'Ορφέως Ζωπύρου τοῦ 'Ηρακλεώτου, τήν τε Εἰς ῞Αιδου κατάβασιν Προδίκου τοῦ Σαμίου. ῎Ιων δὲ ὁ Χῖος ἐν τοῖς Τριαγμοῖς[90] καὶ Πυθαγόραν εἰς 'Ορφέα ἀνενγκεῖν τινα ἱστορεῖ. 'Επιγένης δὲ ἐν τοῖς Περὶ τῆς εἰς 'Ορφέα ποιήσεως Κέρκωπος εἶναι λέγει τοῦ Πυθαγορείου τὴν Εἰς ῞Αιδου κατάβασιν καὶ τὸν 'Ιερὸν λόγον, τὸν δὲ Πέπλον καὶ τὰ Φυσικὰ Βροντίνου. Hence,

[90] Τριαγμοῖς is an emendation of Reinesius; the manuscript reading is Τριγράμμοις.

according to Clement, Ion of Chios, in a work called Τριαγμοί, stated that Pythagoras had attributed certain things to Orpheus. In the context this must mean not merely that Pythagoras had expressed his indebtedness to Orpheus for certain ideas, but that he had published certain poems under the name of Orpheus, or, in other words, that certain poems under the name of Orpheus had really been written by Pythagoras. This is actually stated, more explicitly, by Diogenes Laertius (viii, 8 = *Test.* 248): Ἴων δ' ὁ Χῖος ἐν τοῖς Τριαγμοῖς φησιν αὐτον [Pythagoras] ἔνια ποιήσαντα ἀνενεγκεῖν εἰς Ὀρφέα.

Now, though scholars at the present time do not doubt that the Τριαγμοί was an authentic work of Ion,[91] it is important for our purposes to examine the other evidence for this book. The fullest information about it is supplied by Harpocration, as follows (s.v. Ἴων = *Test.* 229): Ἰσοκράτης ἐν τῷ περὶ τῆς ἀντιδόσεως. Ἴωνος τοῦ τῆς τραγῳδίας ποιητοῦ μνημονεύοι ἂν ὁ ῥήτωρ, ὃς ἦν Χῖος μὲν γένος, υἱὸς δὲ Ὀρθομένους ἐπίκλησιν δὲ Ξούθου. ἔγραψε δὲ μέλη πολλὰ καὶ τραγῳδίας καὶ φιλόσοφόν τι σύγγραμμα τὸν Τριαγμὸν ἐπιγραφόμενον, ὅπερ Καλλίμαχος ἀντιλέγεσθαί φησιν ὡς Ἐπιγένους· ἐν ἐνίοις δὲ καὶ πληθυντικῶς ἐπιγράφεται Τριαγμοί, καθὰ Δημήτριος ὁ Σκήψιος καὶ Ἀπολλωνίδης ὁ Νικαεύς. ἀναγράφουσι δὲ ἐν αὐτῷ τάδε "ἀρχὴ ἥδε μοι τοῦ λόγου. πάντα τρία καὶ οὐδὲν πλέον ἢ ἔλασσον τούτων τῶν τριῶν· ἑνὸς ἑκάστου ἀρετὴ τριάς· σύνεσις καὶ κράτος καὶ τύχη. Here we learn that the book was called Τριαγμός as well as Τριαγμοί; and from the direct quotation which Harpocration gives at the close we obtain more explicit evidence than the title

[91] Diels-Kranz, *Fragmente der Vorsokratiker*, I, 377 ff., No. 36, Ion von Chios.

of the book supplies to show that it was a philosophical treatise concerning the number three. But, besides this, we are told that according to Callimachus the authorship of the book had been contested, and that it was regarded by some as a work of Epigenes. The article in the phrase τὸν Τριαγμὸν ἐπιγραφόμενον, which is not a part of the title, as is shown by its absence with Τριαγμοί immediately below, indicates that Harpocration was aware that the book had been an object of dispute. It was probably Callimachus who settled the question in the library at Alexandria in favor of Ion, recording at the same time the variant opinion which held Epigenes to be the author. Happily the speech of Isocrates, *On the Antidosis*, to which Harpocration refers, is extant, and it is not difficult to find the allusion to Ion which he has in mind. It is this (Isocr. xv, 268): . . . τοὺς λόγους τοὺς τῶν παλαιῶν σοφιστῶν, ὧν ὁ μὲν ἄπειρον τὸ πλῆθος ἔφησεν εἶναι τῶν ὄντων, Ἐμπεδοκλῆς δὲ τέτταρα καὶ νεῖκος καὶ φιλίαν ἐν αὐτοῖς, Ἴων δὲ οὐ πλείω τριῶν, Ἀλκμέων δὲ δύο μόνα, Παρμενίδης δὲ καὶ Μέλισσος ἕν, Γοργίας δὲ παντελῶς οὐδέν. This is direct evidence from the fourth century B.C. of Ion's interest in philosophy, and particularly of his interest in the number three. With this may be quoted by way of corroboration the following statement in Philoponus (*In Aristot. de gen. et corr.* 329a 1, p. 207, 18 Vitelli): πῦρ μὲν καὶ γῆν Παρμενίδης ὑπέθετο, ταῦτα δὲ μετὰ τοῦ ἀέρος Ἴων ὁ Χῖος ὁ τραγῳδοποιός, Ἐμπεδοκλῆς δὲ τὰ τέσσαρα ὑπέθετο. Thus it will be seen that there is little doubt that Ion wrote a philosophical book on the number three, and that its title was Τριαγμός or Τριαγμοί.

It is also apparent that Ion was especially interested in the Pythagorean doctrines which had been brought from the west and were attracting much attention during his lifetime. He was not only struck by the significance of number, but he also saw Pythagorean characteristics in Orphic poems. His interest in Pythagoras is further attested by an epigram which he composed on Pherecydes. This epigram is preserved by Diogenes Laertius (i, 120): Ἴων δ' ὁ Χῖος περὶ αὐτοῦ φησιν·

> Ὣς ὁ μὲν ἠνορέῃ τε κεκασμένος ἠδὲ καὶ αἰδοῖ,
> καὶ φθίμενος ψυχῇ τερπνὸν ἔχει βίοτον·
> εἴπερ Πυθαγόρης ἐτύμως ὁ σοφὸς περὶ πάντων
> ἀνθρώπων γνώμας ᾔδεε κἀξέμαθεν.

Again, there is a Pythagorean flavor in a fragment of two words from Ion's tragedy Ἀλκμήνη, preserved by Hesychius (ii, 437 Schmidt = fr. 6 Nauck): καταφράκτοις ψυχαῖς· ταῖς ἐπεσκοτισμέναις, καὶ μὴ τὸ μέλλον εἰδυίαις. The special interest of the Pythagoreans in the number three is remarked by Aristotle (*De caelo* A 1, 268a 10): καθάπερ γάρ φασι καὶ οἱ Πυθαγόρειοι, τὸ πᾶν καὶ τὰ πάντα τοῖς τρισὶν ὥρισται· τελευτὴ γὰρ καὶ μέσον καὶ ἀρχὴ τὸν ἀριθμὸν ἔχει τὸν τοῦ παντός, ταῦτα δὲ τὸν τῆς τριάδος.

Before leaving the subject of the Τριαγμοί we should glance at another curious twist in the tradition. The longest and fullest list of the works of Orpheus is given by Suidas in the tenth century A.D. The list begins with the words (s.v. Ὀρφεύς = *Test.* 223): ἔγραψε Τριασμούς· λέγονται δὲ εἶναι Ἴωνος τοῦ τραγικοῦ· ἐν δὲ τούτοις τὰ Ἱεροστολικὰ καλούμενα. Lobeck (*Aglaoph.*, I, 389) regards this as a mere blunder on Suidas' part, and offers an ingenious explanation of how he came to make it. But it is not impossible that there was an Orphic work, early or later, bearing the same title as Ion's book, or a similar title.

Twice in the texts which relate to Ion we have encountered the name of Epigenes. According to Harpocration, he was thought by some to be the author of the Τριαγμός; according to Clement, he wrote a book on the poetry of Orpheus. This book on the poetry of Orpheus is mentioned again by Clement in the midst of a long discussion of the wide use of symbolism in the ancient world (*Strom.* v, 8, 49 Stählin = *Fragm.* 33): Τί δ'; οὐχὶ καὶ Ἐπιγένης ἐν τῷ περὶ τῆς Ὀρφέως ποιήσεως τὰ ἰδιάζοντα παρ' Ὀρφεῖ ἐκτιθέμενός φησι 'κερκίσι καμπυλόχρωσι' τοῖς ἀρότροις μηνύεσθαι, 'στήμοσι' δὲ τοῖς αὔλαξι· 'μίτον' δὲ τὸ σπέρμα ἀλληγορεῖσθαι, καὶ 'δάκρυα Διὸς' τὸν ὄμβρον δηλοῦν, 'Μοίρας' τε αὖ τὰ μέρη τῆς σελήνης, τριακάδα καὶ πεντεκαιδεκάτην καὶ νουμηνίαν· διὸ καὶ 'λευκοστόλους' αὐτὰς καλεῖν τὸν Ὀρφέα φωτὸς οὔσας μέρη. πάλιν 'ἄνθιον' μὲν τὸ ἔαρ διὰ τὴν φύσιν, 'ἀργίδα' δὲ τὴν νύκτα διὰ τὴν ἀνάπαυσιν, καὶ 'Γοργόνιον' τὴν σελήνην διὰ τὸ ἐν αὐτῇ πρόσωπον, ' 'Αφροδίτην' δὲ τὸν καιρὸν καθ' ὃν δεῖ σπείρειν, λέγεσθαι παρὰ τῷ θεολόγῳ. τοιαῦτα καὶ οἱ Πυθαγόρειοι ᾐνίσσοντο, Φερσεφόνης μὲν κύνας τοὺς πλανήτας, Κρόνου δὲ δάκρυον τὴν θάλασσαν ἀλληγοροῦντες. Evidently Epigenes devoted his attention, at least in part, to a study of figures of speech and obscurities of language in the Orphic poems, like any other grammarian. There is nothing in the passages quoted by Clement to show that Epigenes was attempting to elucidate esoteric religious or philosphical symbolism in Orpheus. Clement, like all who are obsessed with the thought of symbolism, finds symbols in simple metaphors or indeed in plain statements of fact.

We hear of Epigenes again in connection with Ion. Athenaeus, in the long list of drinking vessels which he discusses in Book XI, includes the *δακτυλωτόν*, with this comment (Athen. xi, 468 C): *δακτυλωτὸν ἔκπωμα οὕτως καλούμενον παρὰ Ἴωνι ἐν Ἀγαμέμνονι* [fr. 1 Nauck]· . . . *Ἐπιγένης μὲν οὖν ἀκούει τὸ ἄμφωτον ποτήριον, εἰς ὃ οἷόν τε τοὺς δακτύλους διείρειν ἑκατέρωθεν.* Here Epigenes is doing for Ion just the kind of thing he did for Orpheus, explaining the meaning of his language. Indeed, the language of Ion, with its new and strange formations and its old words in new meanings, was of special interest to grammarians, and most of the fragments of his poetry owe their preservation to this cause.[92] We cannot say whether Epigenes wrote a commentary on some or all of Ion's poetry or simply made this note in a book on some other subject. Now though it is not absolutely certain that the Epigenes of Clement, the Epigenes of Harpocration, and the Epigenes of Athenaeus are one and the same person, the nexus of circumstantial evidence leaves little doubt in the matter. The juxtaposition of Epigenes, Ion, and Orpheus in Clement, of Epigenes and Ion in Harpocration and Athenaeus, of Ion and Orpheus in Clement and Suidas, can scarcely be accidental.

Who was this Epigenes, and when did he live? The answer to the second question must be sought in the words of Harpocration: *ὅπερ Καλλίμαχος ἀντιλέγεσθαί φησιν ὡς Ἐπιγένους.* The plain meaning is: "whose authenticity,

[92] Schmid, *Gesch. Griech.-Lit.*, I, ii (1934), 518.

says Callimachus, is denied by some, who hold that it is a work of Epigenes." Some commentators strangely understand that it was Callimachus who contested the authorship. Some, dissatisfied with the grammar or thinking it impossible that anyone could have attributed the Τριαγμός to the author of a book on Orphic poetry, resort to emendation.[93] Bergk, followed by Susemihl, changes ὡς to ὑπό. Tannery reads ὡς 'Επιγένης, which he explains thus: "Epigène, parlant du *Triagme* d'Ion de Chios, aurait remarqué que l'authenticité de cet ouvrage avait été contestée par Callimaque." But this is impossible Greek and gives an impossible meaning. Diels prefers to read, ὡς ⟨καὶ⟩ 'Επιγένης, which must mean: "both Callimachus and Epigenes say that the authenticity is doubted"; and certainly Harpocration would not have cited two authorities in support of this assertion. None of these changes is an improvement on the manuscript reading, and no adequate reason for a change has been brought forward. The text is sound, and we must accept what it says.

Epigenes, then, lived before Callimachus, and so long before him that Callimachus can refer to critics who must themselves have been later than Epigenes, since they are already guessing at what he wrote. Now Callimachus was forty years old in 270 B.C. One may agree, therefore, with Lobeck[94] that Epigenes could not have written long after the death of Alexander; but when he adds that he could not have written long before that day, one is uncertain.

[93] Bergk, *Griech. Lit.*, I, 395, n. 235; Susemihl, *Griech. Lit.*, I, 345, n. 96; Paul Tannery, "Orphica," *Rev. de philol.*, XXI (1897), 190–195; Diels-Kranz, *Vorsokr.*, I, 377.

[94] *Aglaoph.*, I, 341.

In fact, all we can say is that the life of Epigenes must lie between 421 B.C. (i.e., soon after the death of Ion) and about 300 B.C. We have no other information of a grammarian of this name flourishing in this period. There were a number of men called Epigenes, but no one has proposed to identify any one of them with our grammarian. This is surprising, because one among them, though he cannot be proved to be our grammarian, is so far a probable candidate that nothing can be said against him and a little can be said in his favor. This is the young associate of Socrates. In the *Apology* of Plato (33 E) Socrates calls attention to the presence in the court of certain men who could testify against him if they believed that he had corrupted their sons. One of these was Ἀντιφῶν ὁ Κηφισιεύς, Ἐπιγένους πατήρ. In the *Memorabilia* of Xenophon (iii, 12) Socrates scolds Ἐπιγένην τῶν συνόντων τινά for not keeping himself fit physically. Unfortunately, Socrates does all the talking, and Epigenes has no opportunity to make revelations about himself. In the *Phaedo* (59 B) we learn that Epigenes made one of that notable company which was present with Socrates at the end. This is all, and not much can be made of it. Epigenes was approximately a contemporary of Plato, forty years old about the year 385 B.C.; little interested in sports and therefore possibly bookish; influenced, perhaps, by the moving discourse of Socrates on the immortality of the soul, to look further into this doctrine and others like it in the books that were available. These things may all be said of the friend of Socrates, and they fit perfectly to what we know of Epigenes the grammarian, who wrote on the poems of Orpheus and attributed some of them to Pythagoreans, and who also occupied himself to some degree with the writings of Ion of Chios, himself a person of Pythagorean leanings. Besides, if Epigenes the grammarian had been the friend of Socrates in his youth, the difficulty concerning the attribution to him of the Τριαγμοί disappears entirely. He is not an Alexandrian grammarian, but a Socratic and possibly a Pythagorean, who might well have written such a book as the Τριαγμοί. Whatever may be the truth of this, it is at any rate clear that whatever was said by Epigenes about the poems of Orpheus belongs to the evidence of classical times.

What do we learn from these two witnesses, Ion and Epigenes, about Orpheus? From Ion we learn that even before 421 B.C. (we learn from Aristophanes, *Peace* 835, that Ion was already dead at this date) doubt had already been expressed concerning some at least of the poems which were ordinarily regarded as the work of Orpheus. From the fact that Ion believed these poems to have been composed by Pythagoras, we must conclude that there was a marked resemblance between their contents and the ideas which were understood to have originated with Pythagoras. Fifty or a hundred years later the Orphic poems were made a subject of special study by Epigenes, who undertook to explain the meaning of their language and to determine their authorship. From Clement's brief allusion to his book we learn the names of four Orphic poems which existed in the fourth century B.C., the Εἰς Ἅιδου κατάβασις, the Ἱερὸς λόγος, the Πέπλος, and the Φυσικά. They must have been definitely Pythagorean in character, since Epigenes maintained that all of them were written by Pythagoreans, the first two by Cercops and the other two by Brontinus. It would seem that Epigenes, who was also interested in the writings of Ion, had accepted Ion's opinion concerning the Orphic poems, but knowing that Pythagoras had written nothing himself, had revised Ion's hasty judgment by attributing the poems to members of the Pythagorean school.

3) We have next to consider some lines of Euripides, a slightly younger contemporary of Ion of Chios. When at the end of the *Alcestis* Admetus returns from the funeral of his wife, so overcome with grief that he cannot bring himself to enter his desolate house, the chorus in their last ode sing of the inexorable power of Ἀνάγκη and can find no consolation to offer except the prediction that all who pass the tomb of Alcestis will do her reverence as if she were a goddess. The ode is planned by the poet as an ironical contrast to the ensuing scene, in which is revealed Heracles' triumph over the inevitable in snatching Alcestis from the tomb. The portion of the ode with which we are concerned is the first strophe (*Alc.* 962–971 = *Test.* 82):

ἐγὼ καὶ διὰ μούσας
καὶ μετάρσιος ᾖξα, καὶ
πλείστων ἁψάμενος λόγων
κρεῖσσον οὐδὲν Ἀνάγκας
ηὗρον, οὐδέ τι φάρμακον
Θρῄσσαις ἐν σανίσιν, τὰς
Ὀρφεία κατέγραψεν
γῆρυς, οὐδ' ὅσα Φοῖβος Ἀσκληπιάδαις ἔδωκε
φάρμακα πολυπόνοις ἀντιτεμὼν βροτοῖσιν.

It is not easy to determine exactly the realities which lie behind Euripides' lyric expression. The sentiments are more appropriate to a reflective Athenian of the fifth century B.C. than to the old men who lived with Admetus in Pherae, and we must suppose that they spring from conditions familiar to the Athenian audience. It is really Euripides who speaks. His studies, he says, in literature, science, and philosophy have led him to conclude that the sovereign power in the universe is Ἀνάγκη, and he has not been able to discover any means of thwarting her decrees. In particular, to give concreteness to his thought, he mentions two sources of aid to which one would naturally turn, but which are both powerless against Ἀνάγκη, the φάρμακα of Orpheus and the φάρμακα which the Asclepiadae received from Apollo. When he says the Asclepiadae, he means of course the medical profession, the scope of whose powers could be known from the actual ministrations of practicing physicians and from such published works on medicine as later were united in the corpus of Hippocrates. But where precisely would he look for the φάρμακα of Orpheus, and what was their character? To the audience, who knew, Euripides' lyric phrase was fully expressive; to us it is obscure.

The inquiry must start from a scholium on the words Θρῄσσαις ἐν σανίσιν (Schol. Eur. *Alc.* 968 Schwartz = *Test.* 82): ὁ δὲ φυσικὸς Ἡρακλείδης εἶναι ὄντως φησὶ σανίδας τινὰς Ὀρφέως, γράφων οὕτως· ‛τὸ δὲ τοῦ Διονύσου κατεσκεύασται ἐπὶ [ἐπί del. Wilamowitz] τῆς Θρᾴκης ἐπὶ τοῦ καλουμένου Αἵμου, ὅπου δή τινας ἐν σανίσιν ἀναγραφὰς εἶναί φασιν ⟨Ὀρφέως⟩. According to the scholiast, *Heracleides said* that there actually were σανίδες of Orpheus; according to Heracleides' own words, as quoted by the scholiast, he said: "*They say* that there are records on σανίδες at a shrine[?] of Dionysus on Mount Haemus." The addition of Ὀρφέως at the close of the quotation, which was made by Wilamowitz, is gratuitous. The scholiast, who made a mistake in reporting the quotation, may have made a mistake also in supposing that it related to Orpheus. In any case, even if Euripides by some freak of information had in mind some σανίδες of Orpheus on Mount Haemus, which Heracleides knew of only at second hand, it is quite certain that the audience would not have understood the bearing of the allusion, unless these σανίδες were more celebrated than we have any right to suppose they were. It is a fair rule to take a sensible author, like Euripides, to mean what his audience must have understood him to mean.

What, then, would an Athenian have thought of when he heard Θρῄσσαις ἐν σανίσιν κτλ? σανίδες are 'boards,' and boards were used for many purposes. Covered with gypsum, they were used in Athens for inscribing public notices of all kinds. But it is doubtful whether 'Thracian boards inscribed by Orpheus' would suggest, even to an Athenian, public notice boards of any sort. φάρμακα of an Orphic type were not likely to be found in such places; at least we have no evidence for such a thing. The σανίδες, it would seem, must be writing tablets. There is no parallel for this use of the word; but πίνακες, a synonym of σανίδες, is so used (e.g., in Aristophanes, *Thesm.* 778 πινάκων ξεστῶν δέλτοι), and there is a passage in the *Iphigenia at*

*Aulis* which bears so close a resemblance to the present one that we may almost believe that Euripides was consciously or unconsciously imitating in the one the form of speech that he had used in the other. The possibility that a legend was false he expresses in these words (*Iph. Aul.* 796 ff.): εἴτ' ἐν δέλτοις Πιερίσιν μῦθοι τάδ' ἐς ἀνθρώπους ἤνεγκαν παρὰ καιρὸν ἄλλως. As the δέλτοι Πιερίδες were books containing mythological poems in the Pierian tradition, so Θρῇσσαι σανίδες must have been books containing magical poems in the Thracian tradition, and it is not likely that the use of σανίδες in this sense, though it is unparalleled, would have seemed too violent in lyric verse.

We come next to the curious phrase, τὰς 'Ορφεία κατέγραψεν γῆρυς, "which the voice of Orpheus filled with writing." A similar collocation of ideas in a lyrical expression is found in a fragment of the *Erechtheus* of Euripides (fr. 369 Nauck), where the chorus prays for a peaceful old age in which, having hung up their shields in the temple of Athena, they may enjoy the pleasures of song and "may unfold the voice of tablets which is rendered illustrious by poets" (δέλτων τ' ἀναπτύσσοιμι γῆρυν ἂν σοφοὶ κλέονται). In dull prose this means 'unfold tablets containing songs by famous poets.' Similarly, the words in the *Alcestis* may mean no more than 'tablets in which are written poems by the singer Orpheus.' The form of expression, however, is somewhat more daring, and it is a little strange that Euripides should invent just such a periphrasis as 'Ορφεία γῆρυς to serve as the subject of κατέγραψεν, however famous Orpheus was as a singer. Another interpretation, which puts no more strain upon the language, may deserve consideration. The meaning may be that the poems with which the tablets were filled were inspired or dictated by the voice of Orpheus and written down by the hand of another. That this may indeed have been in the mind of Euripides is rendered not improbable by certain facts which may now be brought forward.

In a Berlin papyrus (Pap. Berol. 44, ed. Buecheler, in *Berliner Klassikertexte*, V, 1, 8 = *Fragm.* 49), which was written in the first or second century A.D., the opening sentence reads thus, if we accept the restoration of Diels (Orpheus fr. 15a Diels-Kranz):

> ⟨Ὀρφεὺς υἱὸς ἦν Οἰάγ⟩ρου καὶ Καλλιόπης τῆς
> ⟨Μούσης, ὁ δὲ Μουσ⟩ῶν βασιλεὺς Ἀπόλλων τού-
> ⟨τῳ ἐπέπνευσεν, ὅθεν⟩ ἔνθεος γενόμενος
> ⟨ἐποίησεν τοὺς ὕμνους,⟩ οὓς ὀλίγα Μουσαῖος ἐπα-
> ⟨νορθώσας κατέγ⟩ραψεν.

Here is the voice of Orpheus at work, and the hand that writes the poems which he dictates is the hand of Musaeus. This method of composition is perfectly illustrated in the Orphic *Argonautica*, which was probably composed in the fourth century A.D. The poem is composed as the utterance of Orpheus, who, after praying for inspiration to Apollo in the first six lines, thereafter addresses the remainder of the poem to Musaeus. Note particularly vss. 47–49 Dottin:

> Νῦν δ' ἐπεὶ ἀερόφοιτος ἀπέπτατο δήϊος οἶστρος,
> ἡμέτερον δέμας ἐκπρολιπὼν εἰς οὐρανὸν εὐρύν,
> πεύσῃ ἀφ' ἡμετέρης ἐνοπῆς ὅσσα πρὶν ἔκευθον.

Here again is the voice of Orpheus singing the poem which Musaeus must be supposed to have recorded. When Jason came to enlist Orpheus for the expedition he found him preparing his lyre to sing to Musaeus (73):

> ὄφρα κέ σοι μέλπων προχέω μελίγηρυν ἀοιδήν.

Twice Orpheus alludes to earlier poems which he has also dictated to Musaeus:

> Ἄλλα δέ σοι κατέλεξ' ἅπερ εἴσιδον ἠδ' ἐνόησα,
> Ταίναρον ἡνίκ' ἔβην σκοτίην ὁδόν, Ἄϊδος εἴσω [40 f.];

and

> Ὧν πέρι μῦθον ἅπαντ' ἔκλυες, Μουσαῖε δαΐφρον,
> ὥς ποτε Φερσεφόνην τέρεν' ἄνθεα χερσὶ δρέπουσαν
> ἐξάπαφον συνόμαιμοι ἀν' εὐρύ τε καὶ μέγα ἄλσος [1191-93].

The same technique may be observed also in the first two lines of the collection of *Orphic Hymns:*

> Μάνθανε δή, Μουσαῖε, θυηπολίην περισέμνην,
> εὐχήν, ἣ δή τοι προφερεστέρη ἐστὶν ἁπασέων,

and again in the opening lines of the poem called Διαθῆκαι, which are quoted by Ps.-Justinus, *Coh. ad gentil.* 15 (= *Fragm.* 245): Ὀρφεὺς γοῦν, ὁ τῆς πολυθεότητος ὑμῶν, ὡς ἂν εἴποι τις, πρῶτος διδάσκαλος γεγονώς, οἷα πρὸς τὸν υἱὸν αὐτοῦ Μουσαῖον καὶ τοὺς λοιποὺς γνησίους ἀκροατὰς ὕστερον περὶ ἑνὸς καὶ μόνου θεοῦ κηρύττει λέγων, ἀναγκαῖον ὑπομνῆσαι ὑμᾶς. ἔφη δ' οὕτως·

> φθέγξομαι οἷς θέμις ἐστί· θύρας δ' ἐπίθεσθε βέβηλοι
> πάντες ὁμῶς. σὺ δ' ἄκουε, φαεσφόρου ἔκγονε Μήνης,
> Μουσαῖ'· ἐξερέω γὰρ ἀληθέα . . .

Similarly the poet addresses Musaeus in the fourth rhapsode of the *Rhapsodic Theogony* (*Fragm.* 61), and in the Ἐφημερίδες (*Fragm.* 271).

It is clear from these citations that there was a traditional technique in the composition of Orphic poems whereby they were represented as addressed to Musaeus; and it is further clear that the address was not simply a form of dedication, but indicated a kind of dictation by Orpheus, who sang but wrote nothing, to Musaeus, who acted as his amanuensis. We may reasonably conclude that Euripides had this technique in mind when he wrote the lines of the *Alcestis*, and that, therefore, this technique prevailed from the beginning in the writing of Orphic poems. Scholars are in the habit of speaking vaguely of Musaeus as a kind of double of Orpheus, saying often that when Musaeus is named Orpheus is meant. We may now see in what sense this is true. Perhaps every Orphic poem represented itself as, or was understood to be, the joint work of both men; the voice was the voice of Orpheus, but the hand was the hand of Musaeus.[95]

We are not limited to postclassical evidence for support of this theory. There is a red-figured cylix of the fifth century B.C. in the Lewis Collection at Corpus Christi College in Cambridge[96] on one side of which a curious scene is depicted. At the left a young man is seated, writing

[95] On Musaeus see G. Dottin, *Les Argonautiques d'Orphée* (Paris, 1930), p. cli, esp. n. 2: "C'est d'ailleurs l'usage constant dans la littérature ésotérique que les doctrines soient présentées sous forme de révélation à un fils ou à un disciple." This practice was not limited to esoteric literature, as may be seen in the address of Theognis to Cyrnus.

[96] First published by Minervini, "Oracolo di Orfeo e dell' Apollo Napeo in Lesbo: vaso dipinto di fabbrica nolana," *Bulletino Archeologico Napolitano*, n.s., VI (1857), 33–39. Published again, with a plate, by C. D. Bicknell, *Jour. Hellenic Stud.*, XLI (1921), 230.

with a stilus in an open set of tablets, his attention closely concentrated on his work. At the right is the standing figure of a man holding a laurel branch in his left hand. His eyes are fixed on the writer, and his right arm is extended toward him. Between these two figures, under the extended arm of the one and at the feet of the other, is a head, with lips parted and with open eyes gazing up at the writer. On the other side of the cylix are represented two women, one holding a lyre in her right hand, as if she had just picked it up from the ground, the other holding what seems to be the strap by which the lyre had been suspended from the neck of the player. The two scenes have long been connected with Orpheus. The two women are Muses, who have rescued his lyre and its strap after his tragic death; and the head is the singing head of Orpheus. This identification is made certain by a scene on a bronze mirror from Chiusi, probably from the end of the fourth century B.C.[97] The scene as a whole and its Etruscan inscriptions have not been explained satisfactorily; but there is a young man, seated, with stilus and tablets, and at the bottom of the field there is a head looking upward, with an inscription beside it—ΥΡΦΕ. On a number of ancient gems, also, we find a figure, writing, with a head at his feet.[98] On an Attic red-figured hydria, again, in the collection of Professor A. B. Cook, dating from the end of the fifth century B.C.,[99] there is a painting in which a

[97] R. Bianchi Bandinelli, "Clusium, la collezione E. Bonci Casuccini," *Mon. dei Lincei*, XXX (1925), 542–552. Similar scenes are found on other Etruscan mirrors, but without the name of Orpheus.

[98] Furtwängler, *Antike Gemmen* (1900), III, 245 ff.

[99] First published by W. K. C. Guthrie, *Orpheus and Greek Religion* (London, 1935), p. 36 and pl. 5.

male figure is standing in the middle with a laurel branch in his right hand and a lyre in his left, hanging by his side. He is gazing mournfully at a head which is looking up at him from his feet. On either side is the figure of a woman. This single picture combines particulars which are found in the two scenes on the cylix—the figure with the laurel branch, the rescued lyre, the two women, and the head gazing up with open eyes. The figure of the young man writing is absent. In all these graphic representations we have the head of Orpheus still living and singing after his death and dismemberment, and in all but the hydria and some of the gems a young man appears to be writing down the words that proceed from its lips. The earliest instance of this type is the Athenian cylix, which is practically contemporaneous with the *Alcestis*. On the cylix, as in the *Alcestis*, "the voice of Orpheus is covering tablets with writing." The cylix also presents the amanuensis, whom we know from the Berlin papyrus, from the *Argonautica*, and from the other texts quoted, to be Musaeus; and the same texts make it clear that the standing figure with the laurel branch is Apollo, under whose inspiration the head of Orpehus is singing.

But Orpheus is dead. This we know from the picture on the other side of the cylix and from the picture on the hydria, in which the grief of the three figures is manifest. This means that the immortal voice of Orpheus continues to dictate poems even after his death. Thus we find an explanation of the continuous production of new Orphic poems throughout antiquity. Every poet professed to be writing at the dictation of the voice of Orpheus, and perhaps every poet was a Musaeus. The personality of Musaeus, "the servant of the Muses," is completely shadowy, and he may have been created only to serve as the amanuensis of Orpheus.[100] Naturally, hardheaded critics and genealogists and chronologists undertook to bring these fictions into some sort of rational order; but those who continued to write in the Orphic tradition continued to avail themselves of the fanciful technique. How far they deceived themselves into thinking that they were actually composing under the influence of Apollo and Orpheus, we cannot say. It is only a special instance of the inspiration of the Muses, whom all poets since Homer have heard, and from whom Hesiod, as he pastured his lambs beneath holy Helicon, received his verses.

The story of the singing head of Orpheus, the earliest evidence for which is afforded by the fifth-century cylix, is repeated with a number of variations in postclassical literary texts. The first of these is an elegiac poem by the Alexandrian poet Phanocles.[101] As the story is told in this poem, the women of Thrace, after they had slain Orpheus, cut off his head, fastened it to his lyre, and threw both into the sea. The head and the lyre floated ashore on the island of Lesbos, and the air was filled with the clear tones of the lyre. The Lesbians buried the lyre and the head in one tomb, and the result was that Lesbos became the most musical of all islands. Phanocles does not say that the head sings after death, but this detail appears in

[100] André Boulanger ("L'orphisme dans les Argonautiques d'Orphée," *Bull. de l'Assoc. Budé*, No. 22, 1929, pp. 30–46) remarks that Musaeus plays the same part in the Orphic poems that Asclepius or Tat, who receives the instruction of Hermes, plays in the Hermetic treatises.

[101] Ap. Stobaeus iv, 20, 47 (= *Test.* 77).

Vergil, Ovid, Conon, and Lucian.[102] That the head or the lyre or both came to Lesbos is repeated in Ovid, Hyginus, Nicomachus of Gerasa, Lucian, Philostratus, and Proclus;[103] and that they inspired Lesbian music is expressly stated by Hyginus, Nicomachus, and Proclus. Aristides says[104] that the Lesbians attributed the music of their island to the head of Orpheus. Clearly the musical fame of Lesbos was sufficient to supply the storytellers with a motive for bringing the head and the lyre of the great musician to the island.

Two other possible motives appear. Lucian says that the Lesbians buried the head where the Baccheion now stands (*ἵναπερ νῦν τὸ Βάκχειον αὐτοῖς ἐστι*), and dedicated the lyre in the temple of Apollo, where it was long preserved. It is possible that there was a local legend connecting Orpheus with the cult of Dionysus, but Lucian does not say so. It is more likely that the story of the coming of the head and its burial by the Lesbians existed first, and that the grave in course of time was localized in the Baccheion. Philostratus tells a more circumstantial tale. When the head came to Lesbos, it took up its dwelling in a cave and delivered oracles from the earth. The oracle acquired great fame and was visited by people from far and wide. Even Cyrus the Great obtained from it a prediction, in these words, *τὰ ἐμά, ὦ Κῦρε, σά*, which

[102] Vergil, *Georg.* iv, 523 (= *Test.* 131); Ovid, *Metam.* xi, 50 (= *Test.* 132); Conon, xlv, p. 25, 30 Hoefer (= *Test.* 115); Lucian, *Adv. indoct.* 109–111 (= *Test.* 118).

[103] Ovid, *loc. cit.*; Hyginus, *Astron.* ii, 7 (= *Test.* 117); Nicomachus, *Musici Scriptores Graeci*, p. 266 Ian (= *Test.* 163); Lucian, *loc. cit.*; Philostratus, *Heroic.* v, 3, and *Vita Apollon. Tyan.* iv, 14 (= *Test.* 134); Proclus, *In Plat. Rempublicam* i, 174, 27 Kroll (= *Test.* 119).

[104] Aristides xxiv, 55 (= *Test.* 135).

he took to mean that he would conquer Thrace and Greece, but which was really a prophecy that his head would be cut off by the queen of the Massagetae, as the head of Orpheus had been cut off by the women of Thrace. Eventually Apollo became envious of the great fame of the oracle, and standing over Orpheus as he uttered his oracles he ordered him to cease (*ἐφίσταταί οἱ χρησμῳδοῦντι ὁ θεὸς καὶ 'πέπαυσο' ἔφη 'τῶν ἐμῶν, καὶ γὰρ δὴ ⟨καὶ⟩ ᾄδοντά σε ἱκανῶς ἤνεγκα'*). This version of the story differs sharply from the others. There was, at any rate, no oracle of Orpheus in Lesbos in Philostratus' time. If there ever had been one, it had been stilled in the remote past. Clearly it is a variant of the story of the singing head that came to Lesbos, contrived to afford a setting for the two utterances which are so strikingly similar: *τὰ ἐμά, ὦ Κῦρε, σά* and *πέπαυσο τῶν ἐμῶν*. How old the story is, it is impossible to say; but it is significant that there is nothing at all like it in any of the earlier versions, nor is there any other allusion to an oracle of Orpheus.

Minervini interpreted the painting on the Athenian cylix as a representation of this oracle: a consultant is writing down the utterances of the head of Orpheus, and Apollo is standing by. Furthermore, he regarded the oracle as belonging jointly to Orpheus and to Apollo Napaios, who is known to have had a cult in Lesbos; but his arguments to prove a connection with this cult have little weight.

Furtwängler,[105] too, in a very important discussion of the whole matter, held to the belief that there was an oracle of Orpheus in Lesbos, and took the cylix as evi-

[105] *Antike Gemmen*, III, 245 ff.

dence that the cult was well known in Athens in the fifth century B.C. That the pictures on the cylix were connected with the Lesbian cult, he believes to be proved by the presence of Apollo in the one and by the strap held by one of the women on the other, which he supposes was intended for hanging the lyre in Apollo's temple (Lucian reports that the lyre was dedicated in the temple of Apollo). But, aside from the fact that the evidence of an Orphic oracle in Lesbos is unreliable, the presence of Apollo is better explained by the texts which show that Orpheus was always supposed to receive his inspiration from him; and there is nothing in the picture to show that the woman who holds the strap intends to make any use of it. But Furtwängler is not entirely consistent. Though he does not give up the notion of a Lesbian oracle and the connection of the painting on the cylix with it, he wisely points out that the utterances of the head must have been not merely brief prophecies, but something long enough to write in a book. He recalls the use of Orphic books, and concludes that the contents of these books were supposed not only to have been composed by Orpheus while he was still alive, but also to have been dictated by his head after his death. He recognizes the amanuensis as Musaeus, and finds in this circumstance an explanation of the double authorship of the Orphic poems. He cites the passage in the *Alcestis* as an allusion to the tablets which were written by Musaeus at the dictation of Orpheus. All this is sound;[106] but it is an error to

[106] The probability that these conclusions are sound is shown to be greater by the fact that, whereas Furtwängler came to them from the study of certain Italian gems, I arrived at them independently from the opposite approach.

add that the audience were in a position to understand the words of Euripides because they were familiar with such pictures as that on the cylix and with the Lesbian oracle represented by it. The literary technique of the Orphic poems and the story of the singing voice of Orpheus were too wide in their operation and too long-lived to be confined to an obscure and problematical oracle in Lesbos.

Carl Robert[107] abandoned the idea that there was actually an Orphic oracle in Lesbos, but he maintained that there was an old myth which told of such an oracle. This myth was the subject both of the picture on the cylix and of the story related by Philostratus. He points out that the oracle was stopped by Apollo only a short time after the coming of the head to Lesbos (*'Ορφεὺς δὲ ἔχρα μόνος ἄρτι ἐκ Θρᾴκης ἡ κεφαλὴ ἥκουσα*), and draws the inference that the whole incident belongs to the realm of myth. The story of the oracle which was delivered to Cyrus contradicts this; but such self-contradiction is characteristic of Philostratus. Since the whole thing is a myth that does not profess to explain the origin of an oracle which actually existed, it cannot be taken as aetiological and therefore affords no evidence concerning a historical oracle. But the vase painting, he says, is a representation of this very myth: Apollo, with his extended arm, is in the very act of causing the head to cease its prophesying. This is an ingenious way of saving the preconception that the vase painting and Philostratus belong together. But if it were not for this preconception it would not occur to anyone

[107] "Das orakelnde Haupt des Orpheus," *Archaeol. Jahrb.*, XXXII (1917), 146.

that the gesture of Apollo is hostile, and neither the singing head nor the youth who is writing is aware of any prohibition which is being pronounced against them.

The next step is taken by Otto Kern.[108] He agrees that the gesture is hostile, indicating an opposition of some sort between Apollo and Orpheus, but he does not admit that the scene represents an oracle, real or mythical. The head is continuing to sing as Orpheus himself had sung during his lifetime, and the young man is writing down the verses in his tablets. Apollo forbids further composition of poetry of this sort, because at this time the poetry that went under the name of Orpheus was all in the service of Dionysus. There is, of course, nothing in the picture itself to support this extraordinary theory, and it is a pure assumption that Orphic poetry was predominantly Dionysiac in the fifth century B.C. or at any other time.

The results of this survey of the ancient evidence and modern discussion of it may now be summarized. The evidence is not adequate to prove the existence of an actual Orphic oracle in Lesbos.[109] The only allusion to such an oracle in literature is in Philostratus, and it is more likely that his story was a fiction, based on the ancient legend of the coming of the head of Orpheus to Lesbos, and planned to provide a setting for the clever oracle supposed to have been given to Cyrus and for the somewhat similar words which are put into the mouth of Apollo, than that it was an ancient myth. The story that the head of Orpheus remained alive and continued to

---

[108] *Orpheus* (1920), p. 9.

[109] And yet Maass (*Orpheus*, 1895, p. 133) says: "Selten ist ein Totenkult so gut bezeugt, wie dieser aiolisch-lesbische des Orpheus."

sing after his death is well attested in various versions in postclassical literature, and is found as early as the fifth century B.C. in the paintings of the cylix and the hydria. The moment represented in the hydria seems to be immediately after Orpheus' death, when Apollo and the two women are listening mournfully to the voice which comes from the head.[110] Then, in order to establish a connection between the musical island of Lesbos and the greatest of legendary musicians, the story was expanded to tell how the singing head came to the island and conferred upon the islanders the gift of song. An even longer duration was assigned to the activity of the singing head by the poets throughout antiquity who professed that they received their poems from the voice of Orpheus and gave them to the world under his name. This technique appears in the *Alcestis*, in the Berlin papyrus, and in late Orphic poems, and is graphically portrayed on the cylix, on the Etruscan mirrors, and on a number of the Italian gems.

The story that the head of one who has been slain by violence remains alive unspoiled by death and continues to sing as in life bears all the marks of a folk tale. Aristotle (*De partibus animalium*, iii, 10, 673a 17) tells a story of a priest of Zeus in Caria who was murdered by a person unknown: someone reported that he had heard the severed head of the murdered man say repeatedly (in a choliambic verse), "I was slain by Cercidas, I was slain by Cercidas," and in this way the criminal was discovered. Phlegon of Tralles in the second century A.D. tells of simi-

[110] Guthrie seems to think that this picture, too, is a representation of the Lesbian oracle.

lar incidents in his book on *Miracula*. In one of these a general falls in battle and a wolf devours his body, all but the head; when men come to bury the head, it addresses them in verse, bidding them let it alone and predicting disaster.[111] Such stories are not only found in classical antiquity, but they are repeated in countless forms in many parts of the world.[112] One may note in particular certain curious resemblances between the story of the singing head of Orpheus and some of the tales in the collection of the brothers Grimm. In *The Juniper Tree* (No. 47) the wicked stepmother causes her stepson to lean over an open chest and then cuts off his head by bringing down the lid violently on his neck. She then cuts up the body, cooks the parts, and gives them to the father to eat. The sister collects the bones and buries them under a juniper tree, whence a bird flies forth, singing of the murder which has been done. In this tale we have a violent murder by a woman; the head is cut off; the bones are collected by another woman, who is friendly; and the murdered person survives as a voice embodied in a bird. In all these points it resembles the story of Orpheus.[113] Again, in *The Singing Bone* (No. 28), a man is foully murdered and his body is buried. Later by chance a passer-by picks up one of the bones and makes from it a mouthpiece for his horn. When he begins to play upon it, the bone sings of itself, proclaiming the murder and denouncing the

[111] Fr. 32, *F.H.G.*, III, 615.

[112] Cf. G. L. Kittredge, *Gawain and the Green Knight* (1916), pp. 147–194, and W. Deonna, "Orphée et l'oracle de la tête coupée," *Rev. des études grecques*, XXXVIII (1925), 44–69.

[113] It is perhaps too much to find any connection between the laurel branch on the cylix and the hydria and the juniper tree of the folk tale.

criminal. Once more a part of the body of a murdered man has the power of song. A Scandinavian variant of this story[114] tells how two sisters were walking by the sea, and one pushed the other in, so that she drowned. Sailors brought the body to land, and a musician used the breastbone to make a frame for his harp, and the finger bones for pegs, and the golden hair for strings. When he begins to play, the harp itself sings a song denouncing the murderess. Such stories as these show at least that the singing head of the murdered Orpheus and the lyre which goes on playing of itself may belong to the realm of folklore, and that these elements need not have had originally any peculiar and intrinsic connection with the legend of Orpheus.

The study of the singing head of Orpheus has led us beyond the bounds of the classical period. The strictly classical evidence is confined to the text of the *Alcestis* and the paintings of the cylix and the hydria. These documents, interpreted with the aid of later literary and archaeological evidence, yield information both concerning the legend of Orpheus and concerning Orphic poetry. To the legend as it has been recounted in an earlier chapter there must be added as an appendix the story that after his death and dismemberment his head remained alive for a time and continued to sing in the hearing of his mourning friends. Furthermore, the utterances of the head, inspired by Apollo, were recorded in writing. Lastly, the fancy prevailed that some or all of the Orphic poems had been written down in books at the dictation of the

[114] Bolte und Polívka, *Anmerkungen zu den Kinder- u. Hausmärchen der Brüder Grimm* (1913), I, 270.

completely disembodied voice of Orpheus, and this mode of composition was adopted as a literary technique by the poets who wrote Orphic poems. One might suspect that the Orphic poets themselves invented the idea of the living and perennial voice of Orpheus as a sanction for their own productions and gave it picturesque expression in the story of the singing head. But it is more likely that the reverse is true. The story of the singing head was probably an integral part of a folk tale, which included the violent death and dismemberment of a singer, whether Orpheus or another, and was turned to good account by the poets who chose to represent their own productions as the work of Orpheus.

Of the contents of Orphic books Euripides tells us nothing except that they included pharmaka for use in extreme need. We may guess that these pharmaka consisted of charms and incantations with liturgical directions for their use. Some Orphic poems, as we know from the *Republic*, sanctioned practices which insured happiness after death, but the chorus in the *Alcestis* is searching for some means to counteract the inevitability of death itself. Their minds naturally turn to Orpheus and Asclepius. Socrates, in the *Charmides* of Plato (156 D), professes to have learned at Potidaea from one of the physicians of Zamolxis about a pharmakon and an ἐπῳδή to cure headache. These physicians, he adds, are said to produce immortality (λέγονται καὶ ἀπαθανατίζειν). Since Herodotus at an earlier date had already referred to the latter practice,[115] it is possible that Euripides was not

[115] Cf. I. M. Linforth, "ΟΙ ΑΘΑΝΑΤΙΖΟΝΤΕΣ (Herodotus iv. 93–96)," *Class. Philol.*, XIII (1918), 23–33.

unaware of it, and that thinking of means of resisting death he mentions the pharmaka of Thrace. He would introduce the name of Orpheus because he was a Thracian whose utterances, reduced to writing, made Thracian lore accessible. But that Orphic charms were well known in Athens and were available for all kinds of purposes is shown by a passage in the *Cyclops* of Euripides. When Odysseus is confronted with the difficulty of lifting the burning brand and thrusting it into the eye of the Cyclops, the leader of the chorus of satyrs recommends a charm of Orpheus, which will cause the brand to move of itself (646 ff. = *Test.* 83).[116] As Orpheus during his lifetime exercised magical powers by his song, so charms which bore his name had magical powers after his death. They must have formed a considerable part of Orphic literature.[117]

Furtwängler argues, in connection with the *Alcestis* and the cylix painting, that wooden tablets were used for writings which were kept secret, whereas literature which was freely open to the general reader was published in rolls. It is quite clear, however, that the Orphic compositions of the *Alcestis* were freely accessible to Euripides himself, and, as we have seen, Orphic poems formed an important part of the classical literature of the day. Besides, in the text quoted from the *Iphigenia at Aulis*, mythological poetry in general is said to be inscribed on Pierian tablets.

[116] Quoted above, p. 34.

[117] An entirely different interpretation of the passage in the *Alcestis*, which I cannot accept, is given by Leo Weber in his edition of the play (1930) and in his article "Orpheus," *Rhein. Mus.*, LXXXI (1932), 1–19. Cf. also Kern's review of Weber's edition of the *Alcestis* in *Gött gel. Anz.*, CXCVI (1934), 339.

4) In the *Busiris* of Isocrates, from which two citations have been drawn concerning the legend of Orpheus, there is also an illuminating statement about Orphic poetry. Isocrates is criticizing the literary work of Polycrates, to whom his essay is addressed, and besides other things for which he blames him, he says that he shows no regard for the truth but follows the blasphemous stories of the poets concerning the gods and their offspring (xi, 38–40 = *Fragm.* 17): Ἀλλὰ γὰρ οὐδέν σοι τῆς ἀληθείας ἐμέλησεν, ἀλλὰ ταῖς τῶν ποιητῶν βλασφημίαις ἐπηκολούθησας, οἳ δεινότερα μὲν πεποιηκότας καὶ πεπονθότας ἀποφαίνουσι τοὺς ἐκ τῶν ἀθανάτων γεγονότας ἢ τοὺς ἐκ τῶν ἀνθρώπων τῶν ἀνοσιωτάτων, τοιούτους δὲ λόγους περὶ αὐτῶν τῶν θεῶν εἰρήκασιν, οἵους οὐδεὶς ἂν περὶ τῶν ἐχθρῶν εἰπεῖν τολμήσειεν· οὐ γὰρ μόνον κλοπὰς καὶ μοιχείας καὶ παρ' ἀνθρώποις θητείας αὐτοῖς ὠνείδισαν ἀλλὰ καὶ παίδων βρώσεις καὶ πατέρων ἐκτομὰς καὶ μητέρων δεσμοὺς καὶ πολλὰς ἄλλας ἀνομίας κατ' αὐτῶν ἐλογοποίησαν. ὑπὲρ ὧν τὴν μὲν ἀξίαν δίκην οὐκ ἔδοσαν, οὐ μὴν ἀτιμώρητοί γε διέφυγον, ἀλλ' οἱ μὲν αὐτῶν ἀλῆται καὶ τῶν καθ' ἡμέραν ἐνδεεῖς κατέστησαν, οἱ δ' ἐτυφλώθησαν, ἄλλος δὲ φεύγων τὴν πατρίδα καὶ τοῖς οἰκειοτάτοις πολεμῶν ἅπαντα τὸν χρόνον διετέλεσεν, Ὀρφεὺς δ' ὁ μάλιστα τούτων τῶν λόγων ἁψάμενος, διασπασθεὶς τὸν βίον ἐτελεύτησεν· ὥστ' ἢν σωφρονῶμεν, οὐ μιμησόμεθα τοὺς λόγους τοὺς ἐκείνων, οὐδὲ περὶ μὲν τῆς πρὸς ἀλλήλους κακηγορίας νομοθετήσομεν, τῆς δ' εἰς τοὺς θεοὺς παρρησίας ὀλιγωρήσομεν, ἀλλὰ φυλαξόμεθα καὶ νομιοῦμεν ὁμοίως ἀσεβεῖν τούς τε λέγοντας τὰ τοιαῦτα καὶ τοὺς πιστεύοντας αὐτοῖς. Orpheus is represented as a poet whose works contain more instances of outrageous conduct among the gods than the works of any other poet, although no

particular one of the outrages named in Isocrates' list, all of which are found in other poets, can be attributed to him. Some or all of the Orphic poems, therefore, were mythological and contained more myths of a crude and offensive type than are to be found in Homer or Hesiod or in any other early poet. This discreditable preëminence is not assigned to Orpheus by Xenophanes, in the brief fragment in which he accuses Homer and Hesiod of blasphemy against the gods (fr. 11 Diels-Kranz). We might suspect that the Orphic poems which incur the censure of Isocrates had not been written in Xenophanes' time, or that they attained a greater vogue later. But the fragment of Xenophanes is too short to allow us to draw this conclusion; and besides, he may have been content to name the two greatest mythological poets as typical of the practice which he reprobates. It is worth observing that Orpheus is mentioned twice in this essay, and that three things are said about him: he brought back the dead from Hades (7 f.), he was torn to pieces, and he wrote poetry. To Isocrates, therefore, the legendary Orpheus and the poet Orpheus were identical. There were others, as we shall see, who thought differently about this.

5) A text containing the name of Orpheus, which may mean much or little, must be introduced here because, though it tells nothing certain about Orphic poetry or indeed about anything else connected with Orpheus, it has been made to form part of a network of speculations touching Orphic books and rites. It is a verse by Alexis, quoted by Athenaeus as one of a group of passages from the comic poets in which a man called Callimedon is

ridiculed. This personage was cross-eyed, excessively fond of eating fish, and nicknamed Κάραβος or Crayfish. Athenaeus quotes thus (viii, 340 C Kaibel = *Test.* 220): ἐν δὲ Κρατείᾳ

> καί Καλλιμέδων μετ' 'Ορφέως ὁ Κάραβος.

Athenaeus gives on the preceding page another quotation from the same play, in which the full title appears (340 A) : "Αλεξις δ' ἐν Κρατείᾳ ἢ Φαρμακοπώλῃ·

> τῷ Καλλιμέδοντι γὰρ θεραπεύω τὰς κόρας
> ἤδη τετάρτην ἡμέραν. Β. ἦσαν κόραι
> θυγατέρες αὐτῷ ; Α. τὰς μὲν οὖν τῶν ὀμμάτων,
> ἃς οὐδ' ὁ Μελάμπους, ὃς μόνος τὰς Προιτίδας
> ἔπαυσε μαινομένας, καταστήσειεν ἄν.[118]

Kaibel[119] conjectures that the first speaker in this second quotation is the φαρμακοπώλης and that the φαρμακοπώλης is Orpheus himself. It would not be surprising to find Orpheus put into a comedy as a quack doctor, famous as he was for his power of magic and enchantment. But the probability of the conjecture is weakened a little by the pun in the first quotation (which, of course, Kaibel did not fail to perceive). As a κάραβος is a crayfish, so an ὀρφώς is a sea perch; and Callimedon was very fond of fish. It looks as if the opportunity for a pun was a sufficient reason for introducing the name of Orpheus and that he need not have any other part in the play. This does not matter much one way or the other, but there is something more important behind.

[118] In both these passages the proper reading is κρατείᾳ, not κρατεύᾳ, as Kaibel explains in *Hermes*, XXV (1890), 98.

[119] *Hermes*, XXV (1890), 98 f.

The name Κράτεια is attached to the figure of a woman in a vase painting of the fourth century B.C. from the sanctuary of the Cabiri in Thebes.[120] In this picture, at the right, is a bearded figure reclining on a couch and holding out a two-handled cup with his right hand. He wears a crown of ivy and in general resembles the figure of Dionysus in Athenian paintings. Over his head his name is given—ΚΑΒΙΡΟΣ. At his feet, in the middle of the field, stands a nude boy about to dip a pitcher into a mixing bowl, and above his head is the word ΠΑΙΣ. At the left of this boy is another boy with thick lips and woolly hair, looking to the left and bearing the name ΠΡΑΤΟΛΑΟΣ. At the extreme left are two figures, a man and a woman, looking at each other with their faces close together. The man, who has a face of the same type as that of the small boy who is watching him, is named ΜΙΤΟΣ, and the woman, who is represented without caricature, is named ΚΡΑΤΕΙΑ. Kern has interpreted the painting as a representation of certain features in the myth and ritual of the Cabiri.[121] There are also indications, as he believes, that the myth and ritual portrayed had been influenced by the Orphic theogony. In the first place, he recalls that the word *μίτος*, which is found among the Orphic words whose meaning is explained by Epigenes,[122] was used by Orpheus to mean 'seed.' From this he concludes that Μίτος and Κράτεια (the power of the female) are parents of the boy Πρατόλαος, whom he takes to be the first human being. It should be observed, however, that *μίτος* is quite

[120] *Ath. Mitt.*, XIII (1888), Taf. ix. Also reproduced by Guthrie, p. 124.

[121] "Die boiotischen Kabiren," *Hermes*, XXV (1890), 1–16; and *R.-E.*, X (1919), s.v. Kabeiros, 1441, and XVI (1935), s.v. Mysterien, 1278.

[122] See p. 114 above.

definitely explained by Epigenes as meaning seed which is planted in the ground, not the seed of men. In the second place, Kern sees in the two figures of Κάβιρος, who has the characteristics of Dionysus, and the Παίς, who is his son, a resemblance to Dionysus-Phanes and Dionysus-Zagreus of the myth which is commonly thought of as peculiarly Orphic. Lastly, he directs attention to the fact that a large number of toys in terracotta and metal were found in the sanctuary, and these remind him of the toys with which Zagreus was beguiled by the Titans. These coincidences are striking, and it may well be that the features which Kern describes as Orphic were actually to be found in Orphic poetry of the fourth century B.C. Kaibel makes the further inference that Alexis was parodying in his play the rites of Cabirus and introduced Orpheus in connection with them. This, again, is not impossible, though it has only the slender support of the word Κράτεια as the title of the play and as the name of the woman on the vase, together with the part possibly assigned to Orpheus in the play and the resemblance of certain features in the cult of the Cabiri to what was possibly to be found in Orphic poetry. As for direct evidence of the kind we are now concerned with, we have nothing but the single line of Alexis, in which Orpheus is more than half fish. It has been necessary to take cognizance of the interpretation which has been put upon this line; but whether the wider conclusions that are drawn from the play and the vase painting are to be accepted, cannot be decided until the postclassical evidence concerning Orpheus has been studied as well as the classical evidence, not sealed with the name of Orpheus, which may be brought into relation with it.

### DIRECT AND INDIRECT QUOTATIONS

There are about a dozen direct and indirect quotations from Orpheus in the extant works of authors of the fourth century B.C. These all bear the seal of the name. There may be other quotations concealed in authors of the classical period which can in one way or another be proved to have come from his poems; and there may be quotations directly attributed to him by later authors which come from poems already in existence in classical times. Indeed, since the body of Orphic poetry seems to have been large and miscellaneous in content, it is likely that these quotations are numerous, and some can doubtless be recovered. But these do not now concern us. We shall confine our attention to those which are certainly Orphic and were certainly in existence before 300 B.C.

The author of the first speech against Aristogeiton, who may or may not have been Demosthenes, in a passage which has already been discussed (p. 98), quoting indirectly from Orpheus, the founder of teletae, attributes to him the saying that "august and inexorable Dike sits beside the throne of Zeus and watches all humanity" ([Dem.] xxv, 11 = *Fragm.* 23): *καὶ τὴν ἀπαραίτητον καὶ σεμνὴν Δίκην, ἣν ὁ τὰς ἁγιωτάτας ἡμῖν τελετὰς καταδείξας Ὀρφεὺς παρὰ τὸν τοῦ Διὸς θρόνον φησὶ καθημένην πάντα τὰ τῶν ἀνθρώπων ἐφορᾶν* . . . It is possible that this saying was current among those who conducted the teletae and recommended their use, but, even so, it was almost certainly contained in one of the books to which they looked for authority. The idea attributed to Orpheus is found also in Hesiod, *Works and Days* 256 ff.:

> *ἡ δέ τε παρθένος ἐστὶ Δίκη, Διὸς ἐκγεγαυῖα,*
> *κυδρή τ' αἰδοίη τε θεοῖς, οἳ Ὄλυμπον ἔχουσιν.*
> *καί ῥ' ὁπότ' ἄν τίς μιν βλάπτῃ σκολιῶς ὀνοτάζων,*
> *αὐτίκα πὰρ Διὶ πατρὶ καθεζομένη Κρονίωνι*
> *γηρύετ' ἀνθρώπων ἀδίκων νόον, ὄφρ' ἀποτείσῃ.*

It may be idle to ask why the author quotes Orpheus rather than Hesiod, though the answer to the question might be interesting if we could find it. Assuming that he was familiar with both poets, we might guess that he thought the name of Orpheus would be more effective with the audience, because the religious sanctions of justice were stronger in the Orphic poems than elsewhere and the dangers to which the unjust were exposed were more graphically portrayed. Weil[123] points out that in arguing against such a person as Aristogeiton it was necessary to insist solemnly on the moral and religious sanctions of justice in the state. This may have turned the author's mind to an Orphic poem which presented the rewards of the just and the punishments of the unjust. Or it may be that he had recently been reading Orpheus. A little color is given to this supposition by the fact that in three other places in the speech scholars think they have found concealed quotations from Orpheus.[124] This is not the place for an

[123] *Les plaidoyers politiques de Démosthène*, p. 291.

[124] The three places are xxv, 8 (= *Fragm.* 21a); xxv, 37 (= *Fragm.* 23); and xxv, 52 (= *Fragm.* 23).

examination of these three passages, which would carry us far afield; but it may be said that, though the occurrence in a single speech of three suspected quotations from Orpheus is in itself significant, the arguments in support of each one have little weight. Even if it is true that all four passages contain quotations from Orpheus, we are still not warranted in accepting Dieterich's conclusion[125] that the author of the speech was a member of an Orphic congregation which made use of the poems from which the quotations are drawn. The only evidence for anything like Orphic congregations is that which tells of Orphici who avoided animal food. The name of Orpheus was associated with other religious institutions, also, and Orphic poems were numerous and accessible to the public.[126]

Another writer whose evidence concerning Orpheus we have already examined is Epigenes. What we know of his book Περὶ τῆς εἰς Ὀρφέα ποιήσεως comes from two passages in Clement of Alexandria.[127] From one of these (*Strom.* i, 21, 131 Stählin = *Test.* 183, 222) we learn the names of four Orphic poems with which Epigenes was acquainted, the Εἰς Ἅιδου κατάβασις, the Ἱερὸς λόγος, the Πέπλος, and the Φυσικά. In the other (*Strom.* v, 8, 49 Stählin = *Fragm.* 33) Clement cites a number of poetical phrases from Orpheus with Epigenes' explanation of their meaning. Such isolated phrases, which might be found in almost any Greek poet, can tell us little of the content of the poems from which they are taken.

[125] *Nekyia*, p. 139.

[126] Cf. the speculations of F. Ribezzo, "La Δίκη πάρεδρος Διός degli Orfici," *Riv. Indo-Greco-Italica*, IX (1925), fasc. iii and iv, 57.

[127] These texts are quoted above on pp. 110 and 114.

In Plato there are to be found four quotations expressly associated with the name of Orpheus.

Socrates, in the *Cratylus*, after proposing some conjectural etymologies for the word ψυχή, turns next to the word σῶμα (*Crat.* 400 B–C = *Fragm.* 8): ΕΡΜ. Ἀλλὰ δὴ τὸ μετὰ τοῦτο πῶς φῶμεν ἔχειν; ΣΩ. Τὸ σῶμα λέγεις; ΕΡΜ. Ναί. ΣΩ. Πολλαχῇ μοι δοκεῖ τοῦτό γε· ἂν μὲν καὶ σμικρόν τις παρακλίνῃ, καὶ πάνυ. καὶ γὰρ σῆμά τινές φασιν αὐτὸ εἶναι τῆς ψυχῆς, ὡς τεθαμμένης ἐν τῷ νῦν παρόντι· καὶ διότι αὖ τούτῳ σημαίνει ἃ ἂν σημαίνῃ ἡ ψυχή, καὶ ταὺτῃ "σῆμα" ὀρθῶς καλεῖσθαι. δοκοῦσι μέντοι μοι μάλιστα θέσθαι οἱ ἀμφὶ Ὀρφέα τοῦτο τὸ ὄνομα, ὡς δίκην διδούσης τῆς ψυχῆς ὧν δὴ ἕνεκα δίδωσιν, τοῦτον δὲ περίβολον ἔχειν, ἵνα σῴζηται, δεσμωτηρίου εἰκόνα· εἶναι οὖν τῆς ψυχῆς τοῦτο, ὥσπερ αὐτὸ ὀνομάζεται, ἕως ἂν ἐκτείσῃ τὰ ὀφειλόμενα, [τὸ] "σῶμα," καὶ οὐδὲν δεῖν παράγειν οὐδ' ἓν γράμμα. Socrates mentions first two etymologies that have been offered (he does not say by whom), deriving σῶμα from σῆμα, in two senses: according to one, the σῶμα is the "tomb" of the soul, which is supposed to be buried in the body here and now; according to the other, the σῶμα is the sign of the soul, because the soul makes all its communications (σημαίνει) to the outer world by means of the body. He inclines, however, to the view that the word σῶμα was coined by Orpheus and his associates, who, believing that the soul has penalties to pay, regarded the body as an enclosure in which the soul is kept (σῴζηται), as in a prison, until it has paid its due. The first two etymologies are certainly not presented as Orphic in any sense of the word. The Orphic etymology is introduced as if it were offered by a quite different set of persons from the vague *τινες* who are mentioned as offering the first two.[128] The loose phrase *οἱ ἀμφὶ 'Ορφέα* leaves us in some uncertainty. Plato would not have used it if he had been consciously quoting from a poem by Orpheus. He means that the doctrine is associated with Orpheus and those who shared his views—that is, those who coöperated with Orpheus in the institution of the teletae and those who wrote books like the books of Orpheus. In other words, he means that the doctrine belongs to that form of religious thought which finds expression in theology (in a wide sense) and in teletae. But though Plato does not say that the doctrine was set forth in a poem, whether by Orpheus or by Musaeus or by both or by some other poet, it is not reasonable to suppose that, in a form of religion which rested so heavily on books, a doctrine of such importance would not have found expression in writing. We must believe that it was enunciated in a poem by Orpheus or by someone else of his way of thinking.

A little later in the *Cratylus* Socrates quotes two whole lines from Orpheus (*Crat.* 402 B = *Fragm.* 15): *τί οὖν; δοκεῖ σοι ἀλλοιότερον 'Ηρακλείτου νοεῖν ὁ τιθέμενος τοῖς τῶν ἄλλων θεῶν προγόνοις "'Ρέαν" τε καὶ "Κρόνον"; ἆρα οἴει ἀπὸ τοῦ αὐτομάτου αὐτὸν ἀμφοτέροις ῥευμάτων ὀνόματα θέσθαι; ὥσπερ αὖ Ὅμηρος "'Ωκεανόν τε θεῶν γένεσίν" φησιν "καὶ μητέρα Τηθύν·" οἶμαι δὲ καὶ 'Ησίοδος. λέγει δέ που καὶ 'Ορφεὺς ὅτι*

> *'Ωκεανὸς πρῶτος καλλίρροος ἦρξε γάμοιο,*
> *ὅς ῥα κασιγνήτην ὁμομήτορα Τηθὺν ὄπυιεν.*

[128] Cf. Wilamowitz, *Der Glaube der Hellenen*, II (1932), 199: "Platon, Kratyl. 400C, kennt *τοὺς ἀμφὶ 'Ορφέα*, die sagen, daß der Körper *σῶμα* heißt, weil er

Socrates has observed that the names of the gods who were the ancestors of the other gods, Rhea, Cronus, Oceanus, and Tethys, all have meanings that suggest flowing water, and he guesses that these names had been determined by the principle of the Heraclitean flux. The point of the quotation from Orpheus is to show that he, like Homer and Hesiod, represented the gods as sprung from Oceanus and Tethys.

At the close of the *Philebus* Plato gives a graded list of the elements of the good. Having assigned the fifth place to the pure and harmless pleasures, he ends with the following (*Phil.* 66 C = *Fragm. 14*): "Ἕκτῃ δ' ἐν γενεᾷ," φησὶν Ὀρφεύς, "καταπαύσατε κόσμον ἀοιδῆς·" ἀτὰρ κινδυνεύει καὶ ὁ ἡμέτερος λόγος ἐν ἕκτῃ καταπεπαυμένος εἶναι κρίσει. He puts nothing in the sixth place, either because there are no more elements of the good or because their quality is now so attenuated that they are negligible. He, therefore, does not finish with the sixth place, but has finished before he comes to the sixth place. If Orpheus' line is to be understood in the same way, it means: "Bring your song to a close when you come to the sixth generation," in other words, "Stop with the fifth." Scholars have made great efforts to correlate this verse with the generations of the gods in the various Orphic theogonies of which fragments are given by late authors. Professor Nilsson has allowed his preoccupation with this question to mislead him in the interpretation of the words κόσμον ἀοιδῆς.[129]

die Seele σώιζει wie in einem Gefängnis, was die Modernen nicht hindert, das σῶμα σῆμα ψυχῆς für orphisch zu erklären; die Lehre ist pythagoreisch. οἱ ἀμφ' Ὀρφέα sind Orpheus und die ihm folgen."

[129] "Orphism and Kindred Movements," *Harv. Theol. Rev.*, XXVIII (1935), 200.

He translates the line thus: "Let the kosmos of the song cease in the sixth generation," with the following note: "Taken in the usual sense of 'good order,' κόσμον refers to the order of the creation of the world which Orphic poetry tried to establish in a more deliberate manner than earlier cosmogonies." But a κόσμον ἀοιδῆς is simply a song in which art governs the choice and combination of words. We may compare Solon, fr. 2 Diehl αὐτὸς κῆρυξ ἦλθον ἀφ' ἱμερτῆς Σαλαμῖνος, | κόσμον ἐπέων ᾠδὴν ἀντ' ἀγορῆς θέμενος; Parmenides, fr. 8, 52 Diels-Kranz Κόσμον ἐμῶν ἐπέων ἀπατηλόν; Pindar, *Ol.* xi, 13 f. κόσμον . . . ἀδυμελῆ κελαδήσω; Philetas of Cos, fr. 10 Powell ἀλλ' ἐπέων εἰδὼς κόσμον καὶ πολλὰ μογήσας | μύθων παντοίων οἶμον ἐπιστάμενος.

In a passage of the second book of the *Laws* Plato criticizes certain tasteless fashions that have crept into the art of music, among which is the realistic practice of combining the voices of men, the cries of animals, and the noise of instruments in a single composition. Poets who produce such jumbles and confusions, he says, incur the scorn of competent judges (*Laws* ii, 669 D = *Fragm.* 11): ποιηταὶ δὲ ἀνθρώπινοι σφόδρα τὰ τοιαῦτα ἐμπλέκοντες καὶ συγκυκῶντες ἀλόγως, γέλωτ' ἂν παρασκευάζοιεν τῶν ἀνθρώπων ὅσους φησὶν Ὀρφεὺς λαχεῖν ὥραν τῆς τέρψιος. The epic form τέρψιος shows that Plato is quoting the actual words of the Orphic poem. What these words meant in their original context is not certain. ὥραν τῆς τέρψιος may mean either the best time of life for enjoyment, which would presumably be youth, or enjoyment at the moment when it is most perfect, the perfection of enjoyment. Plato uses the words in the latter sense, describing persons of discriminating taste who are capable of discerning and appreciating that which gives the greatest enjoyment. This does not prove that Orpheus did not intend the former meaning, because Plato might have twisted the ambiguous phrase to his own purpose.[130]

Aristotle supplies two indirect quotations from Orphic poetry, throwing doubt on the authorship of both. The first of these is the idea that the generation and growth of an animal is like the weaving of a net (*De gen. animal.* B 1, 734a 16 = *Fragm.* 26): ἢ γάρ τοι ἅμα πάντα γίγνεται τὰ μόρια, οἷον καρδία πλεύμων ἧπαρ ὀρθαλμὸς καὶ τῶν ἄλλων ἕκαστον, ἢ ἐφεξῆς, ὥσπερ ἐν τοῖς καλουμένοις Ὀρφέως ἔπεσιν· ἐκεῖ γὰρ ὁμοίως φησὶ γίγνεσθαι τὸ ζῷον τῇ τοῦ δικτύου πλοκῇ. The second is the idea that the soul is carried by the winds and enters the body from the outer world when the breath is drawn in (*De anima* A 5, 410b 27 = *Fragm.* 27): τοῦτο δὲ πέπονθε καὶ ὁ ἐν τοῖς Ὀρφικοῖς ἔπεσι καλουμένοις λόγος· φησὶ γὰρ τὴν ψυχὴν ἐκ τοῦ ὅλου εἰσιέναι ἀναπνεόντων, φερομένην ὑπὸ τῶν ἀνέμων.

A scholiast has preserved two Orphic verses which were quoted by Philochorus (Schol. Eur. *Alc.* 968 Schwartz = *F. H. G.* fr. 191 = *Fragm.* 332): Φιλόχορος ἐν α' Περὶ μαντικῆς ἐκτίθησιν αὐτοῦ (sc. Ὀρφέως) ποιήματα ἔχοντα οὕτως·

οὔτοι ἀρίστερός εἰμι θεοπροπίας ἀποειπεῖν,
ἀλλά μοι ἐν στήθεσσιν ἀληθεύουσι μενοιναί.

---

[130] This interpretation, which is approximatley that of Lobeck (*Aglaoph.*, II, 948), is rejected by Paul Tannery (*Rev. de philologie*, XXV [1901], 313), who understands the words to mean: "Les musiciens de nos jours feraient rire ceux qui, par exemple, ont entendu Orphée." "Il suffit," he says, "d'admettre que l'hémistiche qu'il reproduit était, dans un hymne orphique circulant de son temps, appliqué aux auditeurs du merveilleux aède, et il me semble qu'il n'y a là aucune difficulté." But there is no reason why we should admit the truth of this guess.

The last word is an emendation of Wilamowitz for the manuscript reading μέλαιναι.

Another verse, which is possibly Orphic, has been preserved by a very indirect tradition. In the second book of the *Geoponica* is a section on the cultivation of beans, which is taken from Didymus of Alexandria. In this section the following passage occurs (*Geopon.* ii, 35, 8 = *Fragm.* 291): Πρῶτος δὲ ἀπέσχετο κυάμων 'Αμφιάραος, διὰ τὴν δι' ὀνείρων μαντείαν. φέρεται δὲ καὶ 'Ορφέως τοιάδε ἔπη· 'Δειλοί, κυάμων ἄπο χεῖρας ἔχεσθε' καὶ 'ἶσόν τοι κυάμους φαγέειν, κεφαλάς τε τοκήων.' The second of these two verses was known to Heracleides Ponticus, if we can believe Joannes Lydus, who writes as follows (*De mens.* iv, 42, p. 99, 17 Wünsch = *Fragm.* 291): ὁ δὲ Ποντικὸς 'Ηρακλείδης φησίν, ὡς εἴ τις τὸν κύαμον ἐν καινῇ (v.l. κενῇ) θήκῃ ἐμβαλὼν ἀποκρύψει τῇ κόπρῳ ἐπὶ τεσσαράκοντα πάσας ἡμέρας, εἰς ὄψιν ἀνθρώπου σεσαρκωμένου μεταβαλόντα τὸν κύαμον εὑρήσει, καὶ διὰ τοῦτο τὸν ποιητὴν φάναι·

ἶσόν τοι κυάμους τε φαγεῖν κεφαλάς τε τοκήων.

The verse, therefore, appears to have been in existence in the fourth century B.C., though the attribution to Orpheus is not found until the fourth century A.D. There are allusions to it in half a dozen other authors: Plutarch quotes it in connection with some remarks about Orphic and Pythagorean doctrines, and Clement of Alexandria in a section concerning the Pythagoreans. We learn from a passage in Diogenes Laertius (viii, 33 = *Test.* 214), whose ultimate source may have been a treatise by a Pythagorean of the fourth century B.C.,[131] that abstinence

[131] See M. Wellman, "Eine pythagoreische Urkunde des IV. Jahrhunderts v. Chr.," *Hermes*, LIV (1919), 225–248.

from beans was recommended by those who conducted teletae (ἀπέχεσθαι . . . καὶ κυάμων καὶ τῶν ἄλλων ὧν παρακελεύονται καὶ οἱ τὰς τελετὰς ἐν τοῖς ἱεροῖς ἐπιτελοῦντες). That Pausanias in the second century A.D. found something about beans in an Orphic poem, we know from his remarks about the temple of Κυαμίτης in Attica (i, 37, 4 = *Test.* 219). After expressing doubt whether Κυαμίτης was the first man who had ever planted beans, or whether he was a hero to whom the discovery of beans was attributed because it could not be attributed to Demeter, he adds the statement: ὅστις δὲ ἤδη τελετὴν Ἐλευσῖνι εἶδεν ἢ τὰ καλούμενα Ὀρφικὰ ἐπελέξατο, οἶδεν ἃ λέγω. But Didymus is the only authority who definitely ascribes the verse which we are considering to Orpheus. It is interesting to note that the other verse quoted by him and also attributed to Orpheus is assigned by Gellius (iv, 11, 9) to Empedocles (fr. 141 Diels), who, he says, followed Pythagorean teaching, and by Callimachus (fr. 128 Schneider) directly to Pythagoras. Doubt is thereby thrown on the statement of Didymus: if he is wrong about the authorship of the first verse, he may be wrong about the second. It would seem that the curious notions about beans which appear not infrequently in ancient authors, and the scraps of verse which touched the subject, were associated indifferently with various persons who were known to have insisted on strange taboos. Since we know that followers of Orpheus in the fifth century B.C. were required to refrain from animal food and to avoid the use of wool in burial, and since Orpheus was recognized as the great originator of teletae, it is not unlikely that the prohibition against beans and the very verse quoted by Heracleides were associated with his name in classical times; but we cannot be sure of this; still less can we be sure that the verse actually appeared in an Orphic poem of the fourth century B.C.

Eudemus, the pupil of Aristotle, was acquainted with an Orphic poem which contained the statement that the beginning of all things was Night. This we know from the Neoplatonic philosopher Damascius, who writes thus (*De prim. princip.* 124, i, 319, 8 Ruelle = *Fragm.* 28): Ἡ δὲ παρὰ τῷ περιπατητικῷ Εὐδήμῳ ἀναγεγραμμένη ὡς τοῦ Ὀρφέως οὖσα θεολογία πᾶν τὸ νοητὸν ἐσιώπησεν, ὡς παντάπασιν ἄρρητόν τε καὶ ἄγνωστον τρόπῳ κατὰ διέξοδόν τε καὶ ἀπαγγελίαν, ἀπὸ δὲ τῆς Νυκτὸς ἐποιήσατο τὴν ἀρχήν, ἀφ' ἧς καὶ Ὅμηρος, εἰ καὶ μὴ συνεχῆ πεποίηται τὴν γενεαλογίαν, ἵστησιν· οὐ γὰρ ἀποδεκτέον Εὐδήμου λέγοντος ὅτι ἀπὸ Ὠκεανοῦ καὶ Τηθύος ἄρχεται (Il. xiv, 302), φαίνεται γὰρ εἰδὼς καὶ τὴν Νύκτα μεγίστην οὕτω θεόν, ὡς καὶ τὸν Δία σέβεσθαι αὐτήν· 'ἅζετο γὰρ μὴ Νυκτὶ θοῇ ἀποθύμια ῥέζοι' (Il. xiv, 261). Ἀλλ' Ὅμηρος μὲν καὶ αὐτὸς ἀρχέσθω ἀπὸ Νυκτός· Ἡσίοδος δέ μοι δοκεῖ πρῶτον γενέσθαι τὸ Χάος ἱστορῶν τὴν ἀκατάληπτον τοῦ νοητοῦ καὶ ἡνωμένην παντελῶς φύσιν κεκληκέναι Χάος, τὴν δὲ Γῆν πρώτην ἐκεῖθεν παράγειν ὥς τινα ἀρχὴν τῆς ὅλης γενεᾶς τῶν θεῶν· εἰ μὴ ἄρα Χάος μὲν τὴν δευτέραν τῶν δυεῖν ἀρχῶν, Γῆν δὲ καὶ Τάρταρον καὶ Ἔρωτα τὸ τριπλοῦν νοητόν, τὸν μὲν Ἔρωτα ἀντὶ τοῦ τρίτου, ὡς κατὰ ἐπιστροφὴν θεωρουμένην. τοῦτο γὰρ οὕτως ὀνομάζει καὶ ὁ Ὀρφεὺς ἐν ταῖς Ῥαψῳδίαις· τὴν δὲ Γῆν ἀντὶ τοῦ πρώτου, ὡς πρώτην ἐν στερεῷ τινι καὶ οὐσιώδει καταστήματι παγεῖσαν, τὸν δὲ Τάρταρον ἀντὶ τοῦ μέσου, ὡς ἤδη πως εἰς διάκρισιν παρακεκινημένου. Whether the statement attributed to Orpheus occurred in a formal theogony, like that of Hesiod, or was merely a passing observation in the midst of a mythological narrative, such as are found in Homer concerning this subject, cannot be determined, because Damascius, who had not seen the Orphic poem himself, proceeds immediately to recall the opinions of both Homer and Hesiod concerning the primal figure in the descent of the gods. The cause of Orpheus' silence concerning the Intelligible, which might be supposed to have preceded the figure of Night, that it is so far beyond speech and knowledge that any description of it is impossible, is, of course, a Neoplatonic invention. It should be observed that Damascius had in his own hands in the fifth century A.D. the so-called *Rhapsodies* of Orpheus and that they were not consistent with the poem referred to by Eudemus.

## CRITICISM CONCERNING THE AUTHORSHIP

Although there was a considerable body of poetry which many, if not most, people unquestioningly believed to have been written by Orpheus, there were not wanting some who expressed critical doubts concerning the authorship of this poetry. Instances of such doubt have appeared in texts which have already been presented, and other texts which are now to be examined will add to the number. The doubt does not seem always to have sprung from the same cause, but the information that is available is too incomplete to allow us to make any proper classification of the critical theories that were advanced.

The possibility that some or all Orphic poems were

supposed to have been inspired by Apollo, dictated by the voice of Orpheus, both before and after his death, and written down by Musaeus has already been considered in connection with a text from the *Alcestis*. This manner of composition may have been openly displayed in some poems by the form in which they were cast, as it was in the late *Argonautica*. In others this formal device may have been omitted. But even if it were generally understood that all Orphic poetry had come into existence in this way, the credit for its authorship would still belong, under Apollo, to Orpheus, and the poems would be currently spoken of as his work.

The opinion expressed by Ion of Chios is a different matter. He, it will be remembered, insisted that some of the Orphic poems had been composed by Pythagoras; and sometime later Epigenes, evidently following the same line of thought, asserted that four definite Orphic poems, which he names, had really been written by certain Pythagoreans, whom he also names. These two men must have been brought to this opinion by some marked resemblance between these poems and the tenets of the Pythagorean school. But this is not enough to explain it. They might have said that Pythagoras and his followers obtained their ideas from Orpheus. Orpheus must have seemed to them a less substantial figure than the real flesh and blood of Pythagoras and the Pythagoreans. Whether or not they acknowledged the existence of any genuine poems of Orpheus, they were certainly prepared to admit that some, if not many, of his poems were composed by authors who published them under his name.

What the initial cause of their doubt was concerning the genuineness of Orphic poems, it is difficult to say. It may have been so generally understood that the Orphic poems with their stereotyped formula of Apollo-Orpheus-Musaeus were the work of a multitude of anonymous poets that no one of any critical judgment recognized any poems as the genuine work of Orpheus. Or they may have been led to regard all Orphic poems as spurious by chronological considerations, of a kind which is now to be considered.

In a text which has already been used as evidence concerning the legend of Orpheus as an Argonaut,[132] we find the curious statement made by Herodorus that there were two men named Orpheus, one of whom sailed with the Argonauts. Besides this, we are told by Olympiodorus (ap. Phot. *Bibl.* 86, Migne CIII, 272 C = Herodorus, fr. 12 Jacoby = *Test.* 230) that Herodorus was the author of a treatise of some kind on Orpheus and Musaeus:[133] *λέγει δὲ ὅτι νῆσος* [sc. *ἡ Ὄασις*] *τὸ παλαιὸν ἦν καὶ ἀπεχερσώθη, καὶ ὅτι ταύτην καλεῖ Ἡρόδοτος Μακάρων νήσους. Ἡρόδωρος δέ, ὁ τὴν Ὀρφέως καὶ Μουσαίου συγγράψας ἱστορίαν, Φαιακίδα ταύτην καλεῖ.* Since Herodorus recognized two men named Orpheus, of whom one was the Argonaut, we may assume that what was known of the other was somehow inconsistent with the Argonautic story. Since Orpheus the Argonaut could overcome the charm of the Sirens, he must have been the legendary singer and magician. Who was the other? Since Musaeus has no part properly in the

[132] See p. 7 above.

[133] Cf. I. M. Linforth, "Diodorus, Herodorus, Orpheus," in *Classical Studies Presented to Edward Capps*, Princeton, 1936, p. 217.

legend of Orpheus, and since the treatise of Herodorus had as its subject Orpheus *and* Musaeus, it seems probable that the Orpheus of the treatise is not the Argonaut but the other one. In view of the well-established association of Orpheus and Musaeus in the composition of poetry, whether as poets dealing with similar themes or as joint authors of the same poems, it seems likely that the 'other Orpheus' was the putative author of the Orphic poems. In answer to the question why Herodorus thought that the poet Orpheus was not the same person as the Orpheus of legend, only a guess can be offered. The guess is this: he believed the Orphic poems to be of later composition than the poems of Homer and Hesiod; he believed that the Orpheus of legend had lived many generations before Homer and Hesiod; and yet he believed that the Orphic poems were written by Orpheus. Confronted with these three facts, he could draw only one conclusion: there were two men named Orpheus. This line of reasoning shows that it is a fair hypothesis to assume that Herodorus, like Ion of Chios,[134] believed the Orphic poems to be younger than Homer and Hesiod.

This hypothesis is supported by a famous passage in Herodotus. Hesiod and Homer, he says (ii, 53 = *Test.* 10), who lived not more than four hundred years ago, created a theogony for the Greeks, giving the gods their epithets, apportioning their honors and functions, and describing their appearance; *οἱ δὲ πρότερον ποιηταὶ λεγόμενοι τούτων τῶν ἀνδρῶν γενέσθαι ὕστερον, ἔμοιγε δοκέειν, ἐγένοντο.* He cannot mean by this statement that there

[134] Cf. Clem. Alex. *Strom.* i, 21, 131 (quoted on p. 110 above).

were no poets before Homer and Hesiod; Demodocus, at least, he would have acknowledged to be earlier than Homer, since Homer himself told of him, and in ii, 23, he gives his opinion that the name of the river Oceanus was introduced into poetry by Homer or some earlier poet (ἤ τινα τῶν προτέρων γενομένων ποιητέων). He must refer to some group of poets whose names naturally came into his mind in this connection and would, he assumed, also occur to the mind of the reader. These would be poets who had composed poems containing theological matter such as was to be found in Homer and Hesiod. Since it is not likely that he was quarreling with the existence before Homer of merely hypothetical poems, we may assume that he was speaking of definite extant poems. His statement may be taken as proof that there existed in his time poems dealing with theological matters which were commonly believed to have been composed before Homer and Hesiod. The authors of these poems, he says, lived after Homer and Hesiod. This is not the same thing as saying that the poems which are attributed to these authors, who themselves lived before Homer and Hesiod, are spurious. Now there can be little doubt that Orpheus and Musaeus were among the poets he was thinking of; there is no record of any other poet more likely. There are, therefore, two possibilities: either Herodotus, saying that Orpheus and Musaeus lived after Homer and Hesiod, not only denied the truth of current genealogies like those of Pherecydes and Hellanicus, but also rejected the legend which made Orpheus an Argonaut; or, acknowledging the existence of an early, legendary Orpheus, he held that the Orphic poems were written by another Orpheus who lived after Homer and Hesiod. It may be that he had not thought the matter through logically. Chiefly concerned with the priority of Homer and Hesiod in the history of Greek theology, he may have intended to say simply: "The theological poems which are attributed to poets who are said to have lived before Homer, were, in my opinion, composed by poets who lived after Homer." But, in any case, he must have believed either that the Orphic poems were composed by a man named Orpheus who was a different person from the legendary Orpheus, or that they were not composed by anyone named Orpheus. In the one case, he would have anticipated the judgment of Herodorus; in the other, his general position would have been the same as that of Ion of Chios and Epigenes, although we do not know that they denied the authenticity of *all* Orphic poems. Still, we do not know why any of these critics denied the antiquity of the Orphic poems, and there is too little foundation to support a profitable guess.

A definite reason for denying that Orpheus had written poetry seems to have been advanced by Androtion, the Athenian historian of the fourth century B.C.; but unfortunately we do not learn how he thought the poems came into existence. All we know is found in the following passage from Aelian (*Var. Hist.* viii, 6 = *Test.* 32): Τῶν ἀρχαίων φασὶ Θρᾳκῶν μηδένα ἐπίστασθαι γράμματα· ἀλλὰ καὶ ἐνόμιζον αἴσχιστον εἶναι πάντες οἱ τὴν Εὐρώπην οἰκοῦντες βάρβαροι χρῆσθαι γράμμασιν. οἱ δὲ ἐν τῇ Ἀσίᾳ ὡς λόγος ἐχρῶντο αὐτοῖς μᾶλλον. ἔνθεν τοι καὶ τολμῶσι λέγειν μηδὲ τὸν Ὀρφέα *σοφὸν γεγονέναι, Θρᾷκα ὄντα, ἀλλ' ἄλλως τοὺς μύθους αὐτοῦ κατεψεῦσθαι.*[135] *ταῦτα 'Ανδροτίων λέγει, εἴ τῳ πιστὸς ὑπὲρ τῆς ἀγραμματίας καὶ ἀπαιδευσίας Θρᾳκῶν τεκμηριῶσαι.* Evidently Androtion said, in some connection, that Orpheus, being a Thracian and therefore illiterate, could not have written the poems ascribed to him. Aelian, in the second century A.D., thinks this is a startling statement and is inclined to doubt the truth of it. It would not have been so surprising in the fourth century B.C.[136] The theory that Orpheus dictated his poems to Musaeus would not have been inconsistent with Androtion's view; but if he had said anything about it Aelian would surely have reported it.

The language used by Aristotle in quoting from the Orphic poems shows that he had no illusion about their authenticity. *ἐν τοῖς καλουμένοις 'Ορφέως ἔπεσιν*, he says in one place; *ἐν τοῖς 'Ορφικοῖς ἔπεσι καλουμένοις*, in another.[137] Philoponus comments on the latter phrase, as follows (*In Aristot. de anima* A 5, 410b 27, p. 186, 24 Hayduck = *Test.* 188): *λεγομένοις εἶπεν, ἐπειδὴ μὴ δοκεῖ 'Ορφέως εἶναι τὰ ἔπη, ὡς καὶ αὐτὸς ἐν τοῖς Περὶ φιλοσοφίας λέγει· αὐτοῦ μὲν γάρ εἰσι τὰ δόγματα, ταῦτα δέ φασιν 'Ονομάκριτον ἐν ἔπεσι κατατεῖναι.* In the lost work *Περὶ φιλοσοφίας*, then, Aristotle said either that the poems were not believed to be by Orpheus, or that he himself did not believe them to be. *δοκεῖ* is more naturally taken in the former sense. Aristotle therefore is reporting the opinion of the critics, but

---

[135] *κατεψεῦσθαι* is an emendation of Perizonius for *καταψεύσασθα*. Cf. Aelian, *Var. Hist.* xii, 36 *πολλὰ καὶ ἄλλα κατέψευσται αὐτοῦ*, "many other things have been falsely attributed to him."

[136] But it was denied even then by Ps.-Alcidamas. See p. 15 above.

[137] See p. 151 above.

he seems to accept it as sound. The last sentence in Philoponus' note cannot be taken with certainty as a report of what Aristotle said, for which *εἶναι* and *ὥς φασιν*[138] should have been used. It may have been added by Philoponus on the authority of later critics (the first clear record of the ascription of Orphic poems to Onomacritus in not earlier than the second century A.D.).

Another reference to the opinion of Aristotle concerning Orphic poetry is found in Cicero (*De natura deorum* i, 107 = *Test.* 13):" Orpheum poetam docet Aristoteles numquam fuisse, et hoc Orphicum carmen Pythagorei ferunt cuiusdam fuisse Cercopis [MSS Cerconis]; at Orpheus, id est imago eius, ut vos vultis, in animum meum saepe incurrit." Cicero's words have given rise to considerable discussion. They occur in a passage intended to prove the insufficiency of the Epicurean doctrine of images to demonstrate the existence of the gods. The case of Orpheus is adduced as an example of the absurdity of the doctrine. The speaker, Cotta, says: "Aristotle declares that the poet Orpheus never existed, and they say that the Orphic poem which we have was written by a certain Cercops; but Orpheus (that is, his image, as you insist) often comes into my mind." Now the fact that Cicero alludes to the *Περὶ φιλοσοφίας* of Aristotle in an earlier passage in this same dialogue (33 "Aristotelesque in tertio de philosophia libro . . .") makes it almost certain that he is recalling here the same work of Aristotle, and indeed has in mind the very passage upon which

[138] *φησιν* (for *φασιν*), which is the reading of Trincavelli, cannot be accepted as proof that it was Aristotle who first attributed the Orphic poems to Onomacritus.

Philoponus was later to write the note which has just been quoted. But according to Philoponus, Aristotle's contention was simply that the Orphic poems were not by Orpheus; and evidently Philoponus did not find in Aristotle any suggestion that Orpheus had never existed at all, because he adds the remark on his own account that the ideas in the poems did originate with Orpheus. According to Cicero, on the other hand, Aristotle seems to say that Orpheus never existed at all, and indeed something like this is the sense that is demanded by the context. Much effort has been expended to reconcile these two texts, mostly by misconstruing Cicero or arguing that he misunderstood or misreported Aristotle. It is probable that he reported Aristotle very accurately. In view of the kind of criticism to which the Orphic poems and the authorship of them were subjected in the fifth and fourth centuries B.C., we may safely conclude that the judgment expressed by Aristotle was in effect this: the so-called Orphic poems were not written by Orpheus —neither by the Orpheus of legend who charmed all nature by his song and accompanied the Argonauts, nor by another person of the same name who has been invented to serve as the author of the poems; there never has been a poet Orpheus. That Cicero had read something like this is indicated by the significant word *poetam* and the reference to a particular poem. The case of Orpheus was rather curious, if one was thinking of the doctrine of images. Here we have a poem, says Cicero, which is commonly thought of as a poem of Orpheus; but, we are told, Orpheus never wrote any poetry and this poem in our hands is really by Cercops: and yet the image of Orpheus keeps coming! The statement that the poem he is thinking of was by Cercops he does not obtain from Aristotle, any more than Philoponus obtained from him the statement that Orphic poetry was written by Onomacritus. That Cicero says one thing and Philoponus another shows that neither was in Aristotle. Both Cicero and Philoponus got their ideas about the authorship of the poems from some other works of literary criticism. We know of the books of Herodorus and Epigenes, and doubtless more of the same kind were produced in the Alexandrian period and later. It is worth noticing that Cicero in the first century B.C. names a Pythagorean as the author, as Ion of Chios and Epigenes had done before him. The suggestion that Onomacritus wrote some or all of the Orphic poems may not have been made until after Cicero's time.

## Conclusions Concerning the Period Before 300 B.C.

We have now completed the review of all the documents, literary and archaeological, earlier than 300 B.C. in which Orpheus appears. Though they certainly do not tell the whole story of what men knew about Orpheus before that date and what they called Orphic, they are all we have. If we had the works of literature and art which are lost we should know more. If we could be sure what documents of later date give true information concerning the earlier period we could add that information immediately to what we have. But, as it is, we are bound to see what we can make of the available early evidence. Nor should we be entirely dissatisfied with the volume of this evidence. It includes sculpture and vase paintings, and it includes texts from all the departments of literature except the epic. Lyric poetry, tragedy, comedy, history, oratory, and philosophy are all represented. It is fair to assume that any picture composed of the elements which are thus supplied would not be unduly distorted. We have the pieces before us: let us see what pattern they make.

Inseparable from Orpheus is the art of music. He is scarcely ever named without some thought of his skill as a musician. Every incident of his legend is in some way touched with music. A Muse is his mother, and Apollo is his father or patron. He is numbered with the great musicians of the legendary past, and like others among them he is supposed to have been a Thracian. When he sailed with the Argonauts, it was his part to set the time for the rowers with his song and to counteract the witchery of the Sirens. When he sought to recover his dead wife, he relied upon the magic of his song to move the inexorable powers of the world below. When he died, he died with his lyre in his hands, struggling helplessly to defend himself with it. Even in Hades, Polygnotus' picture shows him still holding his lyre. Not only men and gods, but beasts and trees and stones yielded to his spell. With him an ᾠδή was an ἐπῳδή. So Amphion, too, built the walls of Thebes with his song. To the Greeks all music was magical and could do wonderful things to soul and body, and the Orpheus whom their fancy created was a singer who had strange power to enthral and charm.

Music in Greece had a wider domain than in the modern world; it included all the arts which were under the patronage of Apollo and the Muses. So Orpheus was not only a singer and a harpist, but also a poet and a prophet. But his poems, too, were thought to possess a magical power like that which he exercised with his own voice. The old men of the chorus in the *Alcestis* sought in the writings of Orpheus for a charm which would restore Alcestis to life, and the satyr in the *Cyclops* professed to know a charm which would cause the glowing log to plunge itself into the eye of the Cyclops. Whether such Orphic charms actually existed or not, they clearly belong to the legendary conception of his music. So also as a prophet or mantis he wielded magical power. It was by a kind of magic that the mantis could declare the truth to men who were groping in perplexity, and even bring to pass what they desired.

The most signal achievement of Orpheus' musical magic was conceived to have been the institution of teletae, which acted like a sacrament to bring purification and release from the consciousness of wrongdoing, to renew the sense of vigor and vitality, and to give assurance of happiness after death. The formulation of such rites was the work of a poet and a prophet. Plato in the *Protagoras* represents Orpheus and Musaeus as occupied with both teletae and oracles. Ephorus says that Orpheus was already distinguished for poetry and song before he learned the arts of the teletae and introduced them into Greece. More than once he is spoken of in the same text as poet and as founder of teletae. Indeed, the features of the legend of Orpheus show complete harmony. In all he does there is music and magic. His activity as a poet and his activity as originator of teletae seem to be closely connected, as if they were two aspects of one undertaking.[139]

We need not ask whether Orpheus ever walked the earth or not. He lived in the legend that men had made of him, a wistful, gentle creature, who with his melody and his magic could do what others could not. The legend was real, if Orpheus was not. But the legend was not the only real thing about him. The teletae which he was believed to have originated were still in use in the real world, and there were real poems of which he was believed to be the author.

Of these poems we know sadly little. There are, as we have seen, a few direct and indirect quotations, which are in substance similar to quotations that might be drawn from the genealogical poets and the early philosophers. The subject matter, we are told, of some of the poems at least, was mythological, and myths were related in them which were highly discreditable to the gods. The names of four of the poems are known, but these again yield little information. The Εἰς Ἅιδου κατάβασις may have contained some account of the rewards and punishments which await the soul after death. Of the Ἱερὸς λόγος, the Πέπλος, and the Φυσικά we can say nothing. But though this poetry must remain obscure to us, it was well known in the Greek world. Orpheus belonged in the company of Homer and Hesiod, with whom he is often named, as one of the classics of literature. Whether his poems were publicly recited or not, they were widely

[139] The subject of Orphic incantation is elaborately developed by P. Boyancé in the earlier chapters of his *Le culte des Muses chez les philosophes grecs* (Paris, 1937).

read and quoted like other secular authors. Though they commanded the respect of certain devout souls, there is no hint that they were kept secret or that their circulation was prohibited. Where you found a copy of Homer or Hesiod, there you were likely to find a copy of Orpheus beside it.

In general the Orphic poems were thought of as older than the poems of Homer and Hesiod. This was a natural conclusion if Orpheus was one of the Argonauts. But there were critics who held other views concerning the age and authorship of the poems. One, insisting that they were composed after the time of Homer and Hesiod, tacitly admitted the necessary implication that they were not the work of the Orpheus of legend. Another, who, presumably, accepted this opinion but still wished to save the tradition, suggested that there were two men named Orpheus. Aristotle, whatever he may have thought of the legendary Orpheus, flatly denied the existence of a poet of that name. An author was found for some of the Orphic poems by Ion of Chios, who said that Pythagoras himself had published some of his poetry under the name of Orpheus. Epigenes stated positively that the *Εἰς Ἅιδου κατάβασις* and the *Ἱερὸς λόγος* were by the Pythagorean Cercops, the *Πέπλος* and the *Φυσικά* by Brontinus, who is also known to have been a Pythagorean. We do not know what reason the critics had for asserting that the Orphic poems were spurious, and we can only guess that there was something in their subject matter which argued a late date. It may have been precisely because they contained ideas which were regarded as Pythagorean.

No argument is needed to convince us that the skeptics were right, and that the poems were not pre-Homeric and were not composed by the Orpheus of legend. This does not alter the fact, however, which is proved by the popular belief in their authenticity, that the poems were such as the Orpheus of legend might have composed. Who, then, did compose them, and why were they represented as the work of Orpheus? The evidence offers no answer to the second question, and no convincing answer to the first. A little guessing on these points may be allowed later. But it may be remarked here that if there had been a recognized Orphic religion of which the Orphic poems were the sacred scriptures, the critics who said that Orpheus himself was not the author would certainly have attributed their composition to adherents of that religion, to "Orphics" in general or to particular Orphics whom they could name, and not to men who are known to have been Pythagoreans.

Besides the poems which Orpheus was believed to have composed, there were also religious rites and practices in actual use for which men understood that they were similarly indebted to him. He was the great benefactor who had devised the saving and healing sacraments of teletae and mysteries. Ephorus says expressly that it was he who first introduced teletae into Greece. If he also says that he learned the art from the Idaean Dactyls, this is only an instance of Greek eagerness to find a foreign origin for everything Greek: as far as Greece is concerned, Orpheus is the originator. This unambiguous statement of Ephorus makes it practically certain that Aristophanes, too, and the author of the speech against Aristogeiton mean the same thing. Elsewhere, however, particular rites and practices are associated with the name of Orpheus. There were certain people who participated in rites which were called Orphic, and who were bound by a rule which required that they should not be buried in woolen garments. Since the arrangements for burial must have been made by survivors of the deceased person, it is likely that these people were organized in groups like burial clubs. There were people (and they may have been the same who were concerned about the mode of burial) who lived what was called the Orphic life, avoiding the use of animal food. There were also men called Orpheotelestae whose profession it was to administer teletae for the remission of sins, and their offices seem to have been available to all alike, not only to individuals, but to whole cities, whenever they were desired. There is no reason to suppose that those who resorted to Orpheotelestae formed a sect of any kind; indeed, the rules requiring avoidance of animal food and the avoidance of wool in burial are quite incongruous with what we know about them. Lastly, there were certain honored Athenian mysteries, presumably a state cult, which were represented as Orphic in the sense that they had been founded by Orpheus.

It would seem that, since Orpheus was the culture hero who had originated teletae and mysteries, any or all rites of this type could on occasion be spoken of as Orphic, and that, at the same time, there were certain rites and practices which were called Orphic in a particular sense, as is indicated by the "Orphic orgia" of Herodotus, the "Orphic life" of Plato, and the Orpheotelestes of Theophrastus. But, as we have seen, these latter rites were not identical: some belonged to special groups of devotees; others were provided by special ministrants for the benefit of all who wished to use them. It is significant that both the public ministrants and the private groups found the authority for their practices in Orphic books, as we know from the *Hippolytus* and the *Republic*. Perhaps, though all teletae were in the wider sense Orphic, the name was applied more particularly to all those which did not belong to a settled cult with fixed traditions, but received their sanction directly from Orphic poems.

It is a curious fact that the only deity who is named as honored in the rites of Orpheus is Persephone, in the Athenian mysteries. In the legend the only deities with whom he is associated are the Muse, his mother, and Apollo, his father or patron. Nowhere, either in the legend or in the rites, is there any connection between him and Dionysus, except in the story of his death as told by Aeschylus, where the relation is one of bitter hostility. There can be little doubt, however, that Dionysiac teletae, like the teletae of other gods, were understood to have been instituted by Orpheus and to have found authority in his poems. It must be only the result of accident that we are not told of them expressly.

Such were Orpheus and his works, on a fair reading of the early evidence. Have we found something that we can call Orphism? Can we discern the core of it in the ideas and practices of the groups who saw to it that their deceased members were not buried in wool and observed a vegetarian diet? Or in the ideas and practices of ministrants to whom all might go to be released from their sins? Or in the great public mysteries of Athens which Orpheus founded? If the core is found in any one of these, it is plain that the others cannot be added to it to fill out this picture of a single institution. There are three institutions here, not one, and there is no justification for saying that one of them alone is the vessel of Orphism. Perhaps the Orphic poems contained a body of doctrine so clearly defined that we should be justified in calling it Orphism. For this there is no evidence whatever. As we have seen, we know very little of the contents of the Orphic poems. They may have contained (and they probably did) myths which were associated with teletae, but since there were many teletae there would be many myths. Certainly the body of Orphic fragments preserved in later authors shows that the poems were miscellaneous in content and often inconsistent. This fact, which makes it difficult to determine what fragments are early and what are late, at the same time makes it probable that the earliest poems did not present a single, coherent creed. If, in spite of all, it is still maintained that there was a particular Orphic religion, it remains clear that the name of Orpheus cannot be used as a touchstone to determine what belonged to it. Still less can we bring into connection with it, on the basis of some fancied resemblance to what it is conceived to be, elements which are not sealed with his name. Even if we assume its existence, we must be at a loss to say what to attribute to it and what not, if the name of Orpheus itself is fallible. It is wiser not to assume its existence. If we must call something Orphism, it must be the entire religion of teletae and mysteries with their magical ritual, the poems of Orpheus and others in which their sacred myths are told, and the ideas concerning god and man which were inherent in poems and ritual. The ancients did not call this religion Orphism, but they said what is in effect the same thing, in the Greek manner, when they said that Orpheus was the inventor and founder of it.

*Chapter* II

# Evidence Later Than 300 B.C. Concerning Orphic Rites and Institutions

THE INVESTIGATION which has now been completed is addressed solely to the evidence obtained from sources earlier than 300 B.C. It will be objected that this arbitrary limitation casts doubt on the validity of the conclusions that have been drawn when so much evidence of a later date still remains behind. The objection is well taken. To attempt a final reconstruction from a fragmentary part of the evidence—*ex pede Herculem*—when many more fragments of the whole are at hand would be futile. But something may be said in defense of the plan which has been adopted. In the first place, there is satisfaction in knowing, on the basis of contemporary evidence which is beyond all suspicion and doubt, precisely what the Greeks before 300 B.C. thought they knew about Orpheus and what they called Orphic; and this, we may say with some confidence, we now know. In the second place, where the whole sum of evidence is so great, it is convenient to set up a tentative hypothesis on the basis of a portion of the evidence. For this purpose it is suitable to use the evidence before 300 B.C., because this period is the earliest in point of time, because it is the period in which we are most eager to learn the nature of

Orphic influence, and because, being terminated by the conquests of Alexander, it forms an organic unit. Now, having made this double use of the early material, it remains to explore the later centuries, and to make such changes, corrections, and readjustments as may be demanded in the tentative picture.

Properly, the inquiry should continue to pursue the three lines which have been followed so far. The Orphic legend, Orphic poetry, and Orphic rites should be studied throughout antiquity, and all should be studied together, since the name of Orpheus must have supplied a certain unity to all that was associated with it. The whole of this, however, is not attempted here. Only one of the three lines will be followed. Our attention will be confined to the documents which supply information concerning Orphic rites and institutions, in the hope that by this menas we may either substantiate the conclusions concerning them which have already been reached on the basis of the early evidence or discover in what respects these conclusions must be modified or corrected.

Here again the arbitrary limitation of the investigation to a portion of the evidence may be disconcerting to the reader. He may object that it is impossible to know what the Orphic religion was without including in the examination all that remains of the Orphic poems. Again it must be granted that the objection is well taken. If the Orphic poems were the sacred scriptures of an Orphic religion, they must contain most important information concerning that religion. But when we say Orphic religion we mean something more than a traditional body or doctrine. We mean a comprehensive institution, so far organized as to be recognizable, maintained by a body of believers who were bound together by a common faith and who gave expression to their faith in common rites and practices. The question is precisely whether there was an Orphic religion that can be described in these terms. To answer this question we must search for traces of all the essential features of such an institution. Unless by these means we can prove its existence it is meaningless to say that the poems provide evidence concerning it. If, on the other hand, we find that it actually existed, we can reasonably assume that the poems belonged to it in some essential way, and we can proceed to amplify our knowledge of it by means of the poems and fragments which we possess.

Still, it may be urged, there is a peculiar thing about the Orphic poems. They are the work, not of a single poet, but of a long line of poets, and this fact in itself argues the existence of an institution. There is undoubtedly force in this argument, and it must not be forgotten. Some community of purpose must have moved the successive poets in the line to publish their works under the name of Orpheus. But this does not in itself prove that they were the adherents of a common religion. It is, in fact, difficult to believe even that they were united in a common doctrine, when we observe the extraordinary diversity in the subject matter of the poems. The poems cover a very wide range of subjects, mythological and otherwise, and the contents of them are miscellaneous and incongruous. Poems so far apart as the Rape of Persephone, the

Διαθῆκαι, and the Λιθικά, for example, can scarcely have been the sacred scriptures of a single sect. The unifying principle inherent in the name of Orpheus must have been something other than participation in the common doctrine of such a sect. Scholars have made persistent efforts to determine what essential Orphic doctrine was, but the results of their efforts remain unconvincing for two reasons. In the first place, as has been remarked before, they have shown a disposition to operate with only a certain portion of the evidence, arbitrarily selected, and to ignore the rest. In the second place, the fact that certain portions of Orphic mythology have been repeatedly cited by later writers because they suited their own particular purposes has led to the unjustifiable conclusion that they held a predominant place in the Orphic poems.

These remarks concerning Orphic poetry are not intended to minimize its importance or the difficulty of interpreting it. Still less is there any intention of hazarding a hasty solution of the many problems which it presents. These can be solved only by a patient examination of all the remains in the light of the changing moods of the world during the long period in which the poems were being composed. All that is urged here is that they should not be treated as the sacred scriptures of a sect until the existence of the sect is proved, and that to determine the existence of a sect we must rely first on evidence other than that of the poems.

With this understanding of the purpose and methods which have been adopted, we can proceed to the inquiry itself. All the available evidence subsequent to 300 B.C.

which throws any light on rites and practices associated with the name of Orpheus has been assembled and is here presented in full. A strict observance of chronology in the arrangement of the multitude of documents would only bewilder the reader. As a matter of convenience they are divided into two groups on a purely objective principle. In the first group are placed the texts in which there is allusion to rites addressed to particular deities, and these are further classified by the names of the deities themselves. The second group is composed of texts in which no deities are named, and these are presented in chronological order. At the end the miscellaneous information which has been obtained is brought into intelligible order by various methods of classification, and the logical conclusions to which it leads are explicitly stated.

## Texts Containing the Names of Particular Deities

### ORPHIC HYMNS

The most important single document to show the wide range of deities with which the name of Orpheus is associated is the collection of short poems known as the *Orphic Hymns*.[1] In Constantinople in 1423 there was found by G. Aurispa a manuscript containing the Homeric hymns and the hymns of Callimachus, Orpheus, and Proclus. This manuscript, which has disappeared again, is the

[1] Last published by Eugenius Abel in *Orphica* (1885), pp. 55–102. The collection sorely needs reëditing and presents many unsolved problems. References to most of the pertinent books and articles can be found in Christ, *Gesch. der griech. Lit.*, revised by Schmid and Stählin, II, 2 (1924), 985; Otto Kern, *R.-E.*, XVI (1935), s.v. Mysterien, 1283; W. K. C. Guthrie, *Orpheus and Greek Religion* (London, 1935), pp. 257–261.

archetype of the existing copies of the *Orphic Hymns*. The first poem in the collection, consisting of fifty-four hexameters, bears the title Εὐχὴ πρὸς Μουσαῖον, and the opening couplet is addressed to Musaeus:

> Μάνθανε δή, Μουσαῖε, θυηπολίην περισέμνην,
> εὐχήν, ἣ δή τοι προφερεστέρη ἐστὶν ἁπασέων.

The next forty-two lines are a prayer addressed by name and epithet to some seventy-five deities, closing with this petition:

> εὐμενέας ἐλθεῖν κεχαρημένον ἦτορ ἔχοντας
> τήνδε θυηπολίην ἱερὴν σπονδήν τ' ἐπὶ σεμνήν.

The remaining ten lines form a separate prayer addressed to Hecate, whose name does not appear in the previous all-embracing list. This hymn to Hecate, which is numbered "i" in Abel's edition, may or may not have been originally independent; it may have been an integral part of the longer poem, or it may have been united with it in the manuscripts by mistake. F. Jacobi[2] believes that the longer poem comprises two distinct hymns, the first addressed to πάντες θεοί, the second to Hecate. However this may be, the introductory poem is followed in the collection by eighty-six hymns, from six to thirty lines in length, each hymn bearing as a title the name of the deity or deities to whom it is addressed, either in the genitive case or in the accusative with εἰς. No two hymns in the eighty-six (or in the eighty-seven, if we include the hymn to Hecate with the others) bear the same title, except

[2] ΠΑΝΤΕΣ ΘΕΟΙ, Diss. Halle, 1930, pp. 72–74.

that *Hymns* xxxi and xxxviii are both addressed to the Curetes. The names of several deities appear more than once in the titles, but they are distinguished by different epithets. For example, *Hymn* xxviii is addressed simply to Hermes, lvii to Hermes Chthonios; *Hymn* xv is addressed to Zeus, xix to Zeus Keraunios, and xx to Zeus Astrapios. Some seven hymns are addressed to Dionysus under one name or another—more than to any other deity. Most of the names in the list of eighty-seven are familar names of Greek cult or myth, including personal gods, personified abstractions, and natural phenomena. Some, however, are less familiar, such as Ἵππα (xlix) and Μίση (xlii). Each hymn, with ten exceptions, has a rubric appended to the title indicating the kind of incense that is prescribed for use in connection with it. One, addressed to Amphietes (liii), besides the incense, has also a regulation requiring a libation of milk.

The greater part of each hymn consists of a mere list of epithets and attributes, and the petition is confined to the last line or two. Most often the petition takes the form of a supplication that the deity addressed shall come among his worshipers in friendly and joyful mood. But the hymns contain, besides, prayers for many other blessings of the kind that men usually pray for—safety in general, peace, health, prosperity, and success; fair voyages; rain and good crops; protection from storms, earthquakes, and disease; a long and happy life, a comfortable old age, and a good end.

In some but by no means all of the hymns, there are words and phrases from the technical vocabulary of the mysteries.[3] Blessings are invoked on the *μύσται* in the closing petition of about a third of the hymns. The word *μυστιπόλοι* appears about six times. The language in three hymns suggests that they were to be sung at the initiation of new members: iv (Uranus) *κλῦθ' ἐπάγων ζωὴν ὁσίην μύστῃ νεοφάντῃ*; xliii (Horae) *ἔλθετ' ἐπ εὐφήμους τελετὰς ὁσίας νεομύστοις εὐκάρπους καιρῶν γενέσεις ἐπάγουσαι ἀμεμφῶς*; lxxxiv (Hestia) *τούσδε σὺ ἐν τελεταῖς ὁσίαις μύστας ἀναδείξαις*. Teletae are mentioned frequently, a *πάνθειος τελετή* three times (xxxv, liii, liv). *ὀργιοφάνταις* (vi) and *ὄργια νυκτιφαῆ* (liv) each appear once. The cult title *βουκόλος* is found twice, once in the hymn to Hecate (i) and in one of the hymns to the Curetes (xxxi).

Everything about the hymns, except what can be learned from the text itself, is a matter of speculation. Lobeck[4] found no allusion to them in ancient literature earlier than Tzetzes, Johannes Diaconus, and Constantine Lascaris. Their date and authorship and the purpose for which they were composed are all uncertain. A consideration of the substance of the hymns, the deities that are named, the theological and philosophical ideas, the significant omissions (e.g., there is no hint of emperor worship) have led various scholars to date them at various times between the second century B.C. and the fourth century A.D.[5] Wilamowitz[6] concludes from an anlysis of

[3] See esp. R. Schöll, "De communibus et collegiis quibusdam Graecorum," in *Satura Philologica Hermanno Sauppio oblata* (1879), pp. 167–180; A. Dieterich, *De hymnis Orphicis*, Diss. Marburg, 1891; W. Quandt, *De Baccho ab Alexandri aetate in Asia minore culto*, Diss. Halle, 1912, p. 254.

[4] *Aglaoph.*, I, 406.

[5] Cf. particularly Lobeck, *Aglaoph.*, I, 389–410; Dieterich, *op. cit.*; Otto Gruppe, in Roscher's *Lexikon*, s.v. Orpheus, p. 1149.

[6] *Der Glaube der Hellenen*, II (1932), 514.

the language and the versification that they cannot be earlier than the second century A.D., and agrees with Van Liempt[7] that the language is in general the same as that of the poets of the third and fourth centuries A.D.

It was Lobeck's opinion that the hymns which form the collection were a purely literary work produced by a scholar in his study. "I know of no festival," he says, "in which so many gods were worshiped."[8] Evidence, however, has come to light since his time, as we shall see, which would probably persuade him to alter his opinion. But even if we consider the hymns alone, we must acknowledge that their form, the prevalence of the technical language of the mysteries, and their inferior literary quality make it far more likely that they were intended for actual ritual use than that they were composed merely as a literary exercise.

If we seek to discover the purpose for which the hymns were intended, we must recognize immediately that there are two possibilities: the whole collection may have been intended for a single purpose, or the several hymns may have been intended for various purposes. If the latter is true, the several hymns would probably have been composed independently, by one or more persons, and subsequently brought together by an editor in the collection as we have it. On this supposition, though it is fairly clear that many of the hymns were composed for actual use in mysteries, we cannot be sure that this was true of all. Wilamowitz,[9] who like most other scholars believes that

---

[7] *De vocabulario hymnorum Orphicorum atque aetate* (1930). [8] *Aglaoph.*, I, 394.

[9] Wilamowitz, *Der Glaube der Hellenen*, II, 515; Kern, *R.-E.*, XVI, s.v. Mysterien, 1283.

the collection was the hymnbook of a single cult society, is disposed to think (and Kern agrees with him) that the poet composed hymns for more gods than the society regularly worshiped. This admission, that certain of the hymns do not really fit in the hymnbook of a cult society, lends a little support to the possibility that our collection was made by an editor who gathered the hymns from various quarters, some being ritual hymns used in the cult of various deities, some being purely literary productions. The other possibility is that the hymns may have formed a single book from the first, composed for a single purpose. A book so predominantly liturgical must have been intended for a state institution in a particular locality, or for a private religious organization which may have been confined to a particular locality or may have had chapters in various parts of the Greek world.

The next question is whether we can discover any state institution or private cult society for whose use the hymns may have been composed. Lobeck, as we have seen, was not aware of any, but the archaeology of the last fifty years has brought to light much that was unknown in his day. Excavations in western Asia Minor have revealed conditions in that part of the ancient world which scholars have been quick to bring into connection with the hymns.[10] Many inscriptions have been discovered containing names and epithets of gods which are also found in the hymns, and in particular they have supplied evidence of the cult of those deities in the hymns which are the least familiar in the Greek world. Many inscriptions also contain some

[10] Otto Kern, "Die Herkunft des orphischen Hymnenbuchs," in *Genethliakon für K. Robert* (Halle, 1910), pp. 89–101.

of the same technical terms of the mysteries which are also used in the hymns. These correspondences make it extremely probable that the hymns were produced for use in one or more mystery cults in western Asia Minor. This fact was established before the excavation of Pergamon by Austrian archaeologists. When the results of these excavations were published, Otto Kern was immediately convinced that he had discovered the actual cult place in which the hymns were used.[11] This place was the precinct of Demeter in Pergamon, in which, as the evidence shows, a mystery cult was maintained. The names of many deities appear in the inscriptions which have been found in this precinct, and among them many are identical with names in the hymns. Such are Νύξ, Ἀσκλήπιος, Athena Nikephoros, Hermes, Heracles, Helios, Ὁμόνοια, τῷ Πανθείῳ. One of the inscriptions has Ἄνεμοι, and there are hymns to Boreas, Zephyros, and Notos. A number of Eleusinian names appear in both hymns and precinct. The deities of the hymns which had already been recognized as Asiatic are also found in the precinct. It is a curious thing, however, that though there are a number of hymns to Dionysus, the precinct has shown no trace of his cult. Still, all these correspondences are striking enough; and since Kern pointed them out, many scholars have accepted his conclusion and are satisfied that our collection is the hymnbook which was used in the precinct of Demeter in Pergamum. The degree of probability is indeed high, but it must be acknowledged that the proof

[11] Otto Kern, "Das Demeterheiligtum von Pergamon und die orphische Hymnen," *Hermes*, XLVI (1911), 431. Quandt, *op. cit.*, adds a little to the evidence brought forward by Kern.

is not final. Wilamowitz, it may be noted, does not admit that the connection between the hymns and the precinct has been proved, though he fully agrees that the home of the hymns is western Asia Minor. What has been demonstrated beyond a doubt is that since there existed a mystery cult lodged in a single precinct but involving a large number of deities, there is no longer any reason to question the possibility that the collection of hymns as a whole was intended for use in such a cult, whether at Pergamon or elsewhere.

Whatever may have been the origin and purpose of the hymns, they are called in the manuscripts the *Hymns of Orpheus*. Who attributed them to the ancient legendary poet? One thinks at first of the possibility that it was an early editor of the collection who for one reason or another published as the work of Orpheus hymns which were anonymous. But it is more likely that they were known from the beginning as poems of Orpheus, that is, that their author or authors had brought them forth under his name. Several things go to show that they belong to the great body of Orphic poetry and were Orphic in the same sense that the other poems were. In the first place, the dedication to Musaeus was, as we have seen, a conventional device by which poets writing under the name of Orpheus gave their readers to understand that their work was Orphic. In the second place, the poet maintains the character of Orpheus by referring to Calliope as his mother, in the hymn to the Nereids (xxiv, 12, Καλλιόπῃ σὺν μητρὶ καὶ Ἀπόλλωνι ἄνακτι) and in the hymn to the Muses (lxxvi, 10, Καλλιόπῃ σὺν μητρὶ καὶ Εὐνομίῃ θεᾷ ἁγνῇ).

Thirdly, there are not a few reminiscences of other Orphic poetry in the language of the hymns, though not so many as some scholars have thought. Kern, who has made a careful examination,[12] finds them mostly in a few hymns, principally in the hymn to Protogonos (vi). Lastly, there may be some significance in the fact that in the margin of one of the manuscripts (cod. Laurentianus 32, 45) by the Εὐχὴ πρὸς Μουσαῖον is found the abbreviation ΘΫΗΠΟ̂.[13] In the Εὐχή itself the word θυηπολίην is used twice, in the first and last lines. Plato, in the *Republic* (ii, 364 E), uses the word θυηπολοῦσιν in connection with teletae. There is a possibility, therefore, that the title Θυηπολικόν, which is included by Suidas in his list of the works of Orpheus, belonged actually to the collection of hymns which is extant.

The question next arises, Why were the hymns attributed by their author or authors to Orpheus? Again we can discern two possibilities. One is that the hymns may have been intended for the use of a society which was in some sense itself Orphic either because it had been founded by Orpheus, or because it used his rites and rules of life, or because it believed in his doctrines. This view is widely accepted. "It was then an Orphic society," says Guthrie, "at least in so far as it was a cult-society, primarily Dionysiac and practising mysteries, which used the name of Orpheus as its patron." A little later he says: "The society was Dionysiac, and Orpheus was its saint, but it was a child of the age in that it was familiar with the

---

[12] "Zu den orphischen Hymnen," *Hermes*, XXIV (1889), 498–508.

[13] This is reported by Kern, *R.-E.*, XVI, s.v. Mysterien, 1283.

current philosophical ideas."[14] Now I submit that there is no evidence for believing that the society was primarily Dionysiac or that Orpheus was its patron or its saint. Guthrie himself is convinced that the home of the society was the precinct at Pergamon, and not only was this a precinct of Demeter, but no trace of Dionysus has been found within it. There are more hymns to Dionysus in the collection than to any other deity, but they do not form more than a tenth of the whole, which is a very small fraction in view of the predominance of Dionysus in mystery cults in general. As for Orpheus, he is nothing whatever but the ostensible author of the poems, neither patron nor saint nor founder—as far as anything in the hymns shows. The existence of parallels with other Orphic poetry proves nothing one way or the other: it is only natural that a poet writing under the name of Orpheus should be familiar with earlier Orphic poetry. The fact is that the only support for the statement that the society was an Orphic society is the unfounded assumption that all Orphic poetry was written for an Orphic society and that every society or cult for which or about which Orphic poetry was written was Orphic.

Still, acknowledging the possibility that the hymns were composed for an Orphic society, even though there is a total lack of proof, we proceed to consider the other possibility. This is that they were intended for a cult or cults which were no more Orphic than other mysteries. This possibility, it may at once be granted, cannot be proved any more than the other, on the basis of the hymns alone,

[14] *Orpheus and Greek Religion*, pp. 258, 259.

but it deserves equal consideration. It requires us to assume that the hymns were given to the world as the work of Orpheus in order to gain the prestige of his name, because he was looked upon as the founder and patron of mysteries in general and the supreme author of theological and liturgical poetry. It requires us to assume that there was a traditional practice of publishing such poetry independently and in connection with the cults of all kinds of deities, under the august name of Orpheus, with the fiction that it was addressed to Musaeus.

Now the decision between these two possibilities cannot be made on the basis of the hymns alone. The whole body of evidence is needed to establish a reasonable probability. But if we assume, for the sake of the whole argument, that there was an Orphic society whose hymnbook the collection was, we must recognize as characteristic of this Orphic society the features which have been described in the discussion of the hymns. It maintained a mystery cult addressed to a very large number of deities, among whom no one can be called really preëminent. It had a ritual involving the use of hymns, incense, and libations. It prayed to its gods to come among them in propitious mood, and it prayed to them for a great variety of purely worldly benefits. The hymns show no hint of any kind of asceticism and no hint of any concern for the afterlife.

## DEMETER AND PERSEPHONE

We have already seen that the author of the *Rhesus* credited Orpheus with the foundation of certain honored mysteries of Persephone at Athens. It may be noted that one of the *Orphic Hymns* (xl) is addressed to Demeter Eleusinia, and that another (xxix) is addressed to Persephone. A number of other texts also show that Orpheus was understood to have been active in the cult of these goddesses.

A passage in Diodorus (i, 96 = *Test.* 96 and *Fragm.* 293), which is very instructive concerning the general conception of Orpheus, represents him as having introduced rites of Dionysus and Demeter from Egypt.[15] It will be recalled that, according to Ephorus, he learned his arts from the Phrygian Dactyls. The theory that Orpheus, like other great Greeks, obtained his instruction in Egypt is a matter which need not concern us at this point in the discussion; we can be quite sure that what he was supposed to have learned there is what was actually attributed to him in Greek tradition.

What Diodorus says is this. The Egyptian priests assert that many of the Greeks who were distinguished for their intellectual attainments studied in Egypt. They name in particular a dozen men, of whom Orpheus is one, and they point out in some detail what each one of them learned. Of Orpheus they say that he carried back with him from their country most of the features of the mystic rites, the ritual of the various religious ceremonies that he encountered in his travels, and the mythological account of Hades. They mention in particular the fact that the rite of Dionysus is the same as that of Osiris, and that the rite of Demeter is very similar to that of Isis (Ὀρφέα μὲν γὰρ τῶν

[15] It is most probable that Diodorus' source here was Hecataeus of Abdera, who visited Egypt in the reign of the first Ptolemy (Schwartz, *R.-E.*, V, 670 s.v. Diodorus).

μυστικῶν τελετῶν τὰ πλεῖστα καὶ τὰ περὶ τὴν ἑαυτοῦ[16] πλάνην ὀργιαζόμενα καὶ τὴν τῶν ἐν Ἅιδου μυθοποιίαν ἀπενέγκασθαι. τὴν μὲν γὰρ Ὀσίριδος τελετὴν τῇ Διονύσου τὴν αὐτὴν εἶναι, τὴν δὲ τῆς Ἴσιδος τῇ τῆς Δήμητρος ὁμοιοτάτην ὑπάρχειν, τῶν ὀνομάτων μόνον ἐνηλλαγμένων).

Diodorus has much more to say concerning the debt of Greek religion to Egypt, especially in connection with the myth of Hades and the achievements of Melampus and Pythagoras, but enough has been quoted for our present purpose.

Stripped of the notion of Egyptian origins, this means that Greek mystic rites in general and various types of ritual were understood to have been instituted by Orpheus, and that among them were rites of Dionysus and rites of Demeter. The latter particularly are mentioned because their striking resemblance to certain Egyptian institutions makes them most apt as evidence to support the theory of Egyptian origin. The rites of Demeter, it should be observed, are definitely distinguished from the rites of Dionysus. If this had not been made clear, the reader who was aware of the close association of Isis and Osiris in Egyptian story would have been led to think that Greek rites were meant, the myth of which involved both Dionysus and Demeter. The identity which is asserted between the Egyptian rite of Osiris and the Greek rite of Dionysus makes it probable that the Greek rite intended was that which was concerned with the dismemberment of Dionysus. What rite of Demeter is re-

---

[16] It has been proposed to change ἑαυτοῦ to Δήμητρος, but this is arbitrary. πλάνη is a normal word for travel (cf. Herodotus i, 30, 2).

ferred to, it is difficult to say; but perhaps the point of resemblance lay in the search which was common to the Egyptian story and the Greek story, the search of Isis for Osiris and the search of Demeter for Persephone. This limited resemblance may be the cause for asserting that the rites of Isis and the rites of Demeter were only "very similar" (ὁμοιοτάτην), whereas those of Osiris and Dionysus were identical (τὴν αὐτήν). If this is so, the writer probably has in mind the mysteries of Eleusis. In any case, rites of Dionysus, rites of Demeter, mysteries in general, and certain types of ritual are all Orphic in the sense that they had been instituted by Orpheus.

Pausanias tells of two cults of Demeter and one of Kore in Laconia with which Orpheus was associated. In Sparta there was a cult of Demeter Chthonia, which the Spartans, as they themselves maintained (though Pausanias thinks they were wrong), had received from Orpheus (παραδόντος σφίσιν Ὀρφέως Paus. iii, 14, 5 = *Test.* 108); and on Mount Taygetus there was a precinct of Demeter Eleusinia, in which was an ancient image (ξόανον) of Orpheus, reputedly of Pelasgian workmanship (Paus. iii, 20, 5 = *Test.* 145). In Sparta, again, there was a temple of Kore Soteira, which according to one tradition had been built by Orpheus of Thrace, according to another by Abaris (Paus. iii, 13, 2 = *Test.* 109).

There were Orphic poems which told the myth of the rape of Persephone, and Orpheus as poet seems to have had some significant connection with Eleusis. This appears particularly in two texts where Orphic poems and Eleusinian rites are brought together.

The first of these is that portion of the inscription on the *Parian Marble* which records the events connected with the institution of the Eleusinian Mysteries (Jacoby, *Griechische Historiker*, 2 B, p. 995 = *Test.* 221, 161). Here it is stated that 1146 years before the date of the inscription (264/3 B.C.) Demeter came to Athens and instituted the cultivation of corn, and the first *προηροσία* was performed under the direction of Triptolemus. In the next year Triptolemus reaped the crop which he had sown in the Rharian plain. Ten years later Orpheus produced the poem in which he told of the rape of Persephone and the search of Demeter.[17] In the following year Eumolpus proclaimed the mysteries in Eleusis (*τὰ μυστήρια ἀνέφηνεν ἐν Ἐλευσῖνι*) and published the poetry of his father Musaeus.[18] The significant things in the version of the legends about the founding of the Eleusinian Mysteries adopted by the author of the inscription are these. Though Orpheus is not represented as the founder of the mysteries, he is accorded a prominent part in the series of events connected with the foundation. He appears as the author of the poem in which the sacred story was told, and this poem was produced before the actual institution of the

[17] The name of Orpheus has been restored here, but Jacoby regards the restoration as certain. The latter part of the paragraph concerning Orpheus, which evidently gives further specifications concerning the contents of the poem, is badly mutilated and has not been successfully restored.

[18] A lacuna after the name of Eumolpus has been tentatively filled by Diels with the words *ὁ Μουσαίου τοῦ ἀπ' Ὀρφέως τετελεσμένου.* This is rejected by Jacoby because if Eumolpus founded the mysteries his father could not have been initiated in them by Orpheus. The restoration is, indeed, quite uncertain, but not on the ground alleged by Jacoby. Musaeus might well have been supposed to have received some form of initiation from Orpheus before the Eleusinian rites were instituted.

mysteries. The function of Orpheus was that of the poet who gave form to the ἱερὸς λόγος.

The second text in which Orpheus is represented as the poet of the Eleusinian Mysteries is in Clement of Alexandria (*Protrept.* ii, 20, 1 – 21, 1 Stählin = *Fragm.* 52). Here Clement tells the story of Demeter and Baubo as an example of the obscenity of Greek mythology. "This," he then adds, "is the sacred myth of the mysteries. It is also recorded by Orpheus; and that you may have the μυσταγωγός as a witness to the obscenity I shall quote his own words." Five hexameters follow. The poem from which these lines were taken, whatever practical use may have been made of it, seems to have been regarded, in some sense, as the official version of the sacred myth. It is by virtue of his function as poet that Orpheus is called *mystagogos*, and not because he took an active part in the ritual.

A curious passage in Proclus represents Orpheus as highly honored at Eleusis. He recalls Socrates' words in Plato's *Apology* (41 A) where he says that it will mean much to him to meet Orpheus, Musaeus, and Ajax in Hades, and by way of explanation of this he suggests that Socrates must have "heard the mysteries at Eleusis singing the praises of him who had revealed the most holy rites" (ἤκουεν γὰρ που καὶ τῶν ἐν Ἐλευσῖνι μυστηρίων ἐξυμνούντων τὸν τὰς ἁγιωτάτας ἐκφήναντα τελετάς, *In Plat. Rempublicam* ii, 312, 16 Kroll = *Test.* 102). The language recalls that of the *Rhesus* and of Ps.-Demosthenes xxv, 11. Whether the "most holy rites" thus mentioned were those of Eleusis in particular, or whether they were mystic rites in general, Proclus, who was steeped in Orphic poetry, has no hesitation about associating Orpheus with Eleusis.

Another author at the end of antiquity states explicitly that Orpheus instituted the Eleusinian Mysteries. Theodoretus (386–456 A.D.), one of the last ancient doctors of the church, writes (*Graecarum affectionum curatio* i, 21, p. 10, 10 Raeder = *Test.* 103): "The rites (τελεταί) of the Dionysia, the Panathenaea, the Thesmophoria, and the Eleusinia were introduced into Athens by Orpheus. He also went to Egypt and transformed the rites (ὄργια) of Isis and Osiris into the rites of Deo and Dionysus. This we learn from Plutarch and Diodorus. Demosthenes, too, alludes to the subject, saying that Orpheus instituted the most holy rites (τελεταί) in Athens." We have already seen the texts in Demosthenes (xxv, 11) and Diodorus (i, 96) which are probably referred to; the passage in Plutarch has not been discovered in his extant works. We are not here concerned with the truth or falsity of Theodoretus' statement, but only with the conception it reveals concerning Orpheus and the kind of institutions that were associated with his name. The tradition, as Theodoretus understands it, is that he introduced the rites of four great Athenian state festivals, and that he adapted to Greek use the rites of Isis and Osiris. The deities who were principally honored in these festivals were Dionysus, Athena, Demeter, and Persephone. The conception of Orpheus that prevailed seems to have been that of an expert in religious ritual, who employed his skill in a wide range of religious institutions.

That Orpheus was thought to have played some part at Eleusis is shown by the texts which have been cited. These texts are scattered over a period of nearly a thousand years. They do not all agree concerning what he had actually done. The earliest, in the *Rhesus*, where it was important to emphasize his benefactions, uses language which suggests, but does not assert, that he was the sole founder of the mysteries. The latest, in Theodoretus, states bluntly that he had introduced them. The *Parian Marble* presents what must have been regarded as a more accurate statement of the facts: Eumolpus established the mysteries, Orpheus composed the poem in which the cult myth was told; and Clement of Alexandria quotes from the poem as the authoritative version of the myth. Proclus indicates that Orpheus was held in high honor at Eleusis, and a slight connection with Eleusis appears also in Diodorus (iv, 25, 1), who says that when Heracles was initiated, Musaeus, the son of Orpheus, presided at the rite. The truth probably is that the native legends at Eleusis were too well established to permit a general belief that he was the founder of the mysteries. But, in view of his fame as a poet and as an organizer of mystic rites, it is not surprising that a few writers should have found some place for him at Eleusis. It is most significant that the notion does not anywhere appear that he introduced something alien or novel into the mysteries. There is no hint that there were two institutions, the Eleusinian Mysteries and Orphic Mysteries, and that the influence of the latter had brought about some transformation in the former. Whatever Orpheus did he did at the beginning, and the Eleusinian Mysteries were Orphic only so far as he had had some part in their institution. This appears to have been the ancient view. The question of Orphic influence at Eleusis, which is much debated by modern scholars, is another matter. To answer it we must know first just what may have exercised this influence in the name of Orpheus, and this is what we are searching for at present.[19]

### EROS AND THE MYSTERIES OF THE LYCOMIDAE

The Athenian family of the Lycomidae, whose seat was in the deme of Phlya,[20] maintained a mystic cult with which Orpheus seems to have been associated, somewhat as he was with the mysteries at Eleusis. The evidence concerning this curious matter, which comes from Pausanias and Hippolytus, should here be examined in some detail.

From one passage in Pausanias (ix, 27, 2 = *Fragm.* 305) we learn that he himself had had an opportunity to read, at the cult place of the Lycomidae, certain poems which the Lycomidae sang in their rites. These, he says, were hymns in epic verse addressed to Eros, and he asserts that they had been composed by Pamphos and Orpheus. Presumably, there was one hymn by Orpheus and one hymn by Pamphos.

Pausanias was convinced, as he informs us in another

[19] Cf. L. Malten, "Altorphische Demetersage," *Archiv für Religionswissenschaft*, XII (1909), 417–446; Wilamowitz, *Der Glaube der Hellenen*, II (1932), 47 ff.; Georges Méautis, *L'âme hellénique d'après les vases grecs* (Paris, 1932), pp. 165–189.

[20] The connection between the Lycomidae and Phlya is proved by Plutarch, *Them.* 1, 112 A. Pausanias (i, 31, 4) gives a list of the cults of Phlya.

passage (ix, 30, 12 = *Fragm.* 304), that the hymns of Orpheus were few in number and brief, and he considered them to be inferior to the hymns of Homer in poetical quality, though superior to them from a religious point of view. The Lycomidae, he says, sing them in their rites. Apparently he thought there were no other hymns of Orpheus except just these. There may, however, have been other hymns generally attributed to Orpheus, the authenticity of which was denied by him, since we know from other statements of his that he was disposed to deny the authenticity of Orphic poems. Perhaps he was persuaded by the authority of the ancient cult of the Lycomidae to admit the authenticity of the Orphic poems which were in their possession. The comparison with Homer suggests that these hymns of the Lycomidae stood in the same relation to the Homeric hymns as that in which an ancient xoanon stood to a cult statue of Pheidias: they were cruder and more primitive, but hallowed by age and the uses of religion.

From two other passages in Pausanias (i, 22, 7, and iv, 1, 5) we learn that the Lycomidae had a hymn to Demeter, which they believed to have been composed for them by Musaeus. This hymn he regarded as the only poem which could be ascribed to Musaeus with certainty. It would seem that he admitted its authenticity for the same reason that he admitted the authenticity of the Orphic hymns of the Lycomidae.

So much is in Pausanias, and we may conclude that in his day there were sung in the ancient rites of the Lycomidae at Phlya a hymn to Demeter, supposed to have been composed by Musaeus, a hymn to Eros, supposed to have been composed by Pamphos, and several hymns supposed to have been composed by Orpheus, of which one was addressed to Eros and the others (presumably) to other deities. *Orphic Hymn* lviii is also addressed to Eros, but there is no reason to suppose that the two are the same.

Hippolytus, in Book V of the *Refutatio omnium haeresium*, discusses certain gnostic sects in whose lore the snake plays an important part, and he undertakes to show that this lore was obtained, not from the Bible, but from pagan authors. The third sect to be examined is that of the Sethiani (v, 20, 4, p. 121, 21 Wendland = *Fragm.* 243). "Their whole doctrine," he says, "is derived from the ancient theologians Musaeus, Linus, and Orpheus, the last of whom was more active than anyone else in the institution of rites and mysteries" (ἔστι δὲ αὐτοῖς ἡ πᾶσα διδασκαλία τοῦ λόγου ἀπὸ τῶν παλαιῶν θεολόγων, Μουσαίου καὶ Λίνου καὶ τοῦ τὰς τελετὰς μάλιστα καὶ τὰ μυστήρια καταδείξαντος Ὀρφέως).

In the passage that follows there are some difficulties in the interpretation, and it will be necessary to transcribe the whole text: ὁ γὰρ περὶ τῆς μήτρας αὐτῶν καὶ τοῦ ὄφεως λόγος καὶ ⟨ὁ⟩ ὀμφαλός, ὅπερ ἐστὶν ἀνδρεία, διαρρήδην οὕτως ἐστὶν ἐν τοῖς Βακχικοῖς τοῦ Ὀρφέως. τετέλεσται δὲ ταῦτα καὶ παραδέδοται ἀνθρώποις πρὸ τῆς Κελεοῦ καὶ Τριπτολέμου καὶ Δήμητρος καὶ Κόρης καὶ Διονύσου ἐν Ἐλευσῖνι τελετῆς, ἐν Φλιοῦντι τῆς Ἀττικῆς· πρὸ γὰρ τῶν Ἐλευσινίων μυστηρίων ἔστιν ἐν τῇ Φλιοῦντι ⟨τῆς⟩ λεγομένης Μεγάλης ὄργια. ἔστι δὲ παστὰς ἐν αὐτῇ, ἐπὶ δὲ τῆς παστάδος ἐγγέγραπται μέχρι σήμερον ἡ [τὰ τῶν] πάντων τῶν εἰρημένων λόγων ἰδέα. πολλὰ μὲν οὖν ἐστι τὰ ἐπὶ τῆς παστάδος ἐκείνης ἐγγεγραμμένα, περὶ ὧν Πλούταρχος ποιεῖται λόγους ἐν ταῖς πρὸς Ἐμπεδοκλέα δέκα βιβλίοις· ἔστι δὲ κτλ. Here follows a description of the pictures and inscriptions. In the first line the manuscript reading is τοῦ Ὀρφέως λόγος. Schneidewin's emendation, τοῦ ὄφεως λόγος, which has been accepted by Wendland, is altogether more satisfactory; but, in any case, the uncertainty of the reading does not affect the present discussion.

The first sentence is translated by Tannery[21] as follows: "Car ce qu'ils disent, ainsi qu'Orphée, sur la matrice et l'ὀμφαλός (*hoc est virilia*), se retrouve clairement et comme suit (οὕτως) dans les rites bachiques (ἐν τοῖς Βακχικοῖς) d'Orphée. Ces rites ont été pratiqués et enseignés aux hommes etc." This interpretation is unsatisfactory for several reasons. In the first place, Bacchic rites of Orpheus cannot, so far as we know, have formed any part of the mysteries at Phlya. Tannery himself admits this when he says: "Ce qui suit se rapporte exclusivement à d'anciens mystères locaux. C'est tout à fait gratuitement que notre auteur considère ces mystères comme *bachiques*, et, du même coup, comme institués par Orphée." In the second place, διαρρήδην is an adverb more appropriate to modify the form of a communication made through a written statement than one made through a piece of ritual. In the third place, οὕτως is strangely placed if it means "as follows," and δέ in the next sentence is inappropriate if the sentence is to fulfill the promise of

[21] *Rev. de philologie*, XXIV (1900), 97 ff.

οὕτως. It is better to take οὕτως as referring to what precedes, and to understand τοῖς Βακχικοῖς as the Orphic poem called *Bacchica*, which is alluded to in a number of texts.[22] The meaning, then, will be: "For what they say about the womb and the snake, as well as the navel, may be found, explicitly in these terms, in the *Bacchica* of Orpheus."

The next sentence goes on to state that the doctrines under discussion (ταῦτα) are to be found also in the ancient mysteries of the Lycomidae at Phlya (Phlyus is plainly a mistake for Phlya). "All this was enacted ritually and thus given to the world at Phlya in Attica before the Eleusinian rite of Celeus, Triptolemus, Demeter, Kore, and Dionysus; for the rites of Megale, as she is called, in Phlya were earlier than the Eleusinian Mysteries."

Next Hippolytus repeats after Plutarch the description of certain pictures and inscriptions at Phlya, in which, he believes, are represented the same ideas and figures that belong to the doctrines of the Sethiani. It would seem that he obtained his evidence to prove that these doctrines were derived from pagan sources either entirely or in part from Plutarch. The Orphic *Bacchica* he may have read for himself, or he may have known something of its contents from allusions and citations in Plutarch.

The myth, then, which Hippolytus believed to be identical with the doctrinal myth of the Sethiani was presented in three forms of art. It was enacted in the ritual

[22] See Kern, *Orphicorum Fragmenta*, pp. 248 ff.

of the mysteries; it was illustrated by pictures on the walls of the sacred building; it was narrated, either the whole of it or significant parts of it, in an Orphic poem. Though it is not expressly said that the mysteries were instituted by Orpheus, it is clearly suggested that he had some part in their institution. The situation is similar to that presented by the *Parian Marble* in connection with the Eleusinian Mysteries. In each case Orpheus is credited with the composition of the poem in which the cult myth is told. In the *Parian Marble* the poem precedes the mysteries. Here, too, the understanding may have been that the myth with its doctrinal implication was first promulgated by Orpheus in his poem, and that the mysteries, when they were organized, presented the same in ritualistic form.[23] About this we cannot be sure. What we learn with certainty from Pausanias and Hippolytus is that Orpheus was associated with the mysteries of the Lycomidae in two ways: an Orphic hymn to Eros and other Orphic hymns were used in them, and the myth of the goddess called Megale, which belonged to them, was told in the Orphic *Bacchica*.

## HECATE

The principal cult in Aegina, according to Pausanias (ii, 30, 2 = *Test.* 110), was that of Hecate, in whose honor a rite (τελετή) was celebrated annually. That this was a

[23] It is not necessary for the present purpose to examine this most interesting cult more closely. For the whole subject see Toepffer, *Attische Genealogie*, pp. 208 ff.; Tannery, *Rev. de philologie*, XXIV (1900), 97 ff.; J. E. Harrison, *Prolegomena*, pp. 641–646; Harriet B. Hawes, "The Ludovisi Throne and the Boston Relief," *Am. Jour. Archaeol.*, XXVI (1922), 278 ff.

mystic cult and involved initiation appears from Origen (*Contra Celsum* vi, 22, ed. Koetschau II, 93, 8) and Libanius (*Orat. pro Aristoph.* xiv, 5). The Aeginetans maintained, as Pausanias also tells us, that the rite had been established by Orpheus (Ὀρφέα σφίσι τὸν Θρᾷκα καταστήσασθαι τὴν τελετὴν λέγοντες).

### RHEA

That Orpheus was supposed to have had some part in the institution of religious rites in Phrygia is suggested by several texts.

In the story told by Apollonius of Rhodes (*Argon.* i, 1134 ff.) the Argonauts, being delayed by storms at Mount Dindymus, were directed by Mopsus, in consequence of a dream of Jason, to conciliate Rhea. Among the ceremonies performed for this purpose was a dance which was recommended by Orpheus (not by Mopsus). One feature of the dance, the use of the rhombos and the tympanum, continued ever after in the rites with which the Phrygians worshiped Rhea (ἔνθεν ἐσαιεὶ ῥόμβῳ καὶ τυπάνῳ Ῥείην Φρύγες ἱλάσκονται). Whether this bit of aetiology was original with Apollonius or not, Orpheus appears in his regular role as an organizer of religious ritual.

There was also a legend that Midas had been a pupil of Orpheus, and that in particular he had been taught religious rites by him, which he then introduced into Phrygia. So in Conon (fr. 1 Jacoby = *Test.* 160 Ὀρφέως κατὰ Πιέρειαν τὸ ὄρος ἀκροατὴς γενόμενος), in Ovid (*Met.* xi, 92 = *Test.* 160 cui Thracius Orpheus orgia tradiderat cum Cecropio Eumolpo), in Justinus (*Hist. Phil. epit.* xi, 7,

14 = *Test.* 160 Mida . . . ab Orpheo sacrorum sollemnibus initiatus Phrygiam religionibus inplevit), and in Clement of Alexandria (*Protrept.* ii, 13, 3 Stählin = *Test.* 160 ὁ Φρὺξ ἐκεῖνος ὁ Μίδας, ὁ παρὰ τοῦ 'Οδρύσου μαθών, ἔπειτα διαδοὺς τοῖς ὑποτεταγμένοις ἔντεχνον ἀπάτην).

Ephorus (ap. Diod. v, 64 = *Test.* 42), on the other hand, tells how the Idaean Dactyls came to Samothrace and impressed the natives greatly with their incantations and mysteries, and how Orpheus became their pupil and was the first to introduce mysteries into Greece.

It may be mentioned, also, that *Orphic Hymn* xiv is addressed to Rhea.

## GODS OF SAMOTHRACE

There is no evidence that Orpheus was ever credited with any part in the institution and maintenance of the Samothracian mysteries, but he is brought into connection with them several times in the Argonautic legend.

According to Apollonius of Rhodes (*Argon.* i, 915), it was on the advice of Orpheus that the heroes landed in Samothrace and were initiated in the mysteries as an insurance of safety amidst the dangers of the sea. This is the only association of Orpheus with mysteries of any kind in the whole poem, though he acts as the adviser of the heroes in religious matters on many occasions.

Diodorus (iv, 43 = *Test.* 105) relates that when a great storm arose and the heroes despaired of their lives, Orpheus, the only one among them who had taken part in the Samothracian rites, offered prayers for safety to the gods of those rites. The storm abated, and two stars settled on the heads of the Dioscuri. Thereafter, sailors in stormy weather always offered their prayers to the Samothracians. Thus, though Orpheus had no connection with the rites except as an initiate, he originated the sailors' custom of praying to the Cabiri in a storm.

In the Orphic *Argonautica* (466 ff. = *Test.* 105), also, it is said that the heroes landed, on the advice of Orpheus, at Samothrace, where awful and secret rites are performed, because these rites were helpful to men and especially to sailors.

### HELIOS AND APOLLO

Early indications of a legendary association between Orpheus and Apollo have already been cited in the first chapter. One text in particular, in the *Catasterismi*, which was attributed to Eratosthenes (24, p. 140 Robert = *Test.* 113), was quoted for what it reveals about the part of Orpheus in a lost play of Aeschylus, but reasons were given for not attributing all that it contains to Aeschylus. In the part, however, which we cannot venture to claim for Aeschylus it is said that Orpheus refused honor to Dionysus and paid his worship to the Sun, whom he called Apollo and held to be the greatest of gods. He used to rise at night and ascend Mount Pangaeum in order to get a first glimpse of the rising sun. The consequence was that Dionysus in anger sent the Bassarides to tear him to pieces.

According to Macrobius (*Saturn.* i, 18, 22 = *Fragm.* 238; cf. also *Fragm.* 239 and 236), on the other hand, Orpheus declared Dionysus and the Sun to be one and the same god and described his vestments in the sacra

Liberalia (item Orpheus Liberum atque Solem unum esse deum eundemque demonstrans de ornatu vestituque eius in sacris Liberalibus ita scribit—here follow twelve hexameters from an Orphic poem). The phrase "in sacris Liberalibus" may belong with the preceding words, so that the meaning is "the vestments used in the rites," or it may be the name of the poem from which the quotation is taken. In either case, liturgical directions for Dionysiac rites are found in an Orphic poem, and in these rites Dionysus and Helios are conceived to be identical.

Hermeias (*In Plat. Phaedrum* 244 A, p. 88, 26 Couvreur = *Test.* 171) says that the tradition about Orpheus represents him as supreme in ritual and prophecy and inspired by Apollo (τελεστικώτατον μὲν γὰρ αὐτὸν καὶ μαντικώτατον παρειλήφαμεν καὶ ὑπὸ τοῦ Ἀπόλλωνος κινούμενον).

*Orphic Hymn* viii is addressed to Helios, and xxxiv to Apollo.

DIONYSUS

In some of the texts already cited the rites of Dionysus have been mentioned in connection with Orpheus. According to Diodorus (i, 96) there was a rite, identical with that of the Egyptian Osiris, which had been imported into Greece by Orpheus; this was probably the rite involving the dismemberment of Dionysus. In the legend told in Ps.-Eratosthenes, *Catasterismi* 24, Orpheus refused to honor Dionysus, and in consequence the god sent the Bassarides to tear him to pieces. According to Macrobius (*Saturn.* i, 18, 22), Orpheus in one of his poems declared Dionysus and the Sun to be one and the same god and described his vestments. Seven of the

*Orphic Hymns* are addressed to Dionysus under various names: xxx Dionysus, xlv Dionysus Bassareus Trieterikos, xlvi Liknites, xlvii Perikionios, l Lysios Lenaios, lii Trieterikos, liii Amphietes. Theodoretus (*Graec. affect. cur.* i, 21) states that Orpheus introduced the Dionysia into Athens and transformed the rites of Osiris into the rites of Dionysus. Elsewhere, in another text, which may be introduced here for convenience, Theodoretus refers again to the importation of Egyptian rites into Greece. Speaking of the cult of the phallus, he says that Orpheus learned it in Egypt, transferred it to Greece, and established the festival of Dionysus (*Graec. affect. cur.* i, 114, p. 31, 24 Raeder = *Test.* 100 *ταῦτα ἐκ τῆς Αἰγύπτου τὰ ὄργια μαθὼν ὁ Ὀδρύσης Ὀρφεὺς εἰς τὴν Ἑλλάδα μετήνεγκε καὶ τὴν τῶν Διονυσίων ἑορτὴν διεσκεύασεν*).

The texts now to be presented are arranged in approximately chronological order, though some are removed from their proper places because of their close association with texts of other dates.

It will be recalled that in the evidence earlier than 300 B.C. no association of Orpheus with Dionysiac rites could be clearly made out. The earliest text in which this association is indubitable is a short elegiac poem of eight lines by Damagetus in the third century B.C. (*Anth. Pal.* vii, 9 = *Test.* 126). The poem recites some of the incidents of the legend of Orpheus and in the fifth line contains the statement that he was the originator of the rites of Bacchus (*τελετὰς μυστηρίδας εὕρετο Βάκχου*). Similarly explicit statements are made by Apollodorus (*Bibl.* i, 15 Wagner = *Test.* 63 *εὗρε δὲ Ὀρφεὺς καὶ τὰ Διονύσου μυστήρια*), by Pomponius Mela (ii, 17 = *Test.* 33 montes interior [sc. Thracia] adtollit Haemon et Rhodopen et Orbelon, sacris Liberi patris et coetu Maenadum, Orpheo primum initiante, celebratos), and by Lactantius (*Divin. Inst.* i, 22, 15–16 Brandt = *Test.* 99 sacra Liberi patris primus Orpheus induxit in Graecia primusque celebrauit in monte Boeotiae Thebis ubi Liber natus est proximo; qui cum frequenter citharae cantu personaret, Cithaeron appellatus est. ea sacra etiamnunc Orphica nominantur, in quibus ipse postea dilaceratus et carptus est).

Another text which may be as early as the third century B.C. tells a story which brings Orpheus into connection with Dionysiac worship in a curious way. This is found in the little book by Palaephatus called Περὶ ἀπίστων (xxxiii = *Mythographi Graeci*, III, 2, p. 50 Festa). The authorship and date of this work, which are discussed at length by Festa, are uncertain, but it may have been composed by a Palaephatus who, according to Suidas, had heard Aristotle. Since the text is not included in Kern's collection, it may be quoted in full: Ψευδὴς καὶ ὁ περὶ τοῦ Ὀρφέως μῦθος, ὅτι κιθαρίζοντι αὐτῷ ἐφείπετο τετράποδα καὶ ἑρπετὰ καὶ ὄρνεα καὶ δένδρα. δοκεῖ δέ μοι ταῦτα εἶναι. Βάκχαι μανεῖσαι πρόβατα διέσπασαν ἐν τῇ Πιερίᾳ, πολλὰ δὲ καὶ ἄλλα βιαίως εἰργάζοντο τρεπόμεναί τε εἰς τὸ ὄρος διέτριβον ἐκεῖ τὰς ἡμέρας. ὡς δὲ ἔμειναν, οἱ πολῖται, δεδιότες περὶ τῶν γυναικῶν καὶ θυγατέρων, μεταπεμψάμενοι τὸν Ὀρφέα μηχανήσασθαι ἐδέοντο, ὃν τρόπον καταγάγοι ἀπὸ τοῦ ὄρους αὐτάς. ὁ δὲ θυσάμενος τῷ Διονύσῳ ὄργια κατάγει αὐτὰς βακχευούσας κιθαρίζων. αἱ δὲ νάρθηκας τότε πρῶτον ἔχουσαι κατέβαινον ἐκ τοῦ ὄρους καὶ κλῶνας δένδρων παντοδαπῶν· τοῖς δὲ ἀνθρώποις τότε *θεασαμένοις τὰ ξύλα θαυμαστὰ ἐφαίνετο καὶ ἔφασαν· "Ὀρφεὺς κιθαρίζων ἄγει ἐκ τοῦ ὄρους καὶ τὴν ὕλην." καὶ ἐκ τούτου ὁ μῦθος ἐπλάσθη.*

This offers an interesting rationalization of the miracle in the legend of Orpheus which told how beasts, birds, creeping things, and trees followed him when he played upon his lyre. To accomplish this rationalization the author brings to bear certain data that are in his possession. He knows that the legend represented Orpheus as a kind of medicine man, a mantis, to whom one could go for aid in strange cases, like the Orpheus in the *Argonautica* of Apollonius of Rhodes. He knows, of course, the story of the Bacchae and their violent conduct in the hills, a story that appears in manifold settings. He knows, besides, that there were Dionysiac rites of a regulated type involving processions of worshipers carrying boughs. Such *δενδροφορίαι* are mentioned by Strabo (x, 3, 10) and elsewhere. The common feature of the moving trees, in the *δενδροφορίαι* and in the legend of Orpheus, suggested to him the origin of the story of Orpheus' miraculous powers, and the explanation would have seemed all the more probable if the Bacchae in the regulated rites followed a leader, as they probably did. It is not essential to the explanatory tale that Orpheus should be supposed to have had some connection with Dionysiac rites. The women were Bacchae before he was called in, and the performances in the mountains were not originated by him. It is true that he performs certain ceremonies in honor of Dionysus (*θυσάμενος τῷ Διονύσῳ ὄργια*) before he leads the women homeward. But this is only a natural preliminary to his trying what he can do with votaries of Dionysus. It is a way of meeting them on their own ground, so that he may have a chance of bringing them under the influence of his music. The story recognizes Orpheus as a mantis and perhaps credits him with the invention of *δενδροφορίαι*, but from this text alone one would not suppose that Orpheus was closely associated in any way with Dionysiac rites.

At the end of the first century B.C., Diodorus in his history of the world brings together many of the speculative theories which had been produced during the three preceding centuries to explain the origins of the ancient myths. The various theories, as he presents them, are not always consistent, nor does he make any great effort to bring them into harmony. Sometimes the source of a theory can be determined, but often it is quite impossible to say where he found it. The myths of Dionysus come in for a particularly large share of attention, and he returns to the subject in a number of different places. In four of the passages in which he deals with Dionysiac myths, Orpheus is mentioned in connection with them. One of these (i, 96) has already been presented (p. 190); the other three must now be studied in some detail.

The first is the twenty-third chapter of the first book. Here, as in i, 96, Orpheus is said to have traveled in Egypt and to have had a part in the institution of a rite of Dionysus which was based on the worship of Osiris. But here there is no hint that the Greek rite was the one involving the dismemberment of Dionysus; indeed, the resemblance between the Greek and Egyptian rites seems to have lain in quite a different feature. The circumstantial story which Diodorus tells is this (i, 23 = *Test.* 95).

Cadmus, who was a native of Thebes in Egypt and familiar with the religious customs of his own land, changed his residence to Thebes in Boeotia. Here his daughter Semele gave birth, at seven months, to a stillborn child. He, observing that the child was exactly like Osiris as the Egyptians conceived him to have been at his birth, recognized an epiphany of Osiris. So he gilded the child's body, performed appropriate sacrifices, and gave it out that the father of the child was Zeus. In consequence, it was reported in the Greek world that Semele, the daughter of Cadmus, had given birth to Osiris, and that Zeus was the father. Long afterward Orpheus enters the story. He enjoyed a great reputation in Greece for his gift of song, for his skill in religious ritual, and for his knowledge of the gods (i, 23, 6 *μεγάλην ἔχοντα δόξαν παρὰ τοῖς Ἕλλησιν ἐπὶ μελῳδίᾳ καὶ τελεταῖς καὶ θεολογίαις*). On one occasion he made a journey to Egypt, took part there in the Dionysiac mysteries, and on his return to Greece repaired to Thebes in Boeotia, where he was received with great honor. Here he heard the old story of Semele and her child, and wishing to gratify the people of Thebes, he brought the birth of the original Osiris, which had occurred thousands of years before, to the time of Cadmus and made Semele the mother of the *original* Osiris. The means by which he accomplished this was to institute a new rite in which the initiates were told that Dionysus was the son of Semele and Zeus (i, 23, 7 *ἐνστήσασθαι καινὴν τελετήν, καθ' ἣν παραδοῦναι τοῖς μυουμένοις ἐκ Σεμέλης καὶ*

*Διὸς γεγεννῆσθαι τὸν Διόνυσον*). The people did not perceive the fraud and were delighted to adopt the new rite because it made the god a Greek. The notion that Dionysus was the son of Zeus and Semele was then taken up by the mythographers and poets; it was constantly repeated in the theaters; and finally it became a fixed belief in the Greek world.

The whole story which Diodorus tells was, obviously, contrived to reconcile the two beliefs, that Dionysus was identical with Osiris, and that he was born of Zeus and Semele in Boeotia. To bring about the reconciliation the author of it had recourse to the legendary figure of Orpheus, and he as much as tells us why when he says that Orpheus enjoyed a great reputation for religious rites and for his knowledge of the gods. Orpheus was the great specialist in these things. In the story of Palaephatus he is called in by distracted husbands and fathers, and he uses his professional skill to restore the Bacchae to sanity. In the present story he takes the initiative himself and generously uses his arts to introduce religious reforms which will please the city that has befriended him. He follows his regular practice in the method of his propaganda. He institutes a new rite which presents the facts about the gods in a new guise. Nothing is said of the composition of a poem in which the revised myth was set forth, but there can be little doubt that the Greek writer and the Greek reader, who were familiar with such rites, would tacitly assume that the sacred myth of the rite was also given a poetical setting. Here, as in Clement of Alexandria, Orpheus was probably thought of as the "poet of the rite," in the full sense of the word ποιητής. Whether the "new rite" was actually performed at Thebes in the real life of historical times or was simply a fiction invented to explain the origin of the familiar story about Dionysus, we cannot say. In either case the Orphic rite in question, imaginary or not, was one in which the most significant feature was that Dionysus was the son of Zeus and Semele.

The first book of Diodorus, in which occur the two passages already studied (i, 23, and i, 96), is given over to the history of Egypt, and in the earlier part of it the myth of Osiris is told at considerable length. It is to this earlier portion of his history that the author refers at the beginning of a very interesting passage in the third book (iii, 62–65), in which he recurs to the subject of Dionysus. We have already given, he says, the Egyptian account of the birth and career of Dionysus; we shall now add the reports that circulate about him among the Greeks. The discussion which ensues may be paraphrased as follows.

The subject is difficult because the stories of the ancient mythographers and poets are inconsistent with one another and full of incredible incidents. Some say there was one Dionysus, some say there were three; others say that he was never born in human form at all, regarding the gift of wine itself as Dionysus. We shall briefly run over the principal features of the several views. The theory of the natural philosophers (φυσιολόγοι) is this. Dionysus is the fruit of the vine, and the vine was produced originally by the earth like other plants: there was no inventor of the vine. The idea that Dionysus had two mothers came from the fact that the planting of the vine stock was reckoned as one birth and the ripening of the grapes was another: the first birth was from the earth, the second from the vine. The mythographers tell of a third birth: the god was the son of Zeus and Demeter, was torn to pieces by the Earthborn (Γηγενεῖς), and boiled; the limbs were collected again by Demeter, and the god was born a child again. This story is based on natural phenomena: the birth from Zeus and Demeter means that the vine which yields the wine is fostered by the earth and the rain; the tearing to pieces refers to the gathering of the grapes by the farmers (i.e., *γεωργοί* = *γηγενεῖς*); the boiling is nothing but the common practice of boiling the wine to improve its flavor; the restoration of the limbs to their original form means that after the gathering of the grapes and the pruning of the vine the cycle is repeated and a new crop is produced in the following year. "Quite in harmony with all this is what we are told in the Orphic poems and what is represented in the rites, with regard to which the uninitiated are not supposed to inquire in any detail" (Diod. iii, 62, 8 = *Fragm.* 301 *σύμφωνα δὲ τούτοις εἶναι τά τε δηλούμενα διὰ τῶν Ὀρφικῶν ποιημάτων καὶ τὰ παρεισαγόμενα κατὰ τὰς τελετάς, περὶ ὧν οὐ θέμις τοῖς ἀμυήτοις ἱστορεῖν τὰ κατὰ μέρος*).

From this interesting account it appears that there were rites in which was enacted a myth telling of the birth of Dionysus from Zeus and Demeter, his dismemberment by the Earthborn, and his restoration to life. The story of these mythical events was also told in Orphic poems. Though the name of Orpheus is attached to the poems and not to the rites, there can be little doubt that the rites too were thought to be Orphic. This is, in fact, definitely proved by another passage in Diodorus (v, 75 = *Fragm.* 210 p. 231 and *Fragm.* 303). The Cretans, he says there, insist that Dionysus, like many other gods, was born in Crete, the son of Zeus and Persephone; it was this Dionysus who was represented by Orpheus in his rites as torn to pieces by the Titans (v, 75, 4 *τοῦτον δὲ τὸν θεὸν γεγονέναι φασὶν ἐκ Διὸς καὶ Φερσεφόνης κατὰ τὴν Κρήτην, ὃν Ὀρφεὺς κατὰ τὰς τελετὰς παρέδωκε διασπώμενον ὑπὸ τῶν Τιτάνων*). These two texts, taken together, furnish good evidence that the poem and the rite were regarded as a single institution, created by a single person. The same myth appears in both, narrated in the one, acted in the other, though in one text the mother of Dionysus is Demeter and in the other Persephone.

Shortly after the passage quoted from the fifth book Diodorus states the belief of the Cretans that their island was not only the birthplace of most of the gods, but also the place where the forms of worship originated which later came into use throughout the world (v, 77, 3 *τὰς δὲ τιμὰς καὶ θυσίας καὶ τὰς περὶ τὰ μυστήρια τελετάς*). As evidence of this they point out that the rites that are celebrated at Eleusis, at Samothrace, and among the Thracian Cicones, are secret, whereas at Cnossus in Crete these rites have always been entirely public.

The words referring to the Thracian rite are these: *τὴν ἐν Θρᾴκῃ ἐν τοῖς Κίκοσιν, ὅθεν ὁ καταδείξας Ὀρφεὺς ἦν* (v, 77, 3; not in Kern), "of which country Orpheus, who instituted the rite, was a native." The point of the relative clause is that the man who introduced the rite from Crete into Thrace was himself a Ciconian. This is evidently a tacit reconciliation of the Cretan claim with a tradition that the originator of the Ciconian rite was Orpheus. Nothing is said of the nature of this Ciconian rite, but it is worth noting that it seems to be thought of as definitely local, like the rites of Eleusis and Samothrace.

We may now return to the passage in the third book, the discussion of which was interrupted to give place to pertinent evidence from the fifth book. After his explanation of the theories of the natural philosophers Diodorus continues with the views of those who believed that Dionysus was the name of one or more real persons (iii, 63–65). The allusion to Orpheus, for which this passage is cited, does not appear till near the end, but it will be necessary to provide a rather long paraphrase of what precedes it in order to give it its proper setting. It must be understood that we are listening to the account of Diodorus until Orpheus comes upon the scene.

The mythographers who represent the god as incarnate all attribute to him the invention of the vine and the making of wine. But they are divided into two classes: one recognizes only one Dionysus, the other recognizes three. According to the views of the first class, one and the same person had taught the making of wine and the use of tree fruits, had led an expedition over the whole civilized world, and had introduced mysteries (iii, 63, 2 τὸν τὰ μυστήρια καὶ τελετὰς καὶ βακχείας εἰσηγησάμενον). According to the second class, there were three separate persons at three different epochs, to each of whom a different set of activities was attributed. The first and eldest Dionysus was an Indian. The vine was native to India, but he taught how to make wine from it. He traveled all over the world with an army and taught men how to cultivate the vine and crush the grapes. For this and for his other inventions he received divine honors after his death. The second Dionysus was the son of Zeus, his mother being, according to some, Persephone, according to others, Demeter. He taught men how to yoke oxen to the plow and how to do other things useful in farming. Thus relieving men of their misery (iii, 64, 1 *ἀπολυθῆναι τοὺς ὄχλους τῆς πολλῆς κακοπαθείας*), he received divine honors after his death and was endowed with immortality. In art he is represented with horns. The third Dionysus was the son of Zeus and Semele in Boeotian Thebes. Born before his due time, he was placed by Zeus in his thigh. When the full time had elapsed, he was entrusted to the nymphs of Nysa in Arabia. Being a child of great beauty, he passed his time at first in dance and play with bands of women. Then he gathered an army of women, armed them with thyrsi, and with them campaigned throughout the world. He instituted the mystic rites and admitted to them those who lived piously and justly; he held festivals and musical contests; and by settling the quarrels between cities and nations he established peace and concord in the place of war and faction (iii, 64, 7 *καταδεῖξαι δὲ καὶ τὰ περὶ τὰς τελετὰς καὶ μεταδοῦναι τῶν μυστηρίων τοῖς εὐσεβέσι τῶν ἀνθρωπων καὶ δίκαιον βίον ἀσκοῦσι, πρὸς δὲ τούτοις πανταχοῦ πανηγύρεις ἄγειν καὶ μουσικοὺς ἀγῶνας συντελεῖν, καὶ τὸ σύνολον συλλύοντα τὰ νείκη τῶν ἐθνῶν καὶ πό-*

*λεων ἀντὶ τῶν στάσεων καὶ τῶν πολέμων ὁμόνοιαν καὶ πολλὴν εἰρήνην κατασκευάζειν*). Some people, however, who said that he took women about with him for licentious purposes and organized his rites in order to get possession of other men's wives (iii, 65, 2 *τὰς δὲ τελετὰς καὶ μυστήρια φθορᾶς ἕνεκα τῶν ἀλλοτρίων γυναικῶν καταδεικνύειν*), were punished by him. Sometimes he made them mad; sometimes he caused them to be torn to pieces (*διαμελίζοντα*) by the women; sometimes he armed the women with spears covered with ivy and led them against his unsuspecting enemies. The most distinguished of those who were punished by him were Pentheus in Greece, Myrrhanus in India, and Lycurgus in Thrace.

The story of Lycurgus is this. Dionysus, being about to lead his army across from Asia into Europe, made a treaty of friendship with Lycurgus. But when he had led the Bacchae into Thrace, Lycurgus gave orders to attack and destroy the party. Dionysus was informed of the treacherous plan by a native named Charops and recrossed into Asia, leaving the Bacchae to be slain by Lycurgus in a place called Nysion. Then he led his main body against Lycurgus, captured him alive, and put him to death with torture. In recognition of the service of Charops, he made him king of Thrace and taught him the ritual of the mysteries. Charops had a son named Oeagrus who succeeded to the kingdom and to the knowledge of the mysteries. Later, Orpheus, the son of Oeagrus, learned the mysteries from his father, and, rising to eminence by virtue of his training and his native ability, he made many alterations in the rites. In consequence of this the rites which had been originated by Dionysus came to be called Orphic (iii, 65, 6 = *Test.* 23 μετὰ δὲ ταῦτα τῷ μὲν Χάροπι χάριν ἀποδιδόντα τῆς εὐεργεσίας παραδοῦναι τὴν τῶν Θρᾳκῶν βασιλείαν καὶ διδάξαι τὰ κατὰ τὰς τελετὰς ὄργια· Χάροπος δ' υἱὸν γενόμενον Οἴαγρον παραλαβεῖν τήν τε βασιλείαν καὶ τὰς ἐν τοῖς μυστηρίοις παραδεδομένας τελετάς, ἃς ὕστερον Ὀρφέα τὸν Οἰάγρου μαθόντα παρὰ τοῦ πατρός, καὶ φύσει καὶ παιδείᾳ τῶν ἁπάντων διενεγκόντα, πολλὰ μεταθεῖναι τῶν ἐν τοῖς ὀργίοις· διὸ καὶ τὰς ὑπὸ τοῦ Διονύσου γενομένας τελετὰς Ὀρφικὰς προσαγορευθῆναι).

From this intricately woven tissue of Euhemeristic invention it is difficult to draw out the true strands of genuine ancient myth and genuine religious institutions. But the language, at least, which is used about the mysteries is instructive. We may take it as certain that some or all of the rites of Dionysus were called Orphic. It might be maintained that the passage affords evidence of two kinds of Dionysiac mysteries, those which were supposed to have been founded by the god himself and to have continued unaltered, and those which were supposed to have been reformed by Orpheus. Such a distinction is unheard of elsewhere, and it is by no means certain that Diodorus has any thought of it here. His language sounds as if Orpheus were understood to have remodeled Dionysiac rites in general. A more likely interpretation is that the story, as it is told, is a device to reconcile the view which prevailed among mythographers that Dionysus had founded the mysteries himself, with the fact that they were called Orphic and the legend that Orpheus was the great originator of mysteries. Even if there were two kinds of Dionysiac mysteries, the pure Dionysiac and the Orphic-Dionysiac, it is worth observing that the moral requirements for initiation (64, 7) belong to the original Dionysiac rites and are not attached particularly to the reformed rites of Orpheus. And yet this moral quality is often expressly attributed by modern writers to the particular mysteries which they call Orphic. Furthermore, the fact that Dionysiac rites were called Orphic does not necessarily imply that they and no others were called Orphic. To be called Orphic may mean no more than to be recognized as instituted by Orpheus.

From Diodorus we proceed to his contemporary, Cicero. A passage in the *De natura deorum* (iii, 58 = *Test.* 94) is evidently based on sources similar to those used by Diodorus in his report of the speculations concerning the myths of Dionysus. What Cicero says is this. "We have many persons called Dionysus: first, the son of Jupiter and Proserpina; second, the son of Nilus, who is said to have slain Nysa; the third, whose father was Cabirus, was king of Asia, as the story goes, and the Sabazia were instituted in his honor; the fourth was the son of Jupiter and Luna, and Orphic rites are believed to be performed in his honor; the fifth, the son of Nysus and Thyone, is believed to have established the Trieterides" (Dionysos multos habemus, primum Iove et Proserpina natum, secundum Nilo, qui Nysam dicitur interemisse, tertium Cabiro patre, eumque regem Asiae praefuisse dicunt, cui Sabazia sunt instituta, quartum Iove et Luna, cui sacra Orphica putantur confici, quintum Nyso natum et Thyone, a quo Trieterides constitutae putantur).

Cicero thus recognizes five distinct gods called Dionysus, whereas in the passage of Diodorus just examined only three are named. To three out of the five he attributes special rites. The text is an important document for the study of the history of Dionysiac myths and the speculations of the learned concerning them, but this large subject cannot be discussed here. We must hold our attention to what can be learned about Orphic rites.

It should be observed, to begin with, that Orphic rites are attributed to the son of Jupiter and Luna, and that no rites at all are attributed to the son of Jupiter and Proserpina, though elsewhere we find Orphic poems and Orphic rites occupied with this Dionysus. Unfortunately the implications of the statement concerning Orphic rites are not clear. In the phrase "putantur confici," "confici" appears to be a translation of τελεῖσθαι, and both verbs are in the present tense, as if the rites were still performed somewhere. The matter, however, may have already become a literary tradition, based on the learned study of myths and cults by the Alexandrians, and the rites may have been only a subject of antiquarian interest. Again, the word "putantur" suggests uncertainty and speculation, but it is not clear to what the doubt appertains. What is "thought" may be either "it is to this god that the Orphic rites are celebrated" or "the rites celebrated in honor of this god are Orphic." The uncertainty may attach to either possible predication. The first implies that all Orphic rites are addressed to this Dionysus, the second that these rites as well as others were Orphic. Evidently, therefore, we cannot be sure what the person who thought about the rites really knew about them beyond their existence. He may have known of one particular rite, called Orphic, from personal acquaintance; he may have heard of sacra Orphica and *supposed* they were one particular rite, whereas the phrase may have simply meant that some or all teletae were called Orphic because Orpheus was regarded as the founder of this kind of ritual and had composed poems associated with it; or he may have known of a *kind* of teletae which for one reason or another were called Orphic. Whether the sacra that he knew were a kind of sacra or a particular rite, he may also have known that they were addressed to Dionysus, though he was not certain which Dionysus it was. He assigns the Sabazia to one, the Trieterides to another, the Orphic to a third. But the general confusion of thought and the obvious juggling of the facts forbid any definite conclusion on these points. Again, it is not clear who it was that thought Orphic rites were performed in honor of the son of Jupiter and Luna. Perhaps it was the general belief among people at large, who were aware of the existence of Orphic rites but knew nothing definite about them. Or, in using "putantur," Cicero may mean that he is quoting the opinion of his source or that in the source itself the idea was pushed still farther back. In any case, there is a disinclination on Cicero's part to make a positive statement on the subject. He seems to know nothing definite about Orphic rites except the name and the opinion about them which he cites. All these uncertainties make the text very unsatisfactory as evidence. In the end, we can say no more than that Cicero had heard of

Orphic rites and was aware of a belief that some or all of them were addressed to Dionysus, son of Jupiter and Luna. His manifest ignorance of the subject suggests that rites which were explicitly called Orphic were not prominent in the world of his day.[24]

There is a curious feature in the text of Cicero which has still to be noticed. The mother of Dionysus to whom Orphic rites were supposed to be addressed is Luna. Nowhere else, apparently, is Luna named as the mother of Dionysus. At the same time it is most surprising that Semele as the mother of Dionysus does not appear anywhere in the list of five. It naturally occurs to one that there may have been some interchange, in the Greek text which Cicero was using or still farther back, between the names Σεμέλη and Σελήνη. But even if this were the case, no emendation, of course, would be admissible in the Latin text of Cicero. There is, in fact, great confusion in the learned speculations about mythological matters. Not only were there widely different opinions, but the various views that were advanced were subjected to shift and change in the reports of later authors and in the works of compilers and epitomizers. An illustration of this is afforded by a comparison of the present passage in Cicero with a text from late antiquity, which may suitably be introduced at this point. The text referred to is in

[24] Carlo Giambelli, in his commentary on the *De natura deorum* (1904), expresses his agreement with Schoemann (whose thought he reports inaccurately) and maintains that the section on Dionysi is in a special and manifest way derived from Orphicism. This extraordinary statement assumes the existence of something called Orphicism, which the writer would not be able to define with any precision, and offers no proof that the ideas in the passage are derived from it.

Joannes Lydus and runs as follows (*De mens.* iv, 51, p. 107 Wünsch = *Test.* 94):

"According to the poets, there were five persons called Dionysus: the first was the son of Zeus and Lysithea; the second, who was the son of Nilus, became king of Libya, Ethiopia, and Arabia; the third, the son of Cabirus, was king of Asia, and the Cabiric rite originated with him; the fourth was the son of Zeus and Semele—the mysteries of Orpheus were celebrated in his honor, and it was he who mixed wine; the fifth, the son of Nisus and Thyone, instituted the Trieteris" (*κατὰ δὲ τοὺς ποιητὰς Διόνυσοι πέντε· πρῶτος Διὸς καὶ Λυσιθέας, δεύτερος ὁ Νείλου, ὁ καὶ βασιλεύσας Λιβύης καὶ Αἰθιοπίας καὶ Ἀραβίας· τρίτος Καβείρου παῖς, ὅστις τῆς ⟨Ἀσίας⟩* [the lacuna has been filled by Creuzer from Cicero] *ἐβασίλευσε, ἀφ' οὗ ἡ Καβειρικὴ τελετή· τέταρτος ὁ Διὸς καὶ Σεμέλης, ᾧ τὰ Ὀρφέως μυστήρια ἐτελεῖτο, καὶ ὑφ' οὗ οἶνος ἐκεράσθη· πέμπτος ὁ Νίσου καὶ Θυώνης, ὃς κατέδειξε τριετηρίδα*).

The resemblances between this and the passage in Cicero are as striking as the divergences, and there can be no doubt that the two passages are somehow related in the literary tradition. In Lydus, as in Cicero, it is the fourth Dionysus to whom Orphic rites are addressed; but in Cicero his mother is Luna, in Lydus Semele. It is impossible to say whether the ultimate source of both Cicero and Lydus had Σεμέλη or Σελήνη. It seems more likely, however, that an original Σελήνη should have been changed to Σεμέλη than that Σεμέλη, the well-known name of the mother of Dionysus, should have been changed to the unfamiliar Σελήνη. It is probable, therefore, that the

Σεμέλη of Lydus is a correction for Σελήνη and that Cicero gives the original name. That a connection between Selene and Orpheus was not unknown may be inferred from Plato (*Rep.* ii, 364 E), who speaks of Musaeus and Orpheus as the offspring of Selene and the Muses (Σελήνης τε καὶ Μουσῶν ἐκγόνων). But it is difficult to see what this could have to do with the notion that Dionysus was the son of Selene. What is clear amidst all this uncertainty is that according to Cicero Orphic rites were performed in honor of the son of Selene, and that according to Lydus, who agrees in this with one account in Diodorus (i, 23), it was the son of Semele in whose honor Orphic mysteries were performed.

A century or more after Cicero we find in Plutarch two or three passages in which Orpheus is associated in one way or another with the rites of Dionysus. In one of these (*Quaest. Symp.* ii, 3, 636 D = *Fragm.* 59), where the subject under discussion is whether the chicken or the egg came first, Plutarch recalls the Orphic doctrine (τὸν 'Ορφικὸν καὶ ἱερὸν λόγον) which not only makes the egg older than the chicken, but indeed makes it the very source and origin of the universe. It is not unreasonable, therefore, he adds, that the egg has been treated as a sacred thing in the rites of Dionysus, since it is a copy of that which generated all things and contained all things within itself. More on this same subject is found in Achilles Statius (*Introd. in Aratum* 6 = *Fragm.* 70), who lived probably somewhat later than Plutarch. Some people, he says, believe that the shape of the universe is conical, others spherical, others oval; and those who perform the

Orphic mysteries (οἱ τὰ Ὀρφικὰ μυστήρια τελοῦντες) adhere to the last opinion. Plutarch, then, recognizes the doctrine of the cosmic egg as Orphic and found it, presumably, in an Orphic poem. Though he also says that an egg was used in Dionysiac rites, he does not call these rites Orphic or necessarily imply that the doctrine of the cosmic egg was involved in them. Seemingly Achilles supplies the missing link which justifies our saying that in certain Dionysiac rites an egg was used and the doctrine of the cosmic egg was taught, and that these rites were called Orphic.[25]

Again, writing of Olympias, mother of Alexander the Great, Plutarch gives the following account of certain conditions in Macedonia (*Alex.* 2, 665 D = *Test.* 206): "All the women of this region have long been addicted to the Orphic rites and to the orgiastic cult of Dionysus. Calling themselves Clodones and Mimallones, they engage in performances which in many ways resemble those of the Edonian women and the Thracian women of Mount Haemus, from which, it is believed, the word θρησκεύειν has come to be applied to excessive and extravagant religious ritual. Olympias, who showed greater devotion to this form of religious intoxication than other women and carried her enthusiasm to wilder extremes, dragged about with her amidst the bands of worshipers huge tame snakes,

[25] On the egg in the cosmogonies and in ritual see J. E. Harrison, *Prolegomena* (1903), pp. 628 ff.; K. Ziegler, "Menschen- und Weltenwerden," *Neue Jahrb. für das klass. Alt.*, XXXI (1913), 529–573; A. Olivieri, "L'uovo cosmogonico degli Orfici," *Atti della R. Accad. di archaeol., lettere e belle arti di Napoli*, n.s., VII (1919); A. B. Cook, *Zeus*, II, pt. ii (1925), App. G; Pierre Boyancé, "Une allusion à l'œuf orphique," *Mélanges d'Archéologie et d'Histoire*, LII (1935), 95–112.

which often caused the men great alarm when they emerged from the ivy and winnowing fans and wound themselves around the thyrsi and wreaths of the women" (ἕτερος δὲ περὶ τούτων ἐστὶ λόγος, ὡς πᾶσαι μὲν αἱ τῇδε γυναῖκες ἔνοχοι τοῖς Ὀρφικοῖς οὖσαι καὶ τοῖς περὶ τὸν Διόνυσον ὀργιασμοῖς ἐκ τοῦ πάνυ παλαιοῦ, Κλώδωνές τε καὶ Μιμαλλόνες ἐπωνυμίαν ἔχουσαι, πολλὰ ταῖς Ἠδωνίσι καὶ ταῖς περὶ τὸν Αἷμον Θρῄσσαις ὅμοια δρῶσιν· ἀφ' ὧν δοκεῖ καὶ τὸ θρησκεύειν ὄνομα ταῖς κατακόροις γενέσθαι καὶ περιέργοις ἱερουργίαις· ἡ δ' Ὀλυμπιὰς μᾶλλον ἑτέρων ζηλώσασα τὰς κατοχάς, καὶ τοὺς ἐνθουσιασμοὺς ἐξάγουσα βαρβαρικώτερον, ὄφεις μεγάλους χειροήθεις ἐφείλκετο τοῖς θιάσοις, οἳ πολλάκις ἐκ τοῦ κιττοῦ καὶ τῶν μυστικῶν λίκνων παραναδυόμενοι καὶ περιελιττόμενοι τοῖς θύρσοις τῶν γυναικῶν καὶ τοῖς στεφάνοις, ἐξέπληττον τοὺς ἄνδρας).

This description is a more circumstantial one than we find in most texts where Orphic rites are referred to. It will be well to repeat the essential features of it: bands (θίασοι) of Macedonian women, carrying ivy, winnowing fans, thyrsi, wreaths, and snakes, and imagining themselves to be Clodones and Mimallones, engaged in extravagant religious activities of an orgiastic type, very similar to those practiced by the women of Thrace. In doing these things they are said to be engaged in Orphic rites and Dionysiac rites. Since the two names are applied to the same things, they must so far be synonymous. The rites may be truthfully called either Orphic or Dionysiac. But this does not mean that the two terms are congruent in their whole extension. If the reader naturally and instinctively understood "Orphic rites" to mean precisely Dionysiac rites, the addition of the second term would seem to be unnecessary. It may be mere redundancy; but it is at least equally possible that "Orphic rites" means more than Dionysiac rites and that the second phrase is added to specify the kind of Orphic rites that are meant. The questions then arise: Why are both terms used? Why is not "Dionysiac rites" sufficient? Why are Orphic rites named at all? The answer probably is that Plutarch had in mind from the start the Thracian character of the women's performances and was consequently reminded of the legend of Orpheus as the founder of Thracian rites. He naturally begins, then, with the statement that they were addicted to Orphic rites; but, feeling that this is not sufficiently clear, since he has not yet mentioned the resemblance to Thracian rites, and since the name of Orpheus was known to his readers to be associated with rites other than Dionysiac, he adds the second phrase for clearer definition. The text shows, therefore, not only that Dionysiac rites of a wild and orgiastic character could be called Orphic, but also, in all probability, that the term "Orphic rites" was not the specific name for them but had a wider range of meaning.

Another text, in a work falsely attributed to Plutarch (*De fluviis* iii, 4 = *Test.* 122), brings the name of Orpheus into connection with the orgiastic rites of Dionysus in rather a curious way. It is there said that after Orpheus had been torn to pieces on Mount Pangaeum, his lyre was made a constellation in the sky, and from his blood there sprang up a plant called cithara. When the Dionysiac rites are celebrated, with fawnskins and thyrsi, this plant gives forth the sound of a lyre.

The legend of Orpheus' tragic death here appears in immediate connection with Dionysiac worship. We have seen this connection elsewhere also. Sometimes no conflict between the legend and his association with Dionysus is recognized, sometimes his death is represented as caused by the hostility of Dionysus. To the former type, besides the text in the *De fluviis*, belongs the reference in Lactantius (see p. 208), who simply says that Orpheus was torn to pieces in the rites of Dionysus which he himself had founded on Mount Cithaeron. Similarly Proclus says that, according to the legend, Orpheus, who was the leader in the rites of Dionysus, suffered a fate similar to that of his god (*In Plat. Rempublicam* i, 174, 30 Kroll = *Test.* 119): ἀλλ' Ὀρφεὺς μὲν ἅτε τῶν Διονύσου τελετῶν ἡγεμὼν γενόμενος τὰ ὅμοια παθεῖν ὑπὸ τῶν μύθων εἴρηται τῷ σφετέρῳ θεῷ (καὶ γὰρ ὁ σπαραγμὸς τῶν Διονυσιακῶν ἕν ἐστιν συνθημάτων). On the other hand, hostility between Dionysus and Orpheus is openly recognized in the *Bassarae* of Aeschylus and in the *Catasterismi* attributed to Eratosthenes. Hyginus, too, reports two explanations that had been offered of the hostility of Dionysus (*Astron.* ii, 7 = *Test.* 117): some said that when Orpheus descended to the lower world he sang the praises of all the gods but Dionysus, who in consequence later sent the Bacchae to tear him to pieces; others said that this fate had befallen him because he had spied on the rites of Dionysus.

The association of Orpheus with rites involving the dismemberment of Dionysus himself, which is alluded to by Proclus in the passage just quoted, we have seen already more than once in Diodorus (i, 96; iii, 62; v, 75).

This association appears again in several late texts, which still remain to be presented.

Clement of Alexandria, in the same chapter on the mysteries from which a citation has already been made concerning Orpheus and the mysteries of Demeter (see p. 194), speaks also of his relation to the mysteries of Dionysus (*Protrept.* ii, 17, 2–18, 1 Stählin = *Fragm.* 34). The mysteries of Dionysus, he says, are thoroughly inhuman: when the god was still a child, the Titans stole upon him, beguiled him with toys, and tore him limb from limb. As evidence of this he quotes two lines from Orpheus, "the poet of the rite," in which are named the toys used by the Titans, and these toys he calls the symbols of the rite (ὡς ὁ τῆς τελετῆς ποιητὴς Ὀρφεύς φησιν ὁ Θρᾴκιος·

> κῶνος καὶ ῥόμβος καὶ παίγνια καμπεσίγυια,
> μῆλά τε χρύσεα καλὰ παρ' Ἑσπερίδων λιγυφώνων).

The phrase ὁ τῆς τελετῆς ποιητής, meaning either poet or maker of the rite, is probably used advisedly to convey both meanings. Orpheus was regarded both as the originator of the ritual of dismemberment and as the author of the poem in which the myth was told.

Arnobius gives a similar account of the Bacchanalia, which he evidently borrowed from Clement (*Adv. nationes* v, 19 = *Fragm.* 34). He refers to an Orphic poem as evidence for the myth, but he does not say that Orpheus was the founder of the rite (cuius rei testimonium argumentumque fortunae suis prodidit in carminibus Thracius talos speculum turbines, uolubiles rotulas et teretis pilas et uirginibus aurea sumpta ab Hesperidibus mala).

Macrobius (*In somn. Scip.* i, 12, 11 = *Fragm.* 240) says that the Orphici understand Dionysus to be the νοῦς ὑλικός, and that in their rites he is torn to pieces by the Titans, the pieces are buried, and he emerges again sound and whole, because the νοῦς thus fulfills its function in the universe by submitting itself to division and again returning to its undivided state (ipsum autem Liberum patrem Orphici νοῦν ὑλικόν suspicantur intelligi, qui ab illo indiuiduo natus in singulos ipse diuiditur. ideo in illorum sacris traditur Titanio furore in membra discerptus et frustis sepultis rursus unus et integer emersisse, quia νοῦς, quem diximus mentem vocari, ex indiuiduo praebendo se diuidendum et rursus ex diuiso ad indiuiduum reuertendo et mundi implet officia et naturae suae arcana non deserit). Two meanings are possible for "traditur": if the phrase "in illorum sacris" is construed with it, the meaning is, "it is disclosed in their rites how Dionysus was torn to pieces, etc."; if the phrase is construed with "discerptus" and "emersisse," the meaning is, "we are told that in their rites Dionysus was torn to pieces, etc." In the latter case, Macrobius knows the rites only from his reading; in the former, he knows them directly, but we cannot be sure whether he obtained his knowledge from the actual rites themselves as performed in his own day or from an Orphic poem in which the ἱερὸς λόγος was told. When the same story is discussed by Diodorus, as we have already seen, he says in one place (iii, 62, 8; see p. 214) that it was represented in teletae and told in Orphic poetry, where he might equally well have said in Orphic teletae and poetry; in another place (v, 75, 4; see p. 215) he says that it was represented in Orphic teletae. The fact seems to be that there were actual mysteries of which this story was the ἱερὸς λόγος, and that since Orpheus was the founder of mysteries in general, and the ἱερὸς λόγος of these particular mysteries was told in Orphic poetry, these mysteries could be, and were, on occasion called Orphic mysteries. As Clement puts it, Orpheus was ὁ τῆς τελετῆς ποιητής.

A similar philosophical interpretation of the dismemberment is given by a writer in the *Mythographi Vaticani* (iii, 12, 5 = *Fragm.* 213). The Giants found Bacchus drunk, tore him to pieces, and buried the pieces. He soon rose again alive and whole. The disciples of Orpheus, as we read, interpreted the story thus (quod figmentum discipuli Orphei interpretati leguntur . . .): Bacchus is the soul of the world (anima mundi), which is divided piecemeal through the bodies of the world but constantly renews itself and restores itself to its undivided state. This story, the books tell us, they represented in his rites (hanc fabulam in sacris eius repraesentasse leguntur). In the last sentence "eius," which is missing in two manuscripts, may be either Orpheus or Bacchus.

## Texts in Which No Particular Deities Are Named

1) There was written in the third century B.C. a book which, if it had been preserved, might have solved many, if not all, of the problems concerning Orphic mysteries. Suidas reports that Apollonius of Aphrodisia, who lived at some time after 266 B.C., wrote a treatise "Concerning Orpheus and His Rites" (Suidas s.v. = *F.H.G.*, IV, 310

= *Test.* 232 Ἀπολλώνιος Ἀφροδισιεύς, ἀρχιερεὺς καὶ ἱστορικός. γέγραφε Καρικά, Περὶ Τράλλεων, Περὶ Ὀρφέως καὶ τῶν τελετῶν αὐτοῦ). Unfortunately the mere title tells us nothing. We do not know whether the teletae are *particular* teletae, distinguished from all others and known as Orphic; or a particular *class* of teletae, thus distinguished; or teletae in general, as the particular form of religious activity originated by Orpheus. The title which is preserved by Suidas would be appropriate for any one of the three.

2) In the first century B.C., Philodemus, in an obscure passage concerning poetical composition (Περὶ ποιημάτων, fr. 41 Hausrath, *Jahrb. für class. Philol., Suppl.* XVII (1889), p. 257 = *Test.* 208), uses the phrase Ὀρφεοτελεστοῦ τυμπάνῳ. We know something already of the Orpheotelestes from the passage in Theophrastus which has been discussed above (see p. 102). The word recurs twice again in later authors. Plutarch (*Apophthegm. Laconic.* 224 E = *Test.* 203) tells a story of a certain Leotychidas, who may have been the king of Sparta who reigned from 491 to 469 B.C. When Philip, the Orpheotelestes, who was an absolute beggar, asserted that those who were initiated with him (οἱ παρ' αὐτῷ μυηθέντες) were happy after death, Leotychidas asked, "Why, then, do you not die immediately and put an end to your misery?" The same story is told, in different language, of Antisthenes by Diogenes Laertius (vi, 1, 4 = *Test.* 203). Once, when Antisthenes was being initiated in the Orphic rites (μυούμενος τὰ Ὀρφικά), and the priest (τοῦ ἱερέως) said that those who are initiated in these rites (οἱ ταῦτα μυούμενοι) enjoy many blessings in Hades, he asked, "Why do you

not die?" The Orpheotelestes who figures in this story is evidently an independent operator, like the one in Theophrastus, and the rites which he performs, like those referred to by Plato in the *Republic*, are supposed to insure happiness after death. It is likely, but not certain, that the Orpheotelestes of Philodemus, who used the drum, performed similar rites.

3) The next document to be considered is a passage of unusual interest in the tenth book of Strabo, on the subject of orgiastic worship. The name of Orpheus appears in it three times, and in order to understand these allusions properly it will be necessary to have the essential features of Strabo's discussion.

The second chapter of the tenth book and part of the third describe Aetolia, Acarnania, and the adjacent islands, and the description closes with an account of the people called Curetes who lived in these regions. Then, with some apology for touching such a subject in a sober work of philosophy, Strabo is led by the identity of the name to introduce a discussion of the Curetes of religion and mythology. He finds very little difference between what is told about them and what is told about the Corybantes, the Cabiri, the Idaean Dactyls, and the Telchines. Recognizing this similarity, he gives a striking account of the type of religion which is associated with all these names. The feature which is always present, he says, is the relaxation characteristic of a festival (*ἄνεσις ἑορταστική*); the other elements, enthusiasm, music, and secrecy, may or may not be present. He then reviews some of the more important instances of this type of religion in Greece and abroad. In Greece it is practiced mostly in the worship of Dionysus, Apollo, Hecate, the Muses, and Demeter. In Crete, besides these gods, Zeus too receives an orgiastic cult. In Phrygia, Rhea is worshiped orgiastically under many names. Like the noisy Phrygian rites are the Cotyttia and the Bendideia in Thrace, where the Orphica too had their origin (x, 3, 16 = *Test.* 160 τούτοις δ' ἔοικε καὶ τὰ παρὰ τοῖς Θρᾳξὶ τά τε Κοτύττια καὶ τὰ Βενδίδεια, παρ' οἷς καὶ τὰ 'Ορφικὰ τὴν καταρχὴν ἔσχε). The music which accompanied these rites reminds Strabo that all music, with its melody, its rhythm, and its instruments, is believed to be Thracian and Asiatic in origin ('από δὲ τοῦ μέλους καὶ τοῦ ῥυθμοῦ καὶ τῶν ὀργάνων καὶ ἡ μουσικὴ πᾶσα Θρᾳκία καὶ 'Ασιᾶτις νενόμισται[26]).Evidence for this is to be found, first, in the fact that the seats of the worship of the Muses were all originally Thracian, and, second, in the fact that the early musicians, Orpheus, Musaeus, and Thamyris among them, were all Thracians (x, 3, 17 = *Test.* 31 οἵ τ' ἐπιμεληθέντες τῆς ἀρχαίας μουσικῆς Θρᾷκες λέγονται, 'Ορφεύς τε καὶ Μουσαῖος καὶ Θάμυρις, καὶ τῷ Εὐμόλπῳ δὲ τοὔνομα ἐνθένδε, καὶ οἱ τῷ Διονύσῳ τὴν 'Ασίαν ὅλην καθιερώσαντες μέχρι τῆς 'Ινδικῆς ἐκεῖθεν καὶ τὴν πολλὴν μουσικὴν μεταφέρουσι). Thracian and Phrygian rites were received in Athens too, as know from Plato and Demosthenes.

After some miscellaneous traditions concerning the Curetes, Cabiri, Corybantes, and Dactyls, the chapter

[26] Jones' translation ("From its melody and rhythm and instruments, all Thracian music has been considered to be Asiatic") misrepresents this passage (H. L. Jones, *The Geography of Strabo*, V [1928], Loeb Classical Library).

closes with another apology for introducing mythological subjects. The discussion is of value, says Strabo, because the ancients expressed their ideas allegorically through myths. These myths are extremely difficult to interpret; but if you assemble a large number of them and compare them, you can sometimes discover resemblances which suggest the real meaning. The present case is an example. The authors of the myths represented religious zealots and even the gods themselves roaming the mountains in a state of inspired ecstasy. Similarly, they represented the gods as dwellers in the sky, occupied principally with the revelation of the future by signs. In all probability, their motive in both representations was the same. (Strabo's reasoning seems to be that since we may assume the reason for making the gods dwellers in the sky to have been the actual reality of celestial phenomena, so we may also assume that there were performances of some sort in the real world which suggested the mountain-roaming and the ecstasy of the myths.) We may guess that in mountain-roaming they saw something akin to the search for metals, wild game, and the other things necessary for life, and in ecstasy, fanaticism, and divination a reflection of the well-known practices of itinerant quacks and magicians. A marked instance of the same kind of thing is to be seen in the Dionysiac arts and the Orphic arts (x, 3, 23; not in Kern: *προήχθημεν δὲ διὰ πλειόνων εἰπεῖν περὶ τούτων καίπερ ἥκιστα φιλομυθοῦντες, ὅτι τοῦ θεολογικοῦ γένους ἐφάπτεται τὰ πράγματα ταῦτα. πᾶς δὲ ὁ περὶ τῶν θεῶν λόγος ἀρχαίας ἐξετάζει δόξας καὶ μύθους, αἰνιττομένων τῶν παλαιῶν ἃς εἶχον ἐννοίας φυσικὰς περὶ τῶν* πραγμάτων καὶ προστιθέντων ἀεὶ τοῖς λόγοις τὸν μῦθον. ἅπαντα μὲν οὖν τὰ αἰνίγματα λύειν ἐπ' ἀκριβὲς οὐ ῥᾴδιον, τοῦ δὲ πλήθους τῶν μυθευομένων ἐκτεθέντος εἰς τὸ μέσον, τῶν μὲν ὁμολογούντων ἀλλήλοις τῶν δ' ἐναντιουμένων, εὐπορώτερον ἄν τις δύναιτο εἰκάζειν ἐξ αὐτῶν τἀληθές· οἷον τὰς ὀρειβασίας τῶν περὶ τὸ θεῖον σπουδαζόντων καὶ αὐτῶν τῶν θεῶν καὶ τοὺς ἐνθουσιασμοὺς εἰκότως μυθεύουσι κατὰ τὴν αὐτὴν αἰτίαν καθ' ἣν καὶ οὐρανίους νομίζουσι τοὺς θεοὺς καὶ προνοητικοὺς τῶν τε ἄλλων καὶ τῶν προσημασιῶν· τῇ μὲν οὖν ὀρειβασίᾳ τὸ μεταλλευτικὸν καὶ τὸ θηρευτικὸν [καὶ] ζητητικὸν τῶν πρὸς τὸν βίον χρησίμων ἐφάνη συγγενές, τῶν δ' ἐνθουσιασμῶν καὶ θρησκείας καί μαντικῆς τὸ ἀγυρτικὸν καὶ γοητεία ἐγγύς. τοιοῦτον δὲ καὶ τὸ φιλότεχνον μάλιστα τὸ περὶ τὰς Διονυσιακὰς τέχνας καὶ τὰς 'Ορφικάς".

The whole passage, of which only a brief outline has been given, is most instructive on the subject of orgiastic religion, its psychological effect, and the esteem in which it was held. With regard to Orpheus certain significant things are said, and there are also significant silences. That he was numbered among the ancient musicians of Thrace is a familiar element of the legend and calls for no further remark. The second passage, however, in which his name appears is more important, since Orphic rites are expressly mentioned: "like the noisy Phrygian rites are the Cotyttia and Bendideia in Thrace, where the Orphica too had their origin." The language suggests that, though the Cotyttia and Bendideia were essentially and permanently Thracian, the Orphica, though they originated in Thrace, were in familiar use in Greece. Strabo seems to assume that his readers will know all about them. A little later, when he speaks of the hospitality of Athens to foreign cults, he says that Plato mentions the Bendideia and Demosthenes the Sabazia, but he says nothing of Orphica in Athens. And yet, as we have seen, the name of Orpheus was associated with certain rites both in Plato and Demosthenes and in other Athenian writers. The reason can only be that the Orphica, though they were supposed to have originated in Thrace, were so well known in Greece that they were not thought of as a foreign cult. It seems probable that Strabo, like Plutarch in his description of the rites of the Macedonian women, is reminded of Orphic rites when he is speaking of Thrace because Orpheus in the legend was a Thracian. As to what is meant precisely by Orphic rites, the text tells us nothing. Let us leave it for a moment and turn to the third passage in which Orpheus' name appears, at the very end of the long discussion.

The immediate context is this: *τοιοῦτον δὲ καὶ τὸ φιλότεχνον μάλιστα τὸ περὶ τὰς Διονυσιακὰς τέχνας καὶ τὰς Ὀρφικάς*. What is the meaning of this puzzling sentence? Jones (*loc. cit.*) translates it thus: "And such also is devotion to the arts, in particular to the Dionysiac and Orphic arts." He also suggests that *τέχνας* is a mistake for *τελετάς*, but he does not introduce *τελετάς* into his text. We must, of course, accept the text without emendation if it yields a satisfactory meaning. The translation, however, errs in one point: *μάλιστα* belongs with *τὸ φιλότεχνον*; if it were intended to be taken with the words which follow it, *μάλιστα δέ* would naturally have been written. The meaning is that *τὸ φιλότεχνον* is a signal example—of something. But the sentence still remains obscure.

The first difficulty lies in the meaning of *τοιοῦτον*. The word asserts a resemblance to something preceding—but a resemblance to what? Elsewhere Strabo describes Orpheus in terms similar to those used in the present passage—*ἄνδρα γόητα, ἀπὸ μουσικῆς ἅμα καὶ μαντικῆς καὶ τῶν περὶ τὰς τελετὰς ὀργιασμῶν ἀγυρτεύοντα* (vii, 330, fr. 18 = *Test.* 40). Here, as always, Orpheus' special activities are music, divination, and ritual, and by virtue of them Strabo thinks of him as a *γόης* and an *ἀγύρτης*. He is, therefore, typical of the profession whose performances Strabo believes to have been reflected in the allegorical myths of the gods. But in the present passage it is clear that Orpheus is not named as an example of *τὸ ἀγυρτικὸν καὶ γοητεία*. The relation indicated by *τοιοῦτον* seems rather to be this. Strabo has just said that human activities such as the search for metals, hunting, sorcery, and magic had supplied subjects for allegorical myths, which, properly interpreted, offer evidence for these very activities. He now adds to these another similar source of myths (*τοιοῦτον*) which has been particularly prolific. This is *τὸ φιλότεχνον τὸ περὶ τὰς Διονυσιακὰς τέχνας καὶ τὰς Ὀρφικάς*. Now *τὸ φιλότεχνον*, "enjoyment of the arts," comes very near to meaning what we mean by the word 'art' itself in the abstract, as it is used, for example, in such a sentence as 'Art plays a large part in his life.' The whole phrase, therefore, means practically "Dionysiac and Orphic art." What Strabo says is that works of art which were produced and enjoyed for their own sake gave rise to myths which had not existed before. This observation is rather profound in its implications. The artist, working in his own medium and eager to produce something which will be artistically successful, originates the whole conception, or certain features of it, which are then, because they are artistically successful, taken up into the general mythological tradition. It is well known that this is precisely what happened in Greek sculpture and painting. Here, however, Strabo is thinking of the influence of art in the particular arts of Dionysus and Orpheus. What were these arts? There can be little doubt that the art of Dionysus was the art of the theater. The creative and formative influence of the drama in the development of myth is quite as clear as that of sculpture and painting. It is equally plain that the Orphic arts can be no other than those that were always associated with his name: music, poetry, and the forms of ritual. The Dionysiac and Orphic arts were closely related and worked with the same materials, but the arts of Dionysus were employed in the theater, the arts of Orpheus in religious rites of the type called *τελεταί, ὄργια, μυστήρια*. The myths which were represented in such rites by symbols and mimetic action, and which were told in the poems connected with the rites, had been in whole or in part created, as Strabo understands it, by the liturgical artist, working under guidance of his own artistic instincts, and public appreciation of his work had made a place for the myth of the rite in the gallery of the national mythology.

If, now, we revert to Strabo's casual remark that the Orphica originated in Thrace, the possibility presents itself that by Orphica he means rites in which the Orphic arts were employed. In view of the fact that most of his material in the entire discussion of orgiastic religion is drawn from literary sources, it is possible that he was thinking especially of liturgical poetry, with which he was doubtless familiar. Now it is certainly true that the Orphic arts were not confined to a particular cult of a particular god. The very gods to whom, as Strabo says, orgiastic worship was offered in Greece—Dionysus, Apollo, Hecate, the Muses, and Demeter—are, as we have seen, all associated with Orpheus. It seems probable, therefore, that when Strabo says that the Orphica originated in Thrace he means that certain arts which were characteristic of all orgiastic cults had been invented by Orpheus in Thrace, and that the body of liturgical poetry which belonged to these cults had been composed by him. If there were special Orphic mysteries, distinguished from all others, it is surprising that Strabo, in so long a study of precisely the kind of religion to which they belong, does not make any clearer allusion to them. And yet the Orphica and the Orphic arts which he does name he evidently assumes to be familiar to his readers. The easiest hypothesis is to assume that they were familiar because Orphic liturgical poetry and the arts of ritual associated with it were familiar, and that special Orphic mysteries do not come in for mention because there were none.

4) Very similar to Strabo's brief mention of the Orphica is a cursory reference in Gregory of Nazianzus. In order to show plainly the contrast between Christianity and paganism, Gregory gives a long, scornful catalogue of Greek and other pagan myths and cults. Toward the end of the list, just after Trophonius, Delphi, the Magi, and

the Chaldaeans, he mentions the rites of the Thracians, from which, he says, the word θρησκεύειν is supposed to be derived, and the rites and mysteries of Orpheus, whom the Greeks admired so greatly for his skill that they even equipped him with a lyre whose tones caused all things to follow him (*Or. in Iulian.* xxxix, 680, Migne XXXVI, 340 B = *Test.* 155 οὐδὲ Θρᾳκῶν ὄργια ταῦτα, παρ' ὧν καὶ τὸ θρησκεύειν, ὡς λόγος· οὐδὲ 'Ορφέως τελεταὶ καὶ μυστήρια, ὃν τοσοῦτον Ἕλληνες ἐπὶ σοφίᾳ ἐθαύμασαν, ὥστε καὶ λύραν αὐτῷ ποιοῦσι, πάντα τοῖς κρούμασιν ἕλκουσαν). As in Strabo, the Thracian and Orphic rites appear side by side and yet distinguished from each other; the reason is doubtless the same in both places. It is interesting that Gregory finds nothing more discreditable to mention in connection with Orphic rites than the legend of the magical lyre.

5) Diodorus, as we have seen, has occasion to mention Orpheus more than once in connection with other matters, but there is one passage, a little less than a page in length, in which, by way of digression, he gives a special statement of the facts of Orpheus' career (iv, 25 = *Test.* 97 and 169). Heracles, before he went to Hades to fetch Cerberus, thought it would be advantageous to partake in the mysteries of Eleusis. So he went to Athens and did so. At the time of his visit Musaeus, the son of Orpheus, presided over the rite. Diodorus seizes this opportunity to introduce his brief digression on Orpheus.[27] In it we find the familiar features of the legend. Orpheus

[27] The possibility that the source of this passage was Herodorus is discussed by me in a paper entitled "Diodorus, Herodorus, Orpheus," in *Classical Studies Presented to Edward Capps* (Princeton, 1936), pp. 217–222.

was a Thracian, the son of Oeagrus, and greatly distinguished for his learning, song, and poetry (παιδείᾳ δὲ καὶ μελῳδίᾳ καὶ ποιήσει πολὺ προέχων τῶν μνημονευομένων). With his song he could even charm beasts and trees. After a period of study in Egypt, he attained to a supreme position among the Greeks in theology, ritual, poetry, and song (μέγιστος ἐγένετο τῶν Ἑλλήνων ἔν τε ταῖς θεολογίαις καὶ ταῖς τελεταῖς καὶ ποιήμασι καὶ μελῳδίαις). He took part in the expedition of the Argonauts, and he was permitted by Persephone to bring back his wife from Hades to the upper world. The resemblance between this last feat and the recovery of Semele by Dionysus is noted, but nothing is said about any connection between Orpheus and Dionysiac mysteries. The absence of any allusion to mysteries specifically Orphic, or indeed to any particular mysteries, is striking. If there were Orphic mysteries, recognized as such and different from others, involving special doctrines recognized as Orphic, it would seem that they must have found a place in this biography, brief as it is.

6) The notion that Orpheus completed his education in Egypt and introduced Egyptian cults into Greece, which is presented by Diodorus in the text just quoted and elsewhere, is found again twice in Eusebius (*Praep. Evang.* i, 6, p. 18 A = *Test.* 98; x, 4, p. 469 B = *Test.* 99a). In both places Eusebius says that Orpheus brought Egyptian mysteries to Greece, as Cadmus had brought the institutions of the Phoenicians. In the second, however, the scope of Orpheus' activity as a culture hero is widened to include almost all religion. Things of religious import, he says—rites and mysteries, the setting up of images,

hymns, chants, and incantation,—all these things were instituted on Egyptian or other models by the Thracian Orpheus or by someone else, Greek or foreign, who thus became the founders of the false doctrines of Greek paganism (*οἷς*—sc. *τοῖς παλαιοῖς Ἕλλησι—τὰ μὲν ἐκ Φοινίκης Κάδμος ὁ Ἀγήνορος, τὰ δ' ἐξ Αἰγύπτου περὶ θεῶν, ἢ καί ποθεν ἄλλοθεν, μυστήρια καὶ τελετάς, ξοάνων τε ἱδρύσεις καὶ ὕμνους, ᾠδάς τε καὶ ἐπῳδάς, ἤτοι ὁ Θρᾴκιος Ὀρφεύς, ἢ καί τις ἕτερος Ἕλλην ἢ βάρβαρος, τῆς πλάνης ἀρχηγοὶ γενόμενοι, συνεστήσαντο*).

7) Plutarch, in his *Life of Caesar*, says that the rites of Bona Dea, which were celebrated by the women of Rome, and to which no men were admitted, corresponded in many respects to the Orphica (*Caesar* 9; not in Kern: *αὗται δὲ καθ' ἑαυτὰς αἱ γυναῖκες πολλὰ τοῖς Ὀρφικοῖς ὁμολογοῦντα δρᾶν λέγονται περὶ τὴν ἱερουργίαν*). Something is known of the rites of Bona Dea, but it is impossible to say what points of resemblance were recognized between them and the Orphica. Plutarch speaks with equal assurance of Orphica here and in the *Life of Alexander*, where he says that Olympias was addicted to the Orphica. One suspects that when a Greek writer had occasion to speak of *foreign* orgiastic ritual and was reminded of *Greek* orgiastic ritual, he was naturally led to refer to the Greek ritual as Orphic. We have seen[28] that similarities were observed between Greek institutions on the one hand and, on the other, Egyptian institutions (first noticed by Herodotus and repeated later), Thracian institutions,

[28] Egyptian, pp. 38, 190, 207, 211; Thracian, pp. 215, 226, 237; Phrygian, pp. 101, 203; Sethiani, p. 199.

Phrygian institutions, and some doctrines of the Sethiani. Sometimes the author is satisfied to point out the similarity; often, however, he takes the next step and maintains that the Greek institution originated abroad or that the foreign institution originated in Greece. If the Greek institution which was called the Orphica was more or less identical with foreign institutions in the lands to the north, south, east, and west of Greece, it would seem that the common bond could have been nothing more precise than the orgiastic and mystical character of all the institutions concerned. Thus, from this point of view again, one comes to the belief that 'Orphica' and 'Greek mysteries' were interchangeable terms.

8) Pausanias, in his description of Boeotia, includes an account of the statues which were to be seen on Mount Helicon. Among these was a statue of Orpheus, with a figure of a Telete standing beside him, surrounded by beasts in marble and bronze listening to his song (ix, 30, 4 = *Test.* 142). The whole group, it may be observed, is a graphic representation of the two essential features of his legend, his magical song and his skill in ritual. The allusion to the statue then leads Pausanias to write about Orpheus at some length. The ensuing page and a half, like the page in Diodorus iv, 25, is given over expressly to him and is as long an account of his legend as can be found in Greek literature. Always skeptical about Orpheus,[29] Pausanias begins by denying the truth of certain things which were generally believed about him: his mother was not the Muse Calliope, but another Calliope,

[29] Cf. i, 14, 3; 37, 4; iii, 14, 5.

the daughter of Pierus: he did not have the power to charm wild beasts; he did not go to Hades alive to recover his wife. The truth is, according to Pausanias, that he surpassed all his predecessors in epic composition, and that he attained great power because he was believed to have invented rites of gods, purifications for unholy deeds, cures for disease, and methods of averting divine wrath (ix, 30, 4; not in Kern: ὁ δὲ Ὀρφεύς, ἐμοὶ δοκεῖν, ὑπερεβάλετο ἐπῶν κόσμῳ τοὺς πρὸ αὐτοῦ καὶ ἐπὶ μέγα ἦλθεν ἰσχύος οἷα πιστευόμενος εὑρηκέναι τελετὰς θεῶν καὶ ἔργων ἀνοσίων καθαρμοὺς νόσων τε ἰάματα καὶ ⟨ἀπο⟩τροπὰς μηνιμάτων θείων). Next are related several stories of the manner of his death, the second of which is that he was struck by lightning on account of the novel doctrines which he taught in the mysteries (ix, 30, 5 = *Test.* 123 κεραυνωθῆναι δὲ αὐτὸν τῶν λόγων ἕνεκα ὧν ἐδίδασκεν ἐν τοῖς μυστηρίοις οὐ πρότερον ἀκηκοότας ἀνθρώπους). Then, after some stories connected with his tomb, Pausanias ends with the statement concerning the hymns of Orpheus and their use by the Lycomidae which we have already examined (p. 198).

It is striking that all the features of this account belong to the legendary past except the few short hymns still extant which Pausanias is willing to allow him. In his lifetime Orpheus was active in mysteries and other forms of religion, but there is no hint in this passage, any more than there is in Diodorus iv, 25, of living Orphic rites. In the two texts the subject of which is Orpheus and nothing else, nothing whatever is said about special Orphic rites. Doubtless both Pausanias and Diodorus would have acknowledged that Orpheus had exercised a formative influence in that department of religion which was characterized by mystic and orgiastic ritual and that his arts were still widely used in the manifold cults of this type. The wide range of his activity is specially noted by Pausanias in his phrase "rites of gods" (τελετὰς θεῶν), and the statue of Telete is a fitting memorial of his life work.

9) In another passage (x, 7, 2 = *Test.* 170) Pausanias makes a somewhat slurring allusion to Orpheus' preoccupation with religion. Speaking of the musical contest at Delphi, in which the competitors sang hymns to the god, he says that, according to the report, though Philammon and Thamyris entered the competition, Orpheus talked solemnly of teletae (σεμνολογίᾳ τῇ ἐπὶ τελεταῖς) and refused to take part, and Musaeus, who imitated Orpheus in everything, also refused. It is natural that the legend should take this form. Though Orpheus was a great musician, his serious devotion to teletae and the religious use of his music would disincline him from taking part in a mere musical contest. One is reminded of Theseus' mockery of this religious aloofness in Euripides' *Hippolytus*. Musaeus, as often, is only a double of Orpheus.

10) Tatian, in a catalogue of inventions and discoveries (*Ad Graecos* 1 = *Test.* 258), attributes to Orpheus not only poetry and song but also the practice of initiation in general (ποίησιν μὲν γὰρ ἀσκεῖν καὶ ᾄδειν Ὀρφεὺς ὑμᾶς ἐδίδαξεν, ὁ δὲ αὐτὸς καὶ μυεῖσθαι).

11) Philostratus, in his account of the oracle of the head of Orpheus in Lesbos, which has been discussed above (p. 129), says that Orpheus attained great power among the Odrysae and among all Greeks who sought

the religious experience afforded by teletae (*Heroic.* v, 3 = *Test.* 134 ὁπόσοι τελεταῖς ἐθείαζον).

12) A passage of great importance for the study of Greek religion and especially its orgiastic forms is to be found in the first seven chapters of the *Protrepticus* of Clement of Alexandria. It is a description of Greek religion from the pen of an enemy, written to show its foulness and absurdity. Clement deals in succession with oracles, mysteries, idolatry, and then, at great length, with the gods of polytheism. In the section on the mysteries (ii, 12–22) Orpheus is mentioned three times: quotations from Orphic poems are introduced in connection with the mysteries of Dionysus and the mysteries of Demeter, and Midas is said to have learned from Orpheus the religion which he established in Phrygia. These passages have already been discussed (pp. 194, 204, 229). The only other allusion to Orpheus is at the very beginning of the book, which opens with a contrast between the legends of old Greek minstrels in Helicon and Cithaeron and the New Song of Christianity in the holy mountain of God. According to Greek story, says Clement, Amphion of Thebes and Arion of Methymna were both minstrels, one of whom used music as bait for a fish, and the other with music built the walls of Thebes; another, who was a Thracian, tamed wild beasts by the sheer power of his song and even transplanted trees with his music. A little later (i, 3 = *Test.* 151), Clement expresses the opinion that these three men, under the guise of music, had done much to degrade human life: they practiced a kind of methodical sorcery, which was disastrous in its results; they gave

ritualistic expression to deeds of violence; they imparted a divine significance to stories of sorrow and suffering; they were the first to bring men to the worship of idols; with their stocks and stones, that is to say with images and paintings, they built up a stupid structure of social custom (*ἐμοὶ μὲν οὖν δοκοῦσιν ὁ Θρᾴκιος ἐκεῖνος* ['Ορφεὺς] *καὶ ὁ Θηβαῖος καὶ ὁ Μηθυμναῖος, ἄνδρες τινὲς οὐκ ἄνδρες, ἀπατηλοὶ γεγονέναι, προσχήματί* ⟨*τε*⟩ *μουσικῆς λυμηνάμενοι τὸν βίον, ἐντέχνῳ τινὶ γοητείᾳ δαιμονῶντες εἰς διαφθοράς, ὕβρεις ὀργιάζοντες, πένθη ἐκθειάζοντες, τοὺς ἀνθρώπους ἐπὶ τὰ εἴδωλα χειραγωγῆσαι πρῶτοι, ναὶ μὴν λίθοις καὶ ξύλοις, τουτέστιν ἀγάλμασι καὶ σκιαγραφίαις, ἀνοικοδομῆσαι τὴν σκαιότητα τοῦ ἔθους, τὴν καλὴν ὄντως ἐκείνην ἐλευθερίαν τῶν ὑπ' οὐρανὸν πεπολιτευμένων ᾠδαῖς καὶ ἐπῳδαῖς ἐσχάτῃ δουλείᾳ καταζεύξαντες*).

There can be no doubt that Clement is thinking, among other things, of mysteries which were associated with the name of Orpheus, such as those of Dionysus and Demeter, which he mentions some pages later. But it is significant that he joins him with Amphion and Arion. He evidently has in mind the influence of poetry and song in the formulation of polytheism and idolatry and names these three because they were supposed to have magical powers as well. In this text he attributes to Orpheus no greater activity in relation to mysteries than to Amphion and Arion. Furthermore, he represents his influence, like that of the other two, as exercised upon the establishment of pagan religion in general.

After this harsh denunciation of Orpheus as one of the founders of paganism, Clement later has occasion to quote from an Orphic poem called the *Διαθῆκαι*, in which pure monotheism is preached, and he finds no difficulty in believing that it was composed by the same Orpheus whom he had previously held up to reprobation. It is surprising that he does not make more of a conversion so miraculous. By way of introduction to the quotation he says: "The Thracian who was at once hierophant and poet, Orpheus the son of Oeagrus, after his disclosure of the mystic rites and his theology of idols, told the truth in a recantation which he published later" (*Protrept.* vii, 74, 3 = *Fragm.* 246 ὁ δὲ Θρᾴκιος ἱεροφάντης καὶ ποιητὴς ἅμα, ὁ τοῦ Οἰάγρου 'Ορφεύς, μετὰ τὴν τῶν ὀργίων ἱεροφαντίαν καὶ τῶν εἰδώλων τὴν θεολογίαν, παλινῳδίαν ἀληθείας εἰσάγει). To call Orpheus a "hierophant" means no more than to call him a religious teacher. Clement calls Moses also the "hierophant of the truth" (*Protrept.* ii, 25, 1), and elsewhere he calls Orpheus "mystagogus" with a similar meaning (*Protrept.* ii, 21). It is evidently the intention of the writer to present both sides of Orpheus' activity, his priestly function in the ordaining of mysteries and his theological function in poetry.

13) The indebtedness of Pythagoras to Orpheus is asserted by Iamblichus in the notable passage which supplied the title for Lobeck's great book, *Aglaophamus* (*De vita Pythag.* xxviii, 145–147 Deubner = *Test.* 249). After relating some instances of the exemplary personal conduct of the Pythagoreans, Iamblichus proceeds to explain the doctrinal foundation for their high moral principles, introducing by way of proof a quotation from the beginning of an apocryphal work attributed to Pythagoras himself. What he says may be paraphrased thus.

If anyone is curious to know whence these men obtained their great piety, it may be stated that a clear model of the Pythagorean number theology was found in Orpheus (παρὰ 'Ορφεῖ). There is no longer any doubt that Pythagoras' book about the gods was based upon Orpheus, and that this was why he entitled it the Holy Doctrine, plucked as it was from the most mystical passage in Orpheus (οὐκέτι δὴ οὖν ἀμφίβολον γέγονε τὸ τὰς ἀφορμὰς παρὰ 'Ορφέως λαβόντα Πυθαγόραν συντάξαι τὸν περὶ θεῶν λόγον, ὃν καὶ ἱερὸν διὰ τοῦτο ἐπέγραψεν, ὡς ἂν ἐκ τοῦ μυστικωτάτου ἀπηνθισμένον παρὰ 'Ορφεῖ τόπου). There is some doubt whether the book was composed by Pythagoras himself or by his son Telauges. But in any case the text makes clear who it was from whom Pythagoras learned his doctrine of the gods. The passage runs thus: "The present work, *Concerning Gods*, is by Pythagoras, son of Mnesarchus. I became acquainted with the doctrine herein contained when I was admitted to certain rites (ὀργιασθείς) at Libethra in Thrace. The celebrant (τελεστής), Aglaophamus, gave me to know that Orpheus, son of Calliope, who was taught by his mother on Mount Pangaeum, declared that the substance of number, itself eternal, is the provident first cause of the whole heaven and the earth and all that is between, and that it is, moreover, the root which supplies the abiding life of divinity, of the great gods and the lesser gods." From this it is plain that he obtained the idea of the substance of the gods as defined by number from Orphic teaching (παρὰ τῶν 'Ορφικῶν παρέλαβεν—in this phrase 'Ορφικῶν may be masculine or neuter).

There is no doubt in Iamblichus' mind that Pythagoras

obtained his doctrine of number theology from Orphic books. He must have recognized the story of Pythagoras' initiation by Aglaophamus as a fictitious and picturesque method of describing his indebtedness to Orpheus. The mythical initiation was probably suggested by Orpheus' reputation as a patron of teletae and seemed natural because of the habit of using the language of mysteries in a figurative sense for philosophical doctrines. Aglaophamus has as much reality as Calliope, no more and no less.

Proclus (*In Plat. Timaeum* v, proem. iii, 168, 11 Diehl = *Test.* 250) repeats the same story of the initiation of Pythagoras by Aglaophamus. Elsewhere (*Theolog. Platon.* i, 6, p. 13, 3 = *Test.* 250) he makes a more sweeping statement, characteristically Neoplatonic: "All theology among the Greeks is sprung from the mystical doctrine of Orpheus. First Pythagoras was taught the holy rites concerning the gods by Aglaophamus; next Plato took over the whole lore concerning these matters from the Pythagorean and Orphic writings" (ἅπασα γὰρ ἡ παρ' Ἕλλησι θεολογία τῆς Ὀρφικῆς ἐστι μυσταγωγίας ἔκγονος, πρώτου μὲν Πυθαγόρου παρὰ Ἀγλαοφήμου τὰ περὶ θεῶν ὄργια διδαχθέντος, δευτέρου δὲ Πλάτωνος ὑποδεξαμένου τὴν παντελῆ περὶ τούτων ἐπιστήμην ἔκ τε τῶν Πυθαφορείων καὶ τῶν Ὀρφικῶν γραμμάτων).

What is to be learned from these texts of Proclus and Iamblichus about the association of Orpheus with mysteries? In the first place, it is clear that in referring to theological and theosophical doctrines, both writers use figuratively the technical terms of the mysteries (μυστικωτάτου τόπου, μυσταγωγία, ὄργια). This was a common practice of the late philosophers and the Christian authors, who, when they refer to mysteries, generally mean the theological doctrines of a school, whether these doctrines were imparted ceremonially to initiates or not. In the present instance it is expressly said that the source of Greek theology, and of the Pythagorean number theology in particular, was to be found in Orphic writings. Only in the purely fictitious account of the initiation of Pythagoras were the Orphic doctrines disclosed in mystic rites. The texts do not supply any evidence of the actual performance of Orphic mysteries in the time of Iamblichus or of Proclus, colored though they are throughout with the language of the mysteries. If there were actual mysteries which these authors were aware of, we can only conclude that the teaching in them was concerned with the philosophical number theory, which Iamblichus describes as the most "mystical" part of the writings of Orpheus, or with the whole range of Greek theology.

14) That Orpheus demanded an oath of secrecy before he disclosed his rites to initiates is asserted by Firmicus Maternus (*Mathes.* vii, 1, 1 Kroll-Skutsch-Ziegler = Kern, p. 312): "When Orpheus revealed his sacred rites to unknown persons, he made no other demand of those whom he initiated than a binding oath, supported by the awful authority of religion, in order that the rites which he had invented and organized might not be betrayed to profane ears" (cum incognitis hominibus Orpheus sacrorum caerimonias ⟨intimaret⟩, nihil aliud ab his quos initiabat in primo vestibulo nisi iurisiurandi necessitatem [et] cum terribili auctoritate religionis exegit, ne profanis auribus inventae ac compositae religiones proderentur).

In this the author is speaking of the legendary practices of Orpheus in his own lifetime, not of an actual procedure in the days of Firmicus Maternus. There was an Orphic poem called Ὅρκοι (see Kern, pp. 312 ff.); and in the Orphic poem called Διαθῆκαι (see Kern, pp. 255 ff.) the first line appears to have been:

φθέγξομαι οἷς θέμις ἐστί· θύρας δ' ἐπίθεσθε βέβηλοι.

Eusebius quotes the line twice from Porphyry as evidence of the solemn pretentiousness of the writer, which, he says, does not impose upon him at all (*Praep. Evang.* iii, 7, p. 97 D = *Fragm.* 247, p. 263 ἄκουε δ' οὖν καὶ τῆς τούτων φυσιολογίας, μεθ' οἵας ἐξενήνεκται τῷ Πορφυρίῳ ἀλαζονείας· Φθέγξομαι ... βέβηλοι, and iii, 13, p. 118 A οὐ γάρ με ἡ ἀλαζὼν ἐκπλήξει φωνή, 'Φθέγξομαι . . . βέβηλοι' φήσασα). Something similar to it appears as early as Plato, who writes in the *Symposium* (218 B = *Fragm.* 13): πύλας πάνυ μεγάλας τοῖς ὠσὶν ἐπίθεσθε. The line is a solemn warning to the unfit to hold aloof as in the presence of a mystery. Whether it was used in an Orphic poem older than Plato or was later adopted by an Orphic poet from some unknown source, it is impossible to say. At the beginning of the Διαθῆκαι it is used to warn the reader that the poem contains matter of solemn import. Similarly, Vettius Valens exacts an oath of secrecy and discretion from the reader (*Anthol.* vii, proem., p. 263, 4 Kroll = Kern, p. 312): χρὴ μὲν οὖν πρὸ πάντων καὶ περὶ ταύτης τῆς βίβλου ὅρκον προτάξαι τοῖς ἐντυγχάνουσιν, ὅπως πεφυλαγμένως καὶ μυστικῶς ἔχωσι τὰ λεγόμενα. From all this it would appear that Firmicus Maternus was aware of the requirement of an oath before initiation into mysteries, of the literary convention which called for a similar oath from the reader at the beginning of a book, and of the employment of this convention in Orphic poems. The text reveals nothing about Orphic mysteries except (and this we should know already) that in whatever rites were called Orphic an oath of secrecy was probably demanded before initiation.

15) Themistius in one of his orations undertakes to show the importance of agriculture in civilization and the advantages of a farmer's life. As witnesses to the truth of his contentions he invokes the gods who are concerned with farming—Dionysus, the Nymphs, the daughter of Demeter, Zeus Hyetius, and Poseidon Phytalmius. In so doing, he says, we are coming close to the sacred rites (πλησιάζομεν ἤδη ταῖς τελεταῖς), and we shall introduce into our discourse the wisdom of Prodicus, who makes all religious ceremonial—mysteries, festivals, and teletae—dependent upon farming, believing that the good will of the gods came to men from this source. He then continues thus (xxx, 349 B = *Test.* 112): "It is no less true that even the rites and ceremonies of Orpheus are not unrelated to the business of the farmer. The legend which tells how all things were affected by his enchantment really means that he tamed all nature and wild animals by means of the cultivated crops which farming produces, and that he tamed and eradicated the animal nature in the soul. Animals were believed to have been charmed by his song because for all sacrifice and divine worship he used the good things that are provided by the farmer. At all events, his fame spread far and wide, and

farming was everywhere adopted" (οὐ μὴν οὐδὲ 'Ορφέως τελετάς τε καὶ ὄργια γεωργίας ἐκτὸς συμβέβηκεν εἶναι, ἀλλὰ καὶ ὁ μῦθος τοῦτο αἰνίττεται, πάντα κηλεῖν τε καὶ θέλγειν τὸν 'Ορφέα λέγων, ὑπὸ τῶν καρπῶν τῶν ἡμέρων ὧν γεωργία παρέχει πᾶσαν ἡμερῶσαι φύσιν καὶ θηρίων δίαιταν, καὶ τὸ ἐν ταῖς ψυχαῖς θηριῶδες ἐκκόψαι καὶ ἡμερῶσαι. καὶ τὰ θηρία γὰρ τῷ μέλει κηλεῖν ἐπιστεύθη θυσίας τε πάσας καὶ τελετὰς διὰ τῶν ἐκ γεωργίας καλῶν εἰς θεοὺς ἀνάγων. πάντες γοῦν ἀνθρώπους ἐπῆλθε τῇ δόξῃ καὶ πάντες ἐδέξαντο γεωργίαν). The author is reminded of Orpheus by his reference to teletae, and he asserts that the rites and ceremonies of Orpheus have some connection with farming. In order to make this point good, he does not describe the features of the rites which he finds significant for his purpose (indeed, one suspects that he does not know anything about them), but has recourse to the legend which tells how Orpheus had the power to charm animals. The legend originated, he says, in the fact that in all rites and sacrifices Orpheus used the domestic products of the farmer. Thus he makes Orpheus a culture hero who brought an end to the wild life of the hunter and introduced the mild and peaceful life of the farmer. All this is, of course, only a literary device in a rhetorical exercise. It was probably based, however, on an older tradition. One is reminded of the text in Aristophanes' *Frogs* which couples together the institution of rites and the injunction against bloodshed, and of Horace's words to similar effect. Kern[30] says that the notion of making Orpheus the originator of agriculture was generated by the Orphic poems on agricultural subjects, but

[30] *Orpheus* (1920), p. 32.

there seems to be no support for this view except the mere fact of the existence of the poems. As for Orphic rites, we can only say that Themistius was aware of them, but it is not certain whether the rites of which he was aware were actually existent in his own day or only a part of the legend of Orpheus.[31]

16) Servius, in a note on Vergil, *Aeneid* vi, 645 (nec non Threicius longa cum veste sacerdos), says that Orpheus was the first to institute mystic rites (*Test.* 58a 'sacerdos' autem, quia et theologus fuit et orgia primus instituit).

17) Hermeias, commenting on the passage in the *Phaedrus* (244) where Socrates describes the four kinds of madness, points to Orpheus as one who was inspired by all these forms of madness in the highest degree. According to the legend, he had the gifts of prophecy, poetry, and love, and besides he showed a special genius in connection with teletae. Musaeus was the great object of his love, which he showed particularly by imparting to him the blessings of religion (*In Plat. Phaedrum* 244 A, p. 88, 26 Couvreur = *Test.* 171 *τελεστικώτατον μὲν γὰρ αὐτὸν καὶ μαντικώτατον παρειλήφαμεν καὶ ὑπὸ τοῦ Ἀπόλλωνος κινούμενον, ἔτι ποιητικώτατον, ὅν γε δι' αὐτὸ τοῦτο καὶ Καλλιόπης υἱὸν γενέσθαι φασίν· ἐρωτικώτατός τέ ἐστιν, ὡς αὐτὸς λέγων φαίνεται, πρὸς τὸν Μουσαῖον καὶ προτείνων αὐτῷ τὰ θεῖα ἀγαθὰ καὶ τελειῶν αὐτόν*).

18) Marinus, in his *Life of Proclus* (sec. 18 Boissonade = *Test.* 239), says that Proclus made constant use of rites

[31] Robert Eisler (*Orphisch-Dionysische Mysteriengedanken in der christlichen Antike*, Leipzig, 1925, pp. 299 ff.) offers an ingenious but unconvincing interpretation of this text.

of purification, sometimes Orphic rites, sometimes Chaldaean (*νύκτωρ τε καὶ μεθ' ἡμέραν ἀποτροπαῖς καὶ περιρραντηρίοις καὶ τοῖς ἄλλοις καθαρμοῖς χρώμενος, ὁτὲ μὲν 'Ορφικοῖς, ὁτὲ δὲ Χαλδαϊκοῖς*). These rites must have been acts of personal devotion for which directions were supplied, either expressly or by implication, in Orphic and Chaldaean writings.

19) A very sweeping phrase for the activity of Orpheus in connection with mysteries is used by Suidas (s.v. *θρησκεύει* = *Test.* 37): "It is said that Orpheus the Thracian was the first to organize the technical rules for the mysteries of the Greeks, and they used the word *θρησκεύειν* for divine worship because the invention was Thracian" (*λέγεται γὰρ ὡς 'Ορφεὺς Θρᾷξ πρῶτος τεχνολογῆσαι τὰ 'Ελλήνων μυστήρια. καὶ τὸ τιμᾶν θεὸν θρησκεύειν ἐκάλεσαν, ὡς Θρᾳκίας οὔσης τῆς εὑρέσεως*). Here are the "Orphic arts" of Strabo. The word *τεχνολογεῖν*, which means "to formulate the rules of an art," as, for example, the art of rhetoric, indicates that there was a particular "art of mysteries." This art Orpheus was supposed to have invented and developed, establishing its regular practices and principles; and in this sense all Greek mysteries were Orphic. Statements similar to that of Suidas are found also in the *Etymologicum Magnum* (455, 10 = *Test.* 37 *θρησκεία παρὰ τὴν τῶν Θρᾳκῶν ἐπιμέλειαν τὴν πρὸς τὸ θεῖον καὶ τὴν 'Ορφέως ἱερουργίαν· οὗτοι γὰρ πρῶτον ἐξεῦρον τὴν περὶ τὸ θεῖον ἔννοιαν*) and in a scholium on Euripides, *Alcestis* 968 (*Test.* 37 *πρῶτος 'Ορφεὺς μυστήρια θεῶν παρέδωκεν· ὅθεν καὶ θρησκεία τὸ μυστήριον καλεῖται, ἀπὸ τοῦ Θρᾳκὸς 'Ορφέως*).

20) Among the works of Orpheus named by Constan-

tine Lascaris (in *Marmora Taurinensia*, Augustae Taurin., 1743, p. 98 = *Test.* 225) appears the phrase Μυστήρια διάφορα. This suggests that a poem could be known as a Mystery; that whether the ritual was also supposed to have been instituted by the poet or not, the poem might continue to exist and be called a Mystery after the practice of the ritual had been given up; and that references to Mysteries, therefore, are not proof of the continued practices of a mystic ritual. Perhaps a poem might be called a Mystery if it told a myth of which a mystic ritual was the representation, or if, not being connected with any ritual, it told a myth which received, or required, allegorical interpretation. Lascaris had heard of more than one such Mystery attributed to Orpheus.

21) A scholium on Aristophanes, *Frogs* 1032, may be quoted for the sake of completeness, though it actually gives no information beyond what may be obtained from the text of Aristophanes itself, which has been discussed above: ὅτι πολλὴ δόξα κατεῖχε περὶ Ὀρφέως, ὡς τελετὰς συντετάχοι. τὸν Μουσαῖον παῖδα Σελήνης καὶ Εὐμόλπῳ Φιλόχορός φησιν· οὗτος δὲ παραλύσεις καὶ τελετὰς καὶ καθαρμοὺς συνέθηκεν. ὁ δὲ Σοφοκλῆς χρησμόλογον αὐτόν φησιν (*Test.* 90).

## *Chapter* III

# Collation of the Evidence

IF THE READER has had the patience to inspect the long array of texts as they have marched past, he will have received a general impression of the kind of religious activities and institutions with which the ancient world associated the name of Orpheus. All the texts touching such activities and institutions in which the name of Orpheus appears have been presented, and the interpretation of the individual texts has been discussed as fully as has seemed necessary. Furthermore, the chronological sequence has been observed in the presentation, except in one respect. The texts later than 300 B.C. have been divided into two groups, those in which the name of Orpheus is associated with the cult of particular deities, and those in which no deities are named. This arrangement makes it possible at a glance to answer the question, Who were the deities with whose cults Orpheus was connected? There are, however, other pertinent questions to which answers may be sought by a collation of the texts. We may now proceed to formulate such questions, to review the texts in order to discover the answers, and so classify the results that sound inferences may be drawn from them.

### REVIEW OF THE TEXTS

Two questions naturally present themselves: first, With what religious activities and institutions was the name of Orpheus actually associated? and second, In what ways was his name associated with them? These two questions will be taken up in order. In recalling particular texts it will not be necessary to quote them again or to repeat the exact specifications; it will be sufficient to refer to the earlier page of this book on which the text is quoted and discussed in full.

## CONSPECTUS OF THE RELIGIOUS ACTIVITIES AND INSTITUTIONS WITH WHICH THE NAME OF ORPHEUS WAS ASSOCIATED

First to be mentioned are a dozen or more local cults and festivals:

a) Certain honored Athenian mysteries of Persephone were founded by Orpheus (Euripides, *Rhesus*, p. 61).

b) According to the *Parian Marble* (p. 193) and Clement of Alexandria (p. 194), the ἱερὸς λόγος of the Eleusinian Mysteries was told in a poem by Orpheus. Elsewhere he is said to have founded these Mysteries (Proclus, p. 194) or introduced them from abroad (Theodoretus, p. 195).

c) The cults of Phrygia are said to have been founded by Midas, who was a pupil of Orpheus (Conon, etc., p. 203).

d) Orpheus was initiated into the Samothracian Mysteries (Diodorus, p. 204).

e) The cult of Dionysus, son of Semele, in Thebes, was founded by him (Diodorus, p. 211).

f) The orgies of the women of Thrace and Macedonia are called Orphic (Plutarch, p. 226).

g) The cult of Demeter Chthonia in Sparta was founded by Orpheus (Pausanias, p. 192).

h) The temple of Kore Soteira in Sparta was built by Orpheus (Pausanias, p. 192).

i) Orpheus was the author of hymns to Eros and other deities, which were used in the mysteries of the Lycomidae at Phlya (Pausanias, p. 197); and the ἱερὸς λόγος of the goddess called Μεγάλη, who was worshiped in these mysteries, was also told in an Orphic poem (Hippolytus, p. 199).

j) The mystery cult of Hecate in Aegina was founded by Orpheus (Pausanias, p. 202).

k) The Dionysia, the Panathenaea, and the Thesmophoria were introduced into Athens by Orpheus (Theodoretus, p. 195).

l) The *Orphic Hymns* (p. 179) were used in a mystery cult which was addressed to eighty-six deities, perhaps in Pergamum.

There is one allusion to a private sect: its members, who were called Orphics, practiced orgia and observed a prohibition against the use of wool in burial (Herodotus, p. 39).

There were rites of private practitioners, open to all, which procured remission of sins and happiness after death: books by Orpheus were in some way authoritative in these rites (Plato, p. 77), the practitioners were called Orpheotelestae (Theophrastus, p. 101; Philodemus, p. 233; Plutarch, p. 233), and the rites were called Orphic (Diogenes Laertius, p. 233).

Persons who avoided the use of animal food were said to lead a life which may have been called Orphic (Euripides, p. 50; Plato, p. 97).

Certain particular forms of ritual were instituted by Orpheus: δενδροφορίαι (Palaephatus, p. 208); purifications for unholy deeds, cures for disease, methods of averting divine wrath (Pausanias, p. 246); the setting up of images, hymns, chants, and incantations (Eusebius, p. 243); apotropaic rites, lustral sprinklings, and purifications (Marinus, p. 257).

Religious activities which appear oftenest, recurring in text after text, are teletae, mysteries, and orgia. Most of the local cults and other institutions already mentioned involve the use of rites of this type. But besides these, there are teletae and mysteries associated with Orpheus in texts which do not supply information that would permit us to assign them to particular local cults.

We hear oftenest of mysteries of Dionysus, the supreme god of mysteries, but there is considerable variety in the kinds of Dionysiac rites associated with Orpheus. Besides those mentioned above (the Theban mysteries of the son of Zeus and Semele, and the orgia of Thracian and Macedonian women), there are mysteries involving the myth of the dismemberment of Dionysus by the Titans (Diodorus, pp. 191, 213, 215; Clement of Alexandria, p. 230; Arnobius, p. 230; Macrobius, p. 231; Proclus, p. 229; *Mythographi Vaticani*, p. 232); mysteries addressed to Dionysus son of Jupiter and Luna (Cicero, p. 220); mysteries whose devotees believed the universe to be oval (Achilles Statius, p. 225); mysteries of Dionysus otherwise undefined (Damagetus, p. 207; Diodorus, p. 219; Apollodorus, p. 207; Pomponius Mela, p. 208; Lactantius, p. 208).

To the mysteries of Demeter mentioned among the local cults may be added the mysteries of this goddess which, according to Diodorus (p. 190), Orpheus introduced from Egypt.

The mysteries may also be recalled in which, according to Iamblichus (p. 250), the number theology of Orpheus was communicated to Pythagoras, and those in which Themistius (p. 255), with recourse to legend, found some connection with farming.

There are many allusions to mysteries which are in no way defined except by association with the name of Orpheus. In a few places the text suggests that particular mysteries are meant: the title of the book by Apollonius of Aphrodisia, "Concerning Orpheus and His Rites" (p. 232); Strabo's statement (p. 235) that the Orphica originated in Thrace; the inclusion by Gregory of Nazianzus (p. 241) of the teletae and mysteries of Orpheus in a long list of cults and myths. When Constantine Lascaris (p. 258) refers to certain Orphic poems which he calls Μυστήρια διάφορα, one may surmise that the subject of each poem was a particular mystery, but that they were not all the same mystery.

A few of the writers, again, clearly have in mind not particular mysteries, but mysteries in general as a type of religious activity. Ephorus (p. 27) says that Orpheus first introduced teletae and mysteries among the Greeks; Tatian (p. 247) says that Orpheus first taught the practice of initiation (μυεῖσθαι); and Suidas (p. 258) says that Orpheus first organized the technical rules for Greek mysteries.

In many texts, if one examines them without prejudice, it is impossible to be sure whether the writer is thinking of particular mysteries, of one or more kinds of mysteries, or of mysteries in general (Aristophanes, p. 67; Plato, p. 71; Ps.-Demosthenes, p. 99; Diodorus, pp. 191, 243; Plutarch, p. 244; Pausanias, pp. 245, 246; Clement of Alexandria, p. 248; Hippolytus, p. 199; Eusebius, p. 243; Philostratus, p. 247; Firmicus Maternus, p. 253; Servius, p. 257; Schol. Euripides, p. 258; *Etym. Magn.*, p. 258).

This survey makes it clear that many rites, of many kinds, addressed to many gods, may, in one sense or another, be properly called Orphic. At one extreme we find certain particular rites closely associated with his name; at the other we find teletae and mysteries in general, as a special class of religious performances, attributed to him in such a way that all teletae and mysteries might be called Orphic. But let us assume for the sake of argument that amongst the multitudinous mysteries in the Greek world there were certain particular mysteries distinguished from all others and recognized as Orphic in a particular sense. How shall we determine which they are? Obviously, all the things that are said about all the mysteries with which Orpheus' name is connected cannot be added together to produce a sum that would have any tolerable or credible unity. The Athenian mysteries of Persephone, the mysteries of Hecate at Aegina, the Dionysiac orgies of Macedonian women, the ministrations of Orpheotelestae, the joint cult of eighty-six deities at Pergamum—all these certainly have nothing in common except a right in the title of mysteries. If *one* among them, or among all the others which we have seen, deserves the name of Orphic above and in distinction from all others, how are we to decide which it is? None seems to be signalized as in any sense more Orphic than another. And if we propose to build up the true Orphic mysteries by accepting some features from some of the mysteries and some from others, and rejecting all the rest, we see immediately that no principle of selection can be discovered and that such a procedure is purely arbitrary. For it must be carefully remarked that nothing is to be inferred from the comparative frequency with which the various myths and other features of the mysteries are alluded to except the comparative interest of the various writers in these matters. It must be admitted that if there were peculiar Orphic mysteries, there seems to be little chance of telling what they were. This renders the assumption unlikely. But the assumption still has some hold on life and must be tested again. We still have to explore the evidence for an answer to the second of the two questions asked at the beginning of this review, In what ways is the name of Orpheus associated with religious activities?

## WAYS IN WHICH THE NAME OF ORPHEUS IS ASSOCIATED WITH RELIGIOUS ACTIVITIES AND INSTITUTIONS

In the great majority of texts in which the name of Orpheus is associated with religious practices, he is represented either as their originator or as a participant in them during his own lifetime. Such activities on his part are conceived, in the Greek manner, to have been characteristic of his legendary career. The general manner of his life is thus described in a half-dozen comprehensive statements. He was occupied, we are told, with teletae and chresmodiae (Plato, p. 72) and lived as a vagabond on what he could make by his music, his prophecy, and his performance of religious rites (Strabo, p. 239). According to Diodorus (pp. 243, 211), he was the greatest of the Greeks in theology, teletae, music, and song. Pausanias (p. 246) says that he attained great power because he was believed to have invented teletae, purifications for unholy deeds, cures for disease, and methods of averting divine wrath. Clement of Alexandria (p. 248) accuses him of practicing sorcery and of introducing deeds of violence into ritual. Philostratus (p. 247) says that he enjoyed great power and influence among all who sought religious experience in teletae. Eusebius (p. 243) attributes to him mysteries and teletae, the setting up of images, hymns, chants, and incantations. A few special incidents are recorded which, though they are as fictitious as the rest of the legend, reveal what kind of person Orpheus appeared to be to the generations of men by whom the legend was shaped. He was said to have worshiped the Sun (Ps.-Eratosthenes, p. 205). He made use of rhombus and tympanum in a dance which was intended to appease Rhea, and these instruments were always used thereafter by the Phrygians in her worship (Apollonius of Rhodes, p. 203). He was the teacher of Midas, who carried religious rites into Phrygia (Conon, p. 203). He restored maddened Bacchantes to their homes; and since they carried boughs of trees as they followed him, the *δενδροφορίαι* continued in use ever afterward (Palaephatus,

p. 208). He was initiated into the Samothracian mysteries (Diodorus, p. 204). He refused to take part in a musical contest, holding himself above it because of the solemnity of his teletae (Pausanias, p. 247). He imposed an oath of secrecy on those whom he initiated (Firmicus Maternus, p. 254). Many texts contain the mere statement, without any legendary elaboration, that particular rites and institutions, or mysteries in general, were founded by him.[1] Sometimes he is represented not as actually originating the rites, but as introducing them from abroad: so in Diodorus (pp. 191, 211), Eusebius (p. 243), Theodoretus (pp. 195, 207). Once he is said to have modified and reformed many of the features in rites which had been instituted by Dionysus himself (Diodorus, p. 218).

In texts which speak of Orpheus as a participator in mysteries or as a founder of mysteries it is not uncommon to find mention of the other great kindred activity on which his fame rests, music and poetry (Ps.-Demosthenes, p. 99; Ephorus, p. 27; Diodorus, pp. 211, 242; Pausanias, p. 245; Tatian, p. 247; Clement of Alexandria, p. 248; Eusebius, p. 243). Often his very function in relation to religious institutions is just that of poet and

[1] The various words which are used in the sense of 'originate' in all the texts referred to above may be noted: *δεῖξαι* (Euripides, p. 61); *καταδεῖξαι* (Aristophanes, p. 67; Ps.-Demosthenes, p. 99; Diodorus, p. 215; Hippolytus, p. 199); *εὑρεῖν*, *εὑρέσθαι* (Damagetus, p. 207; Pausanias, p. 246; Apollodorus, p. 207); *παραδοῦναι* (Diodorus, p. 215; Pausanias, p. 192; Schol. Euripides, p. 258); *ἐνστήσασθαι* (Diodorus, p. 211); *καταστήσασθαι* (Pausanias, p. 203); *συστήσασθαι* (Eusebius, p. 244); *ἐξενεγκεῖν* (Ephorus, p. 27); *διδάξαι* (Tatian, p. 247); *ἐκφῆναι* (Proclus, p. 194); *διασκευάσαι* (Theodoretus, p. 207); *τεχνολογῆσαι* (Suidas, p. 258); primo initiante (Pomponius Mela, p. 208); primus induxit (Lactantius, p. 208); primus instituit (Servius, p. 257).

musician. He is the author of hymns which were composed for use in mysteries (Pausanias, p. 197; *Orphic Hymns*, p. 179); of poems containing liturgical directions (Macrobius, p. 205; many of the titles of poems named by Suidas, s.v. Orpheus = *Test.* 223); of poems in which the ἱεροὶ λόγοι of mysteries were told—of the Eleusinian Mysteries (*Parian Marble*, p. 193; Clement of Alexandria, p. 194), of the mysteries of the Lycomidae (Hippolytus, p. 199), of the mysteries of the dismemberment of Dionysus (Diodorus, p. 213; Clement of Alexandria, p. 230; Arnobius, p. 230); of poems highly regarded by those who avoided animal food (Euripides, p. 50); and of poems used as authority by practitioners of teletae (Plato, p. 77). Sometimes his two activities merge together, and he is named as both the originator of particular mysteries and as the author of the poem in which the ἱερὸς λόγος is told. So Diodorus, who, as we have just seen, refers to Orphic poems which contained the story of the dismemberment of Dionysus, elsewhere calls the teletae involving the dismemberment Orphic (p. 215). Clement of Alexandria (p. 230), quoting two lines from an Orphic poem as evidence for certain features of this same myth, attributes them to the "poet of the rite" (ὁ τῆς τελετῆς ποιητής); and, again (p. 194), quoting from an Orphic poem in which the myth of the Eleusinia was told, he attributes it to the mystagogus. The identity of poet and religious organizer is elsewhere explicitly asserted by the same author (p. 250), when, without reference to a particular myth and rite, he calls Orpheus "at once hierophant and poet."

Thus it is clear that Orpheus is sometimes named as both the poet and the founder of the same mysteries, and that at other times he is only the author of the poems which belong to the mysteries and is not also credited with their institution. There is still another manner of speaking, in which quotations from Orphic poetry are attributed to Orpheus the hierophant when the writer has no thought of real mysteries in mind, and in which doctrines actually found in Orphic poetry are said to belong to the mysteries. In such language, which is purely figurative, the contents, not only of Orphic poems, but of all religious poetry, are treated as something 'mystical' and 'esoteric.' The practice has already been discussed in connection with certain passages in Iamblichus and Proclus (pp. 250 ff.) and may be abundantly illustrated from the works of Proclus and the later Neoplatonists (e.g., Proclus, *Theolog. Platon.* i, 6 = *Test.* 250; *ibid.* v, 35 = *Fragm.* 151; *ibid.* vi, 8 = *Fragm.* 168; *In Plat. Timaeum* 40 E, iii, 161, 1 Diehl = *Test.* 250; *In Plat. Cratylum* 391 D–E, p. 32, 29 Pasquali = *Fragm.* 85). It cannot be assumed, therefore, that such words as τελεταί, μυστήρια, μυστικός, μυσταγωγία, ὄργια, ἱεροφάντης, when they are used by late writers in connection with Orphic poetry and what is found in it, necessarily imply the existence of living mysteries. They are used simply to give sanctity to thoughts which seem too valuable and profound to be divulged to chance comers and unsympathetic listeners.

An interesting example of this use is to be found in the opening lines of the Orphic poem called Διαθῆκαι (p. 254). In this poem the author, under the name of Orpheus, delivers a recantation of polytheism and makes an assertion of the truth of monotheism. It seems impossible that it could have been associated with any kind of mysteries. The poet begins, however, as if he were addressing a company of neophytes, thus:

> φθέγξομαι οἷς θέμις ἐστί· θύρας δ' ἐπίθεσθε βέβηλοι
> πάντες ὁμῶς· σὺ δ' ἄκουε, φαεσφόρου ἔκγονε Μήνης,
> Μουσαῖ'· ἐξερέω γὰρ ἀληθέα· μηδέ σε τὰ πρὶν
> ἐν στήθεσσι φανέντα φίλης αἰῶνος ἀμέρσῃ

The first line obviously contains a formula from the mysteries which seems to have been in use even before Plato. Its use in the Διαθῆκαι, like the address to Musaeus, is a purely literary convention.

The three ways already reviewed in which the name of Orpheus is associated with religious institutions and activities, as participant, originator, and poet, all represent him as personally active. Among the texts which illustrate these several ways there are two which exhibit at the same time yet another way in which the name of Orpheus is attached to religious rites. In this fourth way the rites simply bear the name of Orpheus as a label. When Diodorus (p. 219) says that rites which were instituted by Dionysus himself were afterward reformed by Orpheus, he adds the statement that in consequence of this they were "called Orphic." Similarly, when Lactantius (p. 208) says that Orpheus was the first to introduce the rites of Liber in Greece, and that he celebrated them on Mount Cithaeron, he adds the statement that these rites are still "called Orphic." In these two places it is explained how the label came to be applied; but there are still other texts in which rites and institutions are called Orphic, by one phrase or another, without any hint of why they are given this proper denomination. The texts in question have all been analyzed in previous chapters, but we must now bring them together in a summary review.

Some of these texts reveal little or nothing beyond the fact that the authors were aware of rites which were actually called Orphic. Such are the title of the book by Apollonius of Aphrodisia, "Concerning Orpheus and His Rites" (p. 232); Strabo's statement that the Orphica had their origin in Thrace (p. 235); the list of pagan myths and cults given by Gregory of Nazianzus in which "teletae and mysteries of Orpheus" are included (p. 241).

In the following texts we find particular rites not only called Orphic but defined to a certain degree.

According to Herodotus (p. 39), there was a rule that those who participated in the orgia of the Orphics should not be buried in woolen garments after death.

The teletae administered by an Orpheotelestes, a word which appears in Theophrastus (p. 101), Philodemus (p. 233), and Plutarch (p. 233), may certainly be called Orphic, and these identical rites are expressly called Orphica by Diogenes Laertius (p. 233). All we know of these rites is that they were believed to procure remission of sins and provide for happiness after death. There is nothing to show that all Orpheotelestae used the same ceremonies.

Cicero, in a passage whose meaning is extremely doubtful (p. 220), gives a list of five gods named Dionysus and says that Orphic sacra were addressed to one among them, the son of Jupiter and Luna. Since he attaches other rites to others of the five, it would appear that he did not regard all Dionysiac rites as Orphic. But in attributing Orphic rites to the son of Jupiter and Luna, he may mean either that these rites alone were Orphic, or that they were of a kind called Orphic. The fatal lack of a definite article in Latin makes the sense ambiguous.

When Diodorus (p. 219) says that rites founded by Dionysus and reformed by Orpheus were called Orphic (τελετὰς 'Ορφικάς), he may mean either that some rites of Dionysus were called Orphic or that all were so called.

Plutarch in one place (p. 244) says that there was considerable similarity between the rites of Bona Dea and the Orphica. Elsewhere (p. 226) he reports that the women of Macedonia were addicted to the Orphica, and he explains that these were wild Dionysiac rites involving the use of snakes, ivy, winnowing fans, thyrsi, and wreaths. We have seen reason to believe, however, that he did not regard these as the only rites which were called Orphic.

Those who perform the Orphic mysteries (οἱ τὰ 'Ορφικὰ μυστήρια τελοῦντες), says Achilles Statius (p. 225), believe that the universe is oval in shape. This sounds as if he thought that there were no Orphic mysteries the participants in which did not believe the universe to be oval.

When Lactantius (p. 208) says that the rites of Liber introduced in Greece by Orpheus were still called Orphic, he, like Strabo, may mean some or all Dionysiac rites.

Themistius (p. 255) says that the rites and ceremonies

of Orpheus (Ὀρφέως τελετάς τε καὶ ὄργια) are not unrelated to the business of the farmer. His warrant for this is a rationalistic interpretation of the legend that Orpheus had the power of charming animals.

In the rites of the Orphics (in illorum sacris), says Macrobius (p. 231), Dionysus is torn to pieces by the Titans, the pieces are buried, and the god reëmerges sound and whole. Practically the same thing is said again in the *Mythographi Vaticani* (p. 232).

Joannes Lydus (p. 224), like Cicero, gives a list of five gods named Dionysus, of whom one was the son of Zeus and Semele, and says that the mysteries of Orpheus (τὰ Ὀρφέως μυστήρια) were performed in his honor. The article suggests that these were the only Orphic mysteries of which the author was aware.

Proclus, we are told by Marinus (p. 257), made constant use of rites of purification, sometimes Orphic, sometimes Chaldaean.

This completes the list. In these texts, if anywhere, we should expect to find a clear revelation of the existence of an Orphic religion. If *all* the rites and institutions which we have found to be associated with Orpheus may in some sense be called Orphic, those to which the ancient writers themselves applied this term explicitly must certainly be acknowledged to have an uncontrovertible right to it. But if we consider the characteristic features of the rites presented in these several texts and compare them one with another, it is difficult to believe that they all belong to a single institution. Their diversity is such that if they must be assembled and reconciled with one another in a single institution, no single institution is capacious enough to hold them all except the great comprehensive and all-embracing institution of mysteries, teletae, and orgia itself. In fact, these texts, in which Orphic rites are explicitly named, disclose the same situation that was revealed by the whole collection of texts touching upon the association of Orpheus with rites and mysteries. We must acknowledge even here that we cannot distinguish any particular mysteries which we may venture to call Orphic in the sense that they and they alone were Orphic.

## THE ORPHICS

The review of the ways in which the name of Orpheus is associated with religious institutions and activities is still not quite complete. It will have been observed that in several of the texts which contain references to such activities the persons who are engaged in them are called Orphics (Ὀρφικοί, Orphici). Such language must imply some bond of union or at least some significant point of resemblance between the persons so denominated. We must examine the texts once more and try to discover the nature of the bond. But besides the texts dealing with Orphic rites, already presented, in which Orphics are mentioned, there are others in which such persons are named, but which we have had no occasion to examine because they say nothing of religious rites. For the sake of completeness the review must be expanded to include these texts which have not hitherto been discussed. Furthermore, the examination will not be limited to the words Ὀρφικοί or Orphici, but will also include texts containing phrases of a similar import. In all, there are a dozen or more texts which demand our attention, including those that have already been cited and those that are still to be presented.

Orphics are first mentioned in Herodotus (p. 39), who says that all who shared in their rites observed a rule that no one among them should be buried in woolen garments. The word appears in the dative case, and the gender is open to doubt; but the masculine is the more probable.

The first appearance of the term Ὀρφικοί after Herodotus, and hence the first appearance of it which is beyond question, is in Achilles Statius in the second century A.D. The following passage is found in his *Introduction to the Phaenomena of Aratus* (4, p. 33, 17 Maass = *Fragm.* 70); "The structure which we have recognized in the sphere is similar, say the Orphics, to that of an egg: the sky bears the same part in the universe as the shell in the egg, and as the aether is attached to the curve of the sky, so the inner membrane of the egg is attached to the shell" (τὴν δὲ τάξιν, ἣν δεδώκαμεν τῷ σφαιρώματι, οἱ Ὀρφικοὶ λέγουσι παραπλησίαν εἶναι τῇ ἐν τοῖς ᾠοῖς· ὃν γὰρ ἔχει λόγον τὸ λέπυρον ἐν τῷ ᾠῷ, τοῦτον ἐν τῷ παντὶ ὁ οὐρανός, καὶ ὡς ἐξήρτηται τοῦ οὐρανοῦ κυκλοτερῶς ὁ αἰθήρ, οὕτω τοῦ λεπύρου ὁ ὑμήν). A few pages later, as we have seen (p. 225), he says that those who celebrate the Orphic mysteries (οἱ τὰ Ὀρφικὰ μυστήρια τελοῦντες) believe that the shape of the universe is oval.

Nearly two centuries later Macrobius (p. 231) says that the Orphici understand Liber to be the νοῦς ὑλικός, indivisible and yet divided through the universe, and that their rites, in which they represent his dismemberment by the Titans, carry this meaning.

Iamblichus (p. 251) says that the model for the Pythagorean number theology was to be found in Orpheus (παρὰ 'Ορφεῖ) and that the fundamental idea was obtained παρὰ τῶν 'Ορφικῶν. Though παρὰ 'Ορφεῖ means definitely "in Orphic books," the adjective in the phrase παρὰ τῶν 'Ορφικῶν may be either masculine or neuter: Orphics or Orphic books. A little later, however (*De vita Pythag.* xxviii, 151 Deubner = *Test.* 249a), he uses the same phrase again in a context which shows that the adjective is to be taken as masculine: "Furthermore, they say that the divine philosophy and worship which were instituted by Pythagoras were composite in character, since he had learned something from the Orphics, something from the Egyptian priests, something from the Chaldaeans and the Magi, something from the rite at Eleusis, something at Imbros, Samothrace, and Lemnos (or Delos), something perhaps from the public cults, something among the Celts and in Iberia" (ἔτι δέ φασι καὶ σύνθετον αὐτὸν ποιῆσαι τὴν θεὶαν φιλοσοφίαν καὶ θεραπείαν, ἃ μὲν μαθόντα παρὰ τῶν 'Ορφικῶν, ἃ δὲ παρὰ τῶν Αἰγυπτίων ἱερέων, ἃ δὲ παρὰ Χαλδαίων καὶ μάγων, ἃ δὲ παρὰ τῆς τελετῆς τῆς ἐν 'Ελευσῖνι γινομένης, ἐν Ἴμβρῳ τε καὶ Σαμοθρᾴκῃ καὶ Λήμνῳ [MSS Δήλῳ], καὶ εἴ τι παρὰ τοῖς κοινοῖς, καὶ περὶ τοὺς Κελτοὺς δὲ καὶ τὴν 'Ιβερίαν).

The context, again, shows the adjective to be masculine in Ps.-Galen, *Ad Gaurum* 34, 26 ed. Kalbfleisch (= *Fragm.* 124): τὸν παρὰ μὲν τῷ Πλάτωνι ποτομὸν 'Αμέλητα, παρὰ δὲ τῷ 'Ησιόδῳ καὶ τοῖς 'Ορφικοῖς τὴν Στύγα . . .

Similarly the scholiast on Euripides, *Alcestis* 1 (= *Fragm.* 40) mentions the Ὀρφικοί and other writers who explain why Asclepius was smitten with a thunderbolt: Ἀπολλόδωρος δέ φησι κεραυνωθῆναι τὸν Ἀσκληπιὸν ἐπὶ τῷ τὸν Ἱππόλυτον ἀναστῆσαι, Ἀμελησαγόρας δὲ ὅτι Γλαῦκον, Πανύασσις ⟨δὲ⟩ ὅτι Τυνδάρεων, οἱ δὲ Ὀρφικοὶ ὅτι Ὑμέναιον, Στησίχορος δὲ ἐπὶ Καπανεῖ καὶ Λυκούργῳ . . .

The later Neoplatonists, in their almost countless allusions to Orphic doctrines, usually attribute them simply to Orpheus, using such phrases as ὥς φησιν Ὀρφεύς, τὰ παρὰ τῷ Ὀρφεῖ λεγόμενα, ἡ Ὀρφικὴ θεολογία, αἱ Ὀρφικαὶ παραδόσεις, αἱ Ὀρφικαὶ θεογονίαι. Sometimes they say ὁ θεολόγος Ὀρφεύς or ὁ τῶν Ἑλλήνων θεολόγος or simply ὁ θεολόγος. Most of these imply that the writer had Orphic books in mind. Proclus in a few places uses the term οἱ Ὀρφικοί (so in *Theolog. Plat.* i, 28, p. 68, 2 = *Fragm.* 68; *In Plat. Cratylum* 396 B–C, p. 61, 2 Pasquali = *Fragm.* 90; *In Plat. Parmenidem*, p. 647, 9 Cousin = *Fragm.* 110; *In Plat. Timaeum* 41 A, iii, 209, 4 Diehl = *Fragm.* 168, p. 204). One doctrine, the καταταρτάρωσις, he mentions three times, with three different formulae: in one passage (*In Plat. Rempublicam* i, 93, 22 Kroll = *Fragm.* 122) he refers to it as παρὰ τοῖς Ὀρφικοῖς, the natural meaning of which is "in the works of the Orphics"; in another place (*In Plat. Timaeum* 25 C = i, 188, 26 Diehl = *Fragm.* 122) he says that it is to be found in τὰ παρὰ τῷ Ὀρφεῖ λεγόμενα; a little later in the same text he says simply τὴν Ὀρφικὴν καταταρτάρωσιν. This shows plainly that the three forms are used indifferently for reference to something found in Orphic poetry.

In addition to these instances of the use of Ὀρφικοί we find in a few texts phrases which may be thought of as synonymous with Ὀρφικοί.

Plato twice uses the phrase οἱ ἀμφὶ Ὀρφέα. In the *Protagoras* (p. 71) he says that οἱ ἀμφί τε Ὀρφέα καὶ Μουσαῖον used teletae and chresmodiae as a cloak for their teaching of the sophistic art; in the *Cratylus* (p. 147) he attributes the derivation of σῶμα from σῴζειν to οἱ ἀμφὶ Ὀρφέα. Plutarch, too, uses Plato's phrase with exactly the same meaning (though we have seen reason to believe that he misreported Plato otherwise in this connection) when he attributes to τοὺς περὶ τὸν Ὀρφέα the doctrine that men who have lived good lives are rewarded with eternal drunkenness (p. 87).

Apollonius of Tyana, writing in the first century A.D., says (*Ep.* 16, ed. C. L. Kayser *Philostratus* = *Test.* 85): "you think that the philosophers who are followers of Pythagoras should be called magi, and the followers of Orpheus, too, I dare say" (μάγους οἴει δεῖν ὀνομάζειν τοὺς ἀπὸ Πυθαγόρου φιλοσόφους, ὧδε δέ που καὶ τοὺς ἀπὸ Ὀρφέως).

The author of the *Cohortatio ad gentiles*, which is attributed to Justinus, quotes a passage from the Orphic poem called Διαθῆκαι, in which, as we have seen (p. 271), the poet abandons polytheism and makes a stirring declaration in favor of monotheism. The quotation is introduced with these words (15, p. 15 C = *Fragm.* 245, *Test.* 168): "I must remind you of what Orpheus, the first teacher, as one might say, of polytheism, proclaims at a later time to his son Musaeus and his other true disciples with regard to one sole god" (Ὀρφεὺς γοῦν, ὁ τῆς πολυθεότητος ὑμῶν, ὡς ἂν εἴποι τις, πρῶτος διδάσκαλος γεγονώς, οἷα πρὸς τὸν υἱὸν αὐτοῦ Μουσαῖον καὶ τοὺς λοιποὺς γνησίους ἀκροατὰς ὕστερον περὶ ἑνὸς καὶ μόνου θεοῦ κηρύττει λέγων, ἀναγκαῖον ὑπομνῆσαι ὑμᾶς). The Διαθῆκαι is a late composition, but the writer who quotes from it speaks of it as the work of Orpheus, either because he actually believed it to be so or in order to keep up the pretense of Orphic authorship. In either case the readers or hearers of Orphic poems are called by a name (ἀκροαταί) which was commonly used of the followers or disciples of a philosopher.

A Latin phrase of the same import is used by a writer in the *Mythographi Vaticani* (p. 232). He attributes to the "discipuli Orphei" exactly the same myth of Dionysus, the same interpretation of it, and the same rites which we have just seen attributed by Macrobius to the Orphics.

This, with due allowance for error, completes the list of texts. The questions must now be asked: Whom did these various writers mean when they spoke of Orphics? What was the nature of the bond which justified a common designation?

Whether or not the bond was always precisely the same, it is clear that it appears in several different aspects which are easily recognizable. Plato, in speaking of "Orpheus and his associates," must have had in mind persons whom he understood to have been engaged with Orpheus in the activities for which Orpheus himself was famous. Such persons would be, as the legend has it, minstrels, poets, prophets, founders of mysteries and other forms of ritual. Plato uses the phrase, one may suppose, because, for the moment at least, he conceives that the great religious work which was attributed to Orpheus had really been performed, not by himself alone, but by a group of which he was the most distinguished member. This is doubtless nearer to the truth than the belief, which was so often expressed, that the invention and development of the religion of mysteries and the composition of numerous religious poems, which must have been the slow work of many men, was the achievement of one man alone.

These Orphics of Plato and Plutarch, if we may call them such, lived in the legendary past and are no more than the multiplication of Orpheus' own personality. But the Ὀρφικοί of Herodotus—if the masculine is the true reading—were members of a society in Herodotus' own world, who were bound together by characteristic rites and by the rule concerning burial in wool. This is indeed clear evidence of the existence of a sect which was known by the name of Orpheus. Such a sect must have found authority for its practices in Orphic poems or in a tradition that they had been instituted by Orpheus himself.

The phrase *παρὰ τοῖς Ὀρφικοῖς* in Ps.-Galen and in Proclus, meaning "in the writings of the Orphics," shows that the writers understand the Orphics to be the authors of the Orphic poems. The Ὀρφικοί of the scholium on Euripides, mentioned in a list of literary sources, are no less certainly Orphic poets. The age-old habit of referring to the poems as the works of Orpheus himself gives way to the plain fact that they were actually written by many men at many times.

Apollonius of Tyana, Ps.-Justinus, and the writer in

the *Mythographi Vaticani*, in using the phrases τοὺς ἀπὸ Ὀρφέως φιλοσόφους, ἀκροατὰς Ὀρφέως, and discipuli Orphei, speak as if they were referring to a school of philosophy. In such a school would be included not only the authors of Orphic poems written in the Orphic tradition, but also the readers and hearers of these poems and all who found their philosophical doctrines congenial. The doctrines themselves would be whatever men chose to write in the name of Orpheus. The forging of Orphic poems, as one may see from the example of the Διαθῆκαι, which Ps.-Justinus quotes, was a practice open to all who wished to avail themselves of the authority of the name, and the authority of the name must have been very great if, knowing that it was firmly attached to ancient Greek polytheistic mythology, a poet chose to make use of it for the publication of monotheistic doctrine.

When Iamblichus uses the phrase παρὰ τῶν Ὀρφικῶν and when Proclus attributes ideas to the Ὀρφικοί, it is impossible to say whether they are thinking of the authors of the poems alone or, more broadly, of the members of a school of thought. It makes little difference, because they are clearly referring to the Orphic poems as the source of the ideas with which they are concerned.

In most of the texts in which Orphics are referred to in one form or another, it is not difficult to see what the writers understood them to be. There is some trouble, however, with Macrobius and Achilles Statius.

Macrobius attributes to the Orphics a difficult philosophical doctrine concerning the νοῦς ὑλικός, which could only be expounded in writing, but he says at the same time that this doctrine is symbolically portrayed in their rites of the dismemberment of Dionysus. Here perhaps we may discern a religious sect, called Orphics, as clearly defined as the sect named by Herodotus, devoted to a particular myth, offering a particular interpretation of it, and practicing rites in which its incidents were represented. Or it may be that in using the phrase "in illorum sacris" Macrobius is following the practice, which we have already noted, of speaking of the weighty doctrines of theosophical schools in figurative terms as mysteries. It is true that these particular rites of Dionysus are known to have been in actual use, that their *ἱερὸς λόγος*, like the *ἱεροὶ λόγοι* of other mysteries, was told in Orphic poetry, and that, like other mysteries, they were called on occasion Orphic. But it is quite possible that Macrobius, knowing these things, but being primarily concerned with the subtle doctrine of the *νοῦς ὑλικός*, could have referred to the myth of the dismemberment as an Orphic rite and at the same time have understood by Orphics only those writers of Orphic poems who had worked out the elaborate allegorical interpretation of it. It is difficult to be sure what realities lay behind the apparently simple words of Macrobius.

Achilles Statius presents the same difficulty. When he attributes the learned doctrine concerning the resemblance between the structure of the universe and the structure of an egg to the Orphics, we naturally assume that this doctrine was expounded in an Orphic poem. Indeed, we know from other Orphic fragments that the egg figured in the mythological, theological, and cosmological speculations which formed the subject of this poetry. We may guess that by the Orphics he means the authors of this poetry or, more generally, those who hold the doctrines contained in it. But when, in the second passage, still speaking of the resemblance between the universe and the egg, he asserts that "those who perform the Orphic mysteries" maintain that the universe is oval in shape, we must ask why he changes the form of expression. There are two possibilities. In the first place, the two phrases, *οἱ Ὀρφικοί* and *οἱ τὰ Ὀρφικὰ μυστήρια τελοῦντες*, may be entirely synonymous. If they are, they may both refer to a sect which held the doctrine of the universe and the egg and performed rites somehow connected with it; or they may both refer to the authors of Orphic poetry, conceived as a philosophical school, and called, the second time, in figurative language "those who perform the Orphic mysteries." On either of these suppositions we must conclude that the writer uses the two forms of expression simply for the sake of variety. The second possibility is that, finding the whole doctrine of the egg fully set forth in Orphic poetry and having occasion, in the first passage, to refer to some rather complicated features of it, he attributes it simply to the Orphics; but, being also aware that there were mysteries in which was involved some simple doctrine of the oval shape of the universe, he assumed that these mysteries were Orphic and attributed this doctrine, in the second passage, to those who performed them. Again, as in Macrobius, we cannot be sure how the author's mind was working or what realities he was actually dealing with.

It happens that there are two passages in Plutarch which have an important bearing on the subject and must be examined with some care. A speaker in the *Quaestiones Symposiacae* (ii, 3, 1, 635 E = *Fragm.* 71), remarking that he does not eat eggs, continues thus: "I have caused people to suspect that I am a devotee of Orphic or Pythagorean dogmas and abstain from eggs on religious grounds, looking upon the egg as the source of existence, as others think the brain or the heart to be" (ὑπόνοιαν μέντοι παρέσχον . . . ἐνέχεσθαι δόγμασιν 'Ορφικοῖς ἢ Πυθαγορικοῖς, καὶ τὸ ᾠόν, ὥσπερ ἔνιοι καρδίαν καὶ ἐγκέφαλον, ἀρχὴν ἡγούμενος γενέσεως ἀφοσιοῦσθαι). A little later in the same essay (636 D; see p. 225) Plutarch refers to the Orphic doctrine which makes the egg the source and origin of the universe and adds that the egg was treated as a sacred thing in the rites of Dionysus.

Plutarch's language in the first passage does not make it clear that there was a sect of Orphics who abstained from eggs. It may mean simply that when people saw a man refusing eggs they were reminded of the doctrine of the egg in Orphic poems and suspected that his action might have something to do with that doctrine. If so, there is no allusion to the practice of an Orphic sect, but only to Orphic poems. This is made more likely by the fact that there is no other place in literature where abstinence from eggs is called an Orphic practice, though there are many allusions to it. It is worth observing, too, that Plutarch does not say, what he might easily have said, that the man who avoided eggs was suspected of being an Orphic. This would have been a natural form of expression if there had been an Orphic sect whose members were forbidden to eat eggs. It is highly significant that neither here nor elsewhere in ancient literature is any one person, named or unnamed, called an Orphic. Furthermore, Plutarch's statement in the second passage concerning the rites of Dionysus in which an egg was used does not make it clear that he regarded these rites as Orphic. Indeed, it is added as further evidence of the sacred character of eggs, as if it had no connection with Orphic doctrines. But these rites of Dionysus in which an egg was used may be the very ones that Achilles is thinking of when he speaks of the oval shape of the universe, and which he chooses to call Orphic. It is not surprising that he should do this. Since Orpheus was the founder of mysteries, any or all mysteries might on occasion be associated with his name, and in the passage here discussed there was a strong inducement to call the mysteries in question Orphic because they involved to some degree a doctrine which was completely set forth in Orphic poetry.

One may choose to give easy credence to the plausible inference from the texts of the two writers that there was a religious sect called Orphics who held a doctrine that an egg was the source of all things and that the universe itself resembled an egg, who refused to eat eggs, and who made use of an egg in their mysteries, which were celebrated in honor of Dionysus. It may be thought oversubtle to find flaws in this. But the considerations that have been brought forward in connection with the texts of both authors do something to weaken the inference and must not be disregarded.

We may now revert to the question which was proposed before the study of the texts containing allusions to Orphics was begun. What is the nature of the bond by which men were bound together under this common denomination? We have seen that where the term was actually used, various bonds were recognized. In three places the bond is participation in common rites and common beliefs. In a number of others the Orphics are the authors of Orphic poetry. In still others they are spoken of as if they were the adherents of a school of philosophy whose doctrines were contained in Orphic books. But it cannot be said that there is any unity of practice or belief among those who for one or another of these reasons are called Orphics. There are attributed to them the rule forbidding the use of wool in burial, philosophical doctrines concerning the universe and the egg with rites involving the use of the egg, the doctrine of Dionysus as the *νοῦς ὑλικός* with rites involving the dismemberment of Dionysus by the Titans, the number theology which was appropriated by Pythagoras, and the doctrine of monotheism.

The necessary conclusion is the same as that which was drawn from the texts expressly naming "Orphic rites" and from the whole body of texts containing allusions to rites associated with the name of Orpheus: the use of the term "Orphics" and similar expressions cannot be taken as evidence that there was one Orphic religious institution and one only, of some unity and solidarity, whose members were devoted to a common creed and a common ceremonial. The term has a far wider range and a less precise significance than this. It must be allowed to comprehend all who concerned themselves in one way or another with just the things to which the name of Orpheus is constantly attached—with the books written over many centuries in his name and containing a vast miscellany of myth and religious lore, together with mythological, theological, and cosmological speculation, and with the many religious rites and mysteries which were conceived to have been instituted by him or which found their authority in the Orphic poems. It has been remarked that no ancient author ever calls any man an Orphic. Let us suppose, however, for the sake of argument again, that a certain person had been called an Orphic and that no other information had been supplied: what should we know of such a person? We should know that he was a person of religious temperament devoted to ideas and practices of the kind which were attributed to Orpheus; we should not know what rites he used or what manner of life he led, in what mysteries he found religious satisfaction, or what theological doctrines he held to be true. If this is so, it would seem that modern scholars would be well advised, first, to avoid applying the title of Orphic to any person of the ancient world, and, second, if they insist on doing so, to use the term with a full understanding that it conveys no precise and definite information and is so vague and general in its meaning that it has little utility.

## *Chapter* IV

# Conclusions and Guesses

IN THE TRIAL of the case concerning the existence of an Orphic religion in the sense in which it is generally conceived the evidence is all in, and in the previous chapter something like a judicial summing up has been attempted. We are ready to render a verdict.[1] The verdict, which I hope will meet the approval of the unprejudiced reader, is that we have been unable to discern such a religion. The things associated with the name of Orpheus are so miscellaneous and so disparate that we cannot recognize a comprehensive and unified institution, however loosely organized, with creed, ritual, clergy, and adherents. They form, not a unity, but an aggregation. No idea or practice which is associated with the name of Orpheus by ancient writers can be called Orphic in the sense that it belonged to such an institution; still less can ideas and practices which the ancient writers did not connect with Orpheus be called Orphic in this sense. The unqualified statement that a given idea or practice is Orphic has no meaning if the intention is to assign it to such an institution. The loose use of the term is to be deprecated as false and misleading. If the source of an idea or practice is unknown, to call it Orphic brings not illumination but

[1] References to particular texts are not supplied in the present chapter, because the conclusions and guesses must rest upon the whole digest of the evidence at once and not upon special passages. It is assumed that the reader will have formed an acquaintance with the texts which have been presented in the earlier chapters and will have obtained from the discussion of them some idea of their bearing upon one another.

obscurity. In these brief and categorical statements we have an answer to the question which was the motive for the long examination of the evidence.

However well founded and important this conclusion may be, it is purely negative. It simply means that we must renounce the idea of a single, comprehensive Orphic religion, conscious of itself and recognized by the outside world, and that we may abandon the attempt to define and describe it. There remains, however, the indubitable fact of the name of Orpheus and its clear association with religion. Every item in the evidence, though it denies an Orphic religion, still demonstrates this association. Rites, mysteries, hieratic poems, and the persons who occupied themselves with these things are all called Orphic. There must have been some unity of conception in all this. There must have been some rational pattern in men's thinking about Orpheus and religion, and some recognizable principle which justified them in the use of the word Orphic. If we reject the old pattern, we cannot resist the insistent demand that we shall find a new pattern into which the pieces will fit more neatly. This calls not only for the process of logical inference which was sufficient for the demonstration of the negative, but for both logical inference and imaginative conjecture. In a word, we must guess. Without professing certainty we must offer a new hypothesis which will provide a more satisfactory explanation of the phenomena. This I shall now undertake to do, and with the whole body of evidence in mind I shall try to show in a summary way how it accords with the hypothesis proposed.

I discern two contributory sources to the religious tradition about Orpheus, two independent cells which united to produce it. One of these two elements was the religion of the mysteries. Out of what practices this form of religion sprang and by what steps it grew I do not pretend to say. I do not undertake to discuss here the many speculations of modern scholars concerning this puzzling matter. It is enough to remark that the forms of this religion, from whatever primitive sanctities they emerged, must have been developed and enriched by the successive generations of men and women who administered them. The earliest evidence which we have of them shows that they were widespread and attached to the cults of various deities. Their ritual involved the mimetic and symbolical representation of myths, and only persons who had properly prepared themselves, by purification and otherwise, were allowed to take part in it. The rites were sacramental in character, and by producing immediate contact between the participants and the divine released them from the oppression of guilt, supplied them with a sense of comfort and well-being, and gave them an assurance of escape from the terrors that await the soul after death.

The other of the two elements is the legend of Orpheus the magical singer, who with his song and lyre could charm and subdue men and beasts and all nature, who could even bend the wills of gods of the lower world by the sweetness of his music. Since the legend gave him a part in the Argonautic expedition, he was believed to have lived many generations before Homer. Like other legendary Greek minstrels he was conceived to have been a Thracian and to have belonged to the company of Apollo and the Muses. Like Linos and Thamyris he suffered a tragic fate, being torn to pieces by Thracian women. How the legend originated I do not profess to know. Like other legends it may have had a kernel of reality, but it was enriched with elements drawn from folk lore and developed by the play of the Greek imagination.

The streams from these two independent sources I conceive to have been blended in the following way. Among those who were occupied with the mysteries (*οἱ ἀμφὶ τὰς τελετάς*) there were some, we must believe, who were more deeply stirred than others, and, being Greeks, they yielded naturally to the instinct to develop the lore of the mysteries in a systematic and orderly way. Plato[2] refers, in connection with the mysteries, to the priests and priestesses who have been concerned to give a rational account of the mysteries which they administer. Similarly, many centuries later, it was Greeks who built the tremendous structure of Christian theology out of the materials supplied by the Orient. Such theologically minded Greeks, operating with the materials of the mysteries—the facts of the ritual, the gods to whom it was addressed, and the emotional experience of the participants,—composed poems in which they told the myths on which the rites were based, found a place for these myths in a wider and more comprehensive theology, and explained the manner and significance of the rites themselves. All Greek poetry

[2] *Meno* 81 A.

is full of religion, but this was religious poetry by profession. The next step was determined by the surprisingly common practice in Greece whereby poets sought to obtain prestige for their work by publishing it under the names of poets greater than themselves. So these humble but earnest poets of the mysteries cast about for a name which should give authority to their work. They found it—and here the two streams flow together—in the name of Orpheus. They may have pretended that they had discovered actual poems of Orpheus or that they had received a revelation from him which they themselves put into verse. In any case, his name was suitable for their purpose because he belonged to the remote past and brought them the dignity of age, and because there was a recognizable kinship between his magical music and the elements of the ritual of the mysteries. It must have been *one* man at first who published his poem under the name of Orpheus, but others followed his example and adopted the same fiction. This was enough to start the tradition of centuries whereby religious poetry of every kind was called Orphic poetry. Orpheus was established as the prophet of mysteries and of the religious speculations of those who were devoted to them. We may guess that in course of time some, at least, among the poets who attributed their poems to Orpheus thought less and less that they were merely following an established fiction and came to have some vague notion of an abiding inspiration proceeding from the founder of the mysteries. What the Muses did for men, the Muse's son might also do.

This association of the name of Orpheus with the poetry of the mysteries had another consequence, which, like the first step in the whole process, sprang from a well-known habit of the Greeks. It was their habit to attribute the invention or discovery of the significant things in human life to great legendary personages. A thing so significant and so beneficent as the religion of the mysteries required a hero-founder or originator, a εὑρέτης, and the name of Orpheus was at hand. In a perfectly natural way, therefore, Orpheus, the poet of the mysteries, came to be thought of as the first founder of mysteries—of *all* mysteries—and a great benefactor of humanity. Gradually his name became synonymous with telestic, and he was credited not only with the institution of it but with the invention of all its arts: he became the expert in ritual. Not only the poetry, but the music, the mimetic representation, the symbolism, the whole action of the ritual, which, based on significant myth, leads to ecstasy and religious transport, thus profoundly moving the soul of man, strengthening it and renewing it, were looked upon as the "arts of Orpheus."

So, we may imagine, the gentle singer of the woodland had greatness thrust upon him in the guise of poet, priest, and prophet. It was his music that made men think of him as a poet; it was the magic of his music and its mystical potency that made men attribute to him the magical arts in the ritual of the mysteries. His legend was expanded to make a place for the notion that he was the first of the "devotees of the mysteries," and he became to a certain degree eponymous of the whole succession.

When he attained this position of eminence we cannot say. He is firmly lodged in it when we first encounter his name in connection with religion in the fifth century B.C. For the steps in his rise we have no reliable contemporary evidence whatever. For the later period, from the fifth century B.C. to the end of antiquity, the history of the part which men assigned to him in religious thought and practice is sparsely told in the texts which we have studied. Let us consider again, in a general way, how men used his name in connection with poetry and mysteries.

That he was given the title of hero-founder of the religion of mysteries is in itself no reason why it would have been regarded as anything more than an honorary title, to be recalled at rare intervals by writers who were reminded of the tradition. Actually the title was kept fresh by frequent use. The name of Orpheus, as we have seen, was brought by many writers into association with many mysteries of many deities. The explanation of this is found in the living presence of Orphic poems, which kept alive also the recollection that the mysteries with which they were associated were also the production of Orpheus. But besides the general undifferentiated tradition of Orphic origin, there were other traditions in connection with certain particular mysteries, which had well-known and picturesque legends of their own concerning their foundation and their development. In speaking of such mysteries, circumstances would determine whether a writer would confine himself to the data of their own tradition or allow himself to refer to the general tradition of Orphic origin. Even in reports concerning the Eleusinian

Mysteries, rich as their own legend is, Orpheus is more than once credited with some part in their glory.

In the great majority of places where the name of Orpheus is mentioned in connection with mysteries, both mysteries in general and particular mysteries with traditions of their own, he appears as the founder or as the poet who had composed the poem in which the sacred myth was told. Sometimes, however, writers use the precise adjective and call mysteries Orphic without saying why they are so called. We have seen that among the mysteries thus expressly called Orphic the same diversity prevails that we have also found in the whole number of mysteries associated in one way or another with his name. The use of the precise term does not determine particular mysteries which alone were Orphic. One wonders, therefore, what writers really mean when they say "Orphic mysteries" or use some similar expression. Of course it might be merely tautological, since any mysteries, by virtue of the tradition of the hero-founder, might be called Orphic. But actually it seems as if it were used in a restrictive sense to distinguish a particular kind of mysteries from others. Local institutions, with names of their own, though they may be said to be indebted in some way to Orpheus, are never bluntly called Orphic, whereas all the mysteries that are called Orphic appear to be unattached mysteries. Though the evidence shows this to be true, there is no real reason to believe that the term Orphic was consciously used to mark this contrast. I am inclined to think that when unattached mysteries were called Orphic the cause was to be found in their association with Orphic poems, and that local mysteries, even though they too might have a similar association, were not called Orphic because it was more natural and convenient to use their own proper local designation. Now it happens that most unattached Greek teletae were addressed to Dionysus. This is clearly recognized by Plato in the *Phaedrus* (265 B), where he discusses the different kinds of inspired madness: as the inspiration of prophets comes from Apollo and the inspiration of poets from the Muses, so the inspiration in teletae is from Dionysus. This is, of course, a general statement, and it cannot be said that all teletae were Dionysiac any more than that all prophecy was from Apollo. But in view of the truth of the general statement we should expect that Dionysiac teletae of various types would be called Orphic more often than others, and this we have found to be the fact.

Where mysteries are called Orphic, there is rarely a necessary implication that they and they alone were Orphic. But there are a few texts in which the writer uses the phrase as if it meant particular mysteries of a particular god and no others. Since the whole body of evidence makes it abundantly clear that this assumption cannot be true, we can only suppose that this misuse of the phrase was due to ignorance. Having heard of mysteries called Orphic, a writer who was not aware of the wide use of the term might naturally conclude that it referred to certain particular mysteries which were different from all others and so be led to use it erroneously in this sense.

Thus we see that there was a rather wide range and

diversity in the use of the term. It could be on occasion synonymous with all mysteries, with unattached mysteries in which Orphic poems were used, with all Dionysiac mysteries, and with particular Dionysiac mysteries. This range of meanings, which would have been impossible if there had actually been particular Orphic mysteries different from all others, was rendered possible by the very comprehensiveness of the term. The variation was due to the mood of the writer and the circumstances of the moment. The situation is analogous to that form of practical theology which is called henotheism. As a worshiper at the moment when he is offering prayer and sacrifice to a particular god may act and speak as if there were no other god, though he recognizes the existence of a whole pantheon, so a writer may for his immediate purpose call particular mysteries, or a particular kind of mysteries, Orphic, even though he knows that others, and indeed all, have an equal right to the name. Failure to observe the significance of this subjective element in the evidence has caused hopeless perplexity, concerning the objective reality, in the minds of those who try to maintain the hypothesis of a particular restricted Orphic religion.

Far more tangible and substantial than the legendary tradition that the religion of mysteries had been originated by Orpheus were the poems written in his name, which men could handle and read. What they found in the poems could be called Orphic in the truest sense of the word. We may suppose that the first poems which were composed by the devotees of the mysteries in the name of Orpheus were simple liturgical hymns and metrical versions of the sacred myths. Once the practice had been begun, however, a means of publication was available for untrammeled religious speculation. Though the poems were at first the offspring of the mysteries and though the bond of relationship was never broken, they outgrew their first function, in which they were confined to immediate association with the ritual, and took a wide sweep in the broad domain of theology. From poems concerning the myths of the mysteries and their religious import the writers passed to mythology and mythological speculation in general and ventured at last into the comprehensive field of theogony and cosmogony. Orphic poems on such subjects as these took their place beside the works of religious philosophers whose names we know. They were not kept secret, nor was acquaintance with them confined to the participants in the mysteries; but by virtue of their origin and their name they are constantly spoken of as if they contained esoteric teaching which was not to be divulged to the profane. They were conceived to have been written by one whose prime work was the institution of mysteries, a business of which the writing of poems was a part, but only a part. They could even be used as authority for the validity of the very mysteries in which they had their own root.

The amount of poetry that was written during the course of antiquity by poets who chose to follow the tradition and give their work the prestige of the name of Orpheus was very large. Lobeck states that the number of fragments of Orphic poetry is greater than the number of fragments of any Greek or Roman writer whose works are lost. Can we say that the authors of this vast body of poetry were consciously united in devotion to a common doctrine and that Orphic poetry is proof of the existence of an Orphic religion? Unity there undoubtedly was to a certain degree. Besides the external bond of a common name the poetry is hieratic throughout, occupied with myth, ritual, and religion. But within this capacious frame there is great and unquestionable diversity. The more narrowly liturgical poems are connected with many mysteries; the fragments of the longer poems show a very great mythological range in their contents; there is considerable incongruity even in the various theogonies which were composed in the name of Orpheus. It is true that certain myths and doctrines which found expression in Orphic poetry are referred to by ancient writers with greater frequency than others. But this proves only that they attracted special attention for one cause or another, and not that they were predominant in the Orphic poems themselves. Furthermore, if there was throughout antiquity a recognized body of co-religionists who produced and owed allegiance to a mass of scriptures so vast as the Orphic poems, it is extraordinary that the records do not reveal it to us in the clear, hard outlines of reality and not as a phantom which remains hazy and elusive. We cannot acknowledge the existence of an Orphic school of religious thought unless we can discern and describe an essential and characteristic body of consistent doctrine which is demonstrably peculiar to it in whole or in part. I suspect that this cannot be done: there is too much incongruity within Orphic poetry and too much resemblance between what is called Orphic and what is not called Orphic.

Though the poetry that was written in the name of Orpheus was hieratic in origin and subject matter, it seems to have been as freely accessible to readers as any secular literature. It probably lacked the charm of the great epics, and it seems not to have been admired for its literary qualities; and in these respects its loss need not be greatly regretted. But it commanded respect for its religious earnestness, and so, in classical times, it was given a place with the classics themselves. Most people believed without question that Orpheus was the author of the poems, and in quoting from them they referred to Orpheus by name as naturally as they referred quotations from the *Iliad* and the *Odyssey* to Homer. At the same time, there were not lacking men of critical insight who found it impossible to believe that the poems had been composed by the Orpheus of legend. Some were content with this skeptical position; others, challenged by the undeniable reality of the poems, undertook to solve the problem of authorship. Efforts were made by a series of critical investigators to assign the several poems to definite authors, and a considerable number of names were proposed. But it is a striking fact that no one ever suggested a possible author on the ground that he was an "Orphic," and none of the authors proposed was called an Orphic. None of the guesses ever won general acceptance, and it never became the practice to refer quotations to anyone but Orpheus. The skepticism, however, had its effect. Whereas some writers throughout antiquity followed the tradition and spoke of Orpheus as if he and he alone were the author of all the poems, the earliest and the latest alike, others, more careful in their language, spoke of "Orphic poetry" or Orphica, or, more cautiously still, of "the Orphic poems as they are called." The only exception is that on a few occasions a writer, recognizing the multiple authorship of the poems and understanding that Orpheus' own title in them was only a transparent fiction, called the authors of the poems, new and old, the "Orphics." This is not surprising; indeed, the surprising thing is that it should not have been the universal practice. Nor is it surprising that the amplitude in the use of Orpheus' own name was transferred to the Orphics. As he was the "poet of the mysteries," and the kinship between his poetry and the mysteries was never forgotten, so the Orphics were spoken of, at times, but only rarely, not only as the authors of poems but as devotees of mysteries also. Again, in the later world, which was full of philosphical schools, the analogy of such names as Stoics, Pythagoreans, Chaldaeans, and many similar ones, led sometimes to the use of the term "Orphics" as if the Orphic poems embodied the doctrines of a school. But, as we have seen, it is difficult to believe that there was any common bond uniting those who for one reason or another were called Orphics except a general interest in the religious and theosophical significance of the old mythology and the religious rites associated with it. Orphic practices are so diverse and Orphic poetry is so vast and miscellaneous that we should not expect to find a single faith and order the adherents of which might claim for themselves alone the designation of true and orthodox Orphics.

If we look for a wider unity in the things that bore the name of Orpheus we may perhaps find that they are the expression of a particular aspect of the religious instinct among the Greeks. The practice of the public cults involved little or no religious speculation and was not developed to meet the deeper religious needs of the individual. Greek poetry, epic, lyric, and dramatic, full as it was of gods and myths and profound thought on the relations between gods and men, was secular rather than hieratic. Philosophy, though it touched religion at many points and became more and more a guide for the moral life, was primarily intellectual and divorced from religious practice. Meantime, the common human need required a religion in which practice and belief would be united, a religion which would allay the concern which men individually felt for their spiritual welfare, in this life and the next. This need was met by the things that bore the name of Orpheus, the comfortable rites of the mysteries, with the doctrines that were implicit in them, and the poems which gave expression to the doctrines and supplied authority for the rites. This whole manifestation of the religious instinct, in all its breadth and scope, may fairly be called Orphism, if we wish to use the name, because Orpheus was conceived to be its originator and patron. The term may be safely used if it is allowed to be so comprehensive as to include no less than all the activities of men who occupied themselves with the religion of mysteries—their practices, their myths, and their potencies—and with speculation on the implications of this religion as touching the gods and the souls of men. Possessing a unity of spirit and purpose, but no unity of deity, creed, or rites, it shows itself in a multitude of forms and institutions and is modified during the course of time by influences from within the Greek world and from without. But through all the change and variety Orpheus held tenaciously to his primacy as a prophet of religion. In the end, when paganism was engaged in its death struggle with Christianity, the particular manifestation of the religious spirit which was inherent in the things that bore his name seemed to the Neoplatonists at once so vital and so comprehensive that he was proclaimed by them as the founder of Greek polytheism itself.

*Chapter* V

# Myth of the Dismemberment of Dionysus

IN A PREVIOUS CHAPTER we have seen (pp. 229 ff.) that one form of teletae among the many to which the name of Orpheus was attached involved the myth of the dismemberment of Dionysus by the Titans, and we have also seen that the same myth was told in Orphic poetry. This myth is commonly regarded as essentially and peculiarly Orphic and the very core of the Orphic religion.[1] The Orphic poet is supposed to have told how the Titans, after tearing Dionysus to pieces, ate of his flesh; how they were slain by the thunderbolt of Zeus; how the race of men sprang from their ashes; and how men, in consequence, contain an element of evil inherited from the Titans and an element of goodness and divinity from the substance of Dionysus which had been absorbed by the Titans before their destruction. The belief that this myth transcends in importance all the other things that were contained in the poetry of Orpheus or were otherwise associated with his name probably rests in large part on the assumption that it formed the basis for an

[1] Cf. Rohde, *Psyche*, II, 117: "Die Sage von der Zerreissung des Zagreus durch die Titanen . . . blieb der Zielpunkt, auf den die orphischen Lehrdichtungen ausliefen." "The tales of Dionysus son of Zeus and his sufferings," says Guthrie (*Orpheus and Greek Religion*, p. 107), "must have been for a worshipper the central point of Orphic story." Nilsson ("Orphism and Kindred Movements," *Harv. Theol. Rev.*, XXVIII [1935], 202) speaks of "the cardinal myth of Orphism, the dismemberment of Dionysus-Zagreus."

Orphic doctrine of the divinity of man. The profound significance of such a doctrine, however, is so dazzling and impressive that scholars have been somewhat uncritical in their use of the testimony which is supposed to supply a warrant for it in Orphic religion. It will be worth while, therefore, to reëxamine the pertinent evidence concerning the dismemberment and its consequences, not only that which brings it into connection with the name of Orpheus, but also other evidence of its treatment and interpretation in antiquity.

There are in all some twoscore or more allusions in ancient literature to the story of the dismemberment. About half of them are found in the later Neoplatonists, who sometimes attribute the story to Orpheus, sometimes not. Outside of the Neoplatonists there are only just over half a dozen texts in which Orpheus is named.[2] The fundamental feature of the dismemberment of the god is common to all the texts in which the story is referred to, but within the recognizable framework which it supplies there are many variations in detail. Since modern scholars are disposed to regard as most significant for the supposed Orphic creed that portion of the story which deals with the events subsequent to the dismemberment, it will be sufficient for the present purpose to trace the variations in these events as they appear in the different versions. Though these events are the direct consequence of the dis-

[2] Diodorus i, 96 (= *Fragm.* 293), iii, 62 (= *Fragm.* 301), v, 75 (= *Fragm.* 210); Philodemus, *De pietate* 44 (= *Fragm.* 36); Clement Alex. *Protrept.* ii, 17, 2–18, 1 (= *Fragm.* 34), *Strom.* vi, 2, 26, 1 (= *Fragm.* 206); Arnobius, *Adv. nationes* v, 19 (= *Fragm.* 34); Servius, *In Verg. Georg.* i, 166 (= *Fragm.* 213); Macrobius, *In somn. Scip.* i, 12, 11 (= *Fragm.* 240); *Myth. Vat.* iii, 12, 5 (= *Fragm.* 213).

memberment, they do not actually form a continuous story. Sometimes the mythmakers chose to follow the fortunes of Dionysus, sometimes the fortunes of the Titans; and there was a similar divergence in the religious and philosophical speculations that were based upon the myth. In the many allusions to the story much more attention is paid to Dionysus than to the Titans. There is also more variation in the incidents and more variation in the significance that was attached to them.

The earliest texts which supply sure and explicit information about the myth are found in Diodorus (p. 253) and Philodemus, though the myth itself was in all probability far older, and though there are, as we shall see, some shadowy allusions to it of an earlier date. The statement of Philodemus, indeed, carries us back to the third century B.C., because he quotes from a poem of Euphorion in which the story is told. The same poem of Euphorion, or another in which the story is referred to, is quoted also by the scholiast on Lycophron. Furthermore, this scholiast mentions also a poem by Callimachus containing the story. These fragments of Callimachus and Euphorion, therefore, together with another fragment of Callimachus preserved in the *Etymologicum Magnum*, provide a suitable starting point for a study of the evidence. The texts are as follows:

Philodemus, *De pietate* 44, Gomperz, *Herculanische Studien*, II, 16 (= *Fragm.* 36): ⟨πρώτην τού⟩των τὴν ἐκ τῆς μ⟨ητρός⟩, ἑτέραν δὲ τ⟨ὴν ἐκ⟩ τοῦ μηροῦ, ⟨τρί⟩την δὲ τὴ⟨ν ὅτε δι⟩ασπασθεὶς ὑπὸ τῶν Τιτάνων Ῥέ⟨ας τὰ⟩ μέλη συνθε⟨ίσης⟩ ἀνεβίω [ι]. καὶ [ἐν] Μοψοπίᾳ δ' Εὐ⟨φορί⟩ω⟨ν (fr. 33 Scheidweiler,

*Euphorionis Fragmenta*, Diss. Bonn, 1898) ὁ⟩μολογεῖ ⟨τού⟩τοις, ⟨ὁ⟩ δ' Ὀρ⟨φεὺς ἐν ἅιδου⟩ καὶ πάντα ⟨χρόνον⟩ ἐνδιατρε⟨ίβειν⟩.[3]

Schol. Lycophron 207 Scheer (= *Fragm.* 35): ἐτιμᾶτο δὲ καὶ Διόνυσος ἐν Δελφοῖς σὺν Ἀπόλλωνι οὑτωσί· οἱ Τιτᾶνες τὰ Διονύσου μέλη σπαράξαντες Ἀπόλλωνι ἀδελφῷ ὄντι αὐτοῦ παρέθεντο ἐμβαλόντες λέβητι, ὁ δὲ παρὰ τῷ τρίποδι ἀπέθετο, ὥς φησι Καλλίμαχος (fr. 374 Schneider) καὶ Εὐφορίων (fr. 12 Scheidw.) λέγων ἀν πυρὶ Βάκχαν δίαν ὑπερ φιάλην ἐβάλοντο.

*Etym. Magn.*, p. 406, 46: Ζαγρεύς, ὁ Διόνυσος παρὰ τοῖς ποιηταῖς· δοκεῖ γὰρ ὁ Ζεὺς μιγῆναι τῇ Περσεφόνῃ, ἐξ ἧς χθόνιος ὁ Διόνυσος. Καλλίμαχος· υἷα Διώνυσον Ζαγρέα γειναμένη (fr. 171 Schneider).

The last text offers the occasion for some remarks about the name Zagreus. It is said that Zagreus was a name for Dionysus which was used by the poets; and a line of Callimachus is quoted as an example of the usage. Furthermore, this Dionysus-Zagreus is represented as the son of Zeus and Persephone. Now though the scholiast on Lycophron neither uses the name Zagreus nor mentions the parentage of Dionysus, it is not unlikely that both he and the *Etymologicum Magnum* are referring to the same poem of Callimachus, because the name Zagreus is sometimes used for the god who was torn to pieces by the Titans. This fact is stated explicitly in another scholium on Lycophron (355), where, after certain derivations for the

[3] The last sentence of this fragment is printed as restored by Wilamowitz (*Hermes*, XXXIII [1898], 521). That Εὐφορίων is right is proved by the name *Mopsopia*. The name of Orpheus cannot be accepted as certain (the reading of the papyrus is ΤΟΙΣ.ΔΟΡ), though, in view of the reference in Diodorus iii, 62, 8, to an Orphic poem on the dismemberment, it can be regarded as extremely probable. ἐν ἅιδου and χρόνον have no value as evidence.

name Pallas have been mentioned, another possible one is offered, thus: ἢ παρὰ τὸ παλλομένην τὴν τοῦ Διονύσου καρδίαν ἀνενεγκεῖν τῷ Διί—Διόνυσον γὰρ τὸν καὶ Ζαγρέα καλούμενον υἱὸν Διὸς καὶ Περσεφόνης ὑπάρχοντα μεληδὸν οἱ Τιτᾶνες ἐσπάραξαν οὗ τὴν καρδίαν ἔτι παλλομένην ἀνήνεγκεν. Whether the incident here described concerning Pallas and the heart of Dionysus was in Callimachus or not, we may reasonably suppose that he used the name Zagreus in his story of the dismemberment. The dismembered god is called Zagreus also by Plutarch (p. 318), by Nonnus Abbas (*Orat. ii contra Iulian.* 35, Migne XXXVI, 1053 C = *Fragm.* 210), and by Nonnus (*passim*). It is a curious thing that the name Zagreus does not appear in any Orphic poem or fragment, nor is it used by any author who refers to Orpheus. And yet Kern can say (*Die Religion der Griechen*, I, 228) that, though it has not been proved that Zagreus and Dionysus were one and the same god, the Orphics identified them. The custom of some scholars always to refer to the dismembered god as Zagreus does not seem to be well advised, nor is there justification for treating the name as a characteristic feature of the Orphic story.[4]

Let us return to the three texts which are under consideration. According to the scholiast on Lycophron, the story both in Callimachus and in Euphorion seems to have been this: the Titans tore Dionysus limb from limb, threw the pieces into a caldron and boiled them, and then

[4] One of the arguments, therefore, for bringing the famous fragment of the *Cretans* of Euripides into association with Orpheus cannot be said to have great weight. The whole subject of the connection of supposedly Orphic belief and practice with Crete is discussed by Guthrie (*Orpheus and Greek Religion*, pp. 110 ff.).

gave them into the keeping of Apollo, who stowed them away beside his own tripod at Delphi. According to Philodemus, though it is impossible to be sure how much of what he reports was actually in the poem to which he refers, Euphorion seems to have said that after Dionysus had been torn to pieces his limbs were put together by Rhea, so that he came to life again. Thus, two versions are reported from the Alexandrian poets which seem to be quite distinct: in one the mangled remains of Dionysus are laid away at Delphi, in the other they are brought to life again by Rhea. Still another version seems to be attributed by Philodemus to Orpheus. The story of the dismemberment, therefore, was told by at least three poets before the time of Diodorus and Philodemus, with striking variation in details. Though the myth itself was probably old, it is not impossible that it was first taken over into literature as material for narrative in the Alexandrian age, when so many obscure myths were first brought into literary light. Callimachus and Euphorion were poets who did much of this kind of thing, and the author who wrote in the name of Orpheus may have been such another.

As we trace the story in the allusions of later writers, we find that some of the incidents mentioned in the poems of the third century B.C. recur and that new incidents come to light. These new incidents may already have been contained in the poems of Callimachus and Euphorion and in the early Orphic poem, or they may have been inventions of later writers, Orphic and otherwise.

According to Callimachus and Euphorion, the limbs of

the god were thrown into a caldron before they were given to Apollo for burial, and Euphorion adds that they were placed over a fire. It is expressly said by Diodorus (p. 214) and by Arnobius (*Adv. nationes* v, 19 = *Fragm.* 34) that the limbs were boiled, and Clement of Alexandria (*Protrept.* ii, 18, 1 = *Fragm.* 35) adds that after boiling them the Titans pierced them with spits and roasted them over the fire. No one of these writers, though their accounts are rather circumstantial, says that the Titans ate of the flesh after all the preparation by cooking. Three other authors, however, who say nothing of the cooking, do mention this fact. Plutarch (p. 335) says that they tasted of the blood (*γευσαμένων τοῦ φόνου*), and Olympiodorus (p. 326), quoting from an Orphic poem, says that they ate of the flesh (*τῶν σαρκῶν αὐτοῦ ἀπογεύεσθαι*). As Firmicus Maternus tells the story (*De errore profan. relig.* 6 = *Fragm.* 214), the Titans, in order to remove all traces of their crime, cut up the body, divided the parts amongst themselves, and after cooking them devoured them completely (membra consumunt).

Sometimes one portion of the body of Dionysus was saved from destruction: Athena rescued the heart and carried it to Zeus. This incident appears in the passages of Clement of Alexandria and of Firmicus Maternus just referred to, in Proclus' *Hymn to Athena*, and in the scholium on Lycophron 355 (p. 310); and it is frequently alluded to by the Neoplatonists. There is considerable variety, however, in the treatment of it. According to Clement and the scholium, it explained the derivation of the name Pallas, because the heart was still beating (πάλλειν) when Athena carried it off. The story of Firmicus Maternus is that the father of the murdered boy was so overcome with grief that he had an image of him made in gypsum and placed the heart in the breast of the image. He also instituted in honor of his dead son a cult with wild rites, and on the occasion of the festival the box in which Athena had conveyed the heart to her father was carried in procession. In the *Hymn* of Proclus (vii, 11–15 ed. Abel, *Orphica*) Athena carries the heart to Zeus in order that Dionysus may be born a child again from Semele.

That the remains of the god were buried by Apollo at Delphi appears not only in Callimachus and Euphorion, but also in Clement of Alexandria, who says that the limbs were given to Apollo by Zeus for burial. Plutarch, too, brings the grave of Dionysus at Delphi into direct connection with the dismemberment in the following passage (*De Is. et Os.* 35, 364 F–365 A): ὁμολογεῖ δὲ καὶ τὰ Τιτανικὰ καὶ Νυκτέλια τοῖς λεγομένοις Ὀσίριδος διασπασμοῖς καὶ ταῖς ἀναβιώσεσι καὶ παλιγγενεσίαις· ὁμοίως δὲ καὶ τὰ περὶ τὰς ταφάς. Αἰγύπτιοί τε γὰρ Ὀσίριδος πολλαχοῦ θήκας, ὥσπερ εἴρηται, δεικνύουσι, καὶ Δελφοὶ τὰ τοῦ Διονύσου λείψανα παρ' αὐτοῖς παρὰ τὸ χρηστήριον ἀποκεῖσθαι νομίζουσι, καὶ θύουσιν οἱ ὅσιοι θυσίαν ἀπόρρητον ἐν τῷ ἱερῷ τοῦ Ἀπόλλωνος, ὅταν αἱ Θυιάδες ἐγείρωσι τὸν Λικνίτην.

Generally, the culmination of the fortunes of Dionysus after the tragedy of his dismemberment is the reunion of his severed limbs and his restoration to life. This triumphant close is alluded to in many texts, and it is in harmony with most versions of the incidents that followed the dismemberment. There is, however, no rebirth in Firmicus Maternus, and none seems to be contemplated. The body of the god, all but the heart, is devoured by the Titans, and the heart is lodged in a gypsum image. Elsewhere there is no incongruity between the rebirth and the incidents that precede. But the process of it is variously told. Besides Euphorion, Cornutus, who represents the myth of dismemberment and reunion as an allegory of the vine, gives Rhea as the agent of the restoration (30, p. 62, 11 Lang συνετέθη πάλιν ὑπὸ τῆς 'Ρέας). Diodorus (p. 214), who also reports the allegory of the vine, says that the limbs were collected by Demeter. In the Orphic version which was read by the Neoplatonists it was Apollo who reunited the severed parts. The clearest statement is in Olympiodorus (*In Plat. Phaedon.* 67 C, p. 43, 14 Norvin = *Fragm.* 211): πῶς δὲ ἄρα οὐ τὰ 'Ορφικὰ ἐκεῖνα παρῳδεῖ νῦν ὁ Πλάτων, ὅτι ὁ Διόνυσος σπαράττεται μὲν ὑπὸ τῶν Τιτάνων, ἑνοῦται δὲ ὑπὸ τοῦ 'Απόλλωνος; διὸ συναγείρεσθαι καὶ ἀθροίζεσθαι, τουτέστιν ἀπὸ τῆς Τιτανικῆς ζωῆς ἐπὶ τὴν ἑνοειδῆ. Similarly Apollo is recognized as the agent of the reunion in Olympiodorus, *In Plat. Phaedon.* Βρκη' p. 111, 14 Norvin (= *Fragm.* 209), and in Proclus, *In Plat. Timaeum* 35 B, ii, 198, 11 Diehl (= *Fragm.* 211) and *In Plat. i Alcibiadem* 103 A, p. 391, 9 Cousin (= *Fragm.* 211). Plutarch (p. 314), in speaking of the burial of the remains of Dionysus at Delphi, seems to imply that he came to life again on the occasion of the secret ceremony in the temple of Apollo when the Thyades awaken Lyknites. Macrobius (p. 231) and the writer in the *Mythographi Vaticani* (p. 232), both of whom are quoting an Orphic version, simply say that the severed parts were buried and that the god later reëmerged whole and sound (integer emersisse, vivum et integrum resurrexisse). Julian (*Adv. Christian.* i, p. 167, 7 Neumann) has the whole myth summed up in two words: οἱ Διονύσου σπαραγμοὶ καὶ μελῶν κολλήσεις. Justinus (*c. Tryph.* p. 295 [167], ap. Lobeck 562), who calls the dismembered god the son of Zeus and Semele, makes him not only rise from the dead, but also ascend into heaven (ἀναστῆναι εἰς οὐρανόν τε ἀνεληλυθέναι). So also does Origen (*Contra Celsum* iv, 17, Koetschau I, 286, 12).

In most of the allusions to the dismemberment and restoration of Dionysus the author does not limit himself to reporting the varying incidents of the myth. Usually the myth is cited as an allegorical representation of events quite different from those in the myth itself. Diodorus, as we have seen, reports the theory of certain natural philosophers (φυσιολόγοι) that it is an allegory of the production of wine. When it is said that Dionysus is the son of Zeus and Demeter, the meaning is that the vine derives its life from the earth and the rain; the tearing apart of the god by the Earthborn (γηγενεῖς) is the gathering of the grapes by the farmers (γεωργοί); the boiling of the limbs signifies the boiling of the wine to improve its flavor; the reunion of the limbs and the rebirth of the god correspond to the restoration of the vine—after the mutilation of the vintage—by the slow process of the seasons, until it is ready to yield a new crop in the following year. Cornutus (p. 315) repeats a similar interpretation, though with him the dismemberment is the crushing of the grapes, and the pouring of all the juice into a single container is the reunion of the parts in a single body. When Diodorus adds that this theory is quite in harmony with the story as it is told in Orphic poetry and ritual, it seems clear that since the Orphic version to which Diodorus refers did not contradict this theory, it must either have contained the same theory itself or, what is more likely, the bare incidents of the story were recited in a way which did not forbid this allegory. In either case it cannot have founded upon the myth any doctrine of profound human significance.

A much loftier meaning was attached to the myth by others, as we may see in a striking passage in Plutarch (*De Ei* 9, 388 E). Having just pointed out a fanciful analogy between the number five and the cosmic process described by Heraclitus in the words *πυρός τε ἀνταμοιβὴν τὰ πάντα καὶ πῦρ ἁπάντων* (fr. 90 Diels-Kranz), he continues thus: "If someone asks what this has to do with Apollo, we shall say that it has to do not only with Apollo but with Dionysus also, whose part in Delphi is as great as that of Apollo. We hear from the *θεολόγοι*, both prose writers and poets, that the god is by nature indestructible and eternal, but yet, under the impulsion of some predestined plan and purpose, he undergoes transformations in his being. At one time he sets fire to nature and reduces all things to one likeness; at another, entering upon a state of infinite diversity (such as prevails at present), with varied shapes, sufferings, and powers, he is called Cosmos (to use the name which is best known). The wiser folk (*οἱ σοφώτεροι*), in their secret doctrines which they conceal from the world, call the transformation into fire by the name of Apollo because of the oneness of that state (Ἀπόλλων = ἄ-πολλα), or by the name of Phoebus because of its purity and lack of defilement. But when the god is changed and distributed into winds, water, earth, stars, plants, and animals, they describe this experience and transformation allegorically by the terms 'rending' and 'dismemberment' (διασπασμόν τινα καὶ διαμελισμόν). They apply to him the names Dionysus, Zagreus, Nyctelius, Isodaites, and they construct allegorical myths in which the transformations that have been described are represented as death and destruction followed by restoration to life and rebirth." Thus the old myth was pressed into use in order to figure the great cosmic change which the Stoics conceived as an eternal alternation between the two processes of διακόσμησις and ἐκπύρωσις.[5] Dionysus torn to pieces and dismembered is the universe in a state of multiplicity and diversity, from which periodically it returns to a state of unity as the severed limbs of Dionysus are reunited and his body restored whole and single.

When Neoplatonism in the third century A.D. entered into the inheritance of all ancient philosophies, the old myth of the dismemberment was soon found to be singularly congruent with some of its essential doctrines. Not so much was made of it at first, but the later Neoplatonists, especially Proclus, return to it again and again. In

[5] Roger M. Jones (*The Platonism of Plutarch*, 1916, p. 15) has pointed out the probability that the Stoics allegorized the rending of Dionysus as the breaking up of the unitary substance into the manifold entities of the kosmos (diakosmesis).

general, they were more disposed to find authority for their ideas in the writings of ancient authors than to assert their own originality. The myth of the dismemberment, as well as countless other myths, they found in Orphic poems. These poems, which by this time formed a collection of considerable size, they conceived to be a very ancient work, to which their own master, Plato himself, was indebted. By means of adroit allegorical interpretation they found in the old myths mystical and 'enigmatic' enunciation of the doctrines of Plato and of the still more elaborate and fanciful doctrines which they spun out of the materials which Plato supplied. Sometimes, perhaps, they found the allegorical interpretation ready prepared for them in the Orphic poems. On the other hand, it is not only reasonable to suppose, but there are also actual indications to show, that the new ideas of the first Neoplatonists had been appreciated by subsequent Orphic poets and introduced by them into their poems. When, therefore, after a century or two had passed, the later Neoplatonists read the supposedly ancient works of Orpheus, they had reason to believe that the truth as they conceived it had been perceived long before Plato. The result is that it is extremely difficult to determine, in the allusions to Orphic poetry in Proclus and the others (which are almost as numerous as the allusions in all the other ancient authors put together), whether the idea attributed to Orpheus was in an Orphic poem or not, and, if it was, whether it was simply a reflection of earlier Neoplatonic thought or was derived from some other source. The myth of the dismemberment is a striking instance of this. Illustrating as it did some of the most important Neoplatonic ideas of the constitution of the universe, it was called into requisition with great frequency.

It will be recalled that the Neoplatonists recognized an endless series of gradations between the pure ineffable being of God and the sensible, phenomenal world of matter. The being of God, at one extreme, is characterized by perfect unity; the phenomenal world, at the other, by infinite multiplicity and diversity. Intermediate between these extrems are Mind (νοῦς) and Soul (ψυχή), which are at once inherently indivisible and yet distributed through the material bodies of the world. Thus a paradoxical solution was provided to reconcile an essential monism with an apparent dualism. Of these things Dionysus and his fortunes are the symbols. Dionysus, who, though he is torn to pieces, is reborn whole and sound, is the Soul of the universe, which is divided and yet retains its indestructible unity. The Titans represent the evil principle of division, which is hostile to the abiding aspiration of the universe toward unity (ἐπιστροφή). The heart of Dionysus, which is saved by Athena, is the undivided Mind, which is approximate, but superior, to Soul.

This is an extremely simplified account, but it is sufficient to show the nature of the allegorical interpretation put upon the myth by the Neoplatonists. The analogy is used in countless ways to support and render intelligible their subtle and speculative fancies which pass beyond the bounds of reason.

One of the earliest illustrations of the employment of

the myth in the Neoplatonic manner is to be found in a book by Alexander, later bishop of Lycopolis, which was written before his conversion about 280 A.D. to Christianity. His conception of the allegory is that the dismemberment signifies the division of 'divine power' into matter (Πρὸς τὰς Μανιχαίων δόξας, Lobeck, *Aglaoph.*, 710, οἱ ἐν τούτοις χαριέστεροι τῶν Ἑλλήνων ἀναμιμνήσκουσιν ἡμᾶς ἐκ τῶν οἰκείων, ἐκ μὲν τῶν τελετῶν τὸν κατατεμνόμενον Διόνυσον τῷ λόγῳ ἐπιφημίζοντες ὑπὸ τῶν Τιτάνων, καθάπερ λέγουσιν αὐτοί, την θείαν δύναμιν μερίζεσθαι εἰς τὴν ὕλην· ἐκ δὲ τῶν ποιητῶν τῆς Γιγαντομαχίας, ὅτι μηδὲ αὐτοὶ ἠγνόησαν τὴν τῆς ὕλης κατὰ τοῦ θεοῦ ἄνταρσιν). Macrobius, who was strongly under Neoplatonic influence, attributes to the Orphics, in a text which has already been quoted (p. 231) and often referred to, the notion that Dionysus is the νοῦς ὑλικός, which performs its functions in the universe by passing back and forth between a state of undivided unity and divided multiplicity. It would be both tedious and unnecessary to cite all the texts in the later Neoplatonists in which the myth is mentioned.[6] Two, however, may be quoted by way of illustration.

Olympiodorus, after explaining that the reigns of Uranus, Cronus, Zeus, and Dionysus, of which, he says, an account is given in an Orphic poem, are not chronologically successsive, but that all continue forever and symbolize the various stages of the virtues according to which the soul operates, continues thus (*In Plat. Phaedon.* 61 C, p. 4, 1 Norvin): Dionysus is torn to pieces because the virtues are not reciprocally implied (διότι οὐκ ἀντακολουθοῦσιν

[6] Some of the most pertinent quotations may be found in *Fragm.* 209, 210.

ἀλλήλαις αἱ ἀρεταί). The chewing of his flesh by the Titans typifies multiplication by division (ὁ πολὺς μερισμός), and Dionysus is the administrator of the present world in which the great division prevails in consequence of the distinction between 'thine' and 'mine.' The Titans, by whom he is torn to pieces, represent the individual or particular, as contrasted with the universal. The thunderbolt symbolizes the ἐπιστροφή: as fire mounts upward, so Zeus turns the Titans back to himself.

Proclus, in his discussion of the passage in the *Timaeus* of Plato where it is told how the demiurgus mixed a portion of the indivisible (τῆς ἀμερίστου οὐσίας) with a portion of the divisible (τῆς μεριστῆς) in order to produce soul, devotes some pages to the definition of these two elements (*In Plat. Timaeum* 35 A, ii, 139–147 Diehl). After expounding his views, he expresses the belief (p. 144, 25) that they are all implicit in Plato's own words and that nothing of what he has said is the product of his own fancy. He then goes on to show that what he has found in Plato is entirely in harmony with the Orphic doctrine (p. 145 = *Fragm.* 210), and at the close of his demonstration he asserts the triumphant conclusion that Plato was simply following the Orphic myths and that his purpose was to act as interpreter of the mystical doctrines (τοῖς Ὀρφικοῖς ἑπόμενος μύθοις καὶ οἷον ἐξηγητὴς τῶν ἐν ἀπορρήτοις λεγομένων εἶναι βουλόμενος, p. 146, 20). He assumes that the Orphic poems are familiar to the reader, and in his demonstration his own ideas, the ideas of Plato, and the contents of the Orphic poems are so intricately interwoven that it is almost impossible to disentangle them.

Though Proclus maintains the identity of the three, his laborious efforts to prove the identity make it quite clear that it would not be apparent except in the light of allegorical interpretation. He found the myth of the dismemberment in the Orphic poem, but we cannot say whether the poem also contained an allegorical exposition of the meaning of the myth, or, if it did, whether the Orphic poet who had composed the exposition had himself written under Neoplatonic influence. Proclus' argument is this. The common belief of Orpheus and Plato is that of the three elements, mind, soul, and body, body and soul are divisible and divided into many souls and bodies, but mind remains unified and undistributed, being all things in one and comprehending all intelligible things by a single act of intelligence (*νοῦς δὲ ἡνωμένος μένει καὶ ἀδιαίρετος ἐν ἑνὶ τὰ πάντα ὢν καὶ μιᾷ νοήσει τὰ ὅλα τὰ νοητὰ περιέχων*, p. 145, 23). Mind is the undivided heart of Dionysus. This is proved by a brief quotation from Orpheus: *μούνην γὰρ κραδίην νοερὴν λίπον*. Since the poet explicitly calls the heart *νοερήν*, it must obviously be *νοῦς* or Mind; and not any and every mind, but the mundane mind, "the mind in the cosmos" (*ὁ ἐγκόσμιος*), because the mind, like the other elements, is the creation of the god who is divided. (This seems to mean that since the cosmos, which is the result of division, is the body of Dionysus, that part of the body which is undivided must be in the cosmos and not transcendent.) Body, like mind, is a portion of the god, because his generative power is the divisible life which resides in body, carrying in itself the seeds of reproduction according to the process of nature (*τὸ δὲ* γόνιμον αὐτοῦ τὴν μεριστὴν αὐτὴν περὶ τὸ σῶμα ζωὴν φυσικὴν οὖσαν καὶ σπερμάτων οἰστικήν, p. 146, 4). In support of this he alludes to a passage in Orpheus about Artemis, but it is impossible to discover from his words what the passage may have contained. All the remainder of the god's body is soul-substance, and it is divided into seven parts. This is supported by another brief quotation: ἑπτὰ δὲ πάντα μέλη κούρου διεμοιρήσαντο. The analogy is made clearer, he says, by the resemblance between the words Τιτᾶνες and τεταμένην: "the fact that the soul is extended throughout the cosmos might remind the Orphics of the Titanic division, by which the soul not only envelopes the universe but is extended through all its parts." This form of expression suggests that the etymological figure and the idea of the extension of the soul were not in the Orphic poem. Perhaps, after all, there was nothing in the poem but the bare myth, and Proclus attributed to the Orphic poet his own lofty speculations because he believed them to be implicit in the myth itself.[7]

Having studied that portion of the myth which is concerned with the fortunes of Dionysus, we may now

[7] Rohde (*Psyche*, II, 119) maintains that the myth was contrived by its original author as an allegory of unity and multiplicity. The Titans, he says, represent the power of evil; they tear the One into many parts; as a result of crime the divine unity is lost in the multiplicity of the forms of this world; and unity is restored again in the Dionysus who is born anew from Zeus. As proof that this was the original meaning of the myth, he cites the passage in Plutarch, *De Ei* (p. 355)—which, we have seen reason to believe, reports a Stoic application of the myth—and the doctrine of Anaximander (fragm. 1 Diels-Kranz), according to which "the multitudes of things which emerge from the single ἄπειρον have by this process committed an ἀδικία for which they must pay atonement and punishment." This is only conjecture. In the age-long speculations on the problem of the One and the Many there is no record of the myth of the dismemberment before the Neoplatonists, and we have no right to say that because this allegorical application of the myth *could* have been made by its first author, it was so made.

turn to the fortunes of the Titans. In most of the texts which tell the story of the dismemberment or allude to it nothing is said about what happens to the Titans. Having performed the crime, they are generally of no further interest. It is the subsequent fortunes of Dionysus that engage the attention of most writers, who, as we have seen, find in them sometimes one meaning, sometimes another. In the supposed Orphic creed, however, the most significant event after the dismemberment is the genesis of men from the ashes of the thunder-smitten Titans. We must next, therefore, trace the fortunes of the Titans after their crime and study the treatment of this aspect of the myth.

A few texts mention the punishment of the Titans; but in all the accounts it is of a conventional type, and no importance is attached to it as a significant feature of the myth. Clement of Alexandria (*Protrept.* ii, 18, 2 = *Fragm.* 35), who is almost certainly quoting from an Orphic poem, and Plutarch (*De esu carn.* i, 996 C = *Fragm.* 210), who gives no authority, say that they were smitten by the thunderbolt of Zeus. Arnobius (*Adv. nationes* v, 19 = *Fragm.* 34), who is also quoting from Orpheus, has them overwhelmed by a thunderbolt and hurled to Tartarus. Nonnus (vi, 206 ff.) has them only imprisoned in Tartarus. In the euhemeristic version of Firmicus Maternus (*De errore profan. relig.* 6 = *Fragm.* 214) they are put to death with torture by Jupiter, the king of Crete. Proclus (*In Plat. Timaeum* 24 E, i, 173, 1 Diehl = *Fragm.* 215), referring to the θεολόγοι, says that the Titans suffered in various ways and that, in particular,

Atlas was condemned to hold up the sky. As authority for the special punishment of Atlas he quotes a verse which he may have found in an Orphic poem, though he does not say so. One may suspect that the Orphic poem, as a comprehensive mythological narrative, included an account of punishments which were inflicted on the other Titans.

What happened to the Titans is in fact precisely what one would expect to happen in Greek story. But there is evidence to show that in at least one version of the myth, and that too in an Orphic poem, their punishment led to an event of singular interest. Proclus, reporting what he found in an Orphic narrative (*In Plat. Rempublicam* ii, 338, 10 Kroll = *Fragm.* 224), makes it clear that the punishment of the Titans was followed by the birth from them of all mortal creatures: (*ἦ οὐχὶ καὶ 'Ορφεὺς τὰ τοιαῦτα σαφῶς παραδίδωσιν, ὅταν μετὰ τὴν τῶν Τιτάνων μυθικὴν δίκην καὶ τῶν ἐξ ἐκείνων γένεσιν τῶν θνητῶν τούτων ζῴων κτλ.*). Men and animals, therefore, according to an Orphic version, were somehow sprung from the Titans after their punishment. This portion of the story is told with more circumstantial detail by Olympiodorus in a passage which has been used as one of the foundation stones in the reconstruction of Orphism. The passage is the one in which he discusses the argument of Socrates against suicide (*In Plat. Phaedon.* 61 C, p. 1, 7 Norvin = *Fragm.* 220). Socrates, he says, uses two arguments to prove that it is wrong to commit suicide, of which one is mythical and Orphic, the other dialectical and philosophic. The mythical argument he presents as follows.

In Orpheus we are told of four reigns. The first is the reign of Uranus. He was succeeded by Cronus, who mutilated his father. After Cronus, Zeus became king, when he had imprisoned his father in Tartarus. Finally, Zeus was succeeded by Dionysus. Through the machinations of Hera the Titans tore Dionysus to pieces and ate of his flesh. Enraged at this, Zeus smote them with a thunderbolt. From the soot in the smoke which rose from their smoldering bodies matter was provided from which human beings came into existence. We must not, therefore, take our own lives. The reason, however, is not, as Plato's words seem to imply, that being in the body we are, in a certain sense, under confinement. That this is true is plain enough, and Plato would not speak of it as a secret. The real reason why we should not take our own lives is that our body is Dionysiac: we must be a part of Dionysus if we are made of the soot from the Titans who had tasted his flesh (p. 2, 27 Norvin *καὶ τούτους ὀργισθεὶς ὁ Ζεὺς ἐκεραύνωσε, καὶ ἐκ τῆς αἰθάλης τῶν ἀτμῶν τῶν ἀναδοθέντων ἐξ αὐτῶν ὕλης γενομένης γενέσθαι τοὺς ἀνθρώπους· οὐ δεῖ οὖν ἐξάγειν ἡμᾶς ἑαυτούς, οὐχ ὅτι, ὡς δοκεῖ λέγειν ἡ λέξις, διότι ἔν τινι δεσμῷ ἐσμεν τῷ σώματι, τοῦτο γὰρ δῆλόν ἐστι, καὶ οὐκ ἂν τοῦτο ἀπόῤῥητον ἔλεγεν, ἀλλ' ὅτι οὐ δεῖ ἐξάγειν ἡμᾶς ἑαυτοὺς ὡς τοῦ σώματος ἡμῶν Διονυσιακοῦ ὄντος· μέρος γὰρ αὐτοῦ ἐσμεν, εἴ γε ἐκ τῆς αἰθάλης τῶν Τιτάνων συγκείμεθα γευσαμένων τῶν σαρκῶν τούτου*).

All the incidents subsequent to the dismemberment which are here expressly attributed to Orpheus we have already found in other versions of the story, with the exception of the generation of men from the soot. It may be taken for granted that Proclus too (in the text last quoted) was aware of this manner of generation, though he does not actually mention it. It should not be overlooked, however, that whereas in Proclus all mortal creatures, men and animals included, are sprung from the Titans, Olympiodorus expressly limits his statement to human beings (ἀνθρώπους). He tells the truth but not the whole truth. The significance of this suppression will appear shortly.

Rohde (*Psyche*, II, 116, n. 2) finds an inconsistency in the three versions of the fate of the Titans: that they were annihilated by the thunderbolt, that they were hurled to Tartarus, and that men sprang from their ashes. To account for this inconsistency he supposes that in the true Orphic account the Titans were destroyed by a thunderbolt and men came into being from their ashes, and that the καταταρτάρωσις, which properly belongs to the part of the theogony in which was described the punishment of the Titans after their war against the gods, was brought, by a mistake on the part of the writers who report the story, into connection with their punishment for the dismemberment. This is a precarious argument. The truth may be that there were various versions of the fate of the Titans in different Orphic poems (Atlas, at all events, survived annihilation, according to Orpheus), and that no particular importance was attached to it. But it is worth observing that there may have been no real inconsistency in the Orphic poem which represented the Titans as struck by lightning and also hurled to Tartarus. It depends upon whether the Titans were actually supposed to have been slain and reduced to ashes. Olympiodorus, to be sure, in another passage (Bή) says that the Titans were dead when men were born from them, but his point there is to show the striking contrast between this form of birth and ordinary birth by procreation. In the present passage, where Olympiodorus is quoting directly from the poem, it is not said that the Titans were destroyed. The common form of statement which is used by Rohde, that men sprang from the ashes of the Titans, which would indeed imply their total destruction and the impossibility of their being thereafter confined in Tartarus, is a misinterpretation of Olympiodorus' words. It was from the soot in the smoke which rose from the thunder-smitten bodies of the Titans that men were made. The Titans were, after all, immortals. The mythmaker, by his ingenious invention of the generation from soot, was careful to avoid the inconsistency which Rohde thought he had discovered.

There can be no doubt of the existence of an Orphic poem in which were told the successive incidents of the dismembering of Dionysus by the Titans, of their tasting his flesh, of the blasting of their bodies by the thunderbolt, and of the generation of men from the soot in the smoke which rose from them.[8] But it cannot be said that Olympiodorus had Orphic authority for the corollary

[8] It is curious that Lobeck, who has brought into connection with Orphic poetry so many ideas that are not actually attributed to Orpheus, attached so little importance to this text. "De ἀνθρωπογονίᾳ quid statuerit Orpheus," he says (*Aglaoph.*, I, 579), "sciri non potest. . . . Orphei quaedam singularis refertur sententia, humana corpora de Titanum cineribus conflata esse, sed utrum hoc ex animo crediderit an tantummodo ad declarandam deorum hominumque cognationem poetice finxerit, minus clare liquet."

which he derives from the myth. This corollary, though logically sound, is somewhat fantastic: if the substance of Dionysus was incorporated in the substance of the Titans, there must be a portion of Dionysus in the human body. There can be little doubt that Olympiodorus drew this inference himself in order to contrive an argument against suicide on the basis of the myth: since the body itself is Dionysiac, we should not abandon it willfully or of our own accord. He does not say that he found the idea that the body of man is Dionysiac in an Orphic poem, nor does he present it as if he had. He merely repeats the data of the myth in such a way as to bring to light an implication which he discerns in them. He offers this implication as a conjecture of his own, albeit with customary Neoplatonic assurance. He even allows himself to use in support of it the phrase *μέρος αὐτοῦ ἐσμεν*, the truth of which no Neoplatonist would deny since it really expresses the familiar doctrine that Dionysus is divided and distributed throughout the universe. Here, however, Olympiodorus is concerned solely with the Dionysiac element in men, and it is for this reason that in his summary of the myth he says expressly that men, and not all mortal creatures, were sprung from the Titans. It is an audacious conjecture, because nothing could be more extraordinary than that a Platonist or a Neoplatonist should locate the divine element which is in man anywhere but in the soul. The fanciful and ingenious inference from the myth that the bodies of men are Dionysiac and that men should therefore not seek to depart from them is expressly devised for Olympiodorus' immediate purpose. This purpose is to explain what Plato meant by ὁ ἐν ἀπορρήτοις λεγόμενος λόγος (*Phaedo* 62 B), a puzzle which continues to disturb commentators even to the present day. He assumes that the myth of the dismemberment as he found it in an Orphic poem of his own day was what was in Plato's mind, and he invents a secret or esoteric inference from the myth in order to show how it could have been applicable as an argument against suicide.

The notion that men were generated from the soot in the smoke which rose from the bodies of the Titans after their punishment for the dismemberment of Dionysus appears nowhere in ancient literature except in the Orphic poem which was read by Olympiodorus. It may have been the invention of a late Orphic poet, or it may have been centuries old. But that men were somehow sprung from the Titans, or that they received from them some heritage of good or evil, is almost a commonplace in Greek literature. It appears as early as the Homeric *Hymn to Apollo* in the following lines (334 ff. Allen):

> κέκλυτε νῦν μοι γαῖα καὶ οὐρανὸς εὐρὺς ὕπερθεν,
> Τιτῆνές τε θεοὶ τοὶ ὑπὸ χθονὶ ναιετάοντες
> Τάρταρον ἀμφὶ μέγαν, τῶν ἒξ ἄνδρες τε θεοί τε.

Hera, defying Zeus, appeals to his great enemies, the Titans of the preceding generation, from whom not men only but the gods themselves are born. In Aelian (fr. 89, p. 230 Hercher) the Titans seem to be used almost proverbially for the source of all that mars human life. He speaks of the book of Epicurus, ἣν ὁ Γαργήττιος, ὥσπερ *οὖν τὰ ἐκ* Τιτανικῶν *σπερμάτων φύντα, τῷ βίῳ τῶν ἀνθρώπων κηλῖδα προσετρίψατο.* The idea that the Titans are the source of evil outside men appears in Nicander (*Theriaca*, 8 ff. Schneider), who says that spiders, vipers, and other noxious creatures are sprung from the blood of the Titans (Τιτήνων *ἀφ' αἵματος*). But the Titanic origin brings men good as well as evil. Oppian (*Halieutica* v, 1–10 ed. Lehrs, *Poetae Bucolici et Didactici*), in a rhapsody on the resourcefulness of men, holds that they are a race like gods, although inferior in strength, and he mentions two possible sources for the race: it may have been created by Prometheus, or it may have been born from the blood of the Titans (*εἴτ' ἄρα καὶ λύθροιο θεορρύτου ἐκγενόμεσθα* Τι-*τήνων*). According to the scholiast on this passage, some writers said that men were born from the blood of the Titans when they were warring with the gods of heaven, and that in consequence man is called *βροτός* as being born from *βρότος*. It does not seem likely that Oppian was thinking of this when he suggested that men, to whom he attributes something only short of divinity, were descended from the Titans. It is a mythological invention, parallel to the story of the soot in Olympiodorus, produced to add circumstantial detail to the master idea that men owe their being to the Titans.

Still another version of this master idea is to be found in the Orphic *Argonautica* (17 ff.):

> *ἠδ' ἔργ' ἀΐδηλα*
> Γηγενέων, *οἳ λυγρὸν ἀπ' οὐρανοῦ ἐστάξαντο*
> *σπέρμα γονῆς, τὸ πρόσθεν ὅθεν γένος ἐξεγένοντο*
> *θνητῶν, οἳ κατὰ γαῖαν ἀπείριτον αἰὲν ἔασι.*

Since the introductory lines of the *Argonautica* are generally regarded, quite properly, as giving a review of subjects dealt with in other Orphic poems, it is fair to suppose that this form of the myth had already appeared in one of these other poems. Two Orphic poets, therefore, who said that men are sprung from the seed of the Earthborn that dropped from the sky, presented a version fundamentally different from that of the Orphic poet whose poem was read by Olympiodorus—unless we wish to defend the harmony of Orphic myths by pressing the words τὸ πρόσθεν to mean that there were two creations of man. Even if this be true, it is curious that the author of the *Argonautica* does not take the trouble to mention the second of the two, which is supposed to be so important in Orphic doctrine. The Orphic *Hymn to the Titans* (xxxvii) recognizes that the Titans were the ancestors not only of men but also of all other mortal creatures, on earth, in the sea, and in the air; and nothing is said of the manner of generation:

> Τιτῆνες, Γαίης τε καὶ οὐρανοῦ ἀγλαὰ τέκνα,
> ἡμετέρων πρόγονοι πατέρων, γαίης ὑπένερθεν
> οἴκοις Ταρταρίοισι μυχῷ χθονὸς ἐνναίοντες,
> ἀρχαὶ καὶ πηγαὶ πάντων θνητῶν πολυμόχθων,
> εἰναλίων πτηνῶν τε καὶ οἳ χθόνα ναιετάουσιν·
> ἐξ ὑμέων γὰρ πᾶσα πέλει γενεὴ κατὰ κόσμον.

In an essay of Dio Chrysostom (*Or.* xxx, 10 De Budé) two views of human life are described. According to one, men are descended from the blood of the Titans (τοῦ τῶν Τιτάνων αἵματός ἐσμεν ἡμεῖς ἅπαντες οἱ ἄνθρωποι), and since the Titans made war upon the gods, there can be no friendship between the gods and men. Men are born to punishment and imprisoned for the length of their lives. The prison is the world, with its trials and hardships and dangers. The punishment is complete when they die, but their offspring continue to suffer the same punishment after them. Some men, however, can remove their bonds through the instrumentality of reason, as with a file, and such men sometimes become the assessors of the gods. According to the other view, the human race is descended, not from the Titans or the Giants, but from the gods, and the world is simply a colony of the gods. In the first of these two theories, not only are men descended from the Titans, but they also inherit their guilt and suffer punishment for the wrongdoing of their ancestors by imprisonment in the world for the period of their lives. The wrongdoing of the Titans for which men suffer is expressly described as their hostility to the gods and their warfare against them. There is no hint of the myth of the dismemberment.

Toward the close of his first essay on *The Eating of Flesh* Plutarch recalls that two days earlier, in a discussion about Xenocrates, he had mentioned the further fact that the Athenians had punished the man who had skinned the ram alive,[9] and expresses the opinion that it was not worse to torture the animal than to slaughter it

[9] *De esu carn.* i, 996 A *ἐμνήσθην δὲ τρίτην ἡμέραν διαλεγόμενος περὶ Ξενοκράτους, καὶ ὅτι Ἀθηναῖοι τῷ ζῶντα τὸν κριὸν ἐκδείραντι δίκην ἐπέθηκαν.* Heinze (*Xenocrates*, 1892, p. 151), taking *καί* to mean "and," translates: "am dritten Tage erwähnte ich im Gespräch das Wort des Xenokrates, und daß die Athener den, der dem Widder lebend das Fell abzog, bestraft haben." *περὶ Ξενοκράτους* can scarcely mean "das Wort des Xenokrates."

outright. He had spoken openly on that occasion, he says, about matters of common knowledge, but the real foundation of the belief that it is wrong to eat flesh is of the nature of a mystery, known only to a few and difficult for most people to accept. Though he expresses some reluctance to take up this subject on the present occasion, he proceeds to do so in the last dozen lines of the essay (if the essay is completely preserved), as follows (*De esu carn.* i, 996 B–C): *οὐ χεῖρον δ' ἴσως καὶ προανακρούσασθαι καὶ προαναφωνῆσαι τὰ τοῦ Ἐμπεδοκλέους*·[10] *ἀλληγορεῖ γὰρ ἐνταῦθα τὰς ψυχάς, ὅτι φόνων καὶ βρώσεως σαρκῶν καὶ ἀλληλοφαγίας δίκην τίνουσαι σώμασι θνητοῖς ἐνδέδενται. καίτοι δοκεῖ παλαιότερος οὗτος ὁ λόγος εἶναι· τὰ γὰρ δὴ περὶ τὸν Διόνυσον μεμυθευμένα πάθη τοῦ διαμελισμοῦ καὶ τὰ Τιτάνων ἐπ' αὐτὸν τολμήματα, κολάσεις τε τούτων καὶ κεραυνώσεις γευσαμένων τοῦ φόνου, ᾐνιγμένος ἐστὶ μῦθος εἰς τὴν παλιγγενεσίαν· τὸ γὰρ ἐν ἡμῖν ἄλογον καὶ ἄτακτον καὶ βίαιον οὐ θεῖον ἀλλὰ δαιμονικὸν οἱ παλαιοὶ Τιτᾶνας ὠνόμασαν, καὶ τοῦτ' ἔστι κολαζομένου καὶ δίκην διδόντος.*

The passage may be paraphrased as follows: "It is not unsuitable, perhaps, to introduce the matter by quoting some verses from Empedocles. By these verses he means, though he does not say so directly, that souls are imprisoned in mortal bodies as a punishment for bloodshed, the eating of flesh, and cannibalism. There is reason to believe, however, that this idea is older than Empedocles. The mythical account of the dismemberment of Dionysus, the crime committed upon him by the Titans, their punishment and blasting by lightning, after they had tasted

[10] It has been pointed out that some verses may have been lost from the text after *τὰ τοῦ Ἐμπεδοκλέους*.

of the blood—all this is a myth which in its inner meaning has to do with rebirth. The ancients used the name Titans to describe the irrational, disorderly, and violent element in us, and this—that is, imprisonment in the bodies of men—is the state of one who is undergoing punishment."

Logically, the argument may be expressed thus. There are two traditions about the Titans. One is that they are the irrational element in men. If they are thus lodged in men, they must be in confinement; and since confinement is a form of punishment, they must be regarded as undergoing punishment. The other tradition is that the Titans murdered Dionysus, tasted of his blood, and were punished for their crime by a lightning stroke. If these two traditions are combined, it may be inferred that the crime for which the Titans are imprisoned in men is the murder of Dionysus, and that their lodgment in this prison came about by the process of rebirth. Therefore the course of events is the same as that implied in the poem of Empedocles: the crime of killing and eating is followed by the imprisonment of the Titans in mortal bodies.

Plutarch's procedure in the argument is curious. He is evidently reminded of the story of the dismemberment because it affords an instance of the eating of flesh, to the vigorous condemnation of which his essay is devoted. But he says nothing of the birth of men from the Titans, which, one would suppose, would offer him an easy analogy to the doctrine of Empedocles. He follows instead quite another line. Recalling the old tradition of the "Titans in us," which he presents as something separate and apart from the myth of the dismemberment, he brings the two into association and so obtains from the old myth of the mysteries solemn and impressive authority for the prohibition against eating flesh. Either he was unacquainted with the version of the myth which we first find unmistakably in Olympiodorus, and according to which the birth of men from the Titans was brought into immediate connection with the outrage on Dionysus, or for some cause he suppressed it. If he was acquainted with it, it is strange that he avoided it and felt impelled to make his case in a roundabout way. One is tempted to guess that he himself took the step of uniting the two traditions without precedent. But there is reason to suppose, as we shall soon see, that he found the suggestion in an earlier writer and availed himself of it for his present argument.

Among the scholia to the *Phaedo* of Plato which go under the name of Olympiodorus there appears the following note on the mysterious phrase *ἔν τινι φρουρᾷ ἐσμεν* (62 B): *Ὅτι τούτοις χρώμενοι τοῖς κανόσι ῥᾳδίως διελέγξομεν, ὡς οὔτε τἀγαθόν ἐστιν ἡ φρουρά, ὥς τινες, οὔτε ἡ ἡδονή, ὡς Νουμήνιος, οὔτε ὁ δημιουργός, ὡς Πατέριος, ἀλλ', ὡς Ξενοκράτης, Τιτανική ἐστιν καὶ εἰς Διόνυσον ἀποκορυφοῦται* ([Olympiodorus] Bβ′, p. 84 Norvin = Xenocrates, fr. 20 Heinze). If the statement is to be trusted, Xenocrates interpreted the *φρουρά* as in some sense Titanic. The exact sense of the condensed phrase *εἰς Διόνυσον ἀποκορυφοῦται* is obscure. It seems to mean that the full significance of the Titanic prison is to be discovered in the myth of Dionysus. In any case, there can be no doubt that there is an allusion to the myth of the dismemberment. Unfortunately, we can only guess at the form of the myth to which Xenocrates referred and the interpretation which he put upon it. But one is immediately struck by the strong probability, noticed long ago by Dümmler, that the text of Xenocrates in which the ideas here attributed to him by the scholiast were expressed was in the mind of Plutarch when he wrote the passage about the Titans which we have just examined. Besides the general resemblance between the two, one notices Plutarch's insistence on the daemonic character of the irrational element in man, which sounds like an echo of Xenocrates' theory of daemons. It is well known that Plutarch was familiar with the writings of Xenocrates, and, as we have seen, he refers to a conversation which he had held concerning the philosopher only two days before he wrote the essay on *The Eating of Flesh*. Furthermore, Xenocrates himself wrote a book on the same subject, referred to by Clement of Alexandria (fr. 100 Heinze), in which he argued that since the flesh of animals (*τῶν ἀλόγων*) is affected by their irrational soul, the eating of it is injurious to human reason. We may, therefore, fairly look to Plutarch for light upon the fragment of Xenocrates, and we are justified in drawing the inference that he, like Plutarch, represented the Titans as imprisoned in men as a punishment for their crime against Dionysus.[11] It must be acknowledged that this

[11] The interpretation of the fragment is discussed at length by Heinze (*Xenocrates*, pp. 149–152), who believes it quite possible that Xenocrates compared the *ἄλογον καὶ ἄτακτον καὶ βίαιον* in us with the Titans. His further suggestion however, that the phrase *εἰς Διόνυσον ἀποκορυφοῦται* is to be explained as meaning that the irrational element in man awaits liberation by the *νοῦς* as the Titans await liberation by Dionysus the Liberator, is not convincing.

does not give a satisfactory explanation of Plato's words, *ἔν τινι φρουρᾷ ἐσμεν*, because men are in the one case the prison and in the other the prisoners. But the blame may lie with the scholiast rather than with Xenocrates, whose views are so summarily reported. With Xenocrates, as with Plutarch, the basis for the idea that the punishment of the Titans took the form of imprisonment in men must have been the notion that the irrational, disorderly, and violent element in man is the "Titan in us"; but this notion must have been older than Xenocrates because Plutarch attributes it to *οἱ παλαιοί*, which he would not have done if he had found it stated as something new by Xenocrates. How the idea originated, it would be difficult to discover. The myths about the Titans show that they could be wicked in more ways than one. Conduct like theirs on the part of men might be attributed to the "Titan in us" either because of the very old notion that men are descended from the Titans or simply by a form of language similar to such a phrase as "the Devil is in him." In any case, the idea that men were born from the Titans is clearly avoided by Plutarch; and that it was also avoided by Xenocrates is made the more likely by the fact that according to his view (fr. 59 Heinze), as we learn from Censorinus, the human race had existed forever.

A passage in the *Laws* of Plato in which a comparison is made between the conduct of certain men and the conduct of the Titans has often been supposed to contain an allusion to the myth of the dismemberment. The text is as follows (*Laws* iii, 701 B–C = *Fragm.* 9): Ἐφεξῆς δὴ ταύτῃ τῇ ἐλευθερίᾳ ἡ τοῦ μὴ ἐθέλειν τοῖς ἄρχουσι δουλεύειν *γίγνοιτ' ἄν, καὶ ἑπομένῃ ταύτῃ φεύγειν πατρὸς καὶ μητρὸς καὶ πρεσβυτέρων δουλείαν καὶ νομοθέτησιν, καὶ ἐγγὺς τοῦ τέλους οὖσιν νόμων ζητεῖν μὴ ὑπηκόοις εἶναι, πρὸς αὐτῷ δὲ ἤδη τῷ τέλει ὅρκων καὶ πίστεων καὶ τὸ παράπαν θεῶν μὴ φροντίζειν, τὴν λεγομένην παλαιὰν Τιτανικὴν φύσιν ἐπιδεικνῦσι καὶ μιμουμένοις, ἐπὶ τὰ αὐτὰ πάλιν ἐκεῖνα ἀφικομένους, χαλεπὸν αἰῶνα διάγοντας μὴ λῆξαί ποτε κακῶν.* The first part of this passage is clear. It recounts the successive stages in the degeneracy that results from unrestrained liberty: first, refusal to obey the magistrates; second, disregard of parents and elders; third, rebellion against the laws; last, defiance of the gods. With the words *τὴν λεγομένην παλαιὰν Τιτανικὴν φύσιν* difficulty begins. In the first place, the irregular grammar, which in the earlier part of the paragraph does not obscure the sense, leaves us in doubt about the last two lines. Who are to be understood as the subject of the predications in *ἀφικομένους*, *διάγοντας*, and *λῆξαι*? England holds that it is the Titans, and he takes the clause *ἀφικομένους . . . λῆξαι* as dependent upon the idea of 'saying' in the previous words ("the story which says . . ."). Thus he obtains the translation: "and they present (to the world) the spectacle of the Titanic nature of which the old stories tell us—how they had to return to their old quarters, and pass a cruel time of unending woe." "In the form of the story here referred to," he says, "the Titans were punished for some offence by being sent to Tartarus. They escaped, fought with the Olympian gods (*their* superiors), were beaten, and sent back to Tartarus (or worse), to stay." It is difficult to believe that Plato could have meant this: the verb of saying is not clearly enough implied, *ἐπὶ τὰ αὐτὰ πάλιν ἐκεῖνα* can scarcely be "to their old quarters," and the form of the story which is assumed is not otherwise known. England's only explicit argument in support of his interpretation is that in his opinion it provides the most satisfactory explanation of *πάλιν*. He is followed by R. G. Bury, however, in the Loeb translation. A better interpretation, which is adopted by Jowett and A. E. Taylor, is that the subject of *ἀφικομένους*, *διάγοντας*, and *λῆξαι* is the degenerate liberals. *λῆξαι* is then parallel to the preceding infinitives *ἐθέλειν*, *φεύγειν*, *ζητεῖν*, *φροντίζειν*. The change from the dative *μιμουμένοις* to the accusative *ἀφικομένους* is not more startling than the dative in the phrase *ἐγγὺς τοῦ τέλους οὖσι* above. Throughout the sentence the degenerate liberals appear both in a dative relation to the main verb, which is *ἐστί* or *γίγνεται* understood in the first line (as if *ἐστὶν αὐτοῖς* had been said), and in an accusative relation to the infinitives *ἐθέλειν*, *φεύγειν*, etc. *ἐπὶ τὰ αὐτὰ πάλιν ἐκεῖνα ἀφικομένους*, "coming once more to that same state," means that they revert to the Titanic character. *πάλιν* implies, not that men repeat again what they have already done before, but that the old habit of lawless outrage once exhibited by the Titans is repeated in the conduct of lawless men. This brings us to the second difficulty, which lies in the words *τὴν λεγομένην παλαιὰν Τιτανικὴν φύσιν*. What is it that is "old"? England, as we have seen, says "old stories," and A. E. Taylor says "our old legends." Wilamowitz (*Platon*, 2d ed., II, 398) brackets *παλαιάν*, on the ground that it would be tolerable only if the phrase "the old Titanic nature" were used proverbially. This seems to imply that we actually have to do here with a proverbial phrase, and that Τιτανικὴ φύσις is such a phrase and παλαιὰ Τιτανικὴ φύσις is not. In fact, neither phrase is proverbial, and there is no reason to take λεγομένην as indicating a proverb. The immediate juxtaposition of λεγομένην and παλαιάν means that Plato is referring to some condition or event of the past which is told of in history. On what occasion did the Titans exhibit their character in conduct which resembled the behavior of the liberals when in their lowest state of degradation they defied the gods themselves? We do not need to seek for an allusion to anything more recondite than their war against the gods, which is a familiar subject of story, in Hesiod and elsewhere. The lines, thus construed and interpreted, may be translated as follows: those in the last stage of degeneracy "exhibit and imitate the essential character of the Titans of old, which we hear of in story —having arrived at a state where they reproduce *their* behavior, they lead a life of wretchedness and unbroken misery."

The text under discussion is printed by Kern in his Orphic *Fragmenta Veteriora* (*Fragm.* 9). A. E. Taylor, in a footnote to his translation, says that he takes the passage as an allusion to the Dionysiac myth. Nilsson ("Orphism and Kindred Movements," *Harv. Theol. Rev.*, XXVIII [1935], p. 202) writes as follows: Plato "speaks once of the 'Titanic nature' of man as a proverbial saying in the sense of an innate evil nature, referring to such as are not willing to obey authorities, parents, or laws, and finally do not care for oaths, trustworthiness, and gods. The common myth of the battle of the Titans and the Olympian gods and their imprisonment in Tartarus is not sufficient to explain this proverbial use of the word. For in this myth the Titans are enemies of the Olympian gods, but they are not represented as the principle of evil. Aeschylus had quite another idea of the Titans in writing his Prometheus, which would have been impossible if, in current myth, the Titans had represented the incarnation of evil as they do in the proverbial saying quoted. It is fully understandable only in the light of their rôle in Orphism, their dismembering of the Divine Child, and of the Orphic doctrine that human nature had incorporated a part of the Titans. Even if it is not mathematically demonstrable, it is practically certain that this expression is due to the Orphic myth referred to."

The opinion of these scholars, of whom we may accept Nilsson as the spokesman, takes issue squarely with the interpretation of the passage which has just been advocated. The common myth of the battle of the Titans and the Olympian gods, they say, is not sufficient to explain the proverbial saying, "the Titanic nature in man," which means an innate evil nature. In answer to this it may be pointed out, first, that Plato says nothing of the Titanic nature in man, but does say explicitly that men in their defiance of the gods *imitate* the Titanic nature; second, that the phrase "Titanic nature" is not necessarily proverbial; and, third, that whether the Titans represented the principle of evil in current myth or not, their conduct in warring against the gods was bad enough to offer a perfect analogy to the defiance of the gods on the part of the degenerate liberals.[12] There is nothing to suggest the myth of the dismemberment except the wickedness of the Titans. But they were wicked also in their war against the gods, and in a way which forms a more perfect counterpart to the conduct of godless men than the wickedness of murdering Dionysus. Furthermore, if there was a part of the Titans incorporated in human nature, it was incorporated in all men forever; Plato finds a resemblance to the conduct of the Titans only in the worst element of society. If we insist that there is an allusion to the Dionysiac myth, and that, in spite of the clear import of Plato's words, the Titanic nature means the nature which men inherited from the Titans, we must also acknowledge that this evil quality in men is a thing of the remote past and has long been outgrown and suppressed in ordered society, since Plato is pointing out the possibility of a *recurrence* to that state. This is entirely different from what is generally regarded as the lesson of the myth of the dismemberment, that the heritage from the Titans is a permanent and pervading guilt inherent in all humanity, and that every individual man in every successive generation is born with an inherited portion of evil which he must strive to overcome. These considerations seem to show that Plato did not have the myth in mind, and that the present passage cannot be used as evidence that the myth was known in his day. But even if we were sure that it was known, which is not in itself

[12] It will be remembered (see p. 333, above) that Dio Chrysostom, who says that the entire human race was descended from the blood of the Titans, represents the hostility of the Titans toward the gods as the source of the heritage of guilt which men have received from their godless ancestors.

unlikely, it would still be impossible to believe that Plato was alluding to it.

There is a puzzling fragment of Pindar which must be discussed as one of the texts which may or may not be concerned with the relation between men and the Titans. Neither Dionysus nor the Titans are mentioned, but a strong case can be made out for recognizing an allusion to the story of the dismemberment. The fragment in question (fr. 133 Bergk, 127 Bowra) is preserved in the *Meno* of Plato (81 B–C), in the passage which introduces the enunciation of the doctrine of reminiscence. The passage, which has already been referred to in another connection (p. 294), must be quoted at length. What Plato says here is highly significant for the development of the tradition with which the name of Orpheus is associated, and it is also indispensable for the interpretation of the Pindaric verses.

ΣΩ. . . . ἀκήκοα γὰρ ἀνδρῶν τε καὶ γυναικῶν σοφῶν περὶ τὰ θεῖα πράγματα— ΜΕΝ. Τίνα λόγον λεγόντων; ΣΩ, Ἀληθῆ, ἔμοιγε δοκεῖν, καὶ καλόν. ΜΕΝ. Τίνα τοῦτον, καὶ τίνες οἱ λέγοντες; ΣΩ. Οἱ μὲν λέγοντές εἰσι τῶν ἱερέων τε καὶ τῶν ἱερειῶν ὅσοις μεμέληκε περὶ ὧν μεταχειρίζονται λόγον οἵοις τ' εἶναι διδόναι· λέγει δὲ καὶ Πίνδαρος καὶ ἄλλοι πολλοὶ τῶν ποιητῶν ὅσοι θεῖοί εἰσιν. ἃ δὲ λέγουσιν, ταυτί ἐστιν· ἀλλὰ σκόπει εἴ σοι δοκοῦσιν ἀληθῆ λέγειν. φασὶ γὰρ τὴν ψυχὴν τοῦ ἀνθρώπου εἶναι ἀθάνατον, καὶ τότε μὲν τελευτᾶν—ὃ δὴ ἀποθνήσκειν καλοῦσι—τότε δὲ πάλιν γίγνεσθαι, ἀπόλλυσθαι δ' οὐδέποτε· δεῖν δὴ διὰ ταῦτα ὡς ὁσιώτατα διαβῶναι τὸν βίον·

> οἷσι γὰρ ἂν Φερσεφόνα ποινὰν παλαιοῦ πένθεος
> δέξεται, εἰς τὸν ὕπερθεν ἅλιον κείνων ἐνάτῳ ἔτει

ἀνδιδοῖ ψυχὰς πάλιν, ἐκ τᾶν βασιλῆες ἀγαυοὶ
καὶ σθένει κραιπνοὶ σοφίᾳ τε μέγιστοι
ἄνδρες αὔξοντ᾽· ἐς δὲ τὸν λοιπὸν χρόνον ἥρωες
ἁγνοὶ πρὸς ἀνθρώπων καλέονται.

Ἅτε οὖν ἡ ψυχὴ ἀθάνατός τε οὖσα καὶ πολλάκις γεγονυῖα, καὶ ἑωρακυῖα καὶ τὰ ἐνθάδε καὶ τὰ ἐν Ἅιδου καὶ πάντα χρήματα, οὐκ ἔστιν ὅτι οὐ μεμάθηκεν. . . .

Plato does not say explicitly that the lines are taken from Pindar; but since Pindar is the only poet he has named among the many who have written of the immortality of the soul and palingenesis, there can be little doubt that he had particular poems of Pindar in mind and that the present fragment is a quotation from one of them. There are other allusions to these doctrines in Pindar (e.g., *Ol.* ii, 56 ff., and fragments 129, 130, 131 Schroeder); but since they are couched in poetical and imaginative language, it is difficult to turn them into precise theological formulas and to harmonize them with one another or with the views of other authors on the subject.[13] They provide little assistance for the interpretation of the present fragment.

The general meaning of the verses is clear. Persephone returns the souls of certain persons to the sun of the upper world in the ninth year; they are reborn into what Pindar would regard as the higher stations of life; and they are thereafter known as heroes. There is difficulty, however, with the first line, which determines who these persons are. According to the traditional interpretation, they are those "from whom Persephone accepts atonement for

[13] Rohde, however, undertakes to do this (*Psyche*, II, 204–222).

ancient grief," and πένθος is understood to be used somehow euphemistically for "guilt," though this meaning for the word is unparalleled. Rohde (*Psyche*, II, 208, n. 2) accepts this interpretation, but he adds: "Ein πένθος kann diese Schuld nur genannt werden, insofern die Empfängerin der Busse selbst als durch die schuldvolle That in Leid gestürzt angesehen wird, die That eben der Persephone Leid verursacht hat." This cannot be regarded as satisfactory. Unless there is something behind of which we are totally ignorant, we must acknowledge that a penalty for grief is quite unthinkable. A ποινὰ πένθεος, however, could be a "recompense for grief," in the sense of a compensation for past sufferings. We can understand how rebirth into a higher station in life could be a recompense for the misery of previous existences. But this demands a meaning of δέξεται which is perhaps impossible in itself (though the sense "approve" is not a difficult extension of the meaning of the word, and it may possibly be the meaning in Anacreon, fr. 2, 10 Diehl τὸν ἐμὸν δ' ἔρωτ', ὦ Δεύνυσε, δέχεσθαι) and is almost certainly forbidden by the collocation ποινὰν δέχεσθαι. Another possibility is that the πένθος is itself the ποινή (the genitive being appositional), so that Persephone is said to accept as atonement the misery of previous existences. This would accord with the view expressed by Empedocles (fr. 115 Diels-Kranz), who represents successive incarnations as a punishment for some ill-defined transgression of the soul; and, as has already been pointed out, the resemblance between the latter part of the Pindaric fragment and another fragment of Empedocles (fr. 146) shows that the two poets were operating with similar ideas. Still another possibility has been offered recently by Professor H. J. Rose,[14] who gives the interpretation a new turn by proposing that the "grief" is not the grief of men, or of men and Persephone, but wholly of Persephone. Recalling the story that Dionysus, the son of Persephone, was torn to pieces by the Titans, and that men were sprung from the Titans, he understands that men are punished for the sin of their progenitors and that Persephone is satisfied with the penalty which some men have paid for the grief which had been brought upon her long before by the death of her son. That Pindar's words may be thus interpreted is so obvious that, as Rose says, the only thing which is "puzzling about the phrase is that anyone acquainted with Greek mythology should ever have interpreted it in any other way." It should be remembered, however, that an accomplished mythologist like Rose, with a knowledge ranging over all antiquity, is acquainted with many myths that Pindar never heard of. Furthermore, the very fact that the phrase has not been interpreted hitherto in this way forbids too hasty acceptance, not because the truth in such a matter must have been discovered long ago if it was to be discovered at all, but because all readers of the line have instinctively felt that men paid the penalty for something they had themselves done and that therefore the "grief," whatever it might have been, was their "grief." In order that the line should convey to the reader, or the ancient listener, immediately and without ques-

[14] "A Study of Pindar, Fragment 133 (Bergk), 127 (Bowra)," in *Greek Poetry and Life, Essays Presented to Gilbert Murray* (Oxford, 1936), pp. 79–96.

tion, the meaning which Rose proposes, the story of the dismemberment must have been very well known and familiar, because the actual words offer only a bare reminder of it. The story may have been told in the very poem of which the fragment was a part, but this we do not know. The question is this: Is Rose's construction of the language so inevitably right that we must infer an intimate acquaintance with the story on the part of Pindar and his hearers? There is no other early evidence for the story in the complete form which is implied by Pindar's allusion ("the story of the Titans, their devouring of Zagreus and destruction by the thunderbolts, and the springing of men from their ashes," with the corollary of hereditary guilt and punishment), and our only authorities for it are much later, as Rose acknowledges.[15] It is curious that there is no hint of it in the other eschatological passages in Pindar or in other classical authors. Whether it formed the subject of mysteries or was told in some poem now lost, Orphic or other, we do not know; but if it was, its highly significant doctrine did not find its way into classical literature—except in this single allusion in Pindar, in which full familiarity with it is assumed. Another thing that gives one pause in Rose's suggestion is the very notion that Persephone was grieved by the death of Dionysus. It is natural enough that a mother should have been grieved, if the story was so far humanized as to allow the introduction of such tender feelings. But it is a stiff, hieratic myth: Persephone's only part in it, elsewhere, is to give birth to Dionysus, and she has no

[15] *Loc. cit.*, p. 88.

concern with what happens to him afterward. It is Apollo or Demeter or Rhea or Athena who figures in the essential part of the story. One feels that there is perhaps a note of incongruous sentimentality in the grief of Persephone. But after all, and in spite of these objections, one must acknowledge that there is a high degree of probability in Rose's interpretation. The fragment may be accepted as at least plausible evidence that the story of the dismemberment was known to Pindar. The story as he knew it must have contained these features: Dionysus, the son of Persephone, was murdered by the Titans; men were somehow born from the Titans, inherited their guilt (not otherwise can men be held responsible for the sorrow of Persephone), and suffered punishment for it. It is a curious thing that nowhere else, early or late, is it said or even expressly implied that guilt descended to men in consequence of the outrage committed upon Dionysus. Even Olympiodorus does not say so. In many other connections the Titans were the source of evil things, and it is difficult to believe that this idea was not somewhere brought into relation with the story of the dismemberment. But in any event it was not taken up as a subject suitable for philosophical reflection.

There is another text which at first sight seems to give evidence of the story of the dismemberment at a date a generation earlier than Pindar. Pausanias (viii, 37, 5 = *Test.* 194), having had occasion to mention the Titans, says that they were first introduced into poetry by Homer, and that Onomacritus took the name from Homer, devised orgia for Dionysus, and made the Titans the authors of his sufferings (Τιτᾶνας δὲ πρῶτος ἐς ποίησιν ἐσήγαγεν Ὅμηρος, θεοὺς εἶναι σφᾶς ὑπὸ τῷ καλουμένῳ Ταρτάρῳ· καὶ ἔστιν ἐν Ἥρας ὅρκῳ τὰ ἔπη. παρὰ δὲ Ὁμήρου Ὀνομάκριτος παραλαβὼν τῶν Τιτάνων τὸ ὄνομα Διονύσῳ τε συνέθηκεν ὄργια, καὶ εἶναι τοὺς Τιτᾶνας τῷ Διονύσῳ τῶν παθημάτων ἐποίησεν αὐτουργούς). If we take these words at their face value, they mean that the teletae involving the dismemberment were first instituted by Onomacritus, and presumably that he composed a poem in which the sacred myth of the teletae was told. There is strong reason, however, for suspecting that this is not true. We know that teletae of the dismemberment were attributed to Orpheus (Diodorus, p. 215), and we know that the myth was told in an Orphic poem. Furthermore, we know that critics were busy from the fifth century onward in trying to determine who had composed the poems that passed under the name of Orpheus. That the poems were actually anonymous, and that no one really knew who composed them is clear. But the anonymity was a challenge. Ion of Chios, it will be recalled, suggested that Pythagoras himself was the author of some of the poems, and Epigenes named two followers of Pythagoras as the authors of particular poems which he names. Among the persons to whom Orphic poems were attributed was Onomacritus. The suggestion is first reported by Tatian, a contemporary of Pausanias (*Ad Graecos* 41, p. 42, 4 Schwartz = *Test.* 183). It is repeated by Clement of Alexandria (p. 109) and by Philoponus (p. 161). Sextus Empiricus accepts the conjecture as a certainty (*Pyrrhon. Hypotyp.* iii, 30 = *Test.* 191). Suidas, in his long catalogue of

Orphic works (s.v. Ὀρφεύς = *Test.* 223), assigns only two conjecturally to Onomacritus, the Χρησμοί and the Τελεταί. It is clear, therefore, that Pausanias could have been acquainted with the views of certain critics which were reported by Tatian and the others after him. This being so, it is quite possible that, regarding these views as sound, he bluntly attributed what he found in an Orphic poem to Onomacritus and tacitly ignored the name of Orpheus entirely. That he did so is rendered extremely probable by two circumstances. In the first place, he is always skeptical about Orpheus. He believed in his existence, but he doubted the stories that were told about him and regarded almost all Orphic poetry as spurious. He questions the authenticity of a poem about Triptolemus (οὐδὲ ταῦτα Ὀρφέως ἐμοὶ δοκεῖν ὄντα, i, 14, 3); he uses the phrase τὰ καλούμενα Ὀρφικά in speaking of Κυαμίτης (i, 37, 4); he doubts the tradition that Orpheus introduced the worship of Demeter Chthonia in Sparta (iii, 14, 5); he denies that Orpheus' mother was the Muse Calliope, that he could charm beasts, and that he went to Hades to recover his wife (ix, 30); by insisting that the hymns of Orpheus are few and short he tacitly rejects others of τὰ καλούμενα Ὀρφικά (ix, 30, 4). He is evidently quite ready to do away with Orpheus as a poet almost entirely. In the second place, all allusions to poems by Onomacritus, except the oracles of Musaeus and the epics of Homer, which he is supposed in some sense to have edited, and the Orphic poems which were attributed to him, are to be found in Pausanias (i, 22, 7; viii, 31, 3; ix, 35, 5). In all these places, as in the passage concerning the Titans, he attributes some bit of mythological lore expressly to Onomacritus. No one else throughout antiquity quotes from works of Onomacritus or makes any allusion to them. It is an extremely probable inference from these considerations that when Pausanias says Onomacritus he means Ps.-Orpheus, that all his quotations from Onomacritus are really quotations from Orphic poems, and that there were actually no poems by Onomacritus and never had been. His words cannot be taken as a statement of fact, but only as an echo of speculations concerning the authorship of Orphic poetry. The result of all this is that the text which we are considering is valueless as proof that the story of the dismemberment was known and received literary treatment in the sixth century B.C. Pausanias had in his hands, or was aware of, an Orphic poem which some critic had guessed to have been written by Onomacritus. This does not permit us to determine the date of the composition, and the earliest evidence for the treatment of the myth in an Orphic poem remains the allusions to it in Philodemus and Diodorus. Furthermore, the view which is widely held, that the teletae and the poem of the dismemberment were actually the work of Onomacritus, and that therefore the "Orphic religion" originated in Athens, or was introduced into Athens, in the time of Pisistratus, is deprived of all trustworthy support.

We may now sum up the results of the whole inquiry concerning the myth of the dismemberment. We knew at the outset that the myth was told in Orphic poetry and that it was an essential feature of certain

Dionysiac teletae which like other teletae were associated with the name of Orpheus. We have discovered that the earliest explicit reference to the treatment of the myth by an Orphic poet comes from the first century B.C. Such a reference is found in Diodorus and in Philodemus. That the myth itself and the teletae to which it belonged were much older we may readily believe. Indeed, it is highly probable that it had been told by an Orphic poet long before. If Rose is right, the Pindaric fragment which is preserved in the *Meno* gives evidence of the dismemberment, the birth of men from the Titans, their inheritance of guilt, and their punishment. This in itself is not enough to prove that there was an Orphic setting of the myth earlier than Pindar; but the probability is greatly increased by what we find in the *Cratylus* of Plato. There we learn that according to the belief of people like Orpheus (οἱ ἀμφὶ Ὀρφέα) the soul is a prisoner in the body. Plato indicates that there was a recognized cause for this imprisonment, and though he does not name the cause we must assume that it was guilt of some kind. The guilty soul, which is common to the Pindaric fragment, and the passage in the *Cratylus*, immediately suggest that the guilt for which the soul was imprisoned was the crime of the Titans. We cannot be sure of this, however, because, as we know from Empedocles, the crime of the Titans was not the only cause that had been assigned for the imprisonment of souls in bodies. But even if the unnamed cause of guilt in the *Cratylus* was not the crime of the Titans in the Orphic poem which Plato had in mind, it is overcritical to maintain that there might not have been another Orphic poem in which it actually was the cause. It was precisely ideas of this sort that commanded the interest of the priests and priestesses who, as Plato says in the *Meno* just before quoting the Pindaric fragment, were eager to give a rational account of the mysteries. It is, therefore, not unreasonable to believe that one of these gentry, writing perhaps in the name of Orpheus, had composed a poem earlier than Pindar in which he told of the dismemberment, the birth of men from the Titans, their inheritance of Titanic guilt, and their punishment by imprisonment in human bodies. He was probably operating with a very primitive ritual which involved the dismemberment of an incarnate god and the eating of his flesh, and to the aetiological myth of this rite he added the extraneous ideas of human descent and guilt. Such things, like other teletae and other myths, belonged to the sphere of interest of those who wrote in the name of Orpheus and attributed to him the institution of teletae. It may be true, therefore, in spite of the curious silence about the matter throughout classical times, that the story of the dismemberment in some form continued to be read in Orphic poetry from as early as the sixth century B.C. to the sixth century A.D.

Among the many allusions to the story which are made by writers throughout this long period, we observe many variations in substance and detail. This is not surprising; but it is worth noting that such variations are attested even within Orphic poetry. In the poem referred to by Philodemus, Dionysus seems to have remained permanently in Hades; in Orphic poems referred to by other writers his limbs are reunited, and he is brought to life again, sometimes by Demeter, sometimes by Apollo. The author of the Orphic *Argonautica* completely disregards the theory that men were born from the Titans after the dismemberment, of which he says nothing, and represents them as sprung from the seed of the Giants which fell from the sky. In the Orphic *Hymn to the Titans* all living creatures are born from the Titans, but there is not a hint of the myth of the dismemberment. If this myth occupied a central place in Orphic doctrine, it is strange that these two poets, writing in the name of Orpheus, should neglect it just at the moment when it would most force itself on their attention.

No trouble, then, need be made about admitting that the myth of the dismemberment and its consequences is Orphic if we mean by this that it was told in Orphic poems and belonged to teletae. It is another matter when the assertion is made that it was the very core and center of Orphic doctrine and that the world saw in it the essential and peculiar possession of an organized religion or of a recognized school of thought. There is no hint of this in the ancient writers; it is the assertion of modern scholars. This fact alone immediately places the burden of proof on those who put it forward, and we have a right to ask for better substantiation of it than has been offered. From our survey of the evidence we have discovered certain facts which seem to justify the conclusion that it would be difficult to establish the truth of the assertion. We must repeat what has perhaps been said too often already. In the first place, though the myth is Orphic in the sense that has just been acknowledged, it is only one among the many that Orphic poets dealt with: this is clear enough to anyone who is acquainted with the extant poems and the fragments. In the second place, the teletae to which the myth belonged were only one type of teletae among many that were associated with the name of Orpheus. Important as these facts are, it might still be maintained that these particular teletae and their myth were preeminent in an Orphic religion. We are bound to consider this possibility.

It may at once be acknowledged that the story was not without value and significance in the ancient world. Great play was made with it by persons of a speculative bent. It was available to all comers for allegorical interpretation. But those who made use of it in this way were not men who wrote in the name of Orpheus. They were students and philosophers who were developing views of their own. To most of them it was the fortunes of Dionysus himself, his death and dismemberment, his reintegration and rebirth, that seemed to be significant. The school of myth interpreters who were called *physiologi*, as Diodorus reports, found in the myth a parable of the vine and the making of wine. The Stoics, as we learn from Plutarch, recognized in the fortunes of Dionysus an expression of their own doctrine of the diacosmesis and the ecpyrosis. The Neoplatonists are never tired of illustrating their own views about unity and multiplicity by allusions to the partition and reunion of Dionysus. It is true that they profess to find an expression of these doctrines in Orpheus; but it is not necessary to believe that they did. Determined allegorizers like the Neoplatonists were quite capable of attributing to an Orphic poem a doctrine of their own because they believed that the bare story in the poem carried the meaning which they themselves attached to it. But at the same time it is quite possible that the allegory was actually in the poem itself. References to it are to be found almost entirely in the *later* Neoplatonists. Writers in the name of Orpheus may have incorporated into their poems something of the lore of the earlier Neoplatonists, and when, one or two centuries later, Proclus and his contemporaries read the Orphic poems which they believed to contain doctrines of great antiquity, they found their own views ready to hand. There must have been much of this give and take between philosophers and Orphic writers throughout history, but it is likely that the insignificant poets who concealed their anonymity under the name of Orpheus were almost invariably the borrowers.

It may be well to point out that in all the allegorical interpretations of the fortunes of Dionysus his *παλιγγενεσία* is never treated as a figure of the successive births of the human soul or of the triumph of the soul over death, but always as a cosmic phenomenon. There is no reason to suppose that the rebirth of Dionysus ever supplied the comforting doctrine that "we are risen with Him."

The restoration of Dionysus alive and whole after the dismemberment was the aspect of the myth which most stirred the ancient imagination, but it was not the Orphic poets, so far as we know, who found significance in it. Nor are the edifying doctrines which were based upon it generally asserted today to be part of an Orphic creed. It is the other aspect of the myth which is held to be the essentially Orphic thing, though the record of it is comparatively meager both in Orphic poets and elsewhere. The significant features are found in what may be called the fortunes of the Titans after the dismemberment: the birth of men, their inheritance of Titanic guilt, and their inheritance of goodness and divinity from Dionysus through the substance of the Titans who had eaten of his flesh.

Let us consider first the last of these three features, from which, in the judgment of modern scholars, the Orphic creed receives particular weight and profundity. The fact is that not only is this supposedly Orphic doctrine never attributed to an Orphic poem, but there is never a hint of it in any version of the story whatever. It appears only in the independent speculations of Olympiodorus and seems to have been invented by him as a desperate device to explain a puzzling passage in Plato. Departing from the familiar idea that the soul is the part of man which is closest to the divine and that the body is only its sordid and temporary lodging, he suggests that the body itself is Dionysiac. This, he thinks, is what Plato had in mind when he said that suicide was forbidden by the teaching of the mysteries: a man must not, violently and of his own will, depart from a tenement which is itself divine. This is ingenious, but it is manifestly a guess to explain a passage which still remains unexplained. The further corollary, that the Dionysiac element in the Titanic tissue of human bodies explains the presence of good and evil in humanity and offers the promise of the triumph of the good, is not suggested by Olympiodorus and is merely the gratuitous assertion of modern scholars. All this must be withdrawn from our conception of the ancient story, and with its disappearance the value of the story as a core for the doctrine of a hypothetical Orphic religion sinks low. Furthermore, it is no longer surprising that the profound doctrine of good and evil which is supposed to be at the heart of the Orphic creed was totally disregarded by Plato and others to whom it would have been a matter of supreme interest: it was unknown until the first move toward its enunciation was made by Olympiodorus.

Let us now turn to the two other features of the myth which are supposed to impart such significance to it that it is worthy to be regarded as the heart of an Orphic creed—the birth of men from the Titans, and their inheritance of Titanic guilt. The fundamental notion of a connection between men and the Titans was a commonplace of Greek thought, and it appears in literature in a considerable variety of forms. Since the Titans were typical of violence and disorder, men from early times spoke of the violent and disorderly element in human character and conduct as the "Titan in us." Plutarch fancifully proposed that the Titans are actually incarnate in men, and that this form of imprisonment is a punishment for their crimes. It was often said that men derived their existence from the Titans: they were descended from them by physical generation, they were sprung from the blood which they shed in their war against the gods, they were born from the seed of the Giants which fell from the sky. It was sometimes said that not only men but all living creatures were sprung from the Titans. The heritage from the Titans was generally thought to be bad: the hardships which men suffer are said to be a punishment inflicted upon them because the Titans, their ancestors, made war on the gods; the Titans are the source of all that mars human life; spiders, vipers, and other noxious creatures are sprung from the blood of the Titans. Sometimes, however, the heritage is good: one writer suggests that the power and resourcefulness of men, in which they fall short of the gods only by a little, came to them from the Titans. From all this it is clear, in the first place, that the idea of the generation of men from the Titans, which was as old as the *Homeric Hymn*, was neither original in Orphic poetry nor peculiar to it. The Orphic poets adopted it, but they conceived the manner of generation in various ways, of which the myth of the dismemberment was only one. It is not impossible that it was an Orphic poet who first attached it to this myth, but there is no certainty.

In the second place, the notion that men inherited evil from the Titans is found in many places where there is no thought of the crime of the dismemberment. Here again it is not surprising that it should have been brought into connection with this greatest atrocity of the Titans, and it is possible that it was an Orphic poet who did this. It is also possible that it was an Orphic poet who combined the idea of guilt thus incurred with the other idea, which is also found in other connections, that the soul is imprisoned in the body as a punishment. As we have seen, the only evidence for this is in the Pindaric fragment and the passage of the *Cratylus*, taken together. But the inheritance of evil from the Titans as a consequence of the dismemberment is never again attested for Orphic poetry, and we are never told that the guilt could be removed by participation in teletae. It is difficult to believe that the idea died entirely and that the ministers of the teletae did not profess to be able to cleanse men of the guilt. But the striking thing is that we hear nothing of this, either as a doctrine significant for its own sake or as a characteristic of Orphic thought and practice. No one found it sufficiently impressive to deserve mention. We must conclude, therefore, that of the features of the myth which are supposed to give it momentous importance, one must be denied altogether and the other two must be acknowledged to be less weighty, less unusual, less original, than they are generally supposed to be, both in Orphic poetry and in Greek thought generally.

Doubtless the frequency of the allusions to the various incidents in the myth has helped to establish the belief that it was preëminent in an Orphic system. In fact it affords no real support for the belief. In the first place, there is no reason to suppose that the myth was the peculiar possession of Orphic poets and that all allusions to it must be allusions to Orphic versions of it. It "lay in the midst," for all to use, like other myths. In the second place, there is no reason to suppose that it stood out with particular importance in the multitude of myths which were swept into Orphic poetry. A simple narrative of the incidents would be a sufficient basis for allusions to them on the part of those who found them interesting. In the third place, in all the allusions where some notable significance is attached to the myth the writers seem to have been attracted to it not by its importance in Orphic poetry, but because they found it useful in the exposition of their own ideas. Philosophers made the crude myth into something edifying by the process of allegory, and when the time came to revolt from the traditions of Greek mythology, the Christians found in the story, as it seemed to them, a striking illustration of the vile and degraded character of pagan religion. In the fourth place, there is no cause for surprise that, though the allusions are numerous, there are only a few indications that it was made a subject for literary treatment by other than Orphic poets. It was an ugly story; fit for the contempt of Christians or for the pious manipulation of those who clung to the ancient religion, unfit for reputable Greek poets. It was not, however, repugnant to the lesser poets who wrote in the name of Orpheus. Though there were doubtless some nobler souls among them, many of them, we may believe, had always been attracted by the crude, the fantastic, the tasteless, the indecent in mythology. Isocrates, it will be remembered, asserted that more indecencies and improprieties were attributed to the gods by Orpheus than by the other poets. The serious-minded young Euthyphro of Plato's dialogue, who had fallen under the spell of a perverted religious feeling, alludes to disreputable myths not known to most people which he seems to find edifying. He may have read them in Orphic poems, or a man of his tastes and instincts may have written

Orphic poems himself. The fragments of the poems themselves amply display a fondness for the bizarre and the obscene. It is enough to compare the Orphic version of the myth of Eleusis with the more refined story in the *Homeric Hymn*, and to recall the silly tales about Phanes and Ericepaeus and Heracles in the Orphic theogonies. In all ages there are men and women who like to take their religion strong and who discover an irresistible attraction in ideas and practices which are repellent to the normal, healthy mind. Out of such unwholesome soil there sometimes spring lofty and moving conceptions. That some such conceptions were developed by those who occupied themselves with the mysteries and wrote poems under the name of Orpheus is attested by the fact that Plato did not find them beneath his notice. Some modern scholars have been so impressed by them as to maintain that what they call the Orphic religion is the highest manifestation of the religious spirit in Greece. In asserting such a paradox they yield to the same seduction as that which drew certain persons in the ancient world to look for edification in the fantastic and the unclean, and they are guilty of disrespect to the nobler speculations of the Greeks. It is not surprising that when the Orphic poems had grown to great bulk and had come to form indeed the recognized corpus of Greek mythology, the Neoplatonists, as the defenders of the old, read into them, through their indomitable allegorizing, the meanings of their own elevated philosophy, and the Christians, the champions of the new, took the myths literally and held them up to reprobation as a defilement of religion.

# INDEX OF TEXTS

# Index of Texts

## Archaeological Documents

# PHILOSOPHY
# OF
# PLATO AND ARISTOTLE

## An Arno Press Collection

Aristotle. **Aristotle De Sensu and De Memoria.** Text and Translation with Introduction and Commentary by G[eorge] R[obert] T[hompson] Ross. 1906.

Aristotle. **Aristotle Nicomachean Ethics.** Book Six, with Essays, Notes, and Translation by L. H. G. Greenwood. 1909.

Aristotle. **Aristotle's Constitution of Athens.** A Revised Text with an Introduction, Critical and Explanatory Notes, Testimonia and Indices Revised and Enlarged by John Edwin Sandys. Second Edition. 1912.

Aristotle. **The Ethics of Aristotle.** Edited, with an Introduction and Notes by John Burnet. 1900.

Aristotle. **The Ethics of Aristotle.** Illustrated with Essays and Notes by Alexander Grant. Fourth Edition. 1885.

Aristotle. **The Fifth Book of the Nicomachean Ethics of Aristotle.** Edited for the Syndics of the University Press by Henry Jackson. 1879.

Aristotle. **The Politics of Aristotle.** With an Introduction, Two Prefatory Essays and Notes Critical and Explanatory by W. L. Newman. 1887.

Aristotle. **The Rhetoric of Aristotle.** With a Commentary by Edward Meredith Cope. Revised and Edited for the Syndics of the University Press by Sir John Edwin Sandys. 1877.

Bywater, Ingram. **Contributions to the Textual Criticism of Aristotle's Nicomachean Ethics.** 1892.

Grote, George. **Aristotle.** Edited by Alexander Bain and G. Croom Robertson. Second Edition, with Additions. 1880.

Linforth, Ivan M. **The Arts of Orpheus.** 1941.

Onians, Richard Broxton. **The Origins of European Thought About the Body, the Mind, the Soul, the World, Time, and Fate.** 1951.

Pearson, A. C., editor. **The Fragments of Zeno and Cleanthes.** With Introduction and Explanatory Notes. 1891.

Plato. **The Apology of Plato.** With a Revised Text and English Notes, and a Digest of Platonic Idioms by James Riddell. 1877.

Plato. **The Euthydemus of Plato.** With Revised Text, Introduction, Notes, and Indices by Edwin Hamilton Gifford. 1905.

Plato. **The Gorgias of Plato.** With English Notes, Introduction, and Appendix by W. H. Thompson. 1871.

Plato. **The Phaedo of Plato.** Edited with Introduction, Notes and Appendices by R. D. Archer-Hind. Second Edition. 1894.

Plato. **The Phaedrus of Plato.** With English Notes and Dissertations by W. H. Thompson. 1868.

Plato. **The Philebus of Plato.** Edited with Introduction, Notes and Appendices by Robert Gregg Bury. 1897.

Plato. **Plato's Republic:** The Greek Text, Edited with Notes and Essays by B. Jowett and Lewis Campbell. Volume II: Essays. 1894.

Plato. **The Sophistes and Politicus of Plato.** With a Revised Text and English Notes by Lewis Campbell. 1867.

Plato. **The Theaetetus of Plato.** With a Revised Text and English Notes by Lewis Campbell. 1861.

Plato. **The Timaeus of Plato.** Edited with Introduction and Notes by R. D. Archer-Hind. 1888.

Schleiermacher, [Friedrich Ernst Daniel]. **Introductions to the Dialogues of Plato.** Translated from the German by William Dobson. 1836.

Stenzel, Julius. **Plato's Method of Dialectic.** Translated and Edited by D. J. Allan. 1940.

Stewart, J. A. **Notes on the Nicomachean Ethics of Aristotle.** 1892.